DUMBARTON OAKS
MEDIEVAL LIBRARY

*Jan M. Ziolkowski, General Editor*

ALLEGORIES OF THE ODYSSEY

JOHN TZETZES

DOML 56

# Allegories of the *Odyssey*

## John Tzetzes

Translated by

## ADAM J. GOLDWYN
and
## DIMITRA KOKKINI

DUMBARTON OAKS
MEDIEVAL LIBRARY

HARVARD UNIVERSITY PRESS
CAMBRIDGE, MASSACHUSETTS
LONDON, ENGLAND
2019

*Library of Congress Cataloging-in-Publication Data*

Names: Tzetzes, John, active 12th century, author. | Tzetzes, John, active
    12th century. Allegories of the Odyssey. (Goldwyn and Kokkini) |
    Tzetzes, John, active 12th century. Allegories of the Odyssey. English.
    (Goldwyn and Kokkini) | Goldwyn, Adam J., translator. | Kokkini,
    Dimitra, translator.
Title: Allegories of the Odyssey / John Tzetzes ; translated by Adam J.
    Goldwyn and Dimitra Kokkini.
Other titles: Dumbarton Oaks medieval library ; 56.
Description: Cambridge, Massachusetts : Harvard University Press, 2019. |
    Series: Dumbarton Oaks medieval library ; 56 | Includes bibliographical
    references and index. | Text in Greek with English translation on facing
    pages ; introduction and notes in English.
Identifiers: LCCN 2019007467 | ISBN 9780674238374 (alk. paper)
Subjects: LCSH: Homer. Odyssey. | Homer—Criticism and
    interpretation. | Tzetzes, John, active 12th century. Allegories of the
    Odyssey. | Epic poetry, Greek—History and criticism.
Classification: LCC PA5390 .A6413 2019 | DDC 883/.01—dc23
LC record available at https://lccn.loc.gov/2019007467

# Contents

# Introduction

The *Allegories of the* Odyssey by John Tzetzes is a twelfth-century commentary on Homer's *Odyssey* in fifteen-syllable verse. Though the *Allegories of the* Odyssey can be read as a stand-alone work in its own right, it is preferable to regard it as the successor work to his *Allegories of the* Iliad; this approach reveals Tzetzes's assumption of his audience's increasing familiarity with both the source epics and his allegorical method and style.

The *Allegories of the* Iliad can be divided stylistically into two sections. The first section, consisting of Books 1 to 15, is dedicated to the foreign-born empress Eirene (born Bertha von Sulzbach in Bavaria, she adopted Eirene as her new Greek name when she moved to Constantinople) and was meant to help familiarize her with one of the foundational works of the new Byzantine environment in which she found herself after her marriage to Emperor Manuel I Komnenos in 1146. This section consists of a book-by-book plot summary of Homer's *Iliad* interspersed with Tzetzes's own allegorical interpretation. At Book 16, however, Tzetzes thanks an otherwise unknown Konstantinos Kotertzes for giving him the patronage that would allow him to finish the work; either death, loss of interest, or, more likely, financial concerns had prevented the empress from subsidizing the completion of the work. At this point the style also changes

dramatically: gone are the basic plot-level summaries, re-
placed instead with direct quotations from the *Iliad* that are
then explained in allegorical terms. This new style—the only
major shift in tone in the *Allegories of the* Iliad—is retained
and even intensified in the *Allegories of the* Odyssey. Indeed,
though Tzetzes famously bragged that "my library happens
to be in my head" (Tz. *All. Il.* 15.87), it seems unlikely that the
*Allegories of the* Odyssey could have been written by some-
one without a copy of the *Odyssey* on one side of the desk
and the blank parchment on the other. It seems even more
unlikely that any of Tzetzes's readers would have memorized
the entire *Odyssey* to such an extent that a typical passage,
such as this early one, would be comprehensible:

> '*Where you will*' means wherever in Attic style.
> '*The goddess*' is knowledge and wisdom, the daughter of
> '*Zeus*,' of reason.
> And by 'a nymph' he means a goddess, an island queen.
> '*The gods*' are the stars deciding one's fate, that is, Des-
> tiny.
> 'All *the gods took pity on him except* Poseidon.' (1.32–36)

If his readers did not have their own copies of the *Odyssey*
to study side by side with Tzetzes's *Allegories,* they would
have needed to have such familiarity with the epic that they
could recall quotations of relatively nondescript individual
words and phrases (those italicized in our edition) in isola-
tion from the rest of the poem, and be able to do so for the
entirety of the work. Rather, and perhaps unlike the *Allego-
ries of the* Iliad, it seems more probable that Tzetzes intended
his new volume of allegories to be read alongside a copy of
the *Odyssey*—the survival of some ninety manuscripts of the

epic from the eighth to fifteenth centuries suggests its popularity and the extent to which a work like Tzetzes's *Allegories* would facilitate access to the Homeric epic for the reading public. The *Allegories of the* Odyssey, then, was most likely intended for more advanced readers, who had already mastered both epics as well as Homeric Greek (which, though a core aspect of Byzantine education, was limited to the elite). They could have familiarized themselves with Tzetzes's allegorical method through his *Allegories of the* Iliad and *Exegesis on the* Iliad, which outlined that method. Such an audience could perhaps have included the empress herself, the educated imperial circles in which the work may have circulated, and Tzetzes's students.

This is not to say, however, that the increased reliance on the audience's prior knowledge makes the *Allegories of the* Odyssey more exciting to read or didactic. Compare, for instance, Tzetzes's virtuosic allegorical interpretation of the shield of Achilles in Tz. *All. Il.* 18.671–780 with his seeming boredom with his material through stretches of the *Allegories of the* Odyssey. Book 13.7–11 of the latter, for instance, reads:

> '*To Zeus, god of the dark clouds*' here means to Destiny.
> '*The gods of heaven*' similarly means Destiny,
> and so too '*may the gods grant you prosperity.*'
> '*To father Zeus*' similarly; the gods of heaven
> signify Destiny and they signify the elements as well.

Tzetzes's allegorical interpretation here simply labels four phrases from the *Odyssey* as meaning "Destiny," without further elaboration.

Tzetzes begins his work on the *Odyssey* with a fifty-six line prologue (Prolegomena A) that addresses his patron, not by name, as in the *Allegories of the* Iliad, but only as "my queen" (pro.A.16). In the most elaborate and rhetorically complex passage in the entire work (pro.A.7–56), Tzetzes compares himself to the Persian king Cyrus, since both men took a deep river with a raging current and divided it into small segments across which one could walk without getting wet. In Cyrus's case, this was the river Gyndes in Babylon, which he divided into 360 channels to march his army across; in Tzetzes's case, it is the twenty-four books of the *Odyssey,* which have been simplified and made comprehensible to any and all. This is followed by an introduction that summarizes the *Odyssey* in nineteen lines (Prolegomena B). The remainder of the volume consists of twenty-four books, one for each of the books of the *Odyssey;* each book begins with a five- to ten-line summary of the analogous book of the *Odyssey,* followed by Tzetzes's seemingly arbitrary and unsystematic identification of various words and phrases that he singles out for allegorical interpretation. The books range in length from 37 lines (Book 21) to 340 (Book 1); nearly half the books in the *Allegories of the* Odyssey have fewer than one hundred lines each (Books 2, 7, 14, 15, 16, 17, 18, 19, 21, 22, 23). By contrast, the shortest books of the *Allegories of the* Iliad are 78 lines long (Books 10 and 14), while Book 18 stretches to 789 lines.

## THE DATE OF THE WORK AND THE CIRCUMSTANCES OF ITS COMMISSION

The Bavarian princess Bertha von Sulzbach arrived in Constantinople to wed Manuel Komnenos in 1142, though the marriage did not take place until 1146. Her husband, the future emperor Manuel I (r. 1143–1180), was the fourth son of the emperor John II Komnenos (r. 1118–1143) and, at his father's death in 1143, the younger of John's two surviving sons; he was thus perceived as unlikely to accede to the throne at the time when the marriage was contracted. It was probably during this period, between 1142 and 1146,[1] that the *Allegories of the* Iliad was commissioned either by Bertha herself or on her behalf by those who realized that the foreign-born princess would soon (or had recently) become the empress and therefore needed a proper introduction to Byzantine Greek language and culture and its most important literary works.

Tzetzes concludes the *Allegories of the* Iliad by writing:

> You have the entire epic achievement of the *Iliad*
> complete and allegorized by Tzetzes.
> But time, like a herald, already cries out for another
> work. (24.329–31)

"Another work" is perhaps a reference to the *Allegories of the* Odyssey, and indeed, in the preface to the successor work, he notes that

> . . . we have already allegorized the *Iliad;*
> now we must move to the subject of the much-traveled
> man (pro.A.53–54).

The reference in Tz. *All. Il.* 24.331 could indicate that Tzetzes began the *Allegories of the* Odyssey shortly after completing his *Iliad* volume. If he finished the latter around the time of Bertha-Eirene's marriage in 1146, this would suggest a date for the *Allegories of the* Odyssey in the late 1140s. Yet while this might seem likely, there are several other equally viable possibilities. For example, Tzetzes could have written Books 1 to 15 of the *Iliad* volume at any time before Bertha-Eirene's death in 1159; at the point he finished Book 15 she may have lost interest in the work (and thus Books 16 to 24 were dedicated to Konstantinos Kotertzes), and then renewed her interest for the *Allegories of the* Odyssey, a not uncommon patronage practice in Byzantium.

Yet we cannot be certain that Bertha-Eirene was the patron of the *Odyssey* volume. In the Prolegomena A (line 16), Tzetzes does not identify the dedicatee by name; rather, he calls her "my queen, who was an ornament to womankind," a generalization that leaves the identity of his patron ultimately unknowable. In addition to Bertha-Eirene, two other prominent women stand out as the most likely possibilities: first, Manuel's second queen, Maria of Antioch, whom he married in 1161, two years after his first wife's death. Though Maria would be the only person legitimately entitled to be referred to as "queen" (βασιλίς), Elizabeth Jeffreys notes that the term was "used elastically of all the most senior women in the Komnenian courts" and could therefore apply to other women in the imperial circle. Outstanding among this class of women was the *sebastokratorissa* Eirene, the wife of Manuel's brother Andronikos and perhaps the leading literary patron of her age.[2] She is known to have commissioned Tzetzes's *Theogony* and is the addressee of two of his letters, making her a likely candidate as patron of the *Allegories of the* Odyssey as well.[3] Thus, while the *Allegories of the* Odyssey must have been written after the *Allegories of the* Iliad, the possible date of composition still spans several decades, ranging from the 1140s to 1152 (*sebastokratorissa* Eirene's death), 1159 (Bertha-Eirene's death), or 1182 (Maria of Antioch's death). Ultimately, however, as so often in Byzantine literature, the exact dating and circumstances of composition must remain speculative.

## The Life of John Tzetzes

The details of Tzetzes's life are uncertain; almost all of what is known is derived from his own writings and therefore must be understood in light of Tzetzes's own rather constant self-mythologizing as a misunderstood genius forced into poverty by an anti-intellectual and corrupt world. Tzetzes was most likely born in Constantinople around 1110 CE[4] to "a second-class aristocracy of families which had known better days, or had at least enjoyed a long and continuous tradition of modest inherited wealth and salaried employment," and he had distant blood ties to the imperial family through his maternal grandmother.[5] Tzetzes's paternal line came from less distinguished stock: his paternal grandfather was an illiterate man who had nevertheless amassed a significant fortune—enough to buy a five-story house[6]—and passed on to his son, Michael Tzetzes, a fierce devotion to education. John was himself given a rigorous education by his father, and in a letter compared their relationship to that of a more famous father, Cato the Elder, who taught his son, a reference that finds its way into the *Allegories of the* Iliad when Tzetzes describes their physical resemblance.[7]

For a twelfth-century man of little means but solid education and access to high society, the life of the scholar and grammarian was one of sufficient opportunity if not always of sufficient remuneration;[8] indeed, Tzetzes has been called "one of the first men of European society to live by his pen."[9] While Tzetzes's complaints about his own poverty and that of intellectuals more generally are frequently found in his work,[10] he endured his poverty voluntarily, as it allowed him to remain a scholar rather than a bureaucrat.[11]

Tzetzes was among a class of educated grammarians whose income came primarily from two sources: first, they could make some money by teaching classical literature and rhetoric to students aspiring to serve in the imperial administration.[12] The second income stream came from the intensely competitive world of imperial patronage for literary works. Modern scholars have described Tzetzes as "an irritating literary polymath who felt his ability was insufficiently recognized"[13] and was "always taking the reader behind the scenes of his own genius, always commenting on himself, always right, always taking issue with something or somebody: fraudulent holy men, conniving clerics, fornicating bishops, ungrateful students, stingy and philistine patrons, even the emperor himself, and most of all fellow intellectuals, who are airily dismissed as 'buffaloes,' or paranoically identified as the 'gang' (κουστωδία) out to get Tzetzes."[14] This attitude was surely due in part to the scarcity of commissions and the surplus of writers seeking them out,[15] a situation that led too often to verbal excess and combativeness: "Tzetzes did not control the violence of his language, particularly in praising himself or attacking others."[16] Tzetzes's personal failings have been magnified by the pettiness of the subjects of his literary feuds: "Most of the controversies in which he participated concerned the diachronic vowels, a fairly trivial metrical issue."[17] Ultimately, Tzetzes left the world of patronage and the performance culture of the Byzantine *theatron*—the competitive literary gatherings hosted by a patron where authors recited their works—and made an "ostentatious withdrawal from the courts of the powerful to the security of an independent existence on the margins of monasticism,"[18] that is, by leasing rooms in a monastery.

It is in the context of this competitive world of imperial patronage, and the particular circumstances of the twelfth-century Komnenian court, that Tzetzes produced the *Allegories of the* Iliad, the *Allegories of the* Odyssey, and his other works, the majority of which were on classical themes. They included more theoretical works on Homer, such as the *Exegesis of the* Iliad, as well as retellings of the Trojan War, in the *Antehomerica, Homerica,* and *Posthomerica;* scholia on authors such as Pindar, Aeschylus, Euripides, and Thucydides; and commentaries on, for instance, Aristophanes, Lykophron, and Ptolemy. A prolific letter writer, Tzetzes wrote 107 letters addressed to fictional and historical characters and to his contemporaries, many of which survive in whole or in fragments. Tzetzes is perhaps most famous for *The Histories,* often referred to as the *Chiliades* (that is, the *Thousands [of Verses]*), a monumental commentary in verse on his own letters, which contains much information about his own times and the Byzantine understanding of the classical past.

## TZETZES'S ALLEGORICAL METHOD

Just as Dante, the far more famous allegorist who lived a century after Tzetzes, did not outline his allegorical method in *The Divine Comedy* itself, but rather detailed it in the ancillary *Letter to Cangrande,* so too does Tzetzes provide a

detailed analysis of his method not in the *Allegories* them-
selves, but rather in his *Exegesis,* a commentary on the *Iliad*
meant as an aid to the schoolchildren who had to memorize
Homer for their daily lessons.[19] Here he asserts that

> since [Homer] knew how rare wisdom was in life, and
> unwise men are much more numerous, he abstained
> from believing that he was writing about great things,
> if not about the truth itself, I mean, of natural and as-
> tronomical and magical things and the like, because
> such things were pleasing to the few and, besides, Or-
> pheus and other men have written about such things;
> and he judged in circumspection of his excellent goal
> to write about the events of the Trojan war, so that his
> poems might also become pleasing to everyone.[20]

This allegorical method has the advantage of luring readers
in with an exciting tale, from which the poet hopes that
they will also learn something: "Having made their subject
matter altogether twofold," he writes, "at the same time leg-
endary (as an enchanting attraction to young men and as a
pastime) and also mathematical and natural and philosophi-
cal as bait for more divine souls."[21]

Tzetzes defines the three kinds of allegory as rhetorical,
natural, and mathematical.[22] The rhetorical rationalizes my-
thology as stylistic literary flourish: sirens are musical pros-
titutes (12.12), for instance, or the Cyclopes are Sicilians
(9.131), and the blinding of Polyphemos is the stealing of his
only daughter, Elpe (9.168–70). The natural type of allegory
explains the poem in terms of its climatological, etiological,
and environmental features, as when Artemis and Apollo are

allegorized as acute diseases (15.72–78). The final type, what Tzetzes calls mathematical, is derived from the subject matter of the quadrivium (the study of arithmetic, music, geometry, and astronomy), and thus allegorizes the poem in astrological and astronomical terms. This last may be seen as a particular interest of Tzetzes, who "seems to have served (or wished to serve) as personal diviner to members of the court, perhaps because this was one of the services that professional polymaths could provide to aristocratic clients."[23]

The most important application of allegory is in its treatment of the gods, for the ideologically motivated reason that this was the only way the pagan text could be assimilated into a Christian belief system. The comparison, however, is implicit rather than explicit, as Tzetzes's references to Christianity are extremely sparse. Indeed, the only explicit mention of Christianity in either of the two *Allegories* is at the beginning of Book 13 (lines 6–17) of the *Allegories of the Iliad*, where Tzetzes offers a digression on Skythian *mores* regarding justice and poverty, comparing them favorably with sinning Christians, and adds a now obscure reference to two oath-breaking bishops. These, and scattered and insignificant references to the Christian God (see, for instance, Tz. *All. Il.* pro.488, where the term is used idiomatically in the expression "God willing"), suggest an author whose interest in allegory was antiquarian and literary rather than theological.

Indeed, Tzetzes's focus on the pagan gods is reflected in the detailed rubric for understanding their allegorical treatment that he offers in the *Exegesis*. He lists five methods by which the gods are allegorized: first, as natural elements[24] (as when the adultery of Aphrodite and Ares and their capture by Hephaistos are described in terms of cosmology and weather patterns) and second, as psychological characteristics "such as knowledge, prudence, anger, desire, and the rest."[25] Both the third and fourth ways apply a "euhemeristic approach," that is, interpreting myth in terms of history; thus, Tzetzes rationalizes the gods as (third) ancient kings and (fourth) wise men. The final allegorical interpretation of the gods is as planets; thus, Hermes is the planet Mercury, Aphrodite is Venus, and so on. This last method of interpretation, much of which is derived from Ptolemy's second-century work on astrology and astronomy, the *Tetrabiblos,* is particularly significant for Tzetzes, as evidenced by his detailed astrological readings.[26]

## TZETZES, EUSTATHIOS OF THESSALONIKE, AND HOMERIC CRITICISM IN THE TWELFTH CENTURY

The tradition of allegorical interpretation of Homer has its origins in classical antiquity.[27] It grew in scope and complexity throughout late antiquity and the early Middle Ages[28] and continued, in Greek, at least through the late Byzantine period.[29] During Tzetzes's own lifetime, the competitive milieu of the *theatron* and the general increase in scholarly and literary activity made reading, writing, and teaching about Homer either a profession in and of itself (as it was for Tzetzes) or a gateway to professions far more lucrative in, for instance, the ecclesiastical or imperial hierarchies. Perhaps no two writers exemplify these economic and professional possibilities more than Tzetzes and his rival contemporary, Eustathios of Thessalonike.[30] While the former lived in self-described squalor on the periphery of Byzantine high society, the latter rose to the heights of the church hierarchy and elite Byzantine cultural and political circles, becoming archbishop of Thessalonike (ca. 1178–1195/6) after a long and successful career in Constantinople. In their afterlives, too, Tzetzes has fallen to near obscurity, while Eustathios was canonized in 1988. The competition between the two men was a point of contention during their own lifetimes. Eric Cullhed notes that, though neither of the men refers to each other explicitly, an allusive rhetoric of competitive contempt wends its way through their work. Tzetzes at one point mocks those "standing in the corner in the Stoa or the Rotunda, the mishmash and rabble of this world," with the rotunda being Hagia Sophia with which Eustathios was affiliated.[31]

Such a rivalry was surely about prestige and economics, but just as surely it was ideological, based on two very different visions of what one would expect from a Homeric work so deeply embedded in the political and literary culture of the period. Tzetzes asserts at the conclusion of Prolegomena A that his allegory of the *Odyssey* "makes it possible to discover / a wealth of pearls, precious stones, all kinds of other delights" (pro.A.42–43). Here and elsewhere, however, Tzetzes is essentially vague as to what moral insight or wisdom he hopes his readers will find in the epic. Eustathios, by contrast, lays out the overall meaning of the epic poem from the outset: "The principal aim of this poem is temperance, and the book teaches lawful love of one's husband. [. . .] It also advises to avoid injustice." He adds, too, a methodological statement: "our method of handling the subject will not be through exegesis, which others have concerned themselves with, but through collecting useful passages for those who run through the work and cannot easily permit themselves to go in a leisurely manner into the breadth of the poem."[32] Tzetzes was not only attempting to interpret Homer, but also, unlike Eustathios, attempting to create a work that could stand as a piece of literature in its own right; what he lacks in comprehensiveness and coherence, he makes up for in artistry.

## Note on the Translation

As we prepared this translation of the *Allegories,* the first into any language, we encountered a number of challenges due to the difficulty of the text. Unlike the *Allegories of the* Iliad, which was commissioned for a patron who may have read little Greek, the *Allegories of the* Odyssey is a more advanced work, with the relatively simple passages of summary limited to the first few lines of every book and with more space devoted to often cryptic, complex, and opaque allegorical and astrological interpretations. Throughout, we have attempted to clarify the often syntactically messy allegorical sections and to offer consistent renderings of the discourse-specific vocabulary of allegory and astrology, always with the goal of providing a clear and comprehensible English verse. This means in practice, for example, that we used the Greek names of the gods except when Tzetzes refers to their astrological aspect as planets; in such cases, we opted for the Latin-derived English counterparts, that is, Jupiter for Zeus (1.85), and Mercury for Hermes (1.96). Finally, in order to capture the tenor of Tzetzes's extensive quotations from the *Odyssey,* which would have sounded archaic to his twelfth-century audience, we have used A. T. Murray's similarly old-fashioned 1919 Loeb translation. We have sometimes modified Murray for stylistic reasons to provide a similar juxtaposition in English. We have inserted single quotation marks and italicized Tzetzes's direct citations of the *Odyssey,* while using single quotation marks alone for his rewordings in twelfth-century Greek and his frequent misquotations. The latter may have arisen from his reliance on his own memory rather than on texts (see, for example, his reference to this practice in Tz. *All. II.* 15.87–89), or from the compression resulting from transferring the epic hexameters of Homer to Tzetzes's own fifteen-syllable political verse. To the extent possible, we have endeavored to preserve intact the wording of individual verses, although sometimes the differences between Greek and English grammar have necessitated some transposition of words. We have also occasionally moved words from one line to another in order to equalize verse lengths.

We extend our thanks to Alice-Mary Talbot, who first invited us to submit a proposal for the Dumbarton Oaks Medieval Library, and who, along with Anthony Kaldellis, has painstakingly reviewed our translation; their suggestions were both innumerable and invaluable, and we offer our deepest gratitude as much for their expertise and guidance as for their patience and encouragement. We are also grateful to two Tyler fellows at Dumbarton Oaks, Jake Ransohoff and John Mulhall, for their careful editing and proofreading. We would also like to express our gratitude to Ingela

Nilsson, Eric Cullhed, and Baukje van den Berg for reading drafts of the introduction and for comments on the translation. All mistakes, of course, remain our own.

## NOTES

1  These are the dates suggested by Rhoby, "Ioannes Tzetzes als Auftragsdichter," 160.

2  Elizabeth Jeffreys, "The *Sebastokratorissa* Irene as Patron," in *Female Founders in Byzantium and Beyond,* ed. Lioba Theis, Margaret Mullett, and Michael Grünbart (Vienna, 2013), 177–94 at 189.

3  E. Jeffreys, "*Sebastokratorissa* Irene," 180.

4  His date of birth is derived from the somewhat more certain dates of his other relatives, while his death date of sometime after 1185 is based on a possible reference to the coup of that year, the latest datable reference in his oeuvre (Carl Wendel, *RE* 7A², col. 1960). Subsequent scholarship has questioned the certainty of the late date: Cullhed, "Diving for Pearls," 61, followed by Agapitos, "John Tzetzes and the Blemish Examiners," 2, finds no certainty for any date after the mid-1160s.

5  Magdalino, *The Empire of Manuel I Komnenos,* 321. Much biographical information is also found in *ODB* 3:2136; Gautier, "La curieuse ascendance de Jean Tzetzès"; Browning, "Homer in Byzantium," 26–28; and Carl Wendel, *RE* 7A², cols. 1959–2011. Tzetzes discusses his own lineage, on both his father's and mother's sides, in Tz. *Chiliades* 5.585–630.

6  Gautier, "La curieuse ascendance de Jean Tzetzès," 219.

7  Tz. *All. Il.* pro.724–39. Tzetzes makes the same comparison at Tz. *Chiliades* 5.615.

8  Budelmann, "Classical Commentary in Byzantium," 165.

9  Browning, "Homer in Byzantium," 26.

10  M. Jeffreys, "The Nature and Origins of the Political Verse," 154, and *ODB* 3:2136.

11  Magdalino, *The Empire of Manuel I Komnenos,* 348.

12  Magdalino, *The Empire of Manuel I Komnenos,* 329.

13  Elizabeth Jeffreys, "The Judgement of Paris in Later Byzantine Literature," *Byzantion* 48 (1978) : 112–31 at 126.

14 Magdalino, *The Empire of Manuel I Komnenos,* 402.

15 Though there is evidence, too, that Tzetzes himself had "contempt for gifts and the flattery needed to win them" (M. Jeffreys, "The Nature and Origins of the Political Verse," 154), for which, see Tz. *Chiliades* 10.851.

16 M. Jeffreys, "The Nature and Origins of the Political Verse," 149.

17 M. Jeffreys, "The Nature and Origins of the Political Verse," 150.

18 Magdalino, *The Empire of Manuel I Komnenos,* 403. For the specific circumstances of Tzetzes's patronage, see Budelmann, "Classical Commentary in Byzantium," 166.

19 Browning, "Homer in Byzantium," 26.

20 Tz. *Exegesis of the* Iliad 42.

21 Tz. *Exegesis of the* Iliad 43.

22 See also the note in *ODB* 1:68, and, for a more expansive discussion, Cesaretti, *Allegoristi di Omero a Bisanzio,* esp. 127–95. The basic contours of Tzetzes's allegorical method are described in greater detail in Goldwyn, "Theory and Method."

23 Mavroudi, "Occult Science and Society in Byzantium," 77. For Tzetzes as a practitioner of astrology and dream divination, see Mavroudi, "Occult Science and Society in Byzantium," 73–79.

24 The word translated here as "elements" is *stoicheia,* which does not invoke the fundamentals of mathematics in Euclid's work of the same name, but rather the composite materials of the physical world. For a history of the changing meaning of the word and its associations with both demonology and astrology, see Richard Greenfield, *Traditions and Belief in Late Byzantine Demonology* (Amsterdam, 1988), esp. 191–95.

25 Tz. *Exegesis of the* Iliad 46.

26 For an outline of the relevant aspects of Ptolemy's theories, see, for example, Maria Michela Sassi, *The Science of Man in Ancient Greece* (Chicago, 2001), esp. 164–72.

27 See, for instance, Ford, "Performing Interpretation: Early Allegorical Exegesis of Homer."

28 See Robert Lamberton, ed., *Homer the Theologian. Neoplatonist Allegorical Reading and the Growth of the Epic Tradition* (Berkeley, 1986).

29 See Browning, "A Fourteenth-Century Prose Version of the 'Odyssey.'"

30 The parallel courses of their careers are discussed in Anthony Kaldellis,

*Hellenism in Byzantium: The Transformation of Greek Identity and the Reception of the Classical Tradition* (Cambridge, 2007), 301–16, and, more recently, Agapitos, "John Tzetzes and the Blemish Examiners," 6.

31 Eric Cullhed, *Eustathios of Thessalonike: Parekbolai on Homer's* Odyssey *1–2* (Uppsala, 2014), 22

32 Eustathios of Thessalonike, *Commentary on Homer's Odyssey: Volume One on Rhapsodies A–B,* ed. and trans. Eric Cullhed (Uppsala: Studia Byzantina Upsaliensia, 2016), 11.

# ALLEGORIES OF
# THE *ODYSSEY*

## Ἰωάννου γραμματικοῦ τοῦ
## Τζέτζου Ἀλληγορίαι εἰς τὴν Ὀδύσσειαν


Κύρος μὲν πρὶν τὸν ποταμὸν Γύνδην τῆς Βαβυλῶνος
ναυσίπλουν ὄντα, πνίξαντα λευκὸν ἵππον ἐκείνου,
τριακοσίας ὀρυγὰς ἑξηκοντάδος μέτα—
ἔνθε τὰς ὀγδοήκοντα καὶ ἑκατὸν ὀρύξας,
5 ἐκ μέρους τοῦ ἑτέρου δὲ πάλιν τὰς ἰσαρίθμους—
βατὸν ἐκεῖνον τέθεικε γραυσὶ καὶ βρεφυλλίοις.
Ταῦτα μὲν Κῦρος ὁ καλὸς τοῖς ἀνωτέρω χρόνοις,
κἀγὼ δὲ νῦν τὴν λιγυρὰν Ὁμήρου Καλλιόπην,
τὴν περιτράνως ᾄδουσαν ἡρώων καταλόγους,
10 τὰς Ἰλιάδος μάχας τε καὶ πόλεμον Ἑλλήνων,
ἐχούσας βάθος ἀχανὲς ἐν ταῖς ἀλληγορίαις·
οὐ κατὰ Γύνδην ποταμόν, Ὠκεανὸν δὲ μέγαν,
ἐξ οὗ πᾶς λόγων ποταμὸς ῥεῖ, θάλασσα καὶ φρέαρ,
οὐχ᾽ ἵππον πνίξαντα λευκόν, μέλλοντα δ᾽ ἀποπνίγειν
15 ἐπιθυμίας σκίρτημα λαμπρᾶς· φημὶ πρὸς λόγους
τῆς βασιλίδος τῆς ἐμῆς, ἢ γυναικῶν ἦν κόσμος,
κελεύσει ταύτης σεβαστῇ καὶ δωρεαῖς ἀξίαις,
καὶ δὴ προσλιπαρήσεσι καὶ δώροις ἄλλων φίλων·
ἔστι μὲν ὅπη γεφυρῶν κατὰ τὸν Μανδροκλέα,

# Prolegomena A

When Cyrus reached the river Gyndes of Babylon,
before it was navigable, the river drowned his white horse,
and so he made three hundred and sixty channels —
digging one hundred and eighty channels on one side,
and again the same number on the other side — and made it          5
    fordable for old women and babies alike.
This is what Cyrus the Great did in olden times,
while I now speak of clear-voiced Kalliope of Homer,
she who sang resoundingly of the catalogs of heroes,
the battles of the *Iliad* and the war of the Greeks,          10
battles which have infinite depth in the allegories;
not like the river Gyndes, but like the great Ocean,
from which every river of words flows, every sea and
    channel,
which did not drown the white horse, but was about to
    choke
the skittish bounding of vigorous desire: I speak at the          15
    request
of my queen, who was an ornament to womankind
as a result of her august command, and her worthy gifts,
and, moreover, due to the persistence and gifts of other
    friends;
it is like building bridges in the manner of Mandrokles,

20 ὃς ἀρχιτέκτων Σάμιος ἦν χρόνοις τοῦ Δαρείου,
κατά τε Ἀπολλόδωρον—τὸν Δαμασκόθεν λέγω—,
ὅσπερ ὑπῆρχεν ἄνακτος Τραϊανοῦ ἐν χρόνοις,
οὕτω μὲν ὅπη γεφυρῶν κατὰ τοὺς ἄνδρας τούτους,
πῆ δὲ χερσῶν τὸ πέλαγος κατὰ τὸν Δεξιφάνην,
25 ὃς χρόνοις Κλεοπάτρας ἦν Κνίδον αὐχῶν πατρίδα,
ὅπη δ᾽, ὡς ὁ Μιλήσιος Θαλῆς ἐκεῖνος γέρων
τὸν Ἅλυν μὴ περάσαντα πεπέρακε τὸν Κῦρον,
οὕτω κἀγὼ νῦν τεχνικῶς τὴν κοίτην μετατρέπων,
πῆ δὲ μυρίαις ὀρυγαῖς λεπτοτομῶν τὰ βάθη,
30 ἀβρόχως πᾶσι τέθεικα πάντας περᾶν εἰς χρόνους,
ἐν λέξει γράφων διαυγεῖ, γνωστῇ καὶ τοῖς τυχοῦσιν,
οὐ μὴν καθάπερ ἡ Δημώ, μιμῶ δὲ τοῖς φρονοῦσι,
γύναιον κομπολάκυθον ψευδυψηγορογράφον,
μηδὲν δὲ πρὸς τὸν Ὅμηρον τῶν συντελούντων λέγον.
35 Ἔχεις Δημοῦς τὸ σύγγραμμα καὶ τὸ τοῦ Ἡρακλείτου,
Κορνοῦτον καὶ Παλαίφατον καὶ τὸν Ψελλὸν σὺν τούτοις,
καὶ εἴ τις ἄλλος λέγεται γράψας ἀλληγορίας,
ἀνερευνήσας εὕρισκε καὶ τὰ τοῦ Τζέτζου βλέπε,
εἴτ᾽ οὖν τοῖς πᾶσι ζηλωτὴς καθέστηκεν Ὁμήρου,
40 κἂν τοῖς σαφέσι καὶ ληπτοῖς καὶ παιγνιωδεστέροις
καὶ τοῖς ἀποκαθάρμασι τοῦ λόγου τῆς οἰκίας·
ὥσπερ ἐκεῖνος καὶ αὐτὸς ὄλβον διδοὺς εὑρίσκειν

who was a Samian architect in the time of Darius,                    20
according to Apollodoros—I mean the one from
    Damascus—
who lived in the time of the emperor Trajan,
just like building bridges, I say, as these men did,
turning the sea into dry land like Dexiphanes,
who in Cleopatra's time proudly called Knidos his native      25
    land;
also, just as that old man Thales of Miletus made
passable the river Halys when Cyrus was not able to cross it,
thus I too now, changing the river's bed skillfully,
as though slicing the depths with countless channels,
made it such that all could forever cross without getting      30
    wet,
writing in clear words, comprehensible even to random
    readers,
not like Demo, imitator of those who possess wisdom,
a little braggart woman, writer of false tall tales,
who said nothing that would help to explain Homer.
You have Demo's book and that of Herakleitos,                    35
and moreover Cornutus and Palaiphatos and, with them,
    Psellos,
and if anyone else is said to have written allegories,
after seeking them out, then find and look at Tzetzes's work
    as well,
since he is a zealous admirer of everything Homeric,
both their clear and comprehensible and more playful parts    40
and the filthy by-products of the edifice of speech;
just as Homer did, so too Tzetzes makes it possible to
    discover

μαργάρων, λίθων τιμαλφῶν, ἄλλων τερπνῶν παντοίων,
ἢ ὡς πολλοὶ τῶν νέων τε καὶ τῶν παλαιοτέρων
45  σφῶν τοῖς δοκοῦσι θησαυροῖς, τοῖς διηρμένοις λόγοις,
οἷάπερ τύμβοι φέρουσι σαπρίαν τε καὶ κόνιν.
Οὕτω τὴν Ἰλιάδα μέν, σύμπασαν Καλλιόπην,
λόγοις ἠλληγορήσαμεν εὐλήπτοις, σαφεστάτοις
καὶ συντελοῦσι πρὸς αὐτὴν τὴν συγγραφὴν Ὁμήρου,
50  ἀλλ᾽ οὐ κατά τινας αὐτῶν ψευδυψηγόροις λόγοις,
εἴτ᾽ οὖν σκιαῖς πλὴν ἀμυδραῖς καὶ μερικαῖς δὲ πλέον,
οὐδὲ θεοὺς τὰ Χερουβὶμ καὶ Σεραφὶμ καλοῦντες.
Οὕτως ἠλληγορήσαμεν ἤδη τὴν Ἰλιάδα·
νῦν δὲ πρὸς τὸν πολύτροπον ἄνδρα μεταβατέον
55  καὶ ἀλληγορητέον δὲ πᾶσαν ἀλληγορίαν,
ὅσην ἡ βίβλος κέκτηται τούτου τῶν πλανημάτων.

a wealth of pearls, precious stones, all kinds of other
    delights,
not in the manner of many ancient and more recent writers
who do it rather through their own supposed treasures,      45
    their conflicted speeches,
which are like the contents of tombs, decay and dust.
Thus the *Iliad,* the whole of Kalliope,
we allegorized with easily understandable, very clear words,
which contribute to the very work of Homer,
but not like some of *those* guys, who are deceptive big-      50
    talkers,
or produce only shadows, and obscure and partial ones at
    that,
nor will we be calling the gods Cherubim and Seraphim.
In this way we have already allegorized the *Iliad;*
now we must move to the subject of the much-traveled man
and every allegory needs to be allegorized,      55
as much allegory as this book of his wanderings contains.

Ὑπόθεσις <μὲν> ἐν βραχεῖ τῆς ὅλης Ὀδυσσείας.

Μετὰ τὴν Τροίας πόρθησιν τὸ στράτευμα Ἑλλήνων,
διαλαχόντες λάφυρα καὶ τοὺς δορυαλώτους,
πρὸς τὰς πατρίδας πλέοντες ἀνέμοις τῶν δυσπνόων,
ἄλλος ἄλλῃ ἐξώσθησαν. Οἱ δὲ μετ᾽ Ὀδυσσέως
5  πρῶτα περὶ Μαρώνειαν, τὴν Ἴσμαρον Ὁμήρῳ,
μάχῃ νικῶσι Κίκονας, ἔπειτα δ᾽ ἡττημένοι
φεύγουσι πρὸς τὸ πέλαγος· Βορέαις δ᾽ ἡρπαγμένοι
πρῶτα καταίρουσιν εἰς γῆν ἀνδρῶν τῶν Λωτοφάγων,
εἶτα πρὸς νῆσον Κύκλωπος, ἔπειτα πρὸς Αἴολον,
10  ἑξῆς ἐς Λαιστρυγόνας δέ, αὖθις ὡς πρὸς τὴν Κίρκην,
εἰς Ἅιδην, μετὰ Κίρκην δὲ πάλιν πρὸς τὰς Σειρῆνας,
μικρῷ πρὸς πέτρας τὰς Πλαγκτὰς καὶ Χάρυβδιν καὶ
Σκύλλαν,
μετέπειτα πρὸς νῆσον δὲ τὴν τῶν βοῶν Ἡλίου.
Μετὰ βραχὺ τῆς νήσου δὲ ταύτης ἀποπλεόντων
15  ἡ ναῦς ἐβλήθη κεραυνῷ καὶ φλέγονται μὲν πάντες·
σῴζεται μόνος δ᾽ Ὀδυσσεὺς εἰς Καλυψοῦς τὴν νῆσον,
ἐκεῖθε δὲ πρὸς Φαίακας, ἐκ τούτων δ᾽ εἰς Ἰθάκην,
οὗ πάντας ἄγνωστος ἐλθὼν ἀνεῖλε τοὺς μνηστῆρας.
Καὶ αὕτη μὲν ὑπόθεσις πᾶσα τῆς Ὀδυσσείας.

# Prolegomena B

The subject matter in brief of the entire *Odyssey*.

After the sack of Troy, the Greek army
divided the booty and the captives by lot,
and sailed to their homelands against adverse winds;
they were driven to shore, some here, some there.
Odysseus's companions first near Maroneia (called Ismaros    5
    by Homer)
defeat the Kikones in battle, then, defeated in turn,
flee out to sea; snatched by the North Winds,
they put in first at the land of the Lotus-Eaters,
then at the island of the Cyclops, then the land of Aiolos,
then that of the Laistrygonians, then that of Kirke,    10
and Hades, then after Kirke (again) to the Sirens,
shortly after that to the Planktai and Charybdis and Skylla,
afterward to the island of the Cattle of the Sun.
Soon after they sailed away from this island
the ship was struck by lightning and everyone was    15
    incinerated;
only Odysseus was saved on Kalypso's isle,
and from there he went to the Phaiakians, from them to
    Ithake
where he arrived, unrecognized, and killed all the suitors.
And this is the entire plot of the *Odyssey*.

συνέβη τούτοις δὲ θανεῖν σκηπτοῖς καὶ ναυαγίᾳ,
ἅτε ἡλίου σφῶν ζωῆς καὶ χρόνου πληρωθέντος.
Ὅμηρος, ὧν δεινότατος ἀνθρώπων νουθεσίαις,
25 πάντας ἀνθρώπους νουθετεῖ τοῖς πταίσμασιν ἐκείνων,
μηδέν τι δρᾶν παράνομον βλέποντας πρὸς ἐκείνους.
Καὶ γὰρ παρανομήσασιν ἐκείνοις εἰς τὰς βόας
ἐν ναυαγίᾳ τῇ δεινῇ καὶ τοῖς σκηπτοῖς, οἷς ἔφην,
Ἥλιον λέγει τῆς ζωῆς πικρῶς ἐκπληρωθῆναι.
30 Καὶ πάλιν περὶ τούτου δὲ τοῖς ἔμπροσθε μαθήσῃ,
ὅπουπερ καὶ ὁ Ὅμηρος ταῦτα πρὸς πλάτος γράφει.
'Ἀμόθεν' ὁθενδήποτε τῶν Ἀττικῶν τῷ τρόπῳ.
'Θεὰ' γνῶσις καὶ φρόνησις, 'Διὸς' νοὸς θυγάτηρ.
'Νύμφην' δὲ λέγει σοι θεάν, ἄνασσαν νησιῶτιν.
35 'Θεοὶ' οἱ ἐπικλώσαντες ἀστέρες, Εἱμαρμένη.
'Θεοὶ πάντες ἐλέαιρον νόσφι τοῦ Ποσειδῶνος.'
Στοιχεῖα καὶ ἀστέρες δέ, ἐξ ὧν τὰ εἱμαρμένα,
ἤτοι καλὸν κατάστημα ὑπῆρχεν εὐκαιρίας,
καὶ οἱ ἀστέρες δὲ αὐτοῦ χρηστοὶ τῆς Εἱμαρμένης·
40 θάνατον οὐκ ἐμφαίνοντες, ἡ θάλασσα δὲ μόνη
καὶ τὰ μακρὰ πελάγη δὲ καὶ νῆες μὴ παροῦσαι
κώλυμα ἦσαν Ὀδυσσεῖ νοστῆσαι τῇ πατρίδι.
'Ἀλλ' ὁ μὲν Αἰθίοπας μετεκίαθε τηλόθ' ἐόντας.'
Τίς ἡ παρὰ Αἰθίοπας δαὶς ἡ τοῦ Ποσειδῶνος,
45 καὶ τίς δὲ Ζεὺς καὶ μέγαρον τούτου καὶ οἱ θεοὶ δέ,
καὶ τίνες λόγοι οἱ Διός, καὶ τίς ἡ Ἀθηνᾶ δέ,
ἡ ἀποκρίνεται Διὶ ἀντιτιθεῖσα λόγους,

they died by thunderbolts and shipwreck,
just as if the sun had been repaid with their life and allotted
    time.
Homer, being very skilled in advising men,
advises all men, through the faults of those men,                          25
to do nothing unlawful, looking to the example of those
    others.
Because for those who transgressed the law in the matter of
    the oxen,
Homer says that the Sun was bitterly repaid with their lives
in a fierce shipwreck and storm, of which I spoke.
And again you will learn about this from what has been        30
    written before,
where Homer also writes this in broad strokes.
    '*Where you will*' means wherever in Attic style.
    '*The goddess*' is knowledge and wisdom, the daughter of
        '*Zeus,*' of reason.
    And by 'a nymph' he means a goddess, an island queen.
    '*The gods*' are the stars deciding one's fate, that is, Destiny.  35
    'All *the gods took pity on him except* Poseidon.'
The elements and the stars, from which Destiny emerges,
that is, there was a state of good weather,
and his stars were beneficial for his Destiny:
not indicating death, but the sea alone                                    40
and the wide oceans and the lack of ships
hindered Odysseus on his journey home to his native land.
    '*But Poseidon was visiting the Ethiopians, who lived far away.*'
The meaning of Poseidon's feast among the Ethiopians,
and who is Zeus and his palace and the gods,                              45
and what are Zeus's words, and who is Athena,
who replies to Zeus with words opposed to his,

τίς ὁ Ἑρμῆς τε ὁ σταλεὶς εἰς Καλυψοῦς τὴν 'νῆσον,'
καὶ πῶς αὐτὴ πορεύεται πάλιν πρὸς τὴν Ἰθάκην,
50  καὶ τ' ἄλλα πάντα μάνθανε λεπτῶς, ἠκριβωμένως.
Καιρὸς ἦν ἀναβάσεως Νείλου παρ' Αἰγυπτίοις,
ἤτοι τὸ θέρος ἔληγεν, ἀρχὴ δ' ἦν φθινοπώρου.
Ἡ Νείλου γὰρ ἀνάβασις ἐκ τέλους Ἰουλίου
μέχρι τῆς συμπληρώσεως γίνεται Σεπτεμβρίου.
55  Τοῦ Νείλου τὴν ἀνάβασιν ταύτην δὲ νῦν σοὶ λέγει
εἶναι παρὰ Αἰθίοπας τοῦ Ποσειδῶνος δαῖτα.
'Ταύρους' δὲ τούτου παρεισφρεῖ 'καὶ ἀρνειοὺς' τὴν δαῖτα,
εἰς Ταῦρον ταυρωδέστερον τῶν ποταμῶν ἠχούντων.
Ἑῴους δὲ Αἰθίοπας καὶ ἑσπερίους λέγει,
60  οὐ πρὸς τὸ πᾶν οἰκήσιμον γῆς τοῦτο πλάτος λέγων,
ἀλλὰ πρὸς τὸ Αἰγύπτιον μέρος καὶ τῆς Λιβύης.
Οἱ μὲν τῶν Αἰθιόπων γὰρ εἰς ἔσπερα Λιβύης,
οἱ δ' ἐν Αἰγύπτου μέρεσι τυγχάνουσιν ἑῴοις.
Παντὸς τοῦ κόσμου γὰρ Ἰνδοὶ τυγχάνουσιν ἑῷοι,
65  ἑσπέριοι δὲ Ἴβηρες, οὓς Ἰσπανοὺς καλοῦμεν.
Οὕτω μὲν ἦν ἀνάβασις παρ' Αἴγυπτον τοῦ Νείλου,
ἁπανταχοῦ δ' ἐν οὐρανῷ στοιχείων εὐκρασία.
Οἶκον καὶ μέγαρον 'Ζηνὸς' τὸν οὐρανὸν νῦν λέγει.
'Τοῖσι δὲ μύθων ἦρχε πατὴρ ἀνδρῶν τε θεῶν τε.'
70  Πρόσχες μὴ ἀπατήσῃ σε ὁ γέρων ὁ βαθύνους.
Νῦν οὐ τὸν Δία οὐρανὸν θεῶν πατέρα λέγει,
θεῶν ὁμοῦ ἀνθρώπων τε, ἀλλὰ τὴν Εἱμαρμένην,
ἥπερ ἅπαν εὐτύχημα καὶ πᾶσαν δυσκληρίαν
οἷα πατὴρ ἀπογεννᾷ τοῖς σύμπασιν ἀνθρώποις·

who is Hermes who was sent to Kalypso's '*island*,'
and how Athena traveled again to Ithake,
and everything else, now learn in detail, accurately.                    50
It was the time of the flooding of the Nile among the
    Egyptians,
that is, summer was ending, autumn was beginning.
For the Nile floods from the end of July
until the end of September.
So Homer tells you that this flooding of the Nile              55
is the feast of Poseidon among the Ethiopians.
And he introduces in his feast 'bulls and rams,'
as the rivers bellow in Taurus in a bull-like manner.
And he calls some Ethiopians easterners and some
    westerners,
not meaning that the entire breadth of their land is          60
    habitable,
but those parts close to Egypt and to Libya.
And some of the Ethiopians happen to be to the west of
    Libya,
and the others happen to be in the eastern parts of Egypt.
For the Indians are to the east of the entire world,
while the Iberians, whom we call Spanish, are to the west.         65
Thus there was flooding of the Nile in Egypt,
but a harmony of elements everywhere in the sky.
Here he calls the sky the abode and palace '*of Zeus*.'
    '*With these words the father of men and gods began.*'
Be careful lest the wise old man deceive you.                   70
Here he does not speak of Zeus, the sky, the father of gods,
of gods and men alike, but of Destiny,
which is every good fortune and every misfortune
such as the father generates for all humanity:

75 σοφοῖς, ἀσόφοις, πένησιν, ἄρχουσι, βασιλεῦσιν.
Ἤ ἥτις Εἱμαρμένη μὲν κατὰ Ἑλλήνων δόξαν
ἀνθρώπους τε παρήγαγεν ὁμοῦ καὶ τὰ στοιχεῖα·
εἰ μὴ γὰρ εἱμαρμένον ἦν, οὐκ ἂν ὑπέστη κόσμος,
πολλῷ δὲ μᾶλλον ἄνθρωποι· καὶ ποῦ γὰρ ἂν διῆγον;
80 Ἤ ὅτι οὔτε ἄνθρωπος, οὔτε τι ἔτους μέρος,
ἢ εὐτυχὴς ἢ δυστυχής, ἢ εὔκρατον ἢ δύσπνουν
γένοιτο, ὥσπερ λέγουσιν, εἰ μὴ προεκυρώθη.
Οὕτω τὴν Εἱμαρμένην νῦν ἐν τῷ παρόντι τόπῳ
'ἀνθρώπων' ἅμα 'καὶ θεῶν' δεικνὺς 'πατέρα' λέγειν,
85 καὶ Δία δὲ τὸν πλάνητα, τὸν κάλλιστον ἀστέρα,
θεοὺς τοὺς ἄλλους πέντε δέ, τὴν δ᾽ Ἀθηνᾶν σελήνην.
Καὶ προσωποποιήσας δὲ καὶ λόγους θεὶς προσφόρους
καὶ ἀπατήσας τοὺς παχεῖς πάνυ τῷ μύθῳ μόνῳ,
νοοῦντας Δία φλύαρον καὶ τἄλλα παρομοίως.
90 Τοὺς σοφωτέρους πάλιν δὲ τῷ γνῶναι Εἱμαρμένην
Δία δοκοῦντας πλάνητα, τὴν δ᾽ Ἀθηνᾶν σελήνην,
θεμάτιον νομίζοντας ἔχον καλῶς κειμένους
τὸν Δία καὶ σελήνην τε καὶ τοὺς λοιποὺς ἀστέρας,
τῶν ἄλλων πάντων πλέον δὲ τὸν Δία καὶ σελήνην,
95 οἷσπερ καὶ λόγοις οἴονται τὸν Ὅμηρον προσάψαι

the wise, the unwise, the poor, the rulers, the kings.                    75
Either a Destiny which, according to the belief of the
    Greeks,
generated humankind as well as the elements;
for if it were not destined, the world would not exist,
much less people; for where would they have lived?
Or he means that neither man, nor any part of the year,      80
whether he is fortunate or unfortunate, or it is temperate or
    with contrary winds,
would come to exist, as they say, unless it had been
    predetermined.
Thus now in this present passage he reveals,
by saying that Destiny is the 'father' of 'men and gods' alike,
that Zeus is the planet Jupiter, the most beautiful heavenly    85
    body,
and that the gods are the other five planets and Athena is
    the moon.
And by personifying them and putting suitable words in
    their mouth,
he entirely deceives thickheaded people with the bare
    myth,
since they thought Zeus was a babbler, and the rest
    accordingly.
But those who are wiser at recognizing Destiny                90
believe that Zeus is a planet and Athena is the moon,
and think that a horoscope had placed in a favorable
    position
Jupiter and the moon and the other planets
and especially Jupiter and the moon above all others.
And with these words they also believe that Homer             95
    attributed

τῷ δι' αὐτῶν καὶ δι' Ἑρμοῦ, λέγω δὲ τοῦ ἀστέρος,
ἅπαντα τὰ συνοίσοντα τῷ Ὀδυσσεῖ γενέσθαι.
Οὕτως ὁ γέρων ἀπατᾷ τινὰς ὡς μυθογράφος,
τοὺς δὲ σοφοὺς ἠπάτησε δόξαντας, Εἱμαρμένην,
100 —εἰ τέως τις ἐνόησε—νῦν Εἱμαρμένην λέγειν,
νοεῖν καὶ Δία πλάνητα καὶ Ἀθηνᾶν σελήνην
καὶ τὸν ἀστέρα τὸν Ἑρμῆν· τοῦτο δ' οὐχ οὕτως ἔχει.
Ὀνόματος "μετάβασις" τὸ σχῆμα δὲ καλεῖται,
ᾧ νῦν ὁ γέρων κέχρηται δεινότητος μεθόδῳ.
105 'Πατὴρ ἀνδρῶν' γὰρ 'καὶ θεῶν' καὶ ὁ ἀὴρ καλεῖται,
ἡ Εἱμαρμένη τε αὐτή—καὶ προλαβὼν εἰρήκειν—
καὶ νοῦς 'πατὴρ δὲ τῶν θεῶν καὶ τῶν ἀνδρῶν' καλεῖται.
Ἐμπεδοκλῆς γὰρ Πλάτων τε καὶ ὁ Ἀναξαγόρας
ἄλλοι τε πόσοι τῶν ἐκτὸς νοῦν τὸν Θεὸν καλοῦσιν.
110 Οὗτος νῦν μεταβάσει δέ, ὡς ἔφην, κεχρημένος
ἀνδρῶν πατέρα καὶ θεῶν τὸν ἔννουν ὀνομάζει·
ὡς γὰρ ὁ νοῦς ὁ ὑπὲρ νοῦν ἐκόσμησε τὸν κόσμον,
οὕτω καὶ ἔννους ἄνθρωπος καὶ προορῶν τὸ μέλλον
κόσμῳ καὶ τάξει καὶ ῥυθμῷ πάντα ποιεῖ προσφόρως.
115 Ἐπεὶ γοῦν ἅπαντα λεπτῶς ἤδη σοι διηρθρώκειν,
τανῦν πάνυ σαφέστατα πραγματικῶς σοὶ λέξω·
καιρὸς ἦν ἀναβάσεως παρ' Αἴγυπτον τοῦ Νείλου
ἤτοι τέλος τοῦ θέρους μέν, ἀρχὴ δὲ φθινοπώρου.
Ὁ Μέντης δὲ ὁ Τάφιος, ἔννους ἀνὴρ ὑπάρχων,

to the horoscope through them and through Hermes, I
    mean the planet Mercury,
everything that was about to happen to Odysseus.
In this way the old man deceives some as a writer of myths,
but he deceived the wise who believed that they should now
    call Destiny
Destiny—if anyone understood this in the past—        100
and understand Jupiter as the planet and Athena as the
    moon
and the star as Mercury; but the matter is not like this.
The figure of speech is called "transition" of reference
which the old man now uses with skillful rhetorical
    technique.
For the air is also called '*the father of men* and *gods*,'       105
as is Destiny itself—and I had said this earlier—
but reason is also called the 'father of gods and men.'
For Empedokles and Plato and Anaxagoras
and so many others among the pagans call God reason.
And Homer here, making use of transition, as I said,       110
calls the sensible person the father of men and gods;
for as the reason-that-is-beyond-reason adorned the world,
thus too a sensible man both foresees the future and
makes everything useful through order, sequence, and
    rhythm.
Since everything has already been clearly defined for you in   115
    detail,
I will tell you now of present matters most clearly in a
    historical sense:
it was the time when the Nile floods in Egypt,
that is, the end of summer and beginning of autumn.
Mentes the Taphian, being a sensible man,

120 καὶ προορῶν τὰ μέλλοντα τῇ τῶν φρενῶν πυκνώσει,
καὶ ἐν τοῖς μάλιστα τελῶν τῶν φίλων Ὀδυσσέως,
τῷ τότε χρόνῳ σὺν πολλοῖς εὔφροσιν ἄλλοις φίλοις
εἰς οἶκον οὖσι τὸν αὐτοῦ θυσίαις τερπομένοις.

Ἐπιμνησθεὶς᾽ τῆς τελευτῆς Αἰγίσθου παρ᾽ Ὀρέστου
125 εἰς μέσον λόγους προύθετο περὶ τῆς Εἱμαρμένης,
λέγων, ὡς μάτην ἄνθρωποι τὴν μοῖραν ᾽αἰτιῶνται᾽—
οὐ πάντα γάρ, ἃ γίνεται, εἰσὶν ἐξ Εἱμαρμένης—
ἀλλὰ τὰ πλείω γίνεται κατὰ τὴν Εἱμαρμένην·
πολλὰ καὶ κακοβούλως δὲ τῶν ἀπρεπῶν συμβαίνει,
130 ὡς ὁ Αἰγίσθου θάνατος χερσὶ ταῖς Ὀρεστείαις·
χρησμοῖς γὰρ προδεδήλωτο τὸ πρὶν ἐγγράφως τούτῳ,
καὶ τῇ γραφῇ κατὰ λεπτὸν ἐφερμηνεύσας ἅπαν
οὕτως ἡρμήνευσε χρησμοῖς εἰργνύειν τὴν μοιχείαν·
οὗτος πεισθεὶς δὲ μηδαμῶς ἀπέδωκε τὸ χρέος.

135 Οὕτω τοῦ Μέντου λέξαντος ἔφασαν οἱ φρονοῦντες,
οὓς Ἀθηνᾶν γλαυκώπιδα ὁ ποιητὴς νῦν λέγει·
ἡ Ἀθηνᾶ καὶ φρόνησις λευκῶς καὶ καθαρῶς γὰρ
τὰ πάντα βλέπει καὶ ὁρᾷ, βλέπει τῷ λογισμῷ δέ.
Τί πρὸς τὸν Μέντην ἔφαν δὲ οἱ ἔμφρονες ἐκεῖνοι;
140 "᾽Ὦ πάτερ᾽ βαθυνούστατε, ὑπέροχε ἀρχόντων,
ἢ καὶ σοφῶν ὑπέροχε προβλεπτικῇ καρδίᾳ"—
πατὴρ ὁ ἔννους γὰρ σοφῶν ὑπάρχει καὶ φρονίμων—
"ὁ Αἴγισθος ἀξίως μὲν ἀπώλετο μοιχεύων,
περὶ τοῦ Ὀδυσσέως δὲ θλίψις ἡμῖν μεγίστη,
145 ὃς ἐν τῇ ᾽νήσῳ᾽ Καλυψοῦς, θεᾶς καὶ βασιλίδος,
᾽πάσχει᾽ πολλὰ τὰ δυσχερῆ, μακρόθεν ὢν τῶν ᾽φίλων.᾽"

foreseeing what was about to happen through the focus of    120
    his mind,
was among Odysseus's best friends
who were in his house at that time
enjoying the sacrifices with many other merry friends.
   '*Remembering*' Aigisthos's death at the hands of Orestes,
he offered in their midst a speech about Destiny,    125
saying that men 'blame' fate in vain—
for not everything that happens comes from Destiny—
but most things do happen according to Destiny;
many unseemly deeds happen because of bad advice,
such as Aigisthos's death at the hands of Orestes;    130
for it had been foretold to Aigisthos in written oracles
    before it happened,
and, having interpreted everything in detail in his writing,
thus he interpreted with prophecies how to prevent
    adultery;
but Aigisthos, in no way persuaded, paid the debt.
As Mentes spoke in this way, so too spoke the wise men,    135
those whom the poet here calls flashing-eyed Athena;
for Athena, that is, wisdom, sees brightly and purely
and observes everything, she sees through reasoning.
And what did those wise ones say to Mentes?
   "Most deep-minded '*father*,' distinguished among rulers,    140
or distinguished among the wise because of your
    foresightful heart"
—for the sensible man is a father of the wise and prudent—
"Aigisthos died deservedly because he was an adulterer,
but we feel great sadness about Odysseus,
who on the '*isle*' of Kalypso, a goddess and queen,    145
'*suffers*' many hardships, being far from his '*friends*.'"

Ἡ 'νῆσος' αὕτη μέσον δὲ Ἀτλαντικοῦ πελάγους,
ὥσπερ τίς 'ἐστιν ὀμφαλός,'—ὃ πέλαγος ὁ Ἄτλας
ὁ καὶ πατὴρ τῆς Καλυψοῦς καὶ ἡ πατρὶς ἑκάστου,
150 ὁρίζων γῆς καὶ οὐρανοῦ καθέστηκε τερμάτων.
Τὸν οὖν ὁρίζοντα καλεῖ 'κίονας' μακροτάτας,
Ἄτλαντα δ' 'ὁλοόφρονα' τὸ πέλαγος ἐκεῖνο,
ὡς χαλεπὸν καὶ ἄγριον καὶ δυσχερὲς εἰς πλόον.
Οὕτως, "ὦ Μέντη," ἔλεξαν, "ὁ Ὀδυσσεὺς κρατεῖται
155 ἐν τῷ πελάγει τῷ δεινῷ· ἠκούετο γὰρ τοῦτο.
Σὺ δέ, ὦ Ζεῦ Ὀλύμπιε, σοφέ, ἀστεροσκόπε,
οὐχὶ φροντίζεις, οὐχ ὁρᾷς περὶ τοῦ Ὀδυσσέως,
χρησμοῖς τε καὶ μαντεύμασι καὶ λέγεις, ὃ πρακτέον;
Ἐπίληθος τῶν τούτου δὲ χαρίτων ἐγεγόνεις,
160 ἢ ὧν ἐν Τροίᾳ ἔδρα σοι, εἰ Μέντης ἦν στρατεύσας;
Εἴπερ δ' οὐ συνεστράτευσας Ἕλλησι πρὸς τὴν Τροίαν,
ὧν ἐκ τῆς Τροίας ἔστελλε, σὴν ὡς τιμῶν φιλίαν;
Ὦ Ζεῦ, σὺ νοῦ καὶ φρόνιμε, τί οἱ ὠργίσθης τόσον;"
'Τὴν δ' ἀπαμειβόμενος προσέφη νεφεληγερέτα Ζεύς,'
165 πρὸς τούτους ἀπεκρίνατο Μέντης δὲ ὁ βαθύνους·
"'Ἐμὰ τέκνα καὶ παῖδες μοι τίνας φατὲ τοὺς λόγους;
'Πῶς ἂν' ἐπίληθος 'ἐγὼ' γενοίμην 'Ὀδυσσέως,'
τοῦ συνετοῦ καὶ σώφρονος καὶ ἀρετῶν κανόνος
καὶ πάσαις ἄλλαις χάρισι τῶν ἀρετῶν κομῶντος;"
170 Ἃ νῦν καὶ οὐρανίωνας θεοὺς κατονομάζει,
ὡς οὐρανῷ, τῇ κεφαλῇ, τοῦ λογισμοῦ κειμένου,
κἂν ἄλλοι δογματίζωσιν ἐν τῇ καρδίᾳ κεῖσθαι·
"Πῶς οὖν," φησίν, "ἐπίληθος γενοίμην Ὀδυσσέως;"

The '*isle*' itself lies in the middle of the Atlantic Ocean,
just like some 'kind of *navel*' — this is the sea that Atlas,
who is also Kalypso's father and each man's fatherland,
marked as the boundary between the earth and sky.            150
And so, Homer calls the horizon very tall '*pillars*,'
and he called that sea 'crafty' Atlas,
as it was harsh and fierce and difficult to navigate.
Thus they said, "O Mentes, Odysseus is held captive
amid the terrible sea, for this has been rumored.            155
But you, Olympian Zeus, wise one, stargazer,
are you not concerned, do you not care about Odysseus,
nor reveal in oracles and divinations what needs to be done?
Have you forgotten his offerings of thanksgiving,
or what he did for you in Troy, if it was Mentes who had      160
        marched with the army?
Even though you did not campaign with the Greeks against
        Troy,
<have you forgotten> what he sent you from Troy, in honor
        of your friendship?
O Zeus, intelligent wisdom, why are you so angry with
        him?"
    '*Then Zeus the cloud-gatherer answered her and said*,'
that is, deep-minded Mentes replied to them:                 165
    "My offspring and children, what words are you uttering?
'*How* could *I* have forgotten Odysseus,'
the wise and measured man, the standard of virtue,
who is adorned with all the other graces of the virtues?"
Here he calls the gods heaven dwellers,                      170
as they are in heaven, in one's head, where reason resides,
even though others declare that it resides in the heart;
"And so," he says, "how could I forget Odysseus?"

Ἀλλὰ Ποσειδάων γαιήοχος ἀσκελὲς αἰὲν

175  Κύκλωπος κεχόλωται, ὃν ὀφθαλμοῦ ἀλάωσεν.'

"Ἐγὼ μὲν οὐκ ἐπίληθος τελῶ τοῦ Ὀδυσσέως,

ἐκ μαντειῶν εὑρίσκω δὲ κρατούμενον πελάγει,

καὶ ἐξ ἀφικνουμένων δὲ τοῦτο τινῶν μανθάνω·

διὰ τὸ πλοῖά τε αὐτὸν τὸ σύνολον μὴ ἔχειν—

180  κἂν εὕρῃ δέ—πτοούμενον τὸν Κύκλωπα ἐκπλέειν,

ἀνθ' οὗ τὴν Ἔλπην ἥρπασεν, ἐκείνου θυγατέρα,"

ἣν ὀφθαλμὸν τοῦ Κύκλωπος ἐκβεβλημένον λέγει,

"κἂν πάλιν ταύτην ἔλαβον περὶ Λαιστρυγονίαν

τοῦ Ὀδυσσέως κτείναντες πάντας σχεδὸν ἑταίρους,

185  τοῦ Ὀδυσσέως σὺν μιᾷ μόλις νηὶ φυγόντος."

Ὡς ὅπῃ χρὴ πλατύτερον λέξαι μὲν περὶ τούτων,

οὕτως ἐν τῇ θαλάσσῃ μὲν κατέχεται, ὡς ἔφην,

τῷ φόβῳ τῷ τοῦ Κύκλωπος, ἡ 'Θόωσα' ὃν τίκτει,

'θυγάτηρ μὲν τοῦ Φόρκυνος μιγεῖσα Ποσειδῶνι.'

190  Ὁ Φόρκυς δὲ καὶ Ποσειδῶν ἡ θάλασσα τυγχάνει,

παῖδα θαλάσσης ταύτην δέ φησι καὶ νησιῶτιν.

Πάλιν τὸν Κύκλωπα υἱὸν τοῦ Ποσειδῶνος λέγει,

ὡς ἄγαν ἀγριώτατον ὄντα καὶ θηριώδη.

Οὕτως ἐκεῖσε Ὀδυσσεὺς κατέχεται, ὡς εἶπον,

195  καὶ βραδύνει δὲ πρὸς καιρόν, θαλάσσῃ δ' οὐ βαλεῖται,

ὥσπερ ἐφεῦρον τεχνικῶς χρησμοῖς, ἀστρομαντείαις

καὶ συμβουλαῖς. Εἰ βούλεσθε, σκοπῶμεν ὅπως ἔλθοι.

Οὐκ ἀποπνίξαι γὰρ αὐτὸν θάλασσα δυνηθείη,

θεοὺς ἀστέρας ἀγαθοὺς ἔχοντα γενεθλίους.

200  Οἱ δέ φασιν, εἰ πέπρωται ἄστρασι γενεθλίοις

*'But Poseidon the earth shaker stubbornly was always
angry because of the Cyclops, whose eye Odysseus blinded.'*       175
"I am not forgetful of Odysseus,
I learn from divination that he is held fast by the sea,
and from some men who have come here I learn this:
because he does not have any ships at all, and—even
if he could find them—he is afraid to sail away from the       180
     Cyclops,
from whom he seized Elpe, his daughter,"
whom Homer calls the Cyclops's eye that had been gouged
     out,
"or if again they captured her near the Laistrygonians,
who killed nearly all of Odysseus's companions,
and Odysseus was barely able to flee with a single ship."       185
Since I must speak more broadly concerning these things,
in this way he is detained at sea, as I have said,
by fear of the Cyclops, whom *'Thoösa'* bore,
'the daughter of Phorkys' who 'lay with Poseidon.'
As Phorkys and Poseidon are the sea, Homer says       190
that she is the daughter of the sea and an islander.
Again he calls the Cyclops Poseidon's son,
as he was extremely wild and beastly.
So Odysseus is detained there, as I said,
and delayed for a long time, but not tossed about by the sea,       195
as they skillfully discovered through oracles, star divination
     and
consultations. If you want, let us think about how he may
     return.
For the sea would not be able to drown him,
because he has benevolent birth gods as birth stars.
And they say, if it had been fated by his birth stars       200

τὸν Ὀδυσσέα πρὸς αὐτοῦ τὸν οἶκον ὑποστρέψαι,
γράμματα δοίη μέν τισιν ἀνθρώποις τῶν ἐμπόρων
(οὓς νῦν Ἑρμῆν διάκτορον' καὶ Ἀργειφόντην' λέγει),
ἀποκομίσαι Καλυψοῖ δηλοῦντα πέμπειν τοῦτον
205 ἔχοντα σύζυγον, υἱόν, πατέρα τε καὶ φίλους.
Τίς δ' ἀφ' ἡμῶν σὺν γράμμασιν ἄλλοις πρὸς τὴν Ἰθάκην
πρὸς Ὀδυσσέως τὸν υἱὸν χωρείτω νουθετήσων;
Ταῦτα εἰπόντες Καλυψοῖ καὶ Ὀδυσσεῖ ὡσαύτως
μετὰ ἐμπόρου στέλλουσι γραφὰς τὰς προσηκούσας.
210 Ἑτέραν ἔννουν τε γραφὴν πάλιν πρὸς τὴν Ἰθάκην
μετά τινος ἐστάλκασιν ἀνδρὸς τῶν εὐσυνέτων
ὀτρύνουσαν Τηλέμαχον κήδεσθαι σφῶν πραγμάτων.
Ἢ καὶ αὐτὸς ὁ Μέντης δὲ λαβὼν γραφὴν ἀπῆλθεν,
ἣν Ἀθηνᾶν νῦν Ὅμηρος δεινῶς κατονομάζει,
215 σὺν τῇ γραφῇ τὸν κομιστὴν Ἀθήνην ὀνομάζων.
Τὴν δὲ συνθήκην τῆς γραφῆς 'πέδιλα' ταύτης λέγει
'ἀμβρόσια' καὶ 'χρύσεια,' φέροντα πάντη ταύτην.
Ἡ δὲ γραφὴ φρονήσεως πέδιλόν ἐστιν ὄντως.
Τὴν δέ γε παροτρύνουσαν δύναμιν τῶν γραμμάτων
220 'ἔγχος χαλκοῦν' ὠνόμασε 'δαμάζον' ἐναντίους·
δύναται γὰρ ἀμύνασθαι, ὃς πρῶτος χαλεπήνῃ,
'ὀβριμοπάτρη' φρόνησις οὖσα νοὸς θυγάτηρ·
καὶ τί γὰρ ἰσχυρότερον νοός ἐστιν ἀνθρώποις;
    'Βῆ δὲ κατ' Οὐλύμποιο καρήνων ἀΐξασα'·
225 δοκῶν τι λέγειν ἕτερον νῦν τῆς ὀβριμοπάτρης,
πάλιν νοὸς καὶ λογισμοῦ ταύτην δεικνύει τέκνον.
Ὄλυμπον γὰρ καὶ οὐρανὸν τὴν κεφαλὴν νῦν λέγει,
οὗπερ ὁ Ζεὺς καὶ λογισμὸς μένων ὡς ἐν οἰκίᾳ

for Odysseus to return to his home,
he should give letters to certain merchants
(these he here calls 'Hermes *the messenger*' and '*Argeïphontes*'),
to convey to Kalypso letters declaring that she should send
    him away,
as he has a wife, a son, a father, and loved ones.        205
"Which of us should go with other letters to Ithake
to counsel Odysseus's son?"
Having said this, they send the appropriate letters
with a merchant to Kalypso and Odysseus in this way.
And again they have sent another sensible letter        210
to Ithake with a prudent man,
urging Telemachos to give thought to his own affairs.
Or perhaps Mentes himself departed, taking the letter,
which Homer here gravely calls Athena,
naming Athena as the messenger as well as the letter.        215
He calls the writing of the letter her '*sandals,*'
'*immortal*' and '*golden,*' carrying her everywhere.
Writing is indeed the sandal of wisdom.
As for the power of writing to exhort,
he calls it a 'bronze *spear point*' 'taming' the enemy;        220
for wisdom, '*daughter of a mighty father,*' daughter of the
    mind,
is able to ward off the man who first gets angry;
for what is stronger among men than the mind?
   '*Then Athena went darting down from the peaks of Olympos*':
here he seems to say something else about the daughter of a    225
    mighty father,
again showing that she is the child of mind and reason.
For here he refers to the head as Olympos and sky,
where Zeus, that is, reason, dwells as if in a house,

πᾶσαν γεννᾷ τὴν φρόνησιν γραπτὴν καὶ τῶν ἀγράφων.

230 Οὐ μόνον δὲ τὴν φρόνησιν Ἀθήνην ὀνομάζει,
καὶ ὅσα γίνεται αὐτῇ γραφαῖς εἴτε καὶ πράξει,
ἀλλὰ καὶ ὄργανα αὐτῆς, ὡς κἂν μυρίοις ἄλλοις.
Ὥς φησιν Ἥφαιστον τὸ πῦρ καί γε τοὺς πυρεργάτας,
καὶ ξύλα Ἥφαιστόν φησιν, ὕλην πυρὸς τελοῦντα,

235 ὡς Ἰλιάδι που φησὶ περικρυβέντος δένδρῳ·
'ἀλλ᾽ Ἥφαιστος ἔρυτο· σάωσε δὲ νυκτὶ καλύψας,'
τὰ ξύλα πάντως Ἥφαιστος, νὺξ δὲ τὸ δάσος τούτων.
Οὕτω κἀνθάδε Ἀθηνᾶν τὴν φρόνησιν καλεῖ σοι
καὶ τὴν γραφὴν τὴν ἔννουν δὲ καὶ τὸν κρατοῦντα ταύτην.

240 Καὶ σκόπει μοι σαφέστερον ἐκ τοῦ κειμένου τοῦτο·
'Βῆ δὲ κατ᾽ Οὐλύμποιο καρήνων ἀίξασα,
στῆ δ᾽ Ἰθάκης ἐνὶ δήμῳ ἐπὶ προθύροις Ὀδυσῆος,
οὐδοῦ ἐπ᾽ αὐλείου, παλάμῃ δ᾽ ἔχε χάλκεον ἔγχος.'
Ἐκ κεφαλῆς καὶ λογισμοῦ τὸ γράμμα συνετέθη,

245 ἐδόθη καὶ ἐστάλη δὲ εὐθέως εἰς Ἰθάκην,
ἔστη δ᾽ ὁ ταύτης κομιστής, ὃν Ἀθηνᾶν νῦν λέγει,
οὐδῷ αὐλῆς, κατεῖχε δὲ τῇ σῇ χειρὶ τὸν χάρτην·
ὃν ἔγχος λέγει χάλκεον διὰ τὰ γεγραμμένα,
ἃ ὤτρυνε Τηλέμαχον ἔχεσθαι τῶν πραγμάτων.

250   Τὸ 'βῆ δὲ κατ᾽ Οὐλύμποιο' καὶ ἄλλως νοητέον·
τὸ γράμμα συνετέθη μέν, ἐδόθη τῷ ἀνθρώπῳ
ἐξ ἀνακτόρων τῶν ἐκεῖ, τρέχει πρὸς τὴν Ἰθάκην,

and creates all wisdom, written and unwritten.
It is not only wisdom that he calls Athena, 230
but also all that she creates in writing or in deeds,
and her instruments too, just as for countless other things.
When Homer says that Hephaistos is fire and the
blacksmiths,
he also says that Hephaistos is wood, that constitutes fuel
for fire,
speaking somewhere in *The Iliad* of a man concealed by a 235
tree;
'*but Hephaistos pulled him away; he saved him, enfolding him in
darkness*';
Hephaistos is definitely wood, and night is their forest.
    Thus here too he calls Athena wisdom for you
and the thoughtful letter and the man who holds it.
And see how this becomes clearer from the text: 240
'*Then she went darting down from the peaks of Olympos,
and stood in the land of Ithake at the outer gate of Odysseus,
at the courtyard's threshold, holding in her hand the brazen spear.*'
The letter was created from both the head and from reason,
and was given and sent straight to Ithake, 245
and the person who brought it, whom here he calls Athena,
stood at the courtyard's threshold, holding the letter in her
hand;
this he calls a bronze spear point because of the written
message,
which urged Telemachos to tend to his affairs.
    '*Went down from Olympos*' could also be understood 250
another way:
the letter was composed, was given to the man
from the palace there; he hastened to Ithake,

ἐφεῦρε τοὺς μνηστῆρας δὲ ἄθεσμα δρῶντας πόσα.
Ἰδὼν τοῦτον Τηλέμαχος τῆς δεξιᾶς λαμβάνει
255 καὶ χάρτην, ὅνπερ ἔφημεν χάλκεον ἔγχος, εἷλεν.
   'Οἱ δ' ὅτε δή ῥ' ἔντοσθεν ἔσαν δόμου ὑψηλοῖο,
ἔγχος μέν ῥ' ἔστησε φέρων πρὸς κίονα μακρὴν
δουροδόκης ἔντοσθεν ἐϋξόου, ἔνθα περ ἄλλα
ἔγχε' Ὀδυσσῆος ταλασίφρονος ἵστατο πολλά.'
260 'Ἔγχος,' τὸν χάρτην, 'ἔστησεν' ἐν 'τῇ δορατοθήκῃ,'
ἐν κιβωτῷ κατέθετο, οὗ Ὀδυσσέως χάρται,
ἣ τὴν αὐτὸν ἐγείρουσαν δύναμιν τῶν γραμμάτων
αὐτοῦ ψυχῇ καὶ λογισμῷ τιθεῖ καὶ τῇ καρδίᾳ,
ὡς πρὶν καὶ τούτου ὁ πατὴρ ὁ Ὀδυσσεὺς ἐποίει,
265 πᾶσαν βουλὴν συνοίσουσαν ἐκεῖσε κατακρύπτων.
Λευκῶπιν οἶδας Ἀθηνᾶν τὸν φέροντα τὸ γράμμα,
εἴτε τὸν Μέντην γε αὐτόν, εἴτε τινὰ τῶν Μέντου.
   'Νῦν δ' ἦλθον· δὴ γάρ μιν ἔφαντ' ἐπιδήμιον εἶναι,
σὸν πατέρ'· ἀλλά νυ τόν γε θεοὶ βλάπτουσι κελεύθου.
270 Οὐ γάρ πω τέθνηκεν ἐπὶ χθονὶ δῖος Ὀδυσσεύς,
ἀλλ' ἔτι που ζωὸς κατερύκεται εὑρέι πόντῳ,
νήσῳ ἐν ἀμφιρύτῃ, χαλεποὶ δέ μιν ἄνδρες ἔχουσιν,
ἄγριοι, οἵ που κεῖνον ἐρυκανόωσ' ἀέκοντα.'
Ὁ Μέντης ἢ τῶν Μέντου τις, ὃν Ἀθηνᾶν νῦν λέγει,
275 τῷ Τηλεμάχῳ δίδωσι χρηστὰς τὰς ἀγγελίας.
Εἶναι γὰρ 'ἐπιδήμιόν' φησι τὸν Ὀδυσσέα,
τουτέστιν ἐλπιζόμενον αὐτοῖς ἐπιδημῆσαι.
Θεοὶ καὶ τὰ στοιχεῖά τε ἄνεμοί τε καὶ πόντος,
καὶ 'χαλεποὶ' δὲ βασιλεῖς θεοὶ νοοῦνται τῇδε.

and found the suitors acting very unlawfully.
Seeing him, Telemachos took his right hand
and also the letter which was, as we said, the bronze spear          255
    point.
  *'And when they were within the lofty palace,*
*he set the spear up, bringing it to a tall pillar*
*in a polished spear rack, where many other*
*spears of stouthearted Odysseus were placed.'*
He *'placed'* the *'spear,'* that is, the letter, in the 'spear case,'          260
that is, he placed it in a chest, where Odysseus's papers
    were,
or he places the power of the letters stirring him
in his soul and reason and heart,
as his father Odysseus formerly did,
concealing in there every profitable decision.          265
You know that gray-eyed Athena is the letter carrier,
either Mentes himself or one of Mentes's men.
  *'And now I have come; for they said that your father*
*was home; but in fact the gods are obstructing his return.*
*For godlike Odysseus has not yet perished from the earth,*          270
*but is still alive somewhere and is detained on the broad sea*
*on a seagirt island, and cruel men hold him, savages,*
*who restrain him in some place against his will.'*
Mentes, or one of his men, whom Homer here calls Athena,
gives Telemachos the useful messages.          275
For he says Odysseus *'was home,'*
that is, he was hoping to return home to them.
The gods here are the elements and winds and open sea,
and the *'cruel men'* are the kings, the gods.

280 'Αὐτὰρ νῦν τοι ἐγὼ μαντεύσομαι, ὡς ἐνὶ θυμῷ,'
ὡς Κύκλωψ τε καὶ Λαιστρυγών, Κίρκη καὶ Καλυψὼ δέ
(νῦν καὶ ἡ Εἱμαρμένη δὲ 'θεοὶ' ἂν νοηθεῖεν)
τοῦτον ἂν βλάπτωσιν ἐλθεῖν εἰς τὴν αὐτοῦ πατρίδα.
Μετὰ βραχὺ δ᾽ ἐλεύσεται πλήσων χαρᾶς τὰ τῇδε.

285 'Ἀθάνατοι βάλλουσι καὶ ὡς τελέεσθαι ὀίω·'
εἰσὶν ἀθάνατοι τανῦν αἱ ψυχικαὶ δυνάμεις,
ἤτοι καθὼς τῷ λογισμῷ καὶ διανοίᾳ κρίνω,
ἢ ὡς ἐκ χρησμῳδήματος καὶ μαντειῶν ἐγνώκειν·
καὶ ταῦτα τῆς σοφίας δὲ καὶ ψυχικαὶ δυνάμεις.

290 Ἂν δ᾽ ἐξ ἀστέρων εἴπῃς μοι τοῦτον ἐπεγνωκέναι,
θεοὺς τὴν Εἱμαρμένην μοι καὶ τοὺς ἀστέρας νόει.
'Οὐ μέν τοι γενεήν γε θεοὶ νώνυμνον ὀπίσσω
θῆκαν, ἐπεὶ σέ γε τοῖον ἐγείνατο Πηνελόπεια.'
Ἐνταῦθα πάλιν οἱ 'θεοὶ' ἀστέρες, Εἱμαρμένη.

295 Καὶ πάλιν δὶς εὕροις ἐξῆς θεοὺς τὴν Εἱμαρμένην.
Τὴν Ἀθηνᾶν εἰρήκαμεν τὸν κομιστὴν γραμμάτων.
'Θεοὺς δ᾽ ἐνεμεσίζετο αἰὲν ἐόντας' νόει
ψυχῆς δυνάμεις, ἤτοι γε φιλίαν οὐκ ἐτίμα.
'Ἀλλ᾽ ἤτοι μὲν ταῦτα θεῶν ἐν γούνασι κεῖται,'

300 ἐν τῇ κινήσει δηλαδὴ ἀστέρων, Εἱμαρμένης.
'Μῦθον πέφραδε πᾶσι, θεοὶ δ᾽ ἐπὶ μάρτυροι ἔστων.'
Ποίησον ἐπιφώνημα σύμπασι τοῖς μνηστῆρσι,
μαρτύρων ὄντων σοι θεῶν, φρονίμων καὶ ἀρχόντων,
εἴτε στοιχείων, οὐρανοῦ, γῆς τε καὶ τοῦ ἡλίου.

'*Now I will prophesy to you, as the gods put it in my heart,*'    280
means that the Cyclops and the Laistrygonian, Kirke, and
    Kalypso
(here the '*gods*' can also be understood as Destiny)
would hinder him from returning to his homeland.
But after a short time he will come, filling this place with
    joy.
'*As the immortals put it, and as I think it will happen*':    285
here the immortals are the powers of the soul,
that is, as I judge according to reason and understanding,
or as I had learned from oracles and divinations;
and these powers of the soul are wisdom.
If you said to me that I recognized him from the stars,    290
understand that I mean the gods are Destiny and the stars.
   '*Surely, then, the gods have not made your future lineage*
    *nameless,*
*since Penelope bore you to be a man such as this.*'
Here again the '*gods*' are the stars, Destiny.
And further on you will find twice again that the gods mean    295
    Destiny.
We have said that Athena is the bearer of the letter.
   Understand that '*for he was* angry *at the eternal gods*'
means the powers of the soul, that is, he did not honor
    friendship.
'*But these things* indeed *lie on the knees of the gods,*'
means they depend on the motion of the stars, of Destiny.    300
   '*Speak out to all, and let the gods be your witnesses.*'
Make a declaratory address to all the suitors,
with the gods as your witnesses, that is, the prudent men
    and rulers,
or else the elements, the sky, earth, and sun.

305 Ἄν μάρτυρες οὐ πάρεισιν, εἰπὲ πρὸς τοὺς μνηστῆρας·
"γῆν, οὐρανὸν μαρτύρομαι καὶ ἥλιον πανόπτην."
'Ὄσσαν Διὸς' δὲ βούλεται λέγειν τὰς χρησμῳδίας·
Διὸς καὶ Εἱμαρμένης γὰρ φήμη αἱ χρησμῳδίαι.
'Ὄρνις δ' ὣς ἀνόπαια διέπτατο· τῷ δ' ἐνὶ θυμῷ.'
310 Ταχέως δὲ παρέδραμεν ὡς ὄρνις, ἥνπερ λέγει,
εἴτε ταχέως ἔδραμε, διέπτατο ὡς ὄρνις.
'Οἴσατο θεὸν' ἤτοι σημεῖον θεῖον εἶναι.
'Ἰσόθεος' ὁ ὅμοιος τῷ κάλλει τῶν ἀστέρων.
'Λυγρὸν τὸν νόστον δ' Ἀχαιοῖς' ἐποίησεν 'ἐκ Τροίας
315 Παλλὰς Ἀθήνη,' ὁ ἀὴρ πήλας σφοδροὺς ἀνέμους.
'Δῖα' ἡ εὐτυχέστατος, φρονιμωτάτη πλέον.
Ζεὺς γάρ, ὡς οἶδας, καὶ ὁ νοῦς τοῖς ποιηταῖς καλεῖται,
ὡς καὶ αὐτὸς 'περίφρονα' ταύτην κατονομάζει.
'Θεῖον' σοφὸν ἢ μουσικὸν καθάπερ οἱ ἀστέρες.
320 ''Ἔργ' ἀνδρῶν τε θεῶν τε, τά τε κλείουσιν ἀοιδοί·'
ἰδιωτῶν τε καὶ σοφῶν, κοινῶν καὶ βασιλέων.
'Ἀλλά ποθι Ζεὺς αἴτιος,' αὐτὴ ἡ Εἱμαρμένη.
'Κλαῖεν ἔπειτ' Ὀδυσῆα, φίλον πόσιν, ὄφρα οἱ ὕπνον
ἡδὺν ἐπὶ βλεφάροισι βάλε γλαυκῶπις Ἀθήνη,'
325 ἢ ἔως αὐτὴν ἔτρεψεν εἰς ὕπνον ἐν φρονήσει,
ἢ ἔως ἐξ ὑγρότητος ἀέρος χειμερίου
ὕπνῳ σχεθεῖσα πέπαυτο τῶν τότε δακρυμάτων.
Ἡ φρόνησις 'γλαυκῶπις' μέν, ὡς ἀληθῶς ὁρῶσα,
ὁ δὲ ἀὴρ ὡς ἔγγλαυκον ἔχων αὐτοῦ τὴν θέαν,
330 κἂν ἄμορφα καὶ ἄποια σύμπαντα τὰ στοιχεῖα
ἅπας μεταγενέστερος τῶν φιλοσόφων λέγῃ.

If witnesses are not present, tell the suitors:       305
"I call to witness the earth, the sky, and the all-seeing sun."
   By the *'voice of Zeus'* he means divinations;
for divinations are the utterances of Zeus and Destiny.
   *'She flew like an all-seeing bird; and in his heart.'*
Swiftly she flew like a bird, of which he speaks,      310
or swiftly ran, flew like a bird.
   *'He perceived she was a god,'* that is, a divine sign.
   *'Godlike'* means a man equal in beauty to the stars.
   *'Pallas Athena'* made 'the homecoming *from Troy baneful*
for the Achaians,' that is, the air blew strong winds.     315
   *'Noblest of women'* is the most fortunate one, the most
     wise.
For Zeus, as you know, is also called the mind by the poets,
just as he also calls her 'thoughtful.'
   *'Divine'* is something wise or musical like the stars.
   *'Deeds of men and gods which singers celebrate,'*    320
means of private individuals and wise ones, of commoners
     and kings.
   *'But Zeus is ever to blame,'* that is, Destiny itself.
   *'Then she mourned for Odysseus, her dear husband,*
*until flashing-eyed Athena cast sweet sleep on her eyelids,'*
or until she lulled her to sleep in wisdom,    325
or until from the dampness of the wintry air
taken by sleep, she then ceased her tears.
The *'flashing-eyed'* one is prudence, as she truly sees,
and as the air took on a bluish appearance,
even if every philosopher in later times says that    330
all the elements are entirely unformed and unmade.

'Θεοῖς' ἀλίγκιος 'αὐδήν,' τῇ μουσικῇ ἀστέρων.

"'Θεοὺς' ἐπιμαρτύρομαι" τοῖς ὄπισθεν ἐρρέθη.

'Αἴ κέ ποθι Ζεὺς δῷσι' <νῦν> ἐὰν ἡ Εἱμαρμένη.

335   'Θεοὶ αὐτοἱ' ἡ φρόνησις εἴτε ἡ Εἱμαρμένη,
ὁμοίως καὶ Κρονίωνα τὴν Εἱμαρμένην λέγει.

"Ὡς φάτο Τηλέμαχος, φρεσὶ δ' ἀθανάτην θεὸν ἔγνω,'
τουτέστι φρόνησιν αὐτὸν γενόμενον τὸν ἄνδρα.

'Βούλευε φρεσὶν ᾗσιν ὁδόν, τὴν πέφραδ' Ἀθήνη,'
340   τὴν ἣν αὐτῷ ἐβούλευσεν ὁ δοὺς αὐτῷ τὸ γράμμα.

The '*voice*' is alike '*to the gods,*' that is, to the music of the stars.

"I call the '*gods*' to witness" was said to the men of old.

'*If Zeus might ever grant*' here means if Destiny ever grants.

'*The gods themselves*' are wisdom or Destiny,                    335
and likewise he calls the son of Kronos Destiny.

'*Thus spoke Telemachos, but in his heart he recognized the immortal goddess,*'
that is to say, this man became wisdom.

'*He thought in his mind about the way Athena showed him,*'
that is, the way recommended to him by the man who gave          340
him the letter.

# Β′

Ὑπόθεσις τῆς Βῆτα σοι Ὁμήρου Ὀδυσσείας.


Συναγαγὼν Τηλέμαχος μνηστῆρσιν ἐκκλησίαν
λέγει αὐτοῖς ἐξέρχεσθαι τοῦ Ὀδυσσέως οἴκου.
Αὐτὸς δ᾿ ἐφόδια λαβὼν παρὰ τῆς Εὐρυκλείας
καὶ νῦν παρὰ Νοήμονος λάθρᾳ μητρὸς ἐκπλέει
5  εἰς Πύλον πρὸς τὸν Νέστορα, εἰς Σπάρτην πρὸς
       Μενέλαον,
περὶ τοῦ σφοῦ πατρὸς αὐτοὺς μέλλων ἀνερωτῆσαι.

'Ἦμος δ᾿ ἠριγένεια φάνη ῥοδοδάκτυλος Ἠώς,'
ἐν ᾗ τὰ ἔργα κάλλιστα φαίνεται τῶν δακτύλων,
οὐ μὴν ὁποῖα τῆς νυκτὸς κατά τι βεβλαμμένα.
10  Τοὺς λεξιγράφους ἔα δὲ μυθωδεστέρως γράφειν.
'Θεῷ ἀλίγκιόν' φησιν ὡραῖον ὡς ἀστέρα,
ἢ ὁρατὸν αὐτόχρημα ἐπιθυμίαν ὄντα.
Ὁ 'τῇ παλάμῃ ἔγχος' δὲ Τηλέμαχος κατεῖχεν,
ἢ δόρυ ὡς νομίζουσιν, εἴτε ὃν εἶπον χάρτην,
15  κρατεῖν βουλευτηρίῳ δέ, εἰ δέον δόρυ, σκόπει.
'Θεσπεσίην δ᾿ ἄρα τῷ γε χάριν κατέχευεν Ἀθήνη·'
ταῖς συμβουλαῖς ταῖς τοῦ ἀνδρὸς τεθαρρηκὼς ἐκείνου
ἐκ σκυθρωποῦ ὡραῖος τε καὶ εὔγλωττος ἐφάνη.
Τὸ 'Ζεὺς' ἐνθάδε καὶ 'θεῶν' καὶ τὸ 'Ζηνὸς' ὁμοίως
20  τὴν Εἱμαρμένην νόησον σημαίνειν μοι τὰ τρία.

# Book 2

The subject matter of the second book of Homer's *Odyssey* explained for you.

Telemachos, after assembling the suitors in a meeting,
tells them to leave Odysseus's home.
And after taking supplies from Eurykleia, he now sails away,
in Noëmon's ship, without his mother's knowledge,
to Nestor in Pylos and Menelaos in Sparta,     5
intending to ask them about his father.

   '*As soon as early Dawn appeared, the rosy fingered,*'
means when the most beautiful handicrafts appear,
not such as have been harmed by the night in some way.
Let the wordsmiths write in a manner more like a fable.     10
   Homer says he is handsome '*like a god,*' that is, like a star,
or that he becomes visible immediately, being desire.
This '*spear*' which Telemachos held '*in his hand,*'
or a lance as they think, or a letter as I said, understand
that he holds it in the council, if a spear was needed.     15
   '*Then Athena shed over him divine grace,*'
that is, having gained confidence through that man's
    counsels,
his appearance changed from downcast to handsome and
    eloquent.
   Understand that '*Zeus*' here and '*of the gods*' and likewise
    '*of Zeus*'
all three mean to me Destiny.     20

Πλέον τὸ 'ὑποδείσατε τῇδε θεῶν τὴν μῆνιν'
ὀργὴν στοιχείων νόησον, εἴπερ εἰ οὕτως εἶπε·
"μὴ πῦρ, ἀὴρ καὶ θάλασσα καὶ τὸ Ταρτάρου στόμα
φλέξαν, βροντήσας, βρύξασα, ῥαγὲν ὑμᾶς πως σχῶσι."

25 Καὶ τὸ 'Ζηνὸς' ὁμοίως δὲ τῇδε νοήσεις λέγον·
"ἀντιβολῶ καὶ δέομαι οἰκτραῖς ταῖς ἱκεσίαις
ὑπὲρ τοῦ νοῦ τοῦ ὑπὲρ νοῦν, τουτέστι τῆς προνοίας,
καὶ τῆς δικαιοσύνης δὲ παύθητε δρᾶν τοιάδε."

'Ἀθήνη' νῦν καὶ οἱ 'θεοὶ' αἱ ψυχικαὶ δυνάμεις,
30 ἤτοι ἡ φρόνησις αὐτὴ καὶ μηχανῶν οἱ τρόποι.

'Δαίμων' ἡ Εἱμαρμένη μέν, 'θεοὶ' δὲ τὰ στοιχεῖα·
μαρτύρεται γὰρ ἥλιον καὶ τοὺς λοιποὺς ἀστέρας·
"ἥλιε, γῆ καὶ οὐρανέ, ὕδωρ σὺν τούτοις," λέγων,
"ὑμεῖς ἔφοροι γίνεσθε τῶν εἰς ἐμὲ δρωμένων."

35 'Ζεὺς' ὁ διδοὺς 'παλίντιτα τὰ ἔργα,' Εἱμαρμένη.
'Ὁ Ζεὺς' δ' ὁ πέμπων αἰετοὺς ἀὴρ καὶ οὐρανὸς δέ.
'Ἤδη τάγ' ἴσασι θεοὶ' ἡ Εἱμαρμένη οἶδεν,
ἢ ταῦτα Ἥλιος ὁρᾷ καὶ τὰ λοιπὰ στοιχεῖα.

'Ὄσσαν ἀκούσω ἐκ Διὸς' μοίρας ἢ καὶ φρονούντων.
40 'Εὔχετ' Ἀθήνῃ' βοηθὸν καὶ σύμβουλον ἐπόθει,
οἷος ὁ γράμμα δοὺς ἦν χθὲς κελεύων πλεῖν εἰς Πύλον.

'Σχεδόθεν ἦλθεν' Ἀθηνᾶ 'Μέντορι εἰδομένη'
πλησίον Μέντωρ ἦλθε δὲ ταῦτα ἐπευχομένου
καὶ τούτῳ συνεβούλευσε καὶ πάντα πράττει τούτῳ,
45 ὅσα φησὶ τὴν Ἀθηνᾶν ποιῆσαί τε καὶ λέξαι·

Moreover, the phrase 'fear the *wrath* of the gods' here
means the anger of the elements, as if he spoke in this way:
"May the burning fire, thundering air, roaring sea,
and the sundered mouth of Tartaros not take you in any
    way."
And you will understand that '*of Zeus*' likewise means:     25
"I entreat and beg with piteous prayers,
for the sake of the mind that is beyond mind, that is,
of providence, and of justice, stop doing such things."
   '*Athena*' and '*the gods*' are here the powers of the soul,
that is, wisdom itself and the ways of contrivances.     30
   '*Divine power*' is Destiny, the 'gods' are the elements;
for he calls as witnesses the sun and the other stars,
saying: "Sun, earth and sky, and water too with them,
watch what is being done to me."
   '*Zeus*,' the giver of '*deeds*' of '*requital*,' is Destiny.     35
   '*Zeus*,' the dispatcher of eagles, is the air and the sky.
   The phrase '*now the gods know* of it' means Destiny
    knows,
or the Sun looks upon this, and the other elements as well.
   '*I may hear a rumor from Zeus*' means from fate or even
    from wise men.
   He '*prayed to Athena*' means he yearned for a helper and     40
    advisor,
like the one who delivered the letter yesterday, urging
    Telemachos to sail to Pylos.
   Athena '*drew near to him in the likeness of Mentor*'
means that Mentor approached while Telemachos was
    praying for this,
and advised him and did everything for him,
all the things that he says Athena did and said;     45

τὸν Μέντορα γὰρ λέγει σοι νῦν Ἀθηνᾶν ἐνθάδε,
ὃς ἦν σοφὸς καὶ συνετὸς ἐπίτροπός τε τούτου,
καὶ σὺν αὐτῷ ἀπέπλευσε πρὸς Νέστορα εἰς Πύλον.
Κἂν ἐκ τοῦ Νέστορος εὐθὺς οὗτος ἀνθυπεστράφη,
50  οἷα βυθὸς φρονήσεως καὶ Ἀθηνᾶ τῷ ὄντι,
ὡς ἂν ὁρώμενος αὐτὸς διάγων ἐν Ἰθάκῃ,
μὴ καταλίπῃ μηδαμοῦ μνηστῆρσιν ὑποψίαν.
Τῷ ὅλῳ Βῆτα Ἀθηνᾶν τὸν Μέντορά μοι νόει
καὶ ἐν τῷ Γάμμα τὸν αὐτόν. Νῦν δὲ τινὰ φραστέον·
55  'Ὣς φάτ' Ἀθηναίη, κούρη Διός· οὐδ' ἄρ' ἔτι δήν,'
ὁ εὔφρων Μέντωρ, ὁ σχεδὸν παῖς τοῦ νοὸς ὑπάρχων.
'Θεοῦ δὲ ἔκλυεν αὐδὴν' αὐτοῦ τοῦ σοφωτάτου.
'Θάρσει, μαῖ', ἐπεὶ οὔ τοι ἄνευ θεοῦ ἥδε γε βουλή,'
"μετὰ σοφοῦ συμβούλου γὰρ ἀπέρχομαι, καὶ θάρρει."
60  'Ἔνθ' αὖτ' ἀλλ' ἐνόησε θεὰ γλαυκῶπις Ἀθήνη·
Τηλεμάχῳ ἐικυῖα κατὰ πτόλιν ᾤχετο πάντῃ
καί ῥα ἑκάστῳ φωτὶ παρισταμένη φάτο μῦθον.'
Πάντως ἐρεῖ τις ἐνθαδί, "Τζέτζη, τερατολόγε,
εἰ Μέντωρ ἐστὶν Ἀθηνᾶ, μορφὴν πῶς μεταβάλλει,
65  ὥστε δοκεῖν Τηλέμαχος ἀγείρειν τε πλωτῆρας;"
Οὐ Μέντωρ εἰς Τηλέμαχον μετέβαλλεν οὐδ' ὅλως·
ὡς ἐκ τοῦ Τηλεμάχου δὲ πάντα πλωτῆρσι λέγει
τοὺς ἄνδρας τε κατέπεισε· τί τὰ λοιπὰ δεῖ γράφειν;

for now he tells you that Athena here is Mentor,
who was his wise and intelligent overseer,
and with him he sailed to Nestor in Pylos.
Even if Mentor returned from Nestor immediately,
in his depth of wisdom he was truly Athena,                                50
so that he himself, being seen as he was acting in Ithake,
might not in any way rouse the suitors' suspicion.
For all of Book Two understand that Athena is Mentor,
and in Book Three he is the same. Now it must be said who
     he was:
   '*Thus spoke Athena, daughter of Zeus, nor did he tarry long,*'      55
the sensible Mentor, who was virtually the child of mind
     itself.
   '*He heard the voice of the goddess*' means of the very wise
     man himself.
   '*Fear not, nurse, for my plan is not without a god's backing*'
means "for I leave with a wise counselor, so do not fear."
   '*Then again the goddess, flashing-eyed Athena, took other*'          60
     *counsel;*
*in the likeness of Telemachos she went all through the city,*
*and to each of the men she drew near and said a word.*'
Surely someone will say here, "Tzetzes, you teller of tall
     tales,
if Athena is Mentor, how can he change form,
so that it is Telemachos who seems to assemble the sailors?"          65
No, Mentor did not change into Telemachos at all; but
     rather
he says everything to the sailors as if on behalf of
     Telemachos
and convinced the men; why need I spell out the rest?

70
75
80
85
90

᾽Ένθ᾽ αὖτ᾽ ἄλλ᾽ ἐνόησε θεὰ γλαυκῶπις Ἀθήνη·
βῆ ῥ᾽ ἴμεναι πρὸς δώματ᾽ Ὀδυσσῆος θείοιο·
ἔνθα μνηστήρεσσιν ἐπὶ γλυκὺν ὕπνον ἔχευε,
πλάζε δὲ πίνοντας, χειρῶν δ᾽ ἔκβαλλε κύπελλα.᾽
Μετά γε τὴν ἐξάρτησιν νηὸς καὶ τῶν πλωτήρων
ὡς πρὸς Τηλέμαχον ἐλθὼν ὁ Μέντωρ συμβουλεύει.
Κιρνᾶν κελεύει συνεχῶς· ἐκ τούτου δ᾽ οἱ μνηστῆρες
καρηβαρεῖς ἀπαίρουσι καὶ κάθυπνοι πρὸς οἴκους,
αὐτὸς δὲ καὶ Τηλέμαχος χωροῦσι πρὸς ἀπόπλουν.
᾽Τοῖσιν δ᾽ ἴκμενον οὖρον ἵει γλαυκῶπις Ἀθήνη·᾽
Ἀθήνη νῦν ἀήρ ἐστιν, ἢ πρόεισιν ἀνέμους,
οὐ μὴν ἡ Μέντου φρόνησις, μὴ πλανηθῇς ἐνθάδε.
᾽Στήσαντο κρητῆρας ἐπιστεφέας οἴνοιο,
λεῖβον δ᾽ ἀθανάτοισι θεοῖς αἰειγενέτῃσιν,
ἐκ πάντων δὲ μάλιστα Διὸς γλαυκώπιδι κούρῃ.᾽
Κἀνταῦθα τὸν ἀέρα δὲ γλαυκώπιδά σοι λέγει,
ὅτι λευκὸς ἀήρ ἐστιν, ὡς ἔφημεν πολλάκις,
καὶ τοῦ Διὸς καὶ οὐρανοῦ παῖς ὁ ἀὴρ τυγχάνει.
Ἔθος δ᾽ ἐστὶ τοῖς ναυτικοῖς εἰς πλοῦν εὐθυδρομοῦσιν,
ἱστᾶν κρατῆρα πίνειν τε χαίροντας τῷ ἀέρι.
Ὅθε τοῖς πᾶσιν ἔθυον θεοῖς τε καὶ στοιχείοις,
τῷ δὲ ἀέρι μάλιστα πλέον τῶν ἄλλων πάντων.

*'Then again the goddess, flashing-eyed Athena, took other*
*counsel;*
*she went to the palace of divine Odysseus;*                              70
*there she began to pour sweet sleep upon the suitors,*
*and befuddled them as they drank and knocked the cups from their*
*hands.'*
After provisioning the ships and sailors,
Mentor, coming to Telemachos, counseled him.
He told him to mix wine continuously; because of this             75
the suitors departed drowsy and half-asleep for their
houses,
while he and Telemachos departed on their sea voyage.
*'And flashing-eyed Athena sent them a favorable wind.'*
Athena here is the air, which propels the winds,
not the wisdom of Mentes; don't get this wrong here.             80
*'They set forth mixing bowls brim full of wine,*
*and poured libations to the immortal, eternal gods,*
*and most of all to the flashing-eyed daughter of Zeus.'*
Here Homer tells you the flashing-eyed one is the air,
because it is clear air, as we have said many times,              85
and the air is the child of Zeus and of the sky.
It is customary for sailors who run a straight course at sea
to set up a mixing bowl and to drink, rejoicing in the air.
In that manner they sacrificed to all the gods and elements,
but especially to the air, more than to all of the others.       90

# Γ′

Σὺν Ἀθηνᾷ Τηλέμαχος εἰς Πύλον κατηγμένος
ξενίζεται τῷ Νέστορι θύοντι Ποσειδῶνι.
Περὶ πατρὸς δὲ ἑαυτοῦ πευθόμενος ἐκείνου,
τὰ τῶν Ἑλλήνων σύμπαντα τούτῳ καλῶς μανθάνει,
5  τὸν κατὰ Τρώων πόλεμον σχεδὸν καὶ τὰ τοῦ νόστου.
Μετὰ δὲ τοῦτο Ἀθηνᾷ ὑποχωρεῖ ὡς ὄρνις.
Νέστωρ μετὰ υἱέος δέ, τὴν κλῆσιν Πεισιστράτου,
Τηλέμαχον ἐξέπεμψεν ἐφ' ἅρματος εἰς Σπάρτην,
ὡς εἴποι τι Μενέλαος ὑστέρως ἀφιγμένος.

10  ῾Ήλιος δ' ἀνόρουσε, λιπὼν περικαλλέα λίμνην,
οὐρανὸν ἐς πολύχαλκον, ἵν' ἀθανάτοισι φαείνοι
καὶ θνητοῖσι βροτοῖσιν ἐπὶ ζείδωρον ἄρουραν.'
Ὠκεανόθεν ἥλιος εἰς οὐρανὸν ἀνήει,
ἡμέραν ἄγων τε καὶ φῶς στοιχείοις καὶ ἀνθρώποις.
15  Πολύχαλκον τὸν οὐρανὸν ὡς στερεὸν δὲ λέγει·
καὶ ἡ Γραφὴ 'στερέωμα' τὸν οὐρανὸν καλεῖ δέ.
    ῾Εκ δ' ἄρα Τηλέμαχος νηὸς βαῖν', ἦρχε δ' Ἀθήνη.'
Ἀθήνη ἤτοι Μέντωρ νῦν προύβαινε Τηλεμάχου.

# Book 3

Subject matter of the third book of Homer's *Odyssey*.

Telemachos sailed down to Pylos with Athena
and was welcomed by Nestor, who was sacrificing to
  Poseidon.
Telemachos inquired about his father,
and learned well from him all the deeds of the Greeks,
the war against the Trojans, more or less, and their             5
  homecoming.
After this Athena withdrew, in the form of a bird.
Along with his son, called Peisistratos, Nestor
sent Telemachos off to Sparta in a chariot, so that
  Menelaos,
who had returned even later, might give him further news.

  *'And now the Sun, leaving the beautiful sea, leaped up*        10
*into the brazen heaven, to give light to the immortals*
*and to mortal men on earth, the giver of grain.'*
The sun rose from the ocean to the sky,
bringing day and light to the elements and humankind.
Homer calls the sky brazen as it is solid,                       15
for Scripture calls the sky *'firmament'* as well.
  *'Then Telemachos stepped forth from the ship, and Athena led*
*    the way.'*
Athena, that is, Mentor, now walked before Telemachos.

Ὅσας δ᾽ ἂν ἄγω Ἀθηνᾶς τὸν Μέντορα δηλούσας,
20 εἰ μή που τί καινότερον ἔχουσι, παραδράμω.
'Ἀλλὰ δὲ ὑποθήσεται ὁ δαίμων' καὶ ἡ τύχη.
'Οὔ σε θεῶν ἀέκητι' οὐκ ἄνευ εὐμοιρίας.
Τὸ 'ἀθανάτοις εὔχεσθαι' καὶ τὸ 'θεῶν δὲ πάντες'
ἡλίῳ καὶ ἀέρι δὲ καὶ τοῖς λοιποῖς στοιχείοις.
25 Χατέομεν ἀέρος γάρ, ὡς πνέωμεν καὶ ζῶμεν,
ὕδατός τε καὶ τῶν λοιπῶν διὰ τὰς τούτων χρείας.
Καὶ τὸ 'Κρονίων' εἴπομεν ἐν τόποισι μυρίοις
τὴν σκοτεινὴν καὶ ἄδηλον σημαίνειν Εἱμαρμένην.
'Βῆμεν δ᾽ ἐν νήεσσι, θεὸς δ᾽ ἐκέδασσεν Ἀχαιούς'
30 θεὸς νῦν δύναμις ψυχῆς, ἀνομογνωμοσύνη·
νυκτὶ γὰρ βουλευσάμενοι, 'βεβαρηότες οἴνῳ,'
διχῇ πως διῃρέθησαν, οὐχ᾽ ὁμογνωμοσύνη.
Ὁ τὸν 'λυγρὸν' μηδόμενος 'νόστον' δὲ Ζεὺς τυγχάνει,
ἡ Εἱμαρμένη τε αὐτὴ καὶ οὐρανὸς δὲ πλέον·
35 ἐξ οὐρανοῦ γὰρ πνεουσῶν βιαίων καταιγίδων,
ἐπλήσθη μὲν πᾶν πέλαγος νεκρῶν καὶ ναυαγίων·
ἄλλοι δὲ παρεξώσθησαν πατρίδων πορρωτέρω
εἰς Ἀφρικήν, εἰς Αἴγυπτον, εἰς Κρήτην, Ἰταλίαν,
εἰς ἄλλας χώρας ἔθνη τε καὶ πόλεις τε καὶ τόπους·
40 βραχεῖ τινες ἀφίκοντο πρὸς τὰς αὐτῶν πατρίδας.
'Μήνιος ἐξ ὀλοῆς γλαυκώπιδος ὀβριμοπάτρης,'

However many Athenas I could introduce, meaning
    Mentor,
I should pass over, unless there is something distinctive    20
    about them.
   'The god,' that is, chance, 'will give you different advice.'
   *'Not without the gods' favor have you,'* means not without
    good fortune.
   Then the phrases *'to pray to the immortals'* and 'all need the
    gods'
mean to pray to the sun, the air, and the other elements.
For we have need of the air, so as to breathe and live,    25
and of water and the rest because of our need for these
    things.
   And we explained in countless places that the term
*'son of Kronos'* means dark and obscure Destiny.
   *'And we got in our ships, and a god scattered the Achaians'*:
the god here is the power of the soul, difference of opinion;    30
for having deliberated by night, 'heavy with wine,'
they were divided into two parts somehow, not in
    agreement.
   He who contrived the *'mournful homecoming'* is Zeus,
Destiny itself and also the sky;
for as violent tempests blew from the sky,    35
the entire sea was filled with corpses and shipwrecks;
others were driven even further away from their
    homelands,
to Africa, Egypt, Crete, Italy,
to other lands and peoples and cities and places;
only a few returned to their homelands in a short time.    40
   *'From the deadly wrath of the flashing-eyed goddess, daughter of*
    *a mighty father,'*

ἐκ τοῦ ἀέρος, τῆς ὀργῆς τῆς ἐκ δεινῶν πνευμάτων.
Εἴπομεν τὸν ἀέρα σοι γλαυκώπιδα πολλάκις.
 Ὀβριμοπάτρη᾽ δ᾽ ἰσχυρὸν ἔχουσα τὸν πατέρα·
45 τὸ ὅλον γὰρ στερέωμα, ὁ οὐρανὸς ὁ σύμπας,
ὁ Ζεὺς αὐτός, ὁ ἰσχυρός, πατήρ ἐστιν ἀέρος.
Ὁ γὰρ ἀήρ, ἡ Ἀθηνᾶ, τοῦ οὐρανοῦ τι μέρος.
 Ἥ τ᾽ ἔριν Ἀτρείδῃσι μετ᾽ ἀμφοτέροισιν ἔθηκε.᾽
Πνευμάτων ἐναντίων γάρ, ὄμβρου τε καὶ χαλάζης
50 καὶ καταιγίδων ἄλλων τε πάντων δεινῶν χειμῶνος
ἤδη μελλόντων ἄρχεσθαι, Μενέλαος μὲν ἔφη
πλεῖν τὴν ταχίστην Ἕλληνας πάντας εἰς τὰς πατρίδας.
 Οὐ δ᾽ Ἀγαμέμνονι πάμπαν ἐήνδανε· βούλετο γάρ ῥα
λαὸν ἐρυκακέειν, ῥέξαι θ᾽ ἱερὰς ἑκατόμβας,
55 ὡς τὸν Ἀθηναίης δεινὸν χόλον ἐξακέσαιτο,
νήπιος, οὐδὲ τὸ ᾔδη, ὃ οὐ πείσεσθαι ἔμελλεν·
οὐ γάρ τ᾽ αἶψα θεῶν τρέπεται νόος αἰὲν ἐόντων.᾽
Ὁ Ἀγαμέμνων δὲ αὐτὸς τὸ στράτευμα κατεῖχεν,
ὡς ἂν ἀέρος τοῦ δεινοῦ παῦσιν θυσίαις λάβοι.
60 Ῥᾷστα δ᾽ οὐ μετατρέπεται κρατῆσάν τι στοιχεῖον,
εἴτ᾽ οὖν χειμέριος ἀὴρ εἴτε καὶ θέρους καύσων.
 Νύκτα μὲν ἀέσαμεν χαλεπὰ φρεσὶν ὁρμαίνοντες
ἀλλήλοις· ἐπὶ γὰρ Ζεὺς ἤρτυε πῆμα κακοῖο.᾽
Οὕτως ἐνυκτερεύσαμεν ἐχθραίνοντες ἀλλήλοις·
65 ὁ Ζεὺς καὶ νοῦς γὰρ ὁ ἡμῶν, ὁ τῆς κακοβουλίας,
ἢ καὶ ἡ Εἱμαρμένη δὲ ἡμῶν ταῖς δυσβουλίαις
 ἤρτυε,᾽ κατεσκεύαζε τὴν συμφορὰν τὴν τόσην.

means from the air, from the wrath of the terrible winds.
We told you many times that the air is the flashing-eyed
    one.
  'Daughter of a mighty father' means she has a powerful
      father;
for the entire firmament, the whole sky,                    45
Zeus himself, the mighty one, is the father of the air.
For the air, Athena, is a part of the sky.
  *'And she caused strife between the two sons of Atreus.'*
For when adverse winds, rain and hail
and tempests and all the other terrible aspects of winter   50
were already about to begin, Menelaos said that
all the Greeks should sail very quickly to their homelands.
  *'But he by no means pleased Agamemnon, for he wanted*
  *to hold back the army and sacrifice holy hecatombs,*
  *so that he, the fool, might appease Athena's terrible wrath,*   55
  *and he didn't realize that she would not be persuaded;*
  *for the mind of the eternal gods is not quickly turned.'*
Agamemnon himself held back the army,
that he might stop the terrible weather with sacrifices.
But an element that has prevailed does not change very      60
    easily,
whether stormy air or burning summer heat.
  *'That night we slept, pondering harsh thoughts in our minds*
  *against each other; for Zeus was preparing an evil doom for us.'*
Thus we passed the night, feeling enmity against each
    other;
for Zeus, our mind, the mentality of malicious counsel,     65
or Destiny through our malicious plans
*'was preparing,'* that is, constructing such a great disaster.

'Ἠῶθεν οἱ ἡμίσεις' δὲ ἐν ταῖς ναυσὶν ἐμβάντες
ἐπλέομεν, 'ἐστόρεσε' τὸ πέλαγος 'θεὸς' δέ.

70 Θεὸς τανῦν ὁ οὐρανὸς ἐκ ζάλης αἰθριάσας,
εἴτ' οὖν θεὸς καὶ μοῖρά τις ἐκ τῶν εὐτυχεστάτων,
ἐστόρεσε καὶ ἔπαυσε τὴν ζάλην τοῦ πελάγους.
'Νόστον δ' οὔπω ἐμήδετο ὁ Ζεὺς' ἡ Εἰμαρμένη.
'Δευτέραν ἔριν' γὰρ αὐτοῖς 'αὖθις' ἀναρριπίζει.

75 'Ἡιτοῦμεν τέρας' δεῖξαι δὲ 'θεὸν' τὴν Εἰμαρμένην.
Καὶ τὸ 'θεοὶ' ὁμοίως δὲ 'δύναμιν περιθεῖεν'
καὶ τὸ 'θεοῦ ὀμφῇ' ὡσαύτως δὲ σὺν τούτοις νόει.
'Εἰ γὰρ Ἀθήνη σε φιλεῖ' ἂν φρόνιμος ὑπάρχῃς,
ὡς Ὀδυσσεῖ παρίστατο,' ὡς ἦν φρονῶν ἐκεῖνος.

80 'Οὐ γάρ πω ἴδον ὧδε θεοὺς ἀναφανδὰ φιλεῦντας,
ὡς κείνῳ ἀναφανδὰ παρίστατο Παλλὰς Ἀθήνη,'
οὐκ εἶδον ὄντως ἔγωγε τὰς ψυχικὰς δυνάμεις
λυσιτελούσας προφανῶς, ὡς Ὀδυσσεῖ τὸ ἔμφρον.
'Οὐδ' εἰ θεοὶ θελήσειαν' αὐτὴ ἡ Εἰμαρμένη.

85 Ὑπερβολὴν τὸ σχῆμα δὲ τοῦτο καλεῖν μοι νόει.
'Ἀθήνη' πάλιν Μέντωρ, νῦν θεὸς ἡ Εἰμαρμένη.
'Ὣς τέ μοι ἀθάνατος ἰνδάλλεται εἰσοράασθαι.'
Στοιχείοις ἢ καὶ ἄστρασιν ὡς οὐρανῷ ἡλίῳ·
'μοῖρα θεῶν' ἀρτίως δὲ ἀστέρων Εἰμαρμένη.

90 'Θεῶν βωμοῖς' στοιχείων τε καὶ σὺν αὐτοῖς ἡλίου.
'Φοῖβος Ἀπόλλων ἔπεφνεν,' ὁ ἥλιος ἀνεῖλεν.
Τὰς λοιμικὰς ἁπάσας γὰρ νόσους καὶ τὰς ὀξείας
ἐκ τοῦ ἡλίου γίνεσθαί φησι καὶ τῆς σελήνης.

'*At dawn,* half of us' embarked on the ships
and sailed off; a '*god made*' the sea '*calm.*'
God here is the sky cleared from its tumult,                    70
or god is a most fortunate fate,
that calmed and ended the tumult of the sea.

'Zeus,' Destiny, '*did not yet plan* our return home.'
For he 'again' stirred up among them a 'second strife.'
We asked '*the god,*' Destiny, to give us a '*sign.*'          75
    And similarly understand the phrases the '*gods would
        bestow strength*'
and likewise '*with the voice of a god*' as meaning "with their
    help."

'For if *Athena* loves you,' you are likely to be wise,
'just as she stood by Odysseus,' as he was wise.

'*For I have never seen the gods openly showing love,*            80
*as Pallas Athena did to him, openly standing by his side,*'
means that truly I have not seen the powers of the soul
visibly benefiting anyone as prudence did then Odysseus.

'*Nor* did *the gods* wish it' means nor did Destiny itself.
You should understand that I call this figure of speech          85
    "hyperbole."

'*Athena*' again is Mentor, the goddess here is Destiny.
'*And he seems to me to look like an immortal.*'
To the elements or even the stars he seems like the sky, the
    sun;
'*fate of the gods*' means Destiny from the stars.

'*To the altars of the gods*' means of the elements and of the    90
    sun as well.

'*Phoibos Apollo* struck' means the sun killed them.
For Homer says that all the plagues and severe diseases
come from the sun and the moon.

Πλοῦν 'στυγερὸν Ζεὺς φράσατο' καὶ 'ἀϋτμένα χεῦεν·'
95 ἡ Εἱμαρμένη νῦν αὐτὴ ἢ καὶ ἀὴρ ἐνθάδε.

'Ζεὺς τό γ' ἀλεξήσειε καὶ ἀθάνατοι θεοὶ ἄλλοι,'
ὁ Ζεὺς ὁ πλάνος, ὁ ἀστήρ, καὶ οἱ λοιποὶ ἀστέρες·
ἤτοι μὴ γένοιτο ἐμοὶ τοιαύτη Εἱμαρμένη,
ἢ μὴ παραχωρήσειεν ὁ Ζεὺς γενέσθαι τοῦτο,
100 ὁ πάντα συστησάμενος, ὁ νοῦς ὁ τῆς προνοίας.
Οἱ ἄλλοι νῦν ἀθάνατοι κωλύουσι τὸν Δία,
ἐνθάδε νοῦν, λαμβάνεσθαι προνοίας, ὥσπερ εἶπον.
Ἐπεὶ δ' ἐγράφη, κείσθω σοι· βίβλον χιοῦν οὐ θέλω·
αὕτη γὰρ καὶ σχεδάριον καὶ καθαρόν ἐστί μοι.
105 'Ὡς ἄρα φωνήσασ' ἀπέβη γλαυκῶπις Ἀθήνη
φήνῃ εἰδομένη· θάμβος δ' ἕλε πάντας Ἀχαιούς.'
Οὕτως εἰπὼν ἀπέδραμεν ὁ συνετὸς ὁ Μέντωρ,
ὠκέως φήνης ὄρνιθος ἐξεικασμένος τάχει,
ἢ ἅμα ὑπεχώρει μὲν ὡς πρὸς τὴν ναῦν ὁ Μέντωρ,
110 καὶ φήνη δὲ διέπτατο· οἰωνοσκόποι δ' ὄντες
καὶ γνόντες μάντευμα χρηστὸν τοῦτο τοῦ Τηλεμάχου
δηλοῦν ἀνύσαι τὴν βουλὴν καὶ τὸν σκοπόν, ὃν θέλει,
οἱ πάντες κατεπλάγησαν καὶ Νέστωρ σὺν ἐκείνοις.
Ὅπως δ' ἡ φήνη μάντευμα τοῦ Τηλεμάχου, μάθε·
115 ἡ φήνη τὰ νεόττια τῶν ἀετῶν ἐκτρέφει,
ἐπίτροπος καὶ Μέντωρ δὲ ὑπῆρχε Τηλεμάχου·
οὗ μετὰ τὸ συμβούλευμα πρὸς ναῦν ἀπερχομένου,
ἐπεὶ φήνη διέπτατο, πᾶσι χρηστὸν ἐκρίθη,

'*Zeus* planned a wretched' voyage and '*poured winds*':
here it is Destiny itself or even air in this case.                          95
   '*May Zeus prevent this, and the other immortal gods as well*'
means Jupiter the planet, the star, and the other stars;
that is, may such a Destiny not befall me,
or may Zeus not allow this to happen,
he who established everything, the mind of foresight.              100
Now the other immortals are hindering Zeus,
here preventing the mind from exercising foresight, as I
      said.
Because it is written, let it stand; I don't want a marked-up
      book;
for this is both my draft and my clean copy.
   '*So flashing-eyed Athena spoke and departed in the likeness*      105
*of a vulture; and amazement fell upon all the Achaians.*'
This means that, with these words, the wise Mentor left
      swiftly,
resembling a bird, the vulture, in speed,
or when Mentor was withdrawing to his ship,
a vulture flew by; and since they were bird diviners              110
and knew that this was an auspicious prophecy for
      Telemachos,
showing that he would accomplish his purpose and desired
      goal,
everyone was amazed, and Nestor as well.
Now learn how the vulture was an omen for Telemachos:
the vulture raised the eagles' chicks,                            115
and Mentor was Telemachos's overseer;
after giving his counsel, as he departed for his ship,
because a vulture was flying past, all judged it a good omen,

ὡς καὶ τὸν Νέστορα εἰπεῖν· "'εἰ νέῳ' πεφυκότι
120 τοιαῦτα σοι ἐκπέμπονται σημεῖα ἐξ ἀέρος,
εἴτ' οὖν ἡ Εἱμαρμένη σοὶ τοῖα σημεῖα πέμπει,
ἐλπίζω πᾶν ἀνύειν σε." Τοῦτο δ' οὐκ ἔστιν ἄλλο.
'Ἀλλὰ Διὸς θυγάτηρ, κυδίστη Τριτογένεια.'
Ἡ νῦν πτῆσις τῆς ὄρνιθος οὐκ ἄλλο τι σημαίνει,
125 σοῦ λογισμοῦ δὲ τὴν βουλὴν ἀνύσαι καὶ πληρῶσαι.
'Ἀλλά, ἄνασσ', ἵληθι, δίδωθι δέ μοι κλέος ἐσθλόν,
αὐτῷ καὶ παίδεσσι καὶ αἰδοίῃ παρακοίτι·'
"ἀλλ' ἵλεως καὶ φίλη μοι τοιάδε Εἱμαρμένη
αὐτῷ γενέσθω καὶ παισὶν ἐμῇ τε συμπαρεύνῳ."
130 'Ὣς ἔφατ' εὐχόμενος, τοῦ δ' ἔκλυε Παλλὰς Ἀθήνη.'
Ἢ πάλιν ἐπεφάνη δὲ τὸ ὄρνεον, ἡ φήνη,
δηλοῦν καὶ τούτου τὰς βουλὰς καὶ τοὺς σκοποὺς
    πληροῦσθαι,
εἴτ' οὖν γε ἤκουσεν αὐτοῦ, τουτέστι καὶ ὁ Νέστωρ
ἐπιτυχὴς ἦν ἐν βουλαῖς, ὧν ἤθελε πραγμάτων.
135 'Υἱέος Ὀρτιλόχοιο, τὸν Ἀλφειὸς τέκε παῖδα.'
Τὶς Ἀλφειὸς Ὀρτίλοχον ἐγέννησεν υἱέα·
ἐξ' οὗ ἀνδρὸς τοῦ Ἀλφειοῦ ὁ ποταμὸς ἐκλήθη

so that even Nestor said to him: "'*If*' such signs are sent to you
from the air, although you are '*young*,'                                                120
or Destiny sends you such signs,
I hope that you accomplish everything." This is nothing else.
  '*But the daughter of Zeus, the most glorious Tritogeneia.*'
Here the bird's flight does not mean anything else but
for you to accomplish and fulfill your reasoning and will.          125
  '*But, Queen, be gracious, and grant me noble glory,*
*for myself and my sons and my revered wife.*'
This means "but may such a Destiny be propitious and
friendly to me and my sons and my wife."
  '*So he spoke in prayer, and Pallas Athena heard him.*'                130
Either the bird appeared again, the vulture,
showing that his wishes and his goals would be fulfilled,
or he heard him, which means that Nestor was also
successful in his desires, in the things he wanted.
  '*Of the son of Ortilochos, the child whom Alpheios begot.*'       135
A certain Alpheios sired a son, Ortilochos;
from this man Alpheios the river took its name.

## Δ΄

Αὕτη ἐστὶν ὑπόθεσις τῆς Δέλτα Ὀδυσσείας.

Εἰς Σπάρτην ὁ Τηλέμαχος ἐλθὼν σὺν Πεισιστράτῳ
γάμων καιροῖς ξενίζεται τοῖς οἴκοις Μενελάου·
νόστον ζητῶν δὲ τοῦ πατρὸς τὰ τῶν μνηστήρων λέγει,
καὶ ὁ Μενέλαος αὐτῷ λεπτῶς πᾶν ἐξηγεῖται,
5    τὸν πλοῦν καὶ τὰ μαντεύματα Πρωτέως Αἰγυπτίου,
ἐξ ὧν τὸν Ἀγαμέμνονος θάνατον ἐπεγνώκει,
ὑπάρχειν Ὀδυσσέα δὲ τῆς Καλυψοῦς τῇ νήσῳ.
Ταῦτα κατὰ τὴν Σπάρτην μὲν ἐν οἴκοις Μενελάου.
Τηλέμαχον ἀπόδημον δὲ γνόντες οἱ μνηστῆρες
10   τοῦτον βουλεύονται κτανεῖν· ὃ γνοῦσα Πηνελόπη
ἐξ ὀδυρμῶν περιπαθῶν εἰς ὕπνον παρεσύρη,
περὶ παιδὸς ὀνείροις δὲ χρηστοῖς παραμυθεῖται.

      *Γάμον θεοὶ ἐτέλειον* ἤτοι ἡ Εἱμαρμένη.
      *Εἶδος τῆς Ἀφροδίτης'* δὲ αὐτῆς ἐπιθυμίας.
15      *Ἄνδρε δύω, γενεῇ δὲ Διὸς μεγάλοιο ἔικτον.'*
      *Διὸς μεγάλου'* νῦν υἱοὺς σημαίνει βασιλέως.
      *Ζηνός που τοιήδε γ' Ὀλυμπίου ἔνδοθεν αὐλή·'*
      Ζηνὸς τανῦν ὁ οὐρανός, ὅδε φησί, τοιόσδε,
      ὡς καταστέρῳ οὐρανῷ παρεμφερὴς ὁ δόμος.
20      *Ἀρτέμιδι εἰκυῖα'* δὲ σελήνη κατὰ θέαν.

# Book 4

Subject matter of the fourth book of the *Odyssey*.

Telemachos, coming to Sparta with Peisistratos,
is a guest in the house of Menelaos during a wedding;
asking about his father's homecoming, he mentions the
    suitors,
and Menelaos explains everything to him in detail,
his voyage and the prophecies of the Egyptian Proteus,    5
from which he found out about Agamemnon's death,
and that Odysseus was on Kalypso's isle.
This happened in Sparta in the house of Menelaos.
The suitors, learning that Telemachos has gone away,
devise a plan to kill him; learning this, Penelope    10
was swept away into sleep by her soulful wailings,
but was consoled by benevolent dreams about her child.

    The '*gods*,' that is, Destiny, were 'carrying out the
        wedding.'
    '*The appearance of Aphrodite*' means of desire itself.
    '*Two men that are like the race of great Zeus.*'    15
'Of great *Zeus*' here means the sons of the king.

    '*Of such sort is the court of Olympian Zeus within*':
here the sky of Zeus, Homer says, is of such kind,
just as his hall is like the starry sky.

    '*Like Artemis*' means like the moon in appearance.    20

'Θεοῦ τερπόμεθα αὐδῇ' ὡς μουσικῇ ἀστέρων.
Εἶναι ὁ Μέμνων παῖς 'Ηοῦς' λέγεται τῆς ἡμέρας,
ἢ ὡς περίβλεπτος ἀνὴρ ἡμέρᾳ καὶ τῷ βίῳ,
ἢ ὡς πατρίδα λελοχὼς τὰ μέρη τὰ ἑῷα.
25  'Αὐτίκ' ἄρ' εἰς οἶνον βάλε φάρμακον, ἔνθεν ἔπινον,
νηπενθές τ' ἄχολόν τε, κακῶν ἐπίληθον ἁπάντων.'
Τοὺς ἐν τῷ πότῳ λόγους νῦν Ἑλένης θελκτηρίους
κατονομάζει φάρμακον ληθεδανὸν ἀνίας.
Οὐκ ἀπεικός, καὶ φάρμακα τὴν Αἴγυπτον κεκτῆσθαι
30  ληθεδανὰ καὶ παύοντα τὰς ἀφορήτους θλίψεις·
καὶ γὰρ καὶ τοὺς Αἰθίοπας τοὺς ἀπαθεῖς ἀκούω
μήτε πληγαῖς, μήτε τομαῖς, μὴ καύσεσι, μηδ' ἄλλοις
ἀνιαροῖς ἀλγύνεσθαι, φέρειν δὲ πάντα ῥᾷστα,
ὡς ἄλλου τινὸς πάσχοντος δοκῶ τισι φαρμάκοις.
35  'Θεὸς' αὖ 'Ζεύς,' ὁ 'ἀγαθὸν' καὶ τὸ 'κακὸν' διδοὺς δέ,
ἡ Εἱμαρμένη νῦν ἐστιν, ἡ δέ γε 'Ἀφροδίτη,'
ἢ τῇ Ἑλένῃ δέδωκεν αὐτὰς ἐπιθυμίας.
'Νόσφιν' Ἑλένην ἤγαγεν ἀφ' ἵππου τοῦ δουρείου
'Παλλὰς Ἀθήνη,' φρόνησις αὐτοῦ τοῦ Ὀδυσσέως·
40  φθέγξασθαι γὰρ οὐκ εἴασεν οὐδὲν αὐτὸν ἐν ἵππῳ.
'Αἲ γάρ, Ζεῦ τε πάτερ καὶ Ἀθηναίη καὶ Ἄπολλον,'
εἴθε ἀήρ, πνοῆς δοτήρ, καὶ Ἀθηνᾶ σελήνη
καὶ Ἀπόλλόν τε ἥλιε, φωτὸς βροτοῖς ταμία,
ἤγουν "εἴθε, ὦ οὐρανέ, νύξ, φῶς τε τῆς ἡμέρας."
45  'Αἰγύπτῳ' τὸν Μενέλαον ποῖοι 'θεοὶ' κατέσχον,
οἷστισι καὶ οὐκ ἔρεξεν; Ἀστέρες Εἱμαρμένης,

'*We rejoice in the voice of the god*' as in the music of the
    stars.
Memnon is said to be the child '*of Dawn,*' that is, of day,
either as a man celebrated in his day and in his life,
or as a man coming to rest in the eastern regions as his
    homeland.
'*Straightaway she poured into the wine they drank a drug*       25
*to quiet pain and strife, causing one to forget all misfortunes.*'
Here he calls Helen's soothing words, spoken as they drank,
a drug causing forgetfulness of sorrow.
Probably he means that Egypt had drugs
to cause forgetfulness and end unbearable grief;                30
for I hear that the Ethiopians, who are unaffected by suf-
    fering,
are pained neither by wounds, cuts, nor burns, nor any
    other
afflictions, but they bear everything very easily,
as if someone else were suffering, I believe due to these
    drugs.
Again the '*god Zeus,*' who gives both '*good*' and '*ill,*'        35
is here Destiny, and '*Aphrodite*'
is she who gave these desires to Helen.
'*Pallas Athena,*' Odysseus's wisdom,
led Helen '*far away*' from the wooden horse;
she did not allow him to say anything in the horse.             40
'*If only, O father Zeus and Athena and Apollo,*'
that is, if only, O air, giver of breath, and Athena, moon,
and Apollo, sun, dispenser of light to mortals,
that is, "if only, O sky, night, and light of the day."
Who were the '*gods*' who detained Menelaos '*in Egypt,*'        45
those to whom he did not sacrifice? The stars of Destiny,

ἤτοι οὐ πλεῖν κατήρξαντο χρηστῷ τῷ θεματίῳ.

  'Εἰ μή τίς με θεῶν ὀλοφύρατο καί μ' ἐλέησε,
Πρωτέως ἰφθίμου θυγάτηρ, ἀλίοιο γέροντος,
50 Εἰδοθέη· τῇ γάρ ῥα μάλιστά γε θυμὸν ὄρινα.'

  'Θεῶν' νῦν μάγων καὶ σοφῶν καὶ ὑδρομαντευόντων.
Πρωτέως ὄνομα πλαστὸν καὶ τὸ τῆς Εἰδοθέας,
ὡς Τζέτζης τέως οἴεται, καὶ σκόπει, πῶς σοι λέγει·
Πρωτεὺς τὸ ὕδωρ, πρώτιστον ὑπάρχον τῶν στοιχείων·
55 ὅθεν αὐτὸν καὶ γέροντα καὶ τῶν ἰφθίμων λέγει.
Εἰ δ' ἦν τις ἀνθρωπόμορφος, γέροντα μὲν ἂν εἶπε,
σοφὸν δὲ ἤ τι ἕτερον, οὐ μέντοι τῶν ἰφθίμων.
Οὕτως ὁ Τζέτζης οἴεται τὸν μὲν Πρωτέα ὕδωρ,
τὴν δ' Εἰδοθέαν ὄνομα πρέπον μαντικωτάτοις,
60 ὡς ἀστρολόγοις καὶ λοιποῖς προγνωστικοῖς ἀνθρώποις·
εἰδυῖα πάντα ὡς θεός, ἢ ἡ εἰδυῖα θεῖα·
ταύτην ὁ Τζέτζης μάντιν σοι λέγει τὴν Εἰδοθέαν.
Πρωτέως θυγατέρα δὲ λέγει καλεῖσθαι οὕτω,
ὡς πάντα προγινώσκουσαν ἐξ ὑδρομαντευμάτων.
65 Αὐτὴ τῷ Μενελάῳ δὲ πάντα μαντευσαμένη
Ὁμήρου λόγοις φέρεται, ὡς ἑρμηνεύει τούτῳ
πῶς τὸν Πρωτέα γέροντα ὄντα πατέρα ταύτης,
ὡς ἂν αὐτῷ μαντεύσηται· ὃ καὶ γενέσθαι λέγει.
Τζέτζης ἐκείνην δέ φησι Μενέλαον ἰδοῦσαν·
70 "Πᾶν ὅσον χρήζεις ἐκμαθεῖν, ὑδρομαντείαις δείξω·
καιρῷ γὰρ μεσημβρίας σε πρὸς σπήλαιόν τι ἄξω
καὶ 'τρεῖς' ἑτάρων δὲ τῶν σῶν, οὕσπερ αὐτὸς ἂν θέλῃς,

that is, they didn't set sail under a benevolent horoscope.

*'If one of the gods had not pitied me and showed mercy,*
*the daughter of mighty Proteus, the old man of the sea,*
*Eidothea; for I moved her heart above all others.'*                    50

'*Of the gods*' here means of sorcerers and wise men and
    water diviners.

The names of Proteus and Eidothea are fabricated,
as Tzetzes has long thought, and look at his explanation:
Proteus is water, the first element that came into existence;
wherefore he calls him the old man and mighty.                         55
If he were of human form, he would call him old man,
wise or something else, but not mighty.

Thus Tzetzes thinks Proteus is water,
and Eidothea is a fitting name for the most capable seers,
such as astrologers and the other prognosticators;                     60
for she knows everything as a god, or as the female divinity
    who knows;

Tzetzes tells you that Eidothea is this diviner.
Thus Homer says that she is called the daughter of Proteus,
as she foretells everything from water divination.

She is said, in the words of Homer, to have prophesied               65
everything to Menelaos, as she explains to him
that the old man Proteus was her father,
so that she would prophesy to him; and he says that it
    happened.

Tzetzes says that it was she who saw Menelaos;
"Everything you must learn, I will show you with water               70
    divinations;
for at midday I will lead you to a cave
along with '*three*' of your companions, whomever you may
    wish,

καὶ νεεκδόροις δέρμασι φωκῶν ὑμᾶς καλύψω."
Ἔχει γὰρ ἀντιπάθειαν ἡ φώκη ταῖς μαγείαις
75 καὶ συνεργεῖ δὲ πρὸς πολλὰ τῶν μαγικῶν ὁμοίως.
"Διὰ 'ὀδμὴν' δὲ τῶν 'φωκῶν' ἀρώματα παράσχω,
κειμένων οὕτω δὲ ὑμῶν φώκαις ἐσκεπασμένων,
καὶ φῶκαι ἐξελεύσονται καὶ αὗται δὲ πεσοῦνται.
Εἶτα καταριθμήσασα τὰς φώκας καὶ ὑμᾶς δέ
80 μέσον ὑμῶν καὶ τῶν φωκῶν ὕδωρ θαλάσσης θήσω,
καὶ τότε ἂν ἐγέρθητε καὶ ἴδητε μυρία
ὅσ' ἐπὶ γαῖαν ἑρπετὰ τῷ ὕδατι ἐκείνῳ,
καὶ πῦρ καὶ ὕδωρ καὶ φυτά, πᾶσαν ἁπλῶς τὴν φύσιν.
Δεῖ δὲ πολλῆς στερρότητος, οὐχὶ δειλίας τότε,
85 ἔχειν καὶ ὑπομένειν τε τὸν γέροντα, τὸ ὕδωρ,
καὶ σθεναρῶς ἐγκαρτερεῖν εὐτόνοις εὐψυχίαις.
Εἰ γὰρ μικρὸν ἐνδοίητε καὶ δειλανδρήσητέ μοι,
τῶν ὁρωμένων ταῖς μορφαῖς πάθητε τὸ Πεισάνδρου.
Οὗτος γὰρ ὢν δειλότατος ψυχὴν ἰδεῖν ἐπόθει,
90 ἐν δὲ τῷ θῦσαι κάμηλον φάσμα ψυχῆς ὡς εἶδεν,
ἄψυχος οὗτος καὶ νεκρὸς ὡράθη παραυτίκα.
Οὕτω τῷ τότε τόλμης μέν, ἀλλ' οὐ δειλίας, χρεία.
Ἐπὰν τὸ ὕδωρ πάλιν δὲ ἴδητε ὕδωρ μόνον,
ἤτοι μετὰ ἐκπλήρωσιν ὧν δράσω μαντευμάτων,
95 ἐρώτα, ὅσα βούλει μοι, Μενέλαε, καὶ μάθῃς."
Τὸν νοῦν ἀλληγορήματος ὅλον τοῦ νῦν εἰρήκειν.
    Ἤδη τινὰς δὲ λέξωμεν λέξεις ἀλληγορίας·
'θεάων' νῦν σοφῶν <τινῶν>, τὸ δ' 'ἀθανάτους' νόει
ἀστέρας Εἱμαρμένην τε, 'θεοὶ' πάλιν σοφοὶ δέ.

and I will cover you with the newly skinned pelts of seals."
For seals both counteract magical tricks
and equally facilitate much magic of another type.          75
    "Because of the '*stench* of the seals' I will give you
          fragrances,
and as you are lying down, thus covered with seal pelts,
seals will come out of the sea and lie down.
Then, after counting you and the seals,
between you and the seals I will place the water of the sea,     80
and then you would wake up and see countless reptiles
in that water, as many as there are on the earth,
and fire and water and plants, simply put, the whole of
          nature.
There is need for much resoluteness, not cowardice then,
to hold and endure the old man's attack, namely the water,      85
and to persevere forcefully with vigorous good spirit.
For if you yield even a little or cower before me
at the sight of these shapes, you will suffer the same fate as
          Peisandros.
For he, being most cowardly, longed to see his soul,
and when he saw a soul's phantom as he sacrificed a camel,      90
he immediately became an inanimate corpse as well.
Thus there is need for daring at that time, but not
          cowardice.
And when you see the water once again as merely water,
that is, after the fulfillment of the divinations I will
          perform,
ask me whatever you want, Menelaos, and you will learn."        95
I have revealed the entire sense of the allegory here.
    Let us now engage in some allegory:
by some wise '*goddesses*' here, understand '*the immortal*'
stars and Destiny, the '*gods*' again are the wise men.

100 'Τίς ἀθανάτων με πεδᾷ' ἤτοι τις Εἱμαρμένη.

'Τίς σοὶ θεὸς *συμφράσατο*' φρόνιμος συνετός τε.

'*Διὶ* καὶ *ἄλλοισι θεοῖς*' τῇ Εἱμαρμένῃ λέγει,

καὶ '*ἀθανάτοις*' δὲ '*θεοῖς*' τοῦ οὐρανοῦ ὁμοίως.

Θεοὺς πολλάκις εὕρῃς μοι πάλιν τὴν Εἱμαρμένην.

105 '*Διὸς γαμβρὸς*' Μενέλαος, ὅ ἐστι βασιλέως.

Ἐπεὶ χρησμοῖς δ' ἐς ὕστερον νήσοις μακάρων ἦλθε,

παίζων ὁ γέρων καὶ γαμβρὸν Διὸς κατονομάζων,

—οὐ βασιλέως δὲ Διός, ἀλλὰ θεοῦ τοῦ λήρου—

"οἷα γαμβρός, Μενέλαε, θεοῦ," φησίν, "ὑπάρχων

110 ἀφίξῃ ἐς Ἠλύσιον καὶ τὰς μακάρων νήσους."

Αἴγυπτον Νεῖλον ποταμὸν διιπετῆ δὲ λέγει,

ὡς ὄμβροις αὐξανόμενον χιόσιν Αἰθιόπων.

'*Θεῶν χόλον κατέπαυσα*' τῆς Εἱμαρμένης λέγει.

'Ἔδοσαν '*οὖρον οἱ θεοί*,' μοῖρα καὶ τὰ στοιχεῖα.

115 '*Ἔργον δ' Ἡφαίστοιό*' ἐστι πυρὸς καὶ τοῦ τεχνίτου.

'*Ἀρχὸν* νηὸς '*τὸν Μέντορα*' εἴτε '*θεὸν*' ἐπέγνων,

'*θεὸν*' σοφὸν καὶ σύμβουλον εἴτ' οὖν ἀρχόντων ἕνα.

Ὡσαύτως καὶ τὸ '*εἴ τίς*' μοι '*θεὸς*' ἦν παροτρύνων.

Νῦν Ἀθηνᾶ ἡ φρόνησις, ἣ ἐκ θανάτου σώζει.

120 '*Θεοῖς*' ἀπέχθεσθαι αὐτοὺς ἤτοι τῇ Εἱμαρμένῃ.

Πῶς Ἀθηνᾶ δὲ ἔκλυε; Τίς φαίη Πηνελόπῃ,

ὅτι σωθεὶς Τηλέμαχος φρονήσει ὑπεστράφη;

'*Who* of the immortals binds me' means some Destiny.          100
'*Which* god *took counsel* with you' means a wise and
    intelligent man.
'*To Zeus* and the other gods' means to Destiny,
and 'to the immortal gods' is likewise of the sky.
You will often learn from me that the gods are Destiny
    again.
'*Zeus's son-in-law*' is Menelaos, meaning the king's son-in-          105
    law.
When, according to the prophecies, he came later to the
    isles of the blessed,
the old man Homer, playfully calling him Zeus's son-in-law,
—not the king Zeus, but the foolish god—
says, "O Menelaos, as you are like a god's son-in-law,
you will arrive at Elysium and the islands of the blessed."          110
Homer says that the river Nile in Egypt was swollen by the
    rain,
as it is swollen with floods from Ethiopian snows.
'I put an end to the *wrath of the gods*' means of Destiny.
'The *gods*,' that is, fate and the elements, gave '*a favorable
    wind.*'
'*The work of Hephaistos*' is the work of fire and the          115
    craftsman.
I recognize as '*the leader*' on the ship '*Mentor*' or a '*god*';
'*a god*' is a wise man and a counselor or one of the leaders.
Likewise also the phrase 'whether *some god*' was urging
    me.
Here Athena is wisdom, who saves from death.
That they are hated '*by the gods,*' that is by Destiny.          120
How did Athena hear? Who would say to Penelope
that Telemachos, saved by wisdom, returned?

Τῇ Πηνελόπῃ Ἀθηνᾶ τὸν ὄνειρον ἐκπέμπει,
ἢ ὁ ἀὴρ ὢν κάθυγρος ἐπαγαγών τε ὕπνον,
125 ἢ ὅτι ἃ καθεύδοντες ὀνείρατα ὁρῶμεν
ψυχῆς τε καὶ φρονήσεως ἀνάπλασμα τυγχάνει.
Ἐπεὶ τὴν Δέλτα πᾶσαν δὲ εἶπον ἀλληγορίαν,
μικρόν τι γελαστέον μοι καὶ ἀνερωτητέον
τοὺς πειθομένους τοῖς μωροῖς ἀλληγορογραφοῦσιν·
130 εἰ ὁ Πρωτεύς, ὡς οἴεσθε, ὕλη δοκεῖ τυγχάνειν,
καὶ μὴ ὑδρομαντεία δέ, καθὼς ὁ Τζέτζης λέγει,
πῶς ἐκ τῆς ὕλης, εἴπατε, Μενέλαος μανθάνει,
ὅσα τῷ Ἀγαμέμνονι συμβαίνει καὶ τοῖς ἄλλοις;
Τίνες αἱ φῶκαι ἦσαν τε καὶ τίς ἡ ἀμβροσία,
135 ἣν ταῖς ῥισὶν ἐνέσταξεν αὐτῶν ἡ Εἰδοθέα,
καὶ τίς ἡ Εἰδοθέα δὲ σὺν πᾶσι τοῖς ἑτέροις;
Ψευδαλληγορογράφοις μοι μὴ πείθεσθε μηδ᾽ ὅλως.
Πῶς δ᾽ ἄν τις γνοίη τὰς ψευδεῖς ἀλληγορίας, λέξω·
ἂν πρὸς τὴν ὅλην ἔννοιαν τήν, ἣν ἀλληγοροῦσι,
140 τὸ διαρκὲς οὐκ ἔχωσιν, ἀλλὰ κενολογῶσιν.

Athena sent the dream to Penelope,
means either that the air being very moist brought sleep,
or that the dreams we see when asleep                                      125
are the representation of our soul and good sense.
Since I have told the allegory of the whole of Book Four,
a small point should make us laugh and ask
of those who are hoodwinked by the foolish allegorists:
if Proteus, as you think, seems to be prime matter,                       130
and not water divination, as Tzetzes says,
how did you say that Menelaos learns from prime matter
everything that happened to Agamemnon and the others?
Or who the seals were and what the ambrosia was,
which Eidothea dripped into their nostrils,                                135
and who Eidothea was among all the rest?
Don't be persuaded by false allegorists in any way.
And I will tell you how one might recognize false allegories:
if they do not hold on continuously to the whole concept
they are allegorizing, then they are talking nonsense.                    140

# Ε′

Ὑπόθεσις Ὁμήρου δὲ τοῦ Ε′ τῆς Ὀδυσσείας.

Θεῶν δευτέρας ἀγορᾶς αὖθις γεγενημένης,
ἡ Ἀθηνᾶ τὰς συμφορὰς ἔφασκεν Ὀδυσσέως,
καὶ ὡς κατέχοιτο αὐτὸς τῆς Καλυψοῦς τῇ νήσῳ,
οἱ δὲ μνηστῆρες βούλονται κτεῖναι καὶ παῖδα τούτου,
5 δι' ἀκοὴν τὴν τοῦ πατρὸς εἰς Πύλον ἀφιγμένον.
Ζεὺς δέ φησι πρὸς μὲν αὐτὴν τὴν Ἀθηνᾶν τοιάδε·
"Ὥσπερ ὑπέθου λογισμὸν ἐλθεῖν τὸν Ὀδυσσέα
καὶ τοὺς μνηστῆρας σύμπαντας σὺν δόλοις ἀποκτεῖναι,
ὡς ἀβλαβῆ Τηλέμαχον κόμισον εἰς Ἰθάκην."
10 Πρὸς Ἀθηνᾶν μὲν τοιαδί. Τὸν δὲ Ἑρμῆν κελεύει
ἐλθόντα φάναι Καλυψοῖ, πέμψαι τὸν Ὀδυσσέα,
καὶ δὴ αὐτὸν ἐξέπεμψεν ἐπί τινος σχεδίας·
τῇ ὀκτωκαιδεκάτῃ δὲ ἡμέρᾳ, τὴν σχεδίαν
ὁ Ποσειδῶν διέλυσε μεγάλως χαλεπήνας.
15 Ἰνὼ δὲ κινδυνεύοντα τοῖς κύμασιν ἰδοῦσα,
δοῦσα τὸ κρήδεμνον αὐτῆς γῆν εἰς Φαιάκων σώζει.

Νῦν ἀλληγορητέον δὲ τὰ τῇδε γεγραμμένα.
'Θεῶν φρονούντων,' ἀγορᾶς δευτέρας ἀγοραίας
ὁ Μέντωρ διηγεῖται μὲν τὰ περὶ Ὀδυσσέα,
20 βουλαῖς τῆς Πηνελόπης δὲ οἰκτρᾷ τῇ διηγήσει.
Ὃν Ἀθηνᾶν νῦν Ὅμηρος, ὥσπερ καὶ πρώην, λέγει,

# Book 5

The subject matter of the fifth book of the *Odyssey*.

When the second council of the gods happened then,
Athena spoke of the misfortunes of Odysseus,
and how he was detained on Kalypso's island,
while the suitors planned to kill his son,
who had gone to Pylos to hear tidings of his father.     5
Zeus said this to Athena herself:
"Just as you advised that Odysseus should go
and kill all the suitors with cunning,
so you should bring Telemachos unharmed to Ithake."
Thus he spoke to Athena. He ordered Hermes     10
to go and tell Kalypso to send Odysseus on his way,
and she sent him off on a raft;
on the eighteenth day, Poseidon
broke up the raft, being very angry.
Ino, seeing him in danger from the waves,     15
gave him her veil and brought him safely to Phaiakia.

Now what has been written here should be allegorized.
'The gods in counsel' means in the second assembly
in the agora Mentor is explaining about Odysseus,
in a pitiable story following the wishes of Penelope.     20
Here Homer, just as earlier, calls Mentor Athena,

αὐτὸν μὲν λέγων Καλυψοῦς κατέχεσθαι τῇ νήσῳ,
βουλεύεσθαι μνηστῆρας δὲ καὶ παῖδα τούτου κτεῖναι.
Ταῦτα εἰπόντος Μέντορος, ἀνδρὸς φρονιμωτάτου,
25  ὁ Ζεὺς καὶ ἔννους τις ἀνήρ, οἷος ὁ Ἀλιθέρσης,
φησίν, "ὡς ᾠκονόμησας τὰ περὶ Ὀδυσσέα,
οὕτω στραφῆναι ἀβλαβῆ καὶ παῖδα τούτου σκόπει."
Ταῦτα μὲν πρὸς τὸν Μέντορα, καὶ γράμμα δὲ συντάξας,
ὅπερ "Ἑρμῆν' τε καὶ 'υἱὸν' αὐτοῦ κατονομάζει—
30  ὁ γὰρ προφορικὸς λόγος, τέχνη νοὸς ὑπάρχων,
ὁ ἑρμηνεὺς νοός ἐστι ψυχῆς τε κινημάτων.
Ἑρμῆς καὶ ὁ τὸ γράμμα δέ τισιν ἀποκομίζων
καὶ ὑπουργοῦν πᾶν ὄργανον πρὸς ἔκθεσιν γραμμάτων,
καθάπερ Ἥφαιστος τὸ πῦρ καὶ πυρεργοὶ καὶ ὗλαι.
35  Καὶ γράμμα δὲ συνθέμενος, μετά τινος ἐμπόρου
στέλλει πρὸς νῆσον Καλυψοῦς σθένον, ἐκείνην πεῖσαι,
πρὸς τὴν πατρίδα τὴν αὐτοῦ πέμψαι τὸν Ὀδυσσέα.
Οἶδας τὸν Ποσειδῶνα τε καὶ τὰς ὀργὰς θαλάσσης.
''Ἰνὼ' δὲ καὶ τὸ 'κρήδεμνον' χάρις ἐστὶν Ὁμήρου·
40  παίζων χαριεντίζεται καὶ γὰρ ἐν τοῖς ἐνθάδε.
Πρὸς ὅνπερ μῦθον λέγουσι περὶ Ἰνοῦς τῆς Κάδμου,
θεὰν λεγόντων γὰρ αὐτὴν γενέσθαι τῇ θαλάσσῃ.
Ἐπεὶ συνέβη πλέοντι τῷ Ὀδυσσεῖ σχεδίᾳ
ἐκ τῆς θαλάσσης αἴθυιαν εὐθὺς ἐξαναδῦναι,
45  ἔγγιστα τῆς σχεδίας τε πτερυξαμένην τότε
χωρῆσαι τὴν εἰς Φαίακας κατὰ γραμμὴν ὀρθίαν·
ἐκ ταύτης δ' ἔγνω Ὀδυσσεὺς ἔγγιστα γῆν ὑπάρχειν,
οὗ ἔμελλε καὶ νήξασθαι σχισθείσης τῆς σχεδίας.
Παίζων χαριεντίσμασιν ὁ Ὅμηρος, ὡς εἶπον,

saying that Odysseus is detained on Kalypso's island,
and that the suitors are plotting to kill his son.
When Mentor, a most wise man, said these things,
Zeus, that is, a certain sensible man such as Halitherses,          25
said, "as you handled the matters concerning Odysseus,
so too look out for his son to return unharmed."
This he said to Mentor and, having composed a letter,
which he calls 'Hermes' and his '*son*,'—
for the uttered speech, existing through the skill of the          30
      mind,
is the interpreter of the mind and the movements of the
      soul.
Hermes is the conveyor of the letter to certain people
and every instrument used to write letters,
just as Hephaistos is fire and blacksmiths and wood.
And having composed a letter, a powerful one, he sent it          35
with a merchant to Kalypso's island, to persuade her
to send Odysseus to his homeland.
You know about Poseidon and the wrath of the sea.
'*Ino*' and '*the veil*' are the grace of Homer;
for he is playful and witty in what he says here too.          40
Besides this story, they tell a tale about Kadmos's daughter
      Ino,
saying that she became a goddess in the sea.
When a shearwater suddenly emerged from the sea
before Odysseus as he was sailing on his raft,
and fluttering very near the raft then,          45
it proceeded toward the Phaiakians along a straight course;
from it Odysseus knew that land was nearby, to which
he would have to swim after the raft was split apart.
Homer, playing with witticisms, as I said,

50 Ἰνὼ᾽ λέγει τὴν αἴθυιαν, ῾κρήδεμνον᾽ δέ σοι ταύτης
γραμμὴν τὴν τοῦ πτερύγματος ἐκείνην τὴν ὀρθίαν,
καθ᾽ ἥνπερ ἐκνηχόμενος πρὸς Φαίακας ἐξῆλθεν.
Ἔχεις τὸ ἀλληγόρημα· τοῦτο δὲ νῦν σημειοῦ,
ὡς πλοίοις κινδυνεύουσιν ἂν αἴθυια φανείη,
55 ἐξαναδῦσα τοῦ βυθοῦ, σημεῖον σωτηρίας·
ἐν δὲ πλόου σοι καταρχῇ ἂν αἴθυια φανείη,
εἰσδῦσα μᾶλλον εἰς βυθὸν ἐκ τῆς ἐπιφανείας,
ὄλεθρον τότε τῇ νηὶ σημαίνει καὶ πλωτῆρσι,
κἂν εὐδιῶν τῶν πώποτε βλέπῃς εὐδιωτέραν.
60 Ἂν τοῦτο γοῦν κατίδῃς μοι, φεῦγε πρὸς ἄλλο πλοῖον,
ἂν ἀναγκαῖον τότε σοι καθέστηκε τὸ πλεῦσαι.
Εἰ δ᾽ οὐ μεγάλη βία τις, ἔα μὴ πλεύσῃς τότε.
Ἐπεὶ ταῦτα κατέλεξα, λοιπόν μοι χωρητέον
ἤδη καὶ πρὸς τὸ κείμενον, ὡς τὰ χρειώδη λέξω.
65 ῾Ἠὼς δ᾽ ἐκ λεχέων παρ᾽ ἀγαυοῦ Τιθωνοῖο
ὤρνυθ᾽, ἵν᾽ ἀθανάτοισι φόως φέροι ἠδὲ βροτοῖσιν.᾽
Τὸν τοῦ Πριάμου ἀδελφὸν νῦν, Τιθωνόν, μοι ἔα
καὶ τὴν Ἠὼ δὲ σύνευνον θεὰν νοεῖν ἀθλίαν.
Τὸ πρωϊνὸν κατάστημα νῦν Τιθωνόν μοι νόει,
70 τὰ ὤνια, ἃ τίθεται ταῖς ἀγοραῖς εἰς πρᾶσιν,
ἤτοι ἡμέρα ἤπλωτο ἀνθρώποις καὶ στοιχείοις.
Οἱ δὲ φρονοῦντες καὶ ῾θεοί,᾽ οὓς προλαβὼν εἰρήκειν,
συνέδριον ἐποίησαν, δῆλον ἐν τῇ Ἰθάκῃ,
περὶ μνηστήρων τῆς βουλῆς καὶ περὶ Ὀδυσσέως.
75 ῾Ὑψιβρεμέτην᾽ δὲ τὸν νοῦν, ὡς λόγοις ὑψηγόροις
δίκην βροντῶν ἀντίθετον ἅπαν καταβροντῶντα
καὶ νοημάτων κεραυνοῖς φλέγοντα καὶ πιμπρῶντα.

calls the shearwater '*Ino,*' and her '*veil*' for you is                    50
that straight course of her wings, along which
he swam and went ashore to the Phaiakians.
You have the allegory; now note this,
whenever a shearwater appears to ships in danger,
emerging from the depths, it is a sign of salvation;          55
but if a shearwater ever appears at the start of your voyage,
instead diving into the depths from the surface,
then it signifies destruction for the ship and its sailors,
even if you see better weather than ever before.
And if you observe this, I say leave for another ship,        60
if it is necessary for you to sail at all.
But if there is no great need, do not sail then.
Now that I said this, I must continue already
with the rest of the text, so that I say what is necessary.
 '*Now Dawn arose from her couch beside lordly Tithonos,*      65
*to bear light to the immortals and to mortal men.*'
Here allow me to explain that Tithonos is Priam's brother,
and his wretched wife is the goddess Dawn.
Here I understand the morning weather as Tithonos,
who is goods for sale, which are placed in markets for        70
      purchase,
that is, day was spreading over men and the elements.
 '*The gods*' who sat in counsel, of whom I spoke earlier,
held an assembly, obviously in Ithake,
concerning the intentions of the suitors and Odysseus.
Zeus had a 'loud-thundering' mind, like pompous words         75
thundering down on everything opposing him as if with
      thunder,
aflame and burning with lightning bolts of thought.

Οἱ 'Φαίακες ἀντίθεοι' τῇ ψυχικῇ δυνάμει,
δίκαιοι καὶ οἰκτίρμονες καὶ τῶν συμπαθεστάτων.
80  Ὥσπερ 'θεὸν τιμήσουσι' σοφὸν ἢ βασιλέα.
Τὰ πέντε σημαινόμενα θεοῦ ἐνταῦθα σώζει·
οἷον δ' ἂν εἴποι τις <τανῦν>· ἀπρόσφορον οὐκ ἔστι,
κἄνπερ ἀνάμματόν ἐστιν εἴτε τῶν ἀκανίσκων.
'Διάκτορος' ὁ μηνυτὴς τοῦ νοῦ τῶν κινημάτων.
85  Ὁ λόγος 'Ἀργειφόντης' δὲ ὡς καθαρὸς ἐκ φόνου.
Ὁ τῶν Ἰθακησίων δὲ τῆς συμβουλῆς καὶ πλέον·
εἰς σωτηρίαν γὰρ αὐτοῦ ἐγράφη Τηλεμάχου.
Ἢ ὁ φονεὺς τοῦ Ἄργου δέ, κυνὸς τοῦ πανομμάτου,
ὁ λόγος πᾶσαν γὰρ ὁρμὴν κυνώδη καταστέλλει.
90  'Χρυσᾶ' δὲ 'πέδιλα' Ἑρμοῦ 'γῇ φέροντα, θαλάσσῃ'
αἱ συλλαβαὶ καὶ λέξεις δέ, αἷς συμπληροῦται λόγος.
Χάρταις γραφὲν τὸ γράμμα γὰρ γῇ στέλλεις καὶ θαλάσσῃ.
'Εἵλετο δὲ ῥάβδον, τῇ τ' ἀνδρῶν ὄμματα θέλγει,
ὧν ἐθέλει, τοὺς δ' αὖτε καὶ ὑπνώοντας ἐγείρει.'
95  Ῥάβδον δὲ τὴν νουθέτησιν καλεῖ, τὰς παραινέσεις,
ἢ θέλγει καὶ πραΰνει μὲν ὠμοὺς καὶ θυμουμένους·
νύττουσα τοὺς ῥᾳθύμους δὲ πράττειν τι διεγείρει.
'Τὴν μετὰ χερσὶν ἔχων πέτετο κρατὺς Ἀργειφόντης.'
Τὸ σχῆμα ἐπανάληψις· ἔστι δ' ὁ νοῦς τοιόσδε·
100  τὴν ἣν εἶπον παραίνεσιν ταχέως γεγραμμένην,

The 'Phaiakians equaled the gods' in the power of their
    souls,
just and compassionate and most sympathetic.
    '*They shall honor him*' as '*a god*' means as a wise man or     80
    king.
He has here the five signifiers of a god;
just as one would say now: it is not unsuitable,
even if it is a basket without knots or braids.
    '*The messenger*' is one who reveals the mind's movements.
    The word '*Argeïphontes*' means that he is purified from     85
    murder.
The story of the Ithakans is moreover the story of
    deliberation;
for it was written for the rescue of Telemachos himself.
Or it means the slayer of Argos, the all-seeing dog,
for speech subdues every dog-like rage.
    The 'golden *sandals*' which 'carry' Hermes 'over earth and     90
    sea'
are the syllables and words of which speech is composed.
For the letter written on paper you send over earth and sea.
    '*And he took the wand with which he lulls to sleep the eyes of*
    *men*
*whom he will, while others he awakens even out of slumber.*'
By wand he means warning, exhortations,     95
which lull and soothe fierce and angry men;
prodding the lazy, it stirs them to action.
    '*With this in hand the strong Argeïphontes flew.*'
The figure of speech is called repetition; the meaning is as
    follows:
once the exhortation of which I spoke was swiftly written,     100

ὁ λόγος ἔχων ὁ γραπτός, Ἑρμῆς, ὁ προλεχθείς μοι,
καὶ ὁ γραμμάτων κομιστής, ὡς προλαβὼν εἰρήκειν,
ἐκ τοῦ 'αἰθέρος' καὶ τοῦ νοῦ τῷ χάρτῃ ἐγγραφεῖσαν,
οἱ χάρται καὶ αἱ βίβλοι δὲ πάντως καὶ Πιερίαι,
105   οἷα Μουσῶν καὶ γνώσεως τελοῦσαι κατοικίαι.
Ἐν πόντῳ καὶ θαλάσσῃ δὲ καὶ δι' ὁλκάδος πλεύσας
εἰς Καλυψοῦς ἀφίκετο τὴν νῆσον πλὴν ἐν χρόνῳ.
'Ἔνθα στὰς θηεῖτο διάκτορος Ἀργειφόντης'·
ὁ τῶν γραμμάτων κομιστής, ὅστις ἦν ἂν ἐκεῖνος.
110   'Οὐ γάρ τ' ἀγνῶτες θεοὶ ἀλλήλοισι πέλονται,'
οἱ γὰρ σοφοὶ καὶ φρόνιμοι νοοῦσι τῶν ὁμοίων.
'Ζεὺς ἐμέγ' ἠνώγει δεῦρ' ἐλθέμεν οὐκ ἐθέλοντα,'
σοφοὶ καὶ ἔννους ἄνθρωποί σοι ἀπεστάλκασί με.
'Θεοῖς θυσίας ῥέζουσι,' τουτέστι τοῖς στοιχείοις.
115   'Διὸς' δὲ νῦν 'παρεξελθεῖν' τῆς Εἱμαρμένης λέγει.
'Ἄλλον θεὸν' στοιχεῖόν τι σοφὸν ἢ βασιλέα.
Νῦν 'σχέτλιοί ἐστε, θεοί,' τὴν Εἱμαρμένην λέγει.
'Θεαῖς' ταῖς βασιλίσσαις δέ, 'ἀνδράσι' δὲ τοῖς κάτω.
Θεαῖς καὶ τοῖς στοιχείοις δέ, οἷς ἔστι θῆλυς κλῆσις,
120   ὥσπερ ἡμέρα τε καὶ γῆ, θαλάσσῃ καὶ τοιούτοις.
Ἄν τις δ' "ἡμέραν," ἔροιτο, "Τζέτζη, στοιχεῖον λέγεις;",
"Ναί," φαίην ἂν ὡς πρὸς αὐτόν, "ἡμέρα γὰρ τυγχάνει
φαῦσις πυρὸς ἡλιακοῦ γῆς ἀνωτέροις τόποις."
Ἡμέρα τὸν 'Ὠρίωνα' μῦθοι φασὶν ἐρᾶσθαι,
125   ἀνθ' ὧν ἐν βίῳ καὶ φωτὶ πράξεις λαμπρὰς ἐποίει.
Ἡ Ὀρτυγία νῆσός τις, Δῆλος νῦν καλουμένη.
Ἄρτεμις τὸν Ὠρίωνα κτανεῖν ἐνεμυθώθη,

78

it was bound to the written word, that is, the
    aforementioned Hermes,
the bringer of the letter, as I said beforehand,
so it was now written on paper from the '*ether*,' that is, from
    the mind;
the papers and the books no doubt are the Pierides,
as they are the abodes of the Muses and knowledge.      105
After sailing on the ocean and sea in a merchant ship,
he arrived at Kalypso's island just in time.
   '*And the messenger Argeïphontes stood and marveled*,'
that is, the bringer of the letter, whoever he was.
   '*For not unknown are the gods to one another*,'      110
as the wise and the prudent recognize those like them.
   '*It was Zeus who bade me come here against my will*,'
meaning wise and thoughtful men have sent me to you.
   They '*offer* sacrifices to the gods,' that is, to the elements.
   Here '*to avoid the will of Zeus*' means of Destiny.      115
   By '*another god*' he means some element or a wise king.
   Here '*Cruel you are, O gods*' means Destiny.
   '*For goddesses*' means for queens, while '*with men*' means
    with those of lower rank.
For goddesses and elements are grammatically feminine,
just like day, earth, sea, and such things.      120
If someone were to say, "Tzetzes, are you calling 'day' an
    element?",
"Yes," I would say to him, "for day happens to be
the rising of the solar fire above earth's higher places."
The myths speak of '*Orion*' being loved by Day,
that is, she did magnificent deeds in life and light.      125
Ortygia is an island, now called Delos.
Artemis is said in myth to have killed Orion,

ἀνθ᾽ ὧν σκορπίος ἔκτεινεν αὐτὸν κυνηγετοῦντα.

Ἐκ Κρήτης Ἰασίων μὲν ἦν τῶν φιλογεώργων,

130 ὅθεν αὐτῷ μυθεύονται τὴν Δήμητραν μιγῆναι.

Ἐκεραυνώθη δ᾽ ὁ ἀνήρ, ὅθε φασὶν οἱ μῦθοι,

ὅτι διὰ τὴν Δήμητραν Ζεὺς κεραυνοῖ τὸν ἄνδρα.

Ζεύς, ὁ βαλὼν ἐν κεραυνῷ, νῦν οὐρανὸς τυγχάνει.

'Ἀθάνατον,' 'ἀγήραον' νῦν βασιλέα λέγει,

135 οὐχ ὅτι οὐ γηράσκουσι σώμασι στεφηφόροι,

ἀνθ᾽ ὧν αἱ μνῆμαι τούτων δὲ τοῖς χρόνοις οὐ γηρῶσι.

'Διὸς μῆνιν' σαφέστατα τὴν Εἱμαρμένην λέγει.

'Ἀπέβη Ἀργειφόντης' δὲ ὁ ἔφορος ἐκείνου.

'Ζηνὸς ἀγγελιάων' δὲ γραφῆς τῆς ἐλλογίμου.

140 Δώσω δὲ καὶ τηρήσω σοι οὔρου πνοὴν ἀνέμου.

'Θεοὶ' δὲ νῦν οἱ οὐρανοῦ ἀστέρες, Εἱμαρμένη

καὶ τὰ στοιχεῖα δὲ αὐτά, ἐξ ὧν πνοαὶ ἀνέμων.

Τῷ Ὀδυσσεῖ μὲν βρώματα παρέθεντο ἀνθρώπων,

ἤγουν κοινὰ ἐσόμενα τοῖς σύμπασιν ἀνθρώποις,

145 τῇ Καλυψοῖ δὲ βρώματα τῶν βασιλικωτέρων,

ἅπερ κατονομάζει νῦν 'νέκταρ' καὶ 'ἀμβροσίαν.'

Ἡ Ὀδυσσεῖ μὲν βρώματα παρέθεντο ἐσθίειν,

αὕτη σὺν θεραπαίναις δὲ λόγοις τισὶν ἐτρύφα,

ἃ μᾶλλον τῇδε λέξει τις νέκταρ καὶ ἀμβροσίαν.

150 Τὸν ὃν γὰρ κατηξίωσε τῶν αἰδημονεστέρων,

ἄτοπον φαίνεται τροφῆς μὴ ἀξιοῦν ὁμοίας.

Τίνας φησὶ νῦν 'τὰς θνητὰς' καὶ τίνας ἀθανάτους;

Θνητὰς τῆς κάτω τύχης μέν, θεὰς τὰς βασιλίδας.

that is, a scorpion killed him as he was hunting.
Iasion from Crete was a lover of agriculture,
because of which the myths say Demeter lay with him.          130
The man was struck by lightning, wherefore the myths say
that Zeus struck the man with lightning because of
    Demeter.
Zeus, hurling the lightning bolt, is the sky here.

    Homer now calls the king *'immortal,' 'ageless,'*
not because men wearing crowns do not age in body,          135
but meaning that their memory does not age with time.
    *'The wrath of Zeus'* he calls most clearly Destiny.
    *'Argeïphontes departed'* means an overseer sent by Zeus.
    The *'commands of Zeus'* means writing most eloquently.
I will give and maintain for you a blast of favorable wind.          140
    Here *'the gods'* are the stars in the sky, Destiny,
and the elements themselves, from which come gusts of
    wind.

    They set before Odysseus food suitable for men,
that is, what will be common to all men;
before Kalypso they set royal food,          145
which Homer calls here *'nectar* and ambrosia.'
Or while she delighted in conversation with her attendants,
they set before Odysseus food to eat,
food which one would rather call nectar and ambrosia.
As she deemed him worthy of her intimacy,          150
it seems strange not to deem him worthy of the same food.
    Whom does he here call *'mortal women'* and whom
        immortals?
Mortal women are those of low fortune, goddesses are
        queens.

Σημείωσαι, ὡς Σόλυμοι Ἱεροσολυμῖται,
155 ἐξ ὧν νῦν Ὅμηρός φησιν, οὐ μὴν δὲ οἱ Μιλύαι,
ὡς ἄλλοι γράφουσί τινες ἄνδρες τῶν νεωτέρων.

Καὶ τοῦτο δὲ σημείωσαι περὶ αὐτοῦ Ὁμήρου,
ὡς ὕστερος καθέστηκε Δαβὶδ καὶ Σολομῶντος
ἐκ τοῦ μεμνῆσθαι ὁπωσοῦν ὀνόματος Σολύμων.
160 Δαβὶδ γὰρ ταύτην ἔθετο καὶ Σολομῶν τὴν κλῆσιν
τῇ χώρᾳ, ἥπερ πρότερον ἦν Ἰεβοὺς ἡ κλῆσις.
Λοιπὸν ἀκούων τῶν ἐπῶν ἠκριβωμένως σκόπει.
ʻΤὸν δʼ ἐξ Αἰθιόπων ἀνιὼν κρείων ἐνοσίχθων,
τηλόθεν ἐκ Σολύμων ὀρέων ἴδεν· εἴσατο γάρ οἱʼ·
165 ἔγνως ἐκ τῶνδε ἀκριβῶς, ἃ σημειοῦσθαι εἶπον.

Ἄκουε νῦν δὲ καὶ τὸν νοῦν, ὃν γράφουσι τὰ ἔπη·
ʻΕὖροςʼ θαλάσσῃ κινηθεὶς ἐκ τῆς Αἰθιοπίας,
τῷ Ὀδυσσεῖ τὰς συμφορὰς ἐπήνεγκεν, ἃς γράφει.
Ὡς Ποσειδῶνα φέρει δὲ τὴν θάλασσαν λαλοῦντα,
170 ὅσα ἂν εἶπε Ποσειδῶν κατά τινος ἀνθρώπου,
τὸν ὃν αὐτὸς ἐκώλυε πελάγεσσι θαλάσσης
πρὸς τὴν πατρίδα τὴν αὐτοῦ μὴ θέλων ἀφικέσθαι,
ἰδὼν δʼ αὐτὸν φερόμενον αὔραις οὐριοπνόοις.
ʻΘεοὶ μετεβουλεύσαντοʼ νῦν τὰ στοιχεῖα λέγει.
175 Πῶς δὲ συνάγει Ποσειδῶν ʻνεφέλας,ʼ μάνθανέ μοι.
Τὰ νέφη ἀνιμήσεσι γίνονται τῶν ὑδάτων.
ʻΤρίαινανʼ δέ μοι νόησον εἶναι τὰς τρικυμίας.
Τὸν οὐρανὸν τοῖς νέφεσιν ὁ Ζεὺς περικαλύπτει,
ἀὴρ ὁ ζῳογόνος τε καὶ ἀνασπῶν ἰκμάδας.

Note that Solymians are Jerusalemites,
based on what Homer says here, and not Milyans,                              155
as written by certain other men of more recent times.
   And note this too about the same Homer,
that he lived after David and Solomon,
given that he mentions in some form the name Solymians.
For David and Solomon gave that name                                        160
to the land which had previously been called Jebus.
   Listen then to his words and consider them carefully.
   '*But the glorious Earth shaker, as he came back from the*
        *Ethiopians,*
*beheld Odysseus from afar, from the mountain of Solymoi; he saw*
        *him*';
you learned carefully from these things, which I told you to               165
        note well.
   Listen now to the inner thought which the words record:
   The '*East Wind,*' having moved over the sea from
        Ethiopia,
brought disasters to Odysseus, about which Homer writes.
He calls the sea Poseidon talking,
whatever Poseidon said against a certain man,                               170
the man whom he himself hindered on the open sea,
not wanting him to reach his fatherland,
seeing him carried by favorable winds.
   'The gods changed their mind' here means the elements.
   Learn from me how Poseidon gathers '*the clouds.*'                       175
The clouds are created by the drawing up of the waters.
   Understand that the '*trident*' is mighty waves.
   That Zeus covers the sky with clouds
means the life-giving air, sucking up the moisture.

180　Τὰ τῆς Ἰνοῦς προείπομεν—τίνα Ἰνὼ νῦν λέγει,
　　ὅτι παίζων τὴν 'αἴθυιαν' Ἰνὼ κατονομάζει
　　καὶ λόγους περιάπτει δὲ νῦν προσωποποιήσας,
　　ἠθοποιίας λόγους δὲ τῷ Ὀδυσσεῖ προσάπτει.
　　'Μὴ' νῦν 'ὑφαίνῃ δόλον μοί τις' ἐκ τῶν 'ἀθανάτων,'
185　μὴ πρὸς τὴν πτῆσιν ἀπιδὼν ἀπατηθῶ αἰθυίας.
　　Δόξας βραχύ τι πέλαγος ὡς πρὸς τὴν γῆν ἐκτρέχειν
　　ἡ 'Ἀθηνᾶ' δέ, ὁ ἀὴρ καὶ οὐρανοῦ θυγάτηρ,
　　'Βορέαν' πνέειν εἴασεν, 'ἄλλους' δ' 'ἀνέμους' ἔσχεν.
　　'Ἀθήνη θεῖσα' δ' ἐν 'φρεσὶν' ἡ φρόνησις ὑπάρχει.
190　'Αἰδοῖος μέν τ' ἐστὶ καὶ ἀθανάτοισι θεοῖσιν'
　　οἰκτείρουσι κακούμενον πολλάκις καὶ στοιχεῖα.
　　'Ἀθήνη ὕπνον ἔχευε' νῦν, κἄντε τὸν ἀέρα,
　　κἄνπερ αὐτοῦ τὴν φρόνησιν εἴποις, οὐχ ἁμαρτάνεις.

We spoke already of Ino—here he speaks of a certain Ino,    180
whom he playfully calls the 'shearwater' Ino,
and he uses these words to characterize her here,
attributing a speech in character study to Odysseus.
    The verse '*let no immortal* weave a snare for me' here
means may I not be tricked as I look at a shearwater's flight.    185
He thinks here that a small sea ran up toward the land,
and 'Athena,' that is the air and the daughter of the sky,
let the 'North Wind' blow but held back 'the other winds.'
    'Athena placed' in his '*mind*' means his wisdom.
    '*Reverend even in the eyes of the immortal gods*'    190
means the elements pity him as he suffers greatly.
    Whether you say that '*Athena* poured *sleep* over him' is
        here
the air or his prudence, you would not go wrong.

# Z′

Ὑπόθεσιν νῦν ἄκουε τῆς Ζῆτα Ὀδυσσείας.

Ὄναρ ἡ Ἀλκινόου παῖς, Φαιάκων βασιλέως,
προτρέπεται πρὸς ποταμὸν πλύνειν αὑτῆς ἐσθῆτας.
Μετὰ τὸ πλῦναι παιδιᾷ σφαίρας δὲ τερπομένη
σὺν θεραπαίναις ταῖς αὑτῆς θροῦν ἤγειρε τῷ τότε·
5 ὑφ᾽ οὗ αὐτὸς ὁ Ὀδυσσεὺς ἐξεγερθεὶς τοῦ ὕπνου
καὶ τῆς παιδὸς προσδεηθείς, λαβὼν τροφήν, ἐσθῆτα,
ταύτῃ συνηκολούθησεν εἰς πόλιν τῶν Φαιάκων.

    Ὣς ὁ μὲν ἔνθα καθεῦδε πολύτλας δῖος Ὀδυσσεὺς
    ὕπνῳ καὶ καμάτῳ ἀρημένος· αὐτὰρ Ἀθήνη
10  βῆ ῥ᾽ ἐς Φαιήκων ἀνδρῶν δῆμόν τε πόλιν τε.᾽
    Καὶ μετὰ ἔπη δέ τινα πάλιν φησὶν τοιάδε·
    ῾τοῦ μὲν ἔβη πρὸς δῶμα θεὰ γλαυκῶπις Ἀθήνη,
    νόστον Ὀδυσσῆι μεγαλήτορι μητιόωσα.᾽
    Νῦν Ἀθηνᾶν τὴν φρόνησιν δεῖ σε νοεῖν, τὸ δ᾽ ὅπως,
15  ἄκουε νῦν καὶ μάνθανε σοφῶς, ἠκριβωμένως,
    εἰ ὄντως ὄνειρός ἐστι καὶ μὴ τελῶν ἐκ μέθης,
    ψυχῆς τε καὶ φρονήσεως καὶ λογισμοῦ τις πλάσις,
    εἰκόνας τε καὶ εἴδωλα μελλόντων προδεικνῦσα.
    Ἐπεὶ καὶ Ναυσικάας δὲ ὁ λογισμὸς καὶ φρένες
20  τὸν περὶ γάμου ὄνειρον ἀνέπλασαν ἐκείνῃ,

# Book 6

Now hear the subject matter of the sixth book of
the *Odyssey*.

The daughter of Alkinoös, king of the Phaiakians, had a
    dream
urging her to wash her clothes at the river.
After doing the washing, she delighted in a ball game,
and made a great din with her maidservants,
which awakened Odysseus from his sleep;          5
after entreating the girl, he received food and clothing,
and followed her into the city of the Phaiakians.

  '*So he lay there asleep, the much-enduring goodly Odysseus,*
*overcome with sleep and weariness; but Athena*
*went to the land and city of the Phaiakians.*'          10
  And afterward Homer speaks such words again:
'*To Alkinoös's house went the goddess, flashing-eyed Athena,*
*to contrive the return of greathearted Odysseus.*'
Understand here that Athena is prudence, but in what way
    exactly
hear now and learn wisely, precisely,          15
if indeed it was a dream and not a result of drunkenness,
some figment of his soul and wisdom and reason,
foreshowing images and phantoms of future events.
Since Nausikaa's reason and heart
fashioned her dream regarding marriage,          20

δι' ὃν σὺν ταῖς νεάνισι καὶ ταῖς θεραπαινίσιν
ἐλθοῦσα πλῦναι ποταμῷ σῴζει τὸν Ὀδυσσέα.
Οὕτω φησὶν ὁ Ὅμηρος, δεινὸς ὢν λογογράφος.
Ὁ λογισμός, ἡ φρόνησις δῆλον τῆς Ναυσικάας,
25  νόστον βουλεύων Ὀδυσσεῖ πόλιν Φαιάκων ἦλθεν.
Ὑπέρεια καὶ Μάρινα πόλις τῆς Σικελίας.
Κατ' ἄλλους ἄλλη πόλις δέ, νῆσος δὲ καθ' ἑτέρους.
'Θεοειδὴς' ἐρρέθη μοι ποσάκις πόσοις τόποις.
'Καί γε νηοὺς ἐποίησε θεῶν,' ἄκουε ποίων·
30  στοιχείων καὶ φρονήσεως, αὐτῆς τε Εἱμαρμένης,
καὶ βασιλέων γε ναοὺς καὶ ἡρωεῖα τούτων·
εἰ θέλεις, ἅμα καὶ σοφῶν οὐκ ἀπεικὸς ἐνθάδε.
Τὴν γὰρ πεντάδα σύμπασαν θεοῦ σημειουμένην
νοεῖν νῦν οὐκ ἀνάρμοστον· τὰ πέντε προσφυᾶ γάρ.
35  'Ἀλκίνοος δὲ τότ' ἦρχε, θεῶν ἄπο μήδεα εἰδώς,'
σοφὰ καὶ ἀγχινούστατα ὡς αἱ ψυχῶν δυνάμεις,
ὡς λογισμός, ὡς φρόνησις, ὡς πάντα τὰ τοιάδε.
Τὴν Ναυσικάας 'Ἀθηνᾶν' τὴν ἐν ὀνείροις εἶπον.
'Ἡ μὲν ἄρ' ὣς εἰποῦσ' ἀπέβη γλαυκῶπις Ἀθήνη
40  Οὐλυμπόνδ', ὅθι φασὶ θεῶν ἕδος ἀσφαλὲς αἰεί.'
Ὄλυμπον νῦν καὶ οὐρανὸν ὁ ποιητής σοι λέγει,
τοῦ λογισμοῦ τὸ ὄργανον, τὴν κεφαλὴν αὐτήν σοι,
ἥτις ὁλολαμπής ἐστιν, ἂν ἔχῃ νοῦν, τὸν Δία,

because of which she came with the young girls and her
    servants
to do the wash in the river, and saved Odysseus.
Thus says Homer, being a skilled writer.
Reason, clearly the prudence of Nausikaa, devising
Odysseus's homecoming, came to the city of the     25
    Phaiakians.
   Hypereia is Marina, a Sicilian city.
According to others, it was a different city, an island
    according to yet others.
   *'Godlike'* has been mentioned by me often and in many
    places.
   *'Nausithoös* had made *temples for the gods,'* hear which ones:
for elements and prudence, for Destiny itself,     30
and temples for the kings and hero shrines for them; if you
    wish,
it wouldn't be unreasonable to say even for wise men here.
For it is not unfitting to understand that all five aspects of
    god
are signified here; for all five are suitable.
   *'Alkinoös was then king, made wise in counsel by the gods,'*     35
that is, wise and most sagacious things, as are the powers of
    souls,
such as reason, prudence, and everything of that kind.
   I have spoken of Nausikaa's 'Athena,' the one in her
    dreams.
   *'So saying, the goddess, flashing-eyed Athena, departed*
*to Olympos, where, they say, the gods' abode stands fast forever.'*     40
The poet here tells you that Olympos is the heavens,
the instrument of reason, your head itself,
which is shining all over, if it has sense, that is Zeus,

ἀπόντος ἀφωτίστῳ δὲ κατέχεται τῷ σκότει.

45 Ἔδαφος αὕτη τῶν θεῶν ἐστὶ καὶ κατοικία,
νοὸς Διός, φρονήσεως τῆς Ἀθηνᾶς, Ἑρμοῦ τε,
τοῦ λόγου τοῦ προφορικοῦ, καὶ τῶν λοιπῶν ἁπάντων.
'Ἀνέμοις' οὐ 'τινάσσεται,' οὐ βρέχεται δ' ὑπ' 'ὄμβρων,'
οὐ ταῖς τυχούσαις προσβολαῖς εὐρίπιστος ὑπάρχει,
50 ἀποσοβεῖ τοὺς ὄμβρους δὲ τῶν ἐναντίων λόγων,
οὐδὲ 'χιόνος' συμφορῶν συστέλλεται τῷ ψύχει,
ὁλολαμπὴς καὶ αἴθριος, ὡς ἔφην, δὲ τυγχάνει,
σκοτιζομένη μηδαμῶς ὑπό τινος τοιούτου,
ἀεὶ λευκὴν τὴν αἴγλην δὲ φέρει παρυπηργμένην·
55 πάντα λευκῶς καὶ καθαρῶς ὡς ἔχουσιν ὁρᾷ γάρ.
    'Τῷ ἔνι τέρπονται μάκαρες θεοὶ ἤματα πάντα,
    ἔνθ' ἀπέβη γλαυκῶπις, ἐπεὶ διεπέφραδε κούρῃ.'
Ἐν τούτῳ μὲν τῷ οὐρανῷ, ὡς ἔφην, καὶ Ὀλύμπῳ,
τῇ σφαιρομόρφῳ κεφαλῇ, τῇ καὶ λοιποῖς ὁπόσοις
60 εἰκονιζούσῃ οὐρανόν, ὁ λογισμὸς οἰκεῖ τε,
θεοί τε χαίρουσι λοιπόν, οὕσπερ τανῦν εἰρήκειν,
αἰὲν ἐόντων ὡς ἀεὶ παρυπαρχόντων τούτων.
Ἐκεῖ καὶ ἡ Ἀθήνη δέ, φρόνησις Ναυσικάας,
μετά γε τὴν ἀνάπλασιν ὑπέδυ τοῦ ὀνείρου.
65 Ὄργανον οὕτω λογισμοῦ τὴν κεφαλὴν μοι νόει,
Ὁμήρῳ τε πειθόμενος, πανσόφῳ λογογράφῳ.
Καὶ ἰατρῶν τῇ δόξῃ δὲ σοφῶν τε φιλοσόφων
ὃς τὴν καρδίαν ὄργανον λογιστικοῦ δὲ λέγει,
τὸ ὑλικόν, οὐ τελικὸν ὄργανον οὗτος λέγει.
70 Ἡ γὰρ ἀναθυμίασις αἵματος ἐγκαρδίου,
χωροῦσα πρὸς τὴν κεφαλὴν διὰ τῶν καρωτίδων,

but when that is absent, it is possessed by unlighted
    darkness.
  The head is the foundation of the gods and their dwelling   45
    place,
of the mind of Zeus, the wisdom of Athena, and of Hermes,
of the spoken word and all the rest.
Olympos *'is not shaken by the winds,'* nor is it soaked by 'rain,'
nor is it easily swayed by chance attacks;
it repels the storms of hostile words,   50
nor is it subdued in the cold of 'snowstorms';
it gleams all over and is clear, as I said,
nor is it darkened by anything of such a kind,
but it always bears a present radiant whiteness;
for it sees everything as clearly and purely as they are.   55
  *'Therein the blessed gods delight all their days, and thither*
*went the flashing-eyed one, when she had spoken to the maiden.'*
In this heaven, as I said, in Olympos,
in the sphere-shaped head, which represents the sky,
in it and in so many other things, reason dwells,   60
and the gods rejoice, of whom I have spoken here,
for they are eternal, as these things always exist.
Athena is there too, the wisdom of Nausikaa,
after she took the form of the dream.
Understand that for me the head is the organ of reason,   65
and in this I follow Homer, the all-wise writer.
And in the opinion of doctors and wise philosophers,
he who says the heart is the organ of reasoning
speaks of the material, not the final organ.
For the exhalation of blood from the heart,   70
moving toward the head through the carotid arteries,

θερμαίνει τὸν ἐγκέφαλον καὶ τὰς βουλὰς ἐξάγει.
Ἂν ὑλικὸν οὖν ὄργανόν τις λέγῃ τὴν καρδίαν,
τὴν κεφαλὴν δὲ τελικόν, ἔτι τῶν σωφρονούντων.
75 Εἰ τὴν καρδίαν λέγει δὲ τὸ τελικὸν τυγχάνειν,
Ἀριστοτέλους πάνσοφός τις μαθητὴς τυγχάνει.
Εἴπερ οὖν οὗτος ἰατρῶν οὐ πείθεται τοῖς λόγοις,
καὶ τούτων ἀποδείξεσι μυρίαις ὑπηργμένων,
"αὐτὸς δ᾽ ἔφα," <τανῦν> ληρεῖ, ὡς πρὶν οἱ Πυθαγόρου,
80 τοῦ Τζέτζου τὸ ἀστέϊσμα ἐρώτησον πρὸς τοῦτον,
ποῖον μέρος τοῦ σώματος μετάφρενον καλοῦμεν,
καὶ δείξει μέρος πάντως σοι τὸ μεταξὺ τῶν ὤμων,
ὃ μετὰ κεφαλῆς ἐστι, κοιλίαν ὀπισθίαν.
Εἰπὲ γοῦν τότε μειδιῶν ἐκείνῳ τῷ πανσόφῳ·
85 "εἰ μὴ παρῆν ὁ λογισμὸς τῇ κεφαλῇ καὶ φρένες,
ἀλλ᾽, ὥσπερ λέγεις, ἐν αὐτῇ τῇ θέσει τῆς καρδίας,
μετάφρενα ἂν ἔλεγον οἱ πάντες τὰ πρὸς ἥβην,
εἴτε τὸ στόμα τῆς γαστρός, ὡς μετὰ τὴν καρδίαν,
οὐ μὴν δ᾽ ὥσπερ οἱ ξύμπαντες τὸ μεταξὺ τῶν ὤμων,
90 ὡς μετὰ κεφαλὴν αὐτὴν καὶ φρένας ὑπηργμένον."
'Οἵη δ᾽ Ἄρτεμις εἶσι κατ᾽ οὔρεος ἰοχέαιρα,'
ὥσπερ τοῖς κυνηγέταις δὲ τοῖς τόποις τῆς Ἐφέσου,
εἴτε τῆς Λακεδαίμονος, εἴτε τῆς Ἀρκαδίας
κυνηγετοῦσιν ἐν νυκτὶ τοὺς κάπρους, τὰς ἐλάφους,
95 φαίνεται ὑπερλάμπουσα σελήνη τῶν ἀστέρων,
ἐπιτερπὴς δὲ ἡ 'Λητὼ' καὶ νὺξ ὁρᾶται τότε.
'Παίζουσι κοῦραι δὲ Διός, Νύμφαι τοῦ Αἰγιόχου,'
αἱ νεωστὶ φαινόμεναι ὗλαι δὲ τῶν ὀρέων,

warms the brain and produces deliberation.
So if one should say that the heart is the material organ,
but the head is the final one, he is wise.
If he says that the heart is the final one,                    75
he is a most wise student of Aristotle.
So if indeed he is not persuaded by the words of doctors,
although these are supported by countless proofs,
"he said so," he now babbles, as the Pythagoreans did
         formerly,
ask him about the witticism of Tzetzes,                        80
which part of the body we call the back,
and he will certainly show you the part between the
         shoulders,
which is below the head, behind the belly.
So tell that most wise man with a smile:
"if reason and wisdom were not in the head,                    85
but, as you say, in that very position of the heart,
everyone would call the parts close to the pelvis the back
or the opening of the stomach, as it is behind the heart,
and not, as everyone does, the part between the shoulders,
which is behind the head itself and supports our thinking."    90
   '*Just as Artemis, the archer, roams around the mountains,*'
just as to the hunters in the regions of Ephesos,
or of Lakedaimon, or of Arkadia,
hunting boars or deer in the night,
the moon appears more radiant than the stars,                  95
so too does '*Leto,*' the night, look delightful then.
   'The *daughters* of *Zeus* the aegis bearer are *playing,* the
         *Nymphs,*'
that is, the newly appearing woods on the mountains,

αἷς νέμεται πᾶν ἄγριον, ἃς Ζεὺς ἀὴρ ἐκτρέφει·
100  παίζουσι καὶ συμπαίζουσι καὶ χαίρουσιν ἐκείνῃ.
Ἰδέας τότε νόει μοι γλυκύτητος τυγχάνειν,
τὸ σχῆμα δὲ μεταφορὰν καὶ προσωποποιίαν,
ὅσῳ περιτιθέασιν ἀψύχοις τὰ ἐμψύχων.
Ὡς ἡ σελήνη οὖν ἐστιν ὑπέροχος ἀστέρων,
105  οὕτω καὶ Ναυσικάα δὲ τῶν μετ' αὐτῆς ὑπῆρχεν.
    ʼΈνθ' αὖτ' ἄλλ' ἐνόησε θεὰ γλαυκῶπις Ἀθήνη,
ὡς Ὀδυσεὺς ἔγροιτο, ἴδοι τ' εὐώπιδα κούρην.'
Νῦν Ἀθηνᾶν γλαυκώπιδα νόει μοι τὸν ἀέρα·
ἡ γὰρ φωνή τε καὶ ὁ θροῦς ἀήρ τε πεπληγμένος,
110  οἷς Ὀδυσσεὺς ἐξυπνισθεὶς εἶδε τὴν Ναυσικάαν,
καὶ δι' αὐτὴν τετύχηκε ταύτης πατρὶ καὶ νόστου.
ʼΘεοειδῆ' νῦν 'νόον' μοι, τὸν δίκαιον, νῦν νόει.
Τὸ δίκαιον δυνάμεως δὲ ψυχικῆς τυγχάνει.
    ʼΤῇ' Ναυσικάᾳ 'θάρσος' δὲ ἐνῆκεν ἡ 'Ἀθήνη,'
115  ἤγουν ἡ φρόνησις αὐτῆς· ἦν γὰρ φρονιμωτάτη.
Τὸ δὲ "θεὸς νύ τις ἐσσί;" φάντασμα ἢ σελήνη.
ʼΔαίμων' ἡ Εἱμαρμένη δὲ τῷ ἔπει τῷ ἐνθάδε.
ʼΘεοὶ' τελέθουσι δὲ νῦν στοιχεῖα, Εἱμαρμένη,
ἤγουν τὸ μέγα πέλαγος κατὰ τῆς Εἱμαρμένης.
120  "Σοὶ δὲ θεοὶ τόσα δοῖεν" αὐτὴ ἡ Εἱμαρμένη.
Καὶ ʼΖεὺς' δὲ ὁ 'Ὀλύμπιος' αὐτὴ ἡ Εἱμαρμένη.
ʼΦίλοι γὰρ ἀθανάτοισιν' αὐτῇ τῇ Εἱμαρμένῃ.
Εἴτ' οὖν περιφρουρούμεθα στοιχείῳ, τῇ θαλάσσῃ,
ἢ ὅτι πάνυ σέβομεν τὰ δίκαια καὶ θεῖα.

94

to whom is apportioned all that is wild, which Zeus, the air,
    nurtures;
they play and play together and rejoice in it.          100
   Take it from me that I mean the ideas of sweetness,
and the figure of speech here is metaphor and
    personification,
inasmuch as they bestow the attributes of animate objects
    upon inanimate ones.
As the moon is supreme over the stars,
so too was Nausikaa over her companions.          105
   '*Then the goddess, flashing-eyed Athena, had another plan,*
*that Odysseus might awaken and see the fair-eyed maiden.*'
Here you should understand that flashing-eyed Athena is
    the air;
for the voice and the sound are the stricken air
by which Odysseus was awakened and saw Nausikaa,     110
and because of her he met her father and had his
    homecoming.
Here understand that 'godlike mind' is the just mind.
Justice is a power of the soul.
   '*Athena,*' that is, her prudence, instilled '*courage in*'
Nausikaa; for she was most prudent.          115
   "*Are you some goddess?*" means are you a ghost or the
    moon?
   '*Spirit*' is Destiny, according to what is said here.
   The '*gods*' here become the elements, Destiny.
That is, the great sea against Destiny.
   "*May the gods grant you so much*" means Destiny itself does.   120
   And '*Zeus*' the '*Olympian*' means Destiny itself.
   'For they are dear *to the immortals*' means to Destiny itself.
So either we are protected by an element, the sea,
or we respect very much what is just and divine.

125 'Πρὸς γὰρ Διὸς' οἱ ξύμπαντες 'ξεῖνοι,' 'πτωχοὶ' τελοῦσι,
ξένοι πτωχοί τε γίνονται καὶ γὰρ ἐξ Εἱμαρμένης.
    'Τὸν μὲν Ἀθηναίη θῆκεν, Διὸς ἐκγεγαυῖα,
    μείζονά τ' εἰσιδέειν καὶ πάσσονα, κὰδ δὲ κάρητος
    οὔλας ἧκε κόμας ὑακινθίνῳ ἄνθει ὁμοίας.'

130 Νῦν Ἀθηναίην λέγει σοι, Διὸς ἐκγεγαυῖαν,
αὐτὸ κατὰ μετάληψιν τὸ δένδρον τῆς ἐλαίας·
πάντα τὰ δένδρα γὰρ ὁ Ζεύς, ἤγουν ἀήρ, ἐκτρέφει.
Μᾶλλον τοῦ δένδρου πλέον νῦν τὸ ἔλαιόν σοι λέγει,
ὡς οἶνον καὶ τὴν ἄμπελον Διόνυσον καλοῦμεν.

135 Τοῦτο γὰρ λέγει προφανῶς τοῖς ἔπεσιν, οἷς γράφει,
ὅτι λουθεὶς ὁ Ὀδυσσεὺς καὶ ἐγχρισθεὶς ἐλαίῳ—
οὕτω γὰρ ἦν τὸ παρ' ἡμᾶς σύνθετον τοῦτο σμῆγμα—
καὶ μείζων καὶ παχύτερος ἐφάνη καὶ εὐκόμης.
    Ἡ θάλασσα ξηραίνει γὰρ καὶ ἡ ταλαιπωρία,

140 τὸ δὲ θερμὸν ἂν καὶ γλυκὺ περιχυθὲν ὑγραίνει,
καὶ ἀραιοῦν τοὺς πόρους δέ, τοὺς πόρους τοὺς ἀδήλους,
μείζονα καὶ παχύτερα τὰ σώματα δεικνύει.
    Οὐλίζει καὶ τὰς τρίχας δὲ καὶ χρίσις ἡ ἐλαίου,
τοὺς πόρους παρεμφράττουσα ταύτης παχυμερείᾳ,

145 καὶ συντηροῦσα τὸ ὑγρὸν ἔντοσθε τῶν σωμάτων,
μείζω τε καὶ παχύτερα καὶ τὸ θερμὸν δεικνύει
καὶ μαλακὰ δὲ καὶ στιλπνά· τρέφει δὲ καὶ τὰς κόμας.
    'Ἴδρις, ὃν Ἥφαιστος δέδαεν καὶ Παλλὰς Ἀθήνη'
Ἥφαιστος νῦν τὸ πῦρ ἐστιν, ἡ φρόνησις Ἀθήνη.

150 'Οὐ' τῶν 'θεῶν ἀέκητι' ἀστέρων, Εἱμαρμένης,
ἤγουν οὐ μοίρας ἀγαθῆς ἄνευθεν ἦλθε τῇδε.

'*For from Zeus*' come all the '*strangers,*' the '*beggars*' means      125
that people become strangers and beggars because of
    Destiny too.
  '*Then Athena, born from Zeus, made him*
*taller to look upon and mightier, and from his head*
*she made the locks to flow in curls like hyacinths.*'
Here he tells you that Athena, born from Zeus,      130
is by substitution the olive tree;
for Zeus, that is, the air, nourishes all trees.
Rather, here he means olive oil,
just as we call wine and the vine Dionysos.
For he clearly tells you this with the words he writes,      135
that Odysseus bathed and anointed himself with oil—
for this was our compounded unguent—
and he looked taller and fatter and fair-haired.
For the sea and hardship dry out,
but heat moistens when sweetly poured around,      140
and rarefies the pores, the invisible pores,
and so makes bodies seem bigger and fatter.
Anointing hair with oil makes it curly,
as the oil blocks the pores with its thickness,
and retains moisture inside bodies,      145
while warmth makes them appear taller and fatter
and soft and glistening; and it nourishes the hair as well.
  '*A skillful workman, whom Hephaistos and Pallas Athena*
    *taught*':
Hephaistos here is fire, Athena is wisdom.
  '*Not* without the will of the *gods*' means of the stars, of      150
    Destiny,
that is, he came here not without the aid of a benevolent
    fate.

'Ἀντίθεοι' ἰσούμενοι τῇ ψυχικῇ δυνάμει,
δίκαιοι καὶ φιλόξενοι καὶ ἕτερα ἐν ἄλλοις.
'Νῦν δὲ θεοῖσιν' ἔοικας ἄστρασιν οὐρανίοις.

155    'Ἤ τίς οἱ εὐξαμένη πολυάρητος θεὸς ἦλθεν
οὐρανόθεν καταβάς, ἕξει δέ μιν ἤματα πάντα.'
Θεὸς νῦν βασιλεύς ἐστι, τὸ δ' 'οὐρανόθεν' λέγει
ἐξ οὐρανίας ἐπελθὼν μοίρας καὶ Εἰμαρμένης.
Δήομεν 'ἀγλαὸν ἄλσος Ἀθήνης ἄγχι κελεύθου'·

160    'Ἀθήνης' τε φρονήσεως νῦν δέ, οὐ τοῦ ἀέρος.
Οἱ παλαιοὶ γὰρ ὡς θεοὺς ἐτίμων τὰ στοιχεῖα
καὶ τοὺς ἀστέρας δὲ αὐτούς, αὐτὴν τὴν Εἰμαρμένην,
σοφοὺς ὁμοῦ καὶ βασιλεῖς καὶ ψυχικὰς δυνάμεις.
Ταῦτα ἐτίμων ἄλσεσι καὶ ἐν βωμοῖς ναοῖς τε.

165    Ἀλλ' ἐατέον τὰ λοιπά, τὰ ψυχικὰ λεκτέον.
Ἄρεος μὲν καὶ τοῦ θυμοῦ ναούς τε καὶ εἰκόνας
ἐν τοῖς ἀγροῖς καὶ πόρρωθεν ἵστων τῶν πολισμάτων,
τῆς δ' Ἀθηνᾶς, φρονήσεως, ἀγάλματα ἐποίουν
ἔγγιστα τείχους πόλεως, πρὸ τῶν πυλῶν δὲ πλέον.

170    Διὸ καὶ κατωνόμαζον ἐκείνην πολιάδα.
Ταυτὶ δ' ὑπῆρχε σύμβολα μονονουχὶ βοῶντα,
πρὸς τοὺς ἐκτὸς καὶ πόρρωθε μάχας συνάπτειν δέον,
πρὸς τοὺς ἐντὸς δὲ φρόνησιν ἀσκεῖν καὶ εὐβουλίαν.
'Κλῦθί μευ, αἰγιόχοιο Διὸς τέκος, Ἀτρυτώνη.'

175    Τέκος Διός, νοός, ἐστὶν ἡ φρόνησις Ἀθήνη,

'Equal to the gods' means equal in the power of their soul,
in being just and hospitable and in other things.

'*Now*' you resemble '*the gods*' means you resemble the
heavenly stars.

'*Or some god, much wished for, has come down from heaven*     155
*answering her prayers, and she will have him for all her days.*'
God here is a king, and '*from heaven*' means that
he came by some heavenly fate and Destiny.

We will find '*a splendid grove of Athena near the road*':
here '*of Athena*' means 'of wisdom,' not 'of air.'     160
For the ancients honored the elements as gods
as well as the stars themselves, that is, Destiny itself,
along with wise kings and powers of the soul.
These they honored in sacred groves and in altars and
temples.
But I should set the rest aside and focus on the powers of     165
the soul.
For they let the temples and images of Ares, that is, of
anger,
be in the countryside far away from the cities,
but they made the statues of Athena, that is, of wisdom,
closest to the city wall, right in front of the gates.
Because of this they called her guardian of the city.     170
Here there were symbols all but shouting
that one must battle with those outside the city and far
away, but
exercise prudence and good counsel toward those inside
the walls.

'*Hear me, child of aegis-bearing Zeus, unwearied one.*'
The child of Zeus, of intelligence, that is Athena, wisdom,     175

καὶ Ἀτρυτώνη φρόνησις ὡς μὴ δαμαζομένη,
ὅθε καὶ ἄφθορον αὐτήν φασί τε καὶ παρθένον.
Ὁ Ζεὺς δέ, νοῦς, αἰγίοχος οὕτως ἐκλήθη πάλιν,
ὁ καταιγίσι λογισμῶν κλονῶν τοὺς ἐναντίους,
180 ἢ ὁ ἀκατανόητος καὶ συγκεκαλυμμένος,
ὥσπερ ἐν καταιγίσι τε καὶ γνόφῳ καὶ θυέλλῃ.
Ἡ Ἀθηνᾶ δ᾽ οὐκ ἤκουσε κινδύνοις Ὀδυσσέως·
πᾶσα βουλὴ γὰρ ἄπρακτος πρὸς κλύδωνα θαλάσσης.
Ὣς ἔφατ᾽ εὐχόμενος, τοῦ δ᾽ ἔκλυε Παλλὰς Ἀθήνη·
185 αὐτῷ δ᾽ οὔ πω φαίνετ᾽ ἐναντίον· ἅζετο γάρ ῥα
πατροκασίγνητον· ὁ δ᾽ ἐπιζαφελῶς μενέαινεν
ἀντιθέῳ Ὀδυσῆι, πάρος ἦν γαῖαν ἱκέσθαι.᾽
Τοῦ Ὀδυσσέως ἤκουσε φρόνησις εὐξαμένου,
οὔπω αὐτῷ ἐφάνη γὰρ μετὰ βραχὺν δὲ χρόνον,
190 οὔτε τὸ φρόνημα αὐτοῦ τοῖς Φαίαξιν ἐδείκνυ·
οὕτω μὲν οὔπω φρόνησις τῷ Ὀδυσσεῖ ἐφάνη.
Ὅμηρος παίζων δέ φησι σχῆμα τῇ μεταβάσει·
τὸν γὰρ αὐτῆς πατράδελφον ᾐδεῖτο Ποσειδῶνα.
Πῶς δ᾽, Ὅμηρε, ἡ θάλασσα, Διὸς νοὸς συναίμων,
194α [ὁ Ποσειδῶν μέν, ὁ θυμός, Διὸς νοὸς συναίμων]
195 οὗπερ νοὸς ἡ Ἀθηνᾶ καὶ φρόνησις θυγάτηρ,
οὕτω θυμὸς μὲν Ποσειδῶν, Διὸς νοὸς συναίμων;
Οὗτος δὲ παίζων τοὺς παχεῖς, τοὺς μυθικῶς νοοῦντας
(ἐπεὶ καὶ Ζεὺς ὁ οὐρανὸς καὶ Ζεὺς αὐτὸς τυγχάνει),
σχήματι μεταβάσεως ἀστειοτάτῳ λέγει.

and the unwearied one is prudence, since it cannot be
    subdued,
wherefore they call her pure and a virgin.
And Zeus, that is mind, was again called the aegis bearer,
he who shakes his opponents with storms of reason,
or he who is inconceivable and concealed,               180
as if in storms and in storm cloud and a squall.
    Athena did not hear Odysseus in danger;
for all her advice was futile against the billowing of the sea.
    *'So he spoke in prayer, and Pallas Athena heard him;*
*but she did not yet appear to him* face to face; *for she* feared    185
*her father's brother; but he furiously raged against*
*godlike Odysseus, until at length he reached his own land.'*
Prudence heard Odysseus's prayer,
but she did not appear to him after a short time,
nor did she reveal his thought to the Phaiakians;          190
thus prudence did not appear to Odysseus yet.
Homer playfully speaks with the figure of speech called
    transition;
for Athena feared her paternal uncle Poseidon.
How, O Homer, is the sea a blood relative of Zeus, the
    mind,
[Poseidon, anger, is a blood relative of Zeus, the mind]    194a
of which mind Athena, that is prudence, is the daughter,    195
and thus anger is Poseidon, a blood relative of Zeus, the
    mind?
Homer, playing with the stupid who think in mythical
    terms
(since Zeus is the sky and also happens to be himself),
speaks most jokingly in the figure of speech called
    transition.

200 Ἠιδεῖτο γὰρ πατράδελφον αὐτῆς τὸν Ποσειδῶνα·
ἢ τὸν θυμὸν πατράδελφον φρονήσεως νῦν λέγει,
θυμὸν τοῦ Ποσειδῶνος δέ, τουτέστι τῆς θαλάσσης·
πρὸς γὰρ θαλάσσης τὸν θυμὸν καὶ φρόνησις ἡττᾶται.
Τῷ Ὀδυσσεῖ ὠργίζετο οὗτος γὰρ καὶ μεγάλως,
205 πρὶν ἢ ἐκεῖνον ἀπελθεῖν εἰς τὴν αὐτοῦ πατρίδα.
Φθάσαντι πρὸς πατρίδα γὰρ φόβος οὐκ ἦν θαλάσσης.

For she feared her paternal uncle Poseidon;                    200
or here he calls anger the paternal uncle of prudence,
the anger of Poseidon, that is, of the sea;
for against the anger of the sea even prudence is defeated.
He was greatly enraged at Odysseus,
before he reached his own homeland.                            205
For a man who reaches his homeland does not fear the sea.

# Η΄

Ἡ Ναυσικάα πρὸς αὐτὴν τὴν πόλιν ἀφικνεῖται,
καὶ μετ᾽ ὀλίγον Ὀδυσσεὺς Ἀρήτην ἱκετεύει.
Ἐρωτησάσης δὲ αὐτῆς μετὰ τροφὴν καὶ δεῖπνον,
πόθεν αὐτὸς ὁ Ὀδυσσεὺς ἐσχήκει τὴν ἐσθῆτα,
5  ἄρχεται πᾶν κατὰ λεπτὸν ἐκείνη διηγεῖσθαι
ἀπὸ τῆς νήσου Καλυψοῦς μέχρι καὶ τῶν Φαιάκων.

 Τοῖς 'ἀθανάτοις' ὅμοιοι τοῖς ἄστρασιν εἰς κάλλος.
 'Θεοῦ δ᾽ ὡς δῆμος ἄκουε,' τουτέστιν Εἱμαρμένης,
ἤτοι καθὼς ὑπείκουσι πάντες τῇ Εἱμαρμένῃ,
10 οὕτως ὑπεῖκον Φαίακες αὐτῷ τῷ Ἀλκινόῳ.
 'Καὶ τότ᾽ Ὀδυσσεὺς ὦρτο πόλινδ᾽ ἴμεν· ἀμφὶ δ᾽ Ἀθήνη
πολλὴν ἠέρα χεῦε φίλα φρονέουσ᾽ Ὀδυσῆι.'
 Ἐπ᾽ εὐτυχίᾳ ὁ ἀὴρ τοῦ Ὀδυσσέως τότε
μεστὸς ὀμίχλης γεγονὼς εἶρξε θεᾶσθαι τοῦτον.
15  'Ἀθήνη' πάλιν φρόνησις, 'παρθενικῇ' ὁμοία·
νεᾶνις γὰρ ἡρμήνευσε πάντα τῷ Ὀδυσσῆι·
τὸν Ἀλκινόου οἶκον τε, γυναῖκα, γένος τούτων.
 'Οὐκ εἴα' ἡ 'ἐϋπλόκαμος' 'Ἀθήνη' δὲ ἐκεῖνον—
ἀὴρ ὁ ἀερόστημος, φάναι κατὰ Πισίδην—
20 ὀμίχλην καταχέασα Φαίαξι θεαθῆναι.
 'Θεὰ γλαυκῶπις ἦρχε' δὲ πάλιν 'Ἀθήνη μύθων'·
αὕτη ἡ ἑρμηνεὺς αὐτοῦ, νεᾶνις ἡ ῥηθεῖσα.

# Book 7

The subject matter of the seventh book of Homer's *Odyssey*.

Nausikaa arrives at the city,
and shortly thereafter Odysseus supplicates Arete.
After a meal and dinner, when she asked Odysseus
where he had acquired his clothing,
he begins to relate everything to her in detail,                    5
from the island of Kalypso up to the Phaiakians.

    Like the '*immortals*' means equal to the stars in beauty.
    '*The people listened to him like a god,*' that is, like Destiny,
which means that just as everyone yields to Destiny,
thus did the Phaiakians yield to Alkinoös.                          10
    '*And then Odysseus got up to go to the city; and Athena,*
*with kindly purpose, cast about him a thick mist.*'
To Odysseus's good fortune then, the air
filled with mist and prevented them from seeing him.
    '*Athena*' again is wisdom, in the form of '*a maiden*';           15
for the girl explained everything to Odysseus:
Alkinoös's house, his wife, their family.
    '*Fair-tressed Athena did not* permit' him to be seen
by the Phaiakians, pouring down mist—
that is the air of the weather, to use a word from Pisides.          20
    'The flashing-eyed goddess Athena' was again 'the first to
        speak';
the aforementioned maiden was his guide.

Ὅρα δὲ νῦν τὸν Ὅμηρον, πῶς ἐν φρενὶ πανσόφῳ
παίζων παραλογίζεται φωναῖς ταῖς ὁμωνύμοις,
25  τῇ μεταβάσει χρώμενος συχνῶς τῶν ὀνομάτων.
    'Ναυσίθοον μὲν πρῶτα Ποσειδάων ἐνοσίχθων
    γείνατο καὶ Περίβοια, γυναικῶν εἶδος ἀρίστη.'
    Οὐκ ἐνοσίχθων Ποσειδῶν ἐγέννησεν ἐκεῖνον,
    ἄνθρωπος δέ τις, Ποσειδῶν καλούμενος τὴν κλῆσιν.
30  Ὅμηρος μεταβάσει δὲ παίζει τῶν ὀνομάτων.
    'Ὀξεῖς θανάτους ἔγνωκεν Ἀπόλλωνος' τοξείας.
    'Θεὸν ὡς εἰσορόωντες' ὁποίαν τὴν σελήνην,
    εἴτε καὶ ἕκαστος αὐτὴν ὡς σφὴν ψυχὴν προβλέπει,
    ὡς καὶ αὐτὸς τοῖς ἔπεσιν οὕτω προερμηνεύει.
35  'Ὣς κείνη περὶ κῆρι τετίμηταί τε καὶ ἔστιν.'
    'Ὣς ἄρα φωνήσασ' ἀπέβη γλαυκῶπις Ἀθήνη
    δῦνε δ' Ἐρεχθῆος πυκινὸν δόμον. Αὐτὰρ Ὀδυσσεύς...'
    Οὕτω τοὺς δύο στίχους μοι τοὺς μέσους ὀβελίσας—
    νόθοι καὶ γάρ εἰσι—γράψον, ὡς καὶ αὐτὸς νῦν γράφω.
40  Ὁ νοῦς τῶν στίχων δέ ἐστιν· ἀπέβη ἡ νεάνις,
    πρὸς δὲ τὸν δόμον ἔδυνε πλασθέντος Ἐρεχθέως,
    ναυπηγικοῦ τινος ἀνδρός, κροτοῦντος ναυπηγίαις.
    "Ἐρέχθω" οἶδας τὸ "ἠχῶ" καὶ "κρότους ἀνεγείρω."
    Οὐκ Ἀττικοῖς ἐν δόμοις γὰρ εἰς Ἐρεχθέως δῆμον
45  μυθώδη δαίμονά τινα νῦν ἀπιέναι λέγει,
    ἀλλ', ὥσπερ εἶπον, χρώμενος οὕτω τῇ μεταβάσει.
    'Κύνες χρυσοῖ καὶ ἀργυροῖ' φυλάσσοντες τὸ δῶμα,
    καὶ 'κοῦροι' δὲ οἱ 'χρύσεοι' βαστάζοντες λαμπάδας,
    ἀπὸ ἀργύρου καὶ χρυσοῦ κατασκευαὶ τοιαῦται,
50  τῶν μὲν κυνῶν καὶ φυλακῆς δόκησιν ἐμποιοῦσαι.

Look at Homer now, how in his all-wise mind
he playfully misleads with homonyms,
by often making use of name transition.                               25
   *'Nausithoös at the first was born from the earth-shaker*
*Poseidon and Periboia, the prettiest of women.'*
He was not born to Poseidon the earth shaker,
but to a man, called Poseidon by name.
Homer plays with names through transition.                            30
      He knew that the sharp arrows of 'Apollo' are death.
   *'Looking upon Arete as a goddess,'* like the moon,
or even that each man foresees in it his own soul,
just as Homer predicts with his words.
      *'So heartily is she honored and has ever been.'*             35
      *'So saying, flashing-eyed Athena departed*
*and entered the well-built house of Erechtheus. But Odysseus . . .'*
Thus I have excised the two middle lines —
for they are spurious — write it as I write here.
The meaning behind the lines is: the maiden departed,                40
she entered the house which Erechtheus fashioned;
he was a shipwright, making a din with his shipbuilding,
You know "I rend" means "I make noise" and "I raise up a
      din."
He does not mean here that some mythical god
went into Attic houses in the city of Erechtheus,                     45
but, as I said, he makes use of transition this way.
   'Gold and silver *dogs*' guarding the house,
and 'golden *youths*' bearing torches,
such furnishings made of silver and gold,
look like dogs and guards.                                            50

Οἱ νέων ἀνδριάντες δέ, κηροπαγεῖς τελοῦντες,
πᾶσι φῶς βλέπειν ἐν νυκτὶ παρεῖχον δαιτυμόσι.
Διὰ τὸ μακροχρόνιον καλεῖ δὲ 'ἀθανάτους.'
    'Τοῖ' ἄρ' ἐν Ἀλκινόοιο θεῶν ἔσαν ἀγλαὰ δῶρα,'
55 ἐκ τῶν στοιχείων τε αὐτῶν καί γε τῆς Εἱμαρμένης.
Στοιχείων εὐφορίαι τε ὁμοῦ καὶ εὔκαρπίαι,
ἐκ δ' Εἱμαρμένης τὸ πλουτεῖν καὶ τὸ κρατεῖν Φαιάκων.
Ἀέρα χεῦεν Ἀθηνᾶ· νῦν ὁ ἀὴρ ὁμίχλην,
αὐτός τε συγκρυπτόμενος φρονήσει τῇ οἰκείᾳ.
60 'Δία' νῦν 'τερπικέραυνον' τὴν Εἱμαρμένην λέγει.
Καὶ τὸ 'θεοῖσι ῥέξομεν' στοιχείοις, Εἱμαρμένη.
    'Εἰ δέ τις ἀθανάτων γε κατ' οὐρανοῦ εἰλήλουθεν,
ἄλλο τι δὴ τόδ' ἔπειτα θεοὶ περιμηχανόωνται·
αἰεὶ γὰρ τὸ πάρος γε θεοὶ φαίνονται ἐναργεῖς.'
65 Εἰ δέ 'τις ἀθανάτων γε,' σοφῶν ἢ βασιλέων,
'ἐξ οὐρανοῦ,' καὶ μοίρας δέ φημι τῆς οὐρανίου,
ἢ ἀνακτόρων ὑψηλῶν μεταφορικωτέρως.
'Θεοὶ δὲ μηχανόωνται' πληροῖ ἡ Εἱμαρμένη.
Θεοὶ ὁρῶνται ἐναργεῖς· σοφοὶ καὶ βασιλέες
70 ἔρχονται πόδῳ τοῦ ἰδεῖν χώραν τὴν ἡμετέραν.
    'Δεινὴ θεὸς' ἡ 'Καλυψὼ' νῦν βασιλὶς μεγάλη.
Θεοὺς ἀνθρώπους τέ φησι σοφοὺς καὶ ἰδιώτας.
Ὁ 'Ζεὺς' 'ἐκέασε' τὴν ναῦν σκηπτὸς καὶ Εἱμαρμένη.
'Ἀθάνατον' ἀγήραον τοῖς ὄπισθεν ἐρρέθη.
75 'Ζηνὸς ὑπ'' ἀγγέλου δὲ φρονίμων μηνυμάτων.
Τὸ 'οὖρον δὲ προέηκεν' ἔπεμψε δὲ τότε,
ὁπότ' ἂν ἄνεμος φορός, ἐμοὶ χρειώδης, ἔπνει.
'Ζεῦ πάτερ' Ἀθηναίη' τε καὶ 'Ἀπόλλον' ἐρρέθη.

The statues of youths, made of wax,
provided all the guests with light to see in the night.
Because they last a long time, he calls them *'immortals.'*
  *'Such were the gods' glorious gifts in Alkinoös's palace,'*
namely gifts from the elements and from Destiny.     55
From the elements came fertility and fruitfulness,
from Destiny came the wealth and power of the Phaiakians.
*'Athena poured air'*—here the air pours mist,
itself being hidden in its own wisdom.
   Here he calls *'Zeus who delights in thunder'* Destiny.   60
   *'We will sacrifice to the gods'* means to the elements,
      Destiny.
   *'But if he is one of the immortals come down from heaven,*
*then the gods are planning some new thing;*
*for always up to now the gods appeared to us in bodily form.'*
But if *'one of the immortals'* means of the wise men or kings,   65
then *'from heaven,'* I say, means from heavenly fate,
or, in a more metaphorical way, from lofty palaces.
The gods are planning means Destiny fulfills.
*'The gods appear in bodily form'* means the wise and the
      kings
come on foot to see our land.       70
   *'Kalypso, a dread goddess'* is here a great queen.
   Homer says that the gods are both wise and ordinary
      men.
   *'Zeus had smitten'* the ship means a thunderbolt and Fate.
   *'Immortal'* has been said previously to mean ageless.
   *'From Zeus'* means from a messenger of wise messages.   75
   *'He sent forth a favorable wind'* means he sent it to me then,
whenever a favorable wind, which I needed, was blowing.
   *'Father Zeus,'* *'Athena,'* and *'Apollo'* have been explained.

# Θ′

Τῆς Ὀδυσσείας Θῆτα δὲ ὑπόθεσις τοιάδε.


Δι᾽ Ὀδυσσέα Φαίαξίν ἐστι νῦν ἐκκλησία,
καὶ ναῦς τις εὐτρεπίζεται πρὸς ἐκπομπὴν ἐκείνου.
Παρ᾽ Ἀλκινόου δ᾽ ἄριστοι Φαιάκων ἐστιῶνται.
Εἶτα καὶ ἀγωνίζονται, καὶ Ὀδυσσεὺς σὺν τούτοις.
5   Ἄιδει δὲ ὁ Δημόδοκος ἐπιβολῇ μὲν πρώτῃ
μοιχείαν τὴν τοῦ Ἄρεος ὡς πρὸς τὴν Ἀφροδίτην,
εἶτα τὴν Τροίας πόρθησιν ὑφ᾽ ἵππου τοῦ δουρείου.
Κλαίοντος Ὀδυσσέως δὲ πυνθάνεται Ἀλκίνους,
τίς ὢν καὶ τίνος ἔνεκα τούτων ἀκούων κλαίει.

10   ‘Πλησίον· ἡ δ᾽ ἀνὰ ἄστυ μετῴχετο Παλλὰς Ἀθήνη,
εἰδομένη κήρυκι δαΐφρονος Ἀλκινόοιο,
νόστον Ὀδυσσῆι μεγαλήτορι μητιόωσα,
καὶ ῥα ἑκάστῳ φωτὶ παρισταμένη φάτο μῦθον.’
Παλλὰς Ἀθήνη φρόνησις τανῦν τοῦ Ὀδυσσέως,
15   εἴτε καὶ ἡ τοῦ κήρυκος αὐτοῦ τοῦ Ἀλκινόου,
ἢ καὶ αὐτὸς ὢν φρόνιμος φρονίμως συνεκάλει.
Δαΐφρων νῦν πολεμικὸς οὐκ ἔστιν ὁ Ἀλκίνους,
ὁ πάντα δὲ λεπτοτομῶν φρονήσει καὶ συνέσει.
Τὸ ‘δέμας ἀθανάτοισιν’ ὅμοιος βασιλεῦσι.
20   Τίς Ἀθηνᾶ ἡ ‘πάσσονα,’ ‘μακρότερον’ τιθεῖσα;
Ἡ τοῦ ἐλαίου ἔγχρισις καὶ τὸ λουτρὸν ἐκεῖνο,

# Book 8

The subject matter of the eighth book of the *Odyssey*.

Now there is an assembly of the Phaiakians because of
    Odysseus,
and a ship is made ready to send him home.
The elite of the Phaiakians feast alongside Alkinoös.
Afterward they engage in competition, and Odysseus with
    them.
As an introduction Demodokos sings          5
of the adultery of Ares and Aphrodite,
then of the sack of Troy by the wooden horse.
As Odysseus was weeping, Alkinoös inquired
who he was and why he wept as he listened to this.

    '*Close together; and Pallas Athena went through the city*    10
*in the likeness of the herald of wise Alkinoös,*
*devising a return for greathearted Odysseus.*
*To each man's side she came and spoke and said.*'
Pallas Athena here is Odysseus's wisdom,
or even that of Alkinoös's herald,          15
or he himself, being wise, wisely issued a summons.
Alkinoös here is not warlike and combative,
he who analyzes everything with wisdom and prudence.
    '*In form like unto the immortals*' means like kings.
    Who was Athena who made him '*sturdier*' and '*taller*'?    20
It was the anointing with oil and that bath,

ἢ καὶ ἡ φρόνησις αὐτοῦ· θαρσήσας γὰρ ἐκείνη,
μηκέτι συστελλόμενος τῇ δέους ὑποψίᾳ,
μείζων τε καὶ παχύτερος αὐτὸς αὐτοῦ ἐφάνη.
25    Θεὸς ὁ ʻδοὺς τὴν ἀοιδὴνʼ γνῶσις, ἡ Εἱμαρμένη.
ʻΘεῶν δαιτὶ θαλείῃʼ τε γνώσει τῆς Εἱμαρμένης,
ἢ ψυχικῶν δυνάμεων, τέρψεως, εὐφροσύνης.
ʻΔιὸς μεγάλουʼ δὲ ʻβουλὰςʼ τῆς Εἱμαρμένης λέγει.
Τὸ δὲ ʻθεὸς στέφει μορφὴνʼ καὶ ὡς "θεὸν" ὁρῶσι
30    γνῶσιν καὶ φρόνησιν δηλοῖ, τὰ δʼ ἄλλα Εἱμαρμένην.
ʻΤέρματαʼ καὶ σημεῖα δὲ τίς ʻἔθηκεν Ἀθήνηʼ;
Ἡ Ὀδυσσέως φρόνησις ἢ καί τινων Φαιάκων·
τοῦτον γὰρ θεραπεύοντες ἢ καὶ ὀρθῶς φρονοῦντες
ἔλεγον· "ʻξεῖνε, καὶ τυφλὸς τὸ σῆμα διακρίνει.ʼ"
35    ʻΟἵ ῥα καὶ ἀθανάτοισιν ἐρίζεσκον περὶ τόξωνʼ
εὐστόχως κατετόξευον ἐπίσης τῷ ἡλίῳ.
Ἀνεῖλε δὲ τὸν Εὔρυτον νόσημα τῶν ὀξέων.
Ὅθε φασὶν Ἀπόλλωνα τοῦτον ἀνῃρηκέναι,
ἅτε αὐτῷ ἐρίζοντα τοξεύμασιν εὐστόχοις.
40    ʻΟἷαʼ δʼ ὁ ʻΖεὺς ἔργα τιθεῖʼ ἐστὶν ἡ Εἱμαρμένη.
ʻἈμφ' Ἄρεος φιλότητος ἐυστεφάνου τʼ Ἀφροδίτης,
ὡς τὰ πρῶτα μίγησαν ἐν Ἡφαίστοιο δόμοισι.ʼ
Ἐνταῦθα παίζων Ὅμηρος τὰ περὶ κόσμου γράφει
κατὰ τὴν δόξαν τῶν σοφῶν τῶν παλαιῶν Ἑλλήνων,
45    ὅτι μετὰ διάρθρωσιν τῆς ὕλης ὡς πρὸς εἶδος
καὶ τὴν ὑπόστασιν αὐτὴν πάσης τῆς κοσμουργίας,
πρὸ τοῦ τὸν ἥλιον λαβεῖν δρόμους εὐτάκτους σφαίρᾳ,
δεινὴ ζάλη καὶ σύγχυσις ὑπῆρχε τῶν στοιχείων,

or even his wisdom; having taken courage from her,
he was no longer held back by the onset of fear;
he appeared greater and stouter there.

God who 'gave him *song*' is knowledge, Destiny.                    25
'*At a rich feast of the gods*' means by knowledge of Destiny,
or of the powers of the soul, of delight, of mirth.

With '*the will of great Zeus*' he means of Destiny.
'*But the god sets a crown of beauty*' and they see him as a '*god*'
signifies knowledge and wisdom; the rest means Destiny.           30

And who is the '*Athena*' who '*placed the marks*' and the
         signs?
The wisdom of Odysseus or that of certain Phaiakians;
for the men attending upon him or even those thinking
         rightly
said: "'*Guest,* even a blind man could distinguish *the mark.*'"

'*Who strove even with immortals in archery*' means               35
they shot arrows accurately in the face of the sun as well.
A virulent disease killed Eurytos.
Because of this they say that Apollo had killed him,
as if he were striving against him with well-aimed arrows.

'*What deeds Zeus* sets up' is Destiny.                            40
'*Of the love of Ares and Aphrodite of the fair crown,
how first they lay together in the house of Hephaistos.*'
Here Homer playfully writes about the world,
according to the belief of the wise men of the ancient
         Greeks,
that after the articulation of matter by species                  45
and the composition of all of creation, before
the sun took up its well-ordered course across the celestial
         sphere,
terrible distress and confusion arose among the elements;

ὁτὲ ὑπερνικῶντος μὲν ἀέρος τοῦ καθύγρου,

50 ὁτὲ εὐκρατοτέρου δὲ ἀέρος καὶ φιλίου.

Ὁ Ἀφροδίτην ἔφασαν οἱ πάλαι μυθογράφοι

καὶ τοῦ Ἡφαίστου καὶ θερμοῦ σύζυγον πεφυκέναι.

Οὕτω πῶς μετετρέπετο ἡ φύσις τοῦ ἀέρος;

Ποτὲ δὲ φλεκτικώτερον τὸ πῦρ ἐξαναθρῶσκον

55 τὴν εὐκρασίαν ἔφθειρε, τὴν σύζυγον Ἡφαίστου.

Ἡλίου θέρμη δ᾽ εὔκρατος ἔσχεν ὁρμὰς ἀτάκτους,

ἀφ᾽ οὗ τὸν σφαίρας εὔτακτον δρόμον ἐτάχθη τρέχειν·

Ἥφαιστον ὅθε λέγουσι τὸν Ἄρεα δεσμῆσαι.

Ταῦτα δὲ ἠλληγόρησα πρὶν ἰαμβείῳ μέτρῳ,

60 καὶ νῦν συνεπειγμένως δὲ πάντα τὸν νοῦν εἰρήκειν,

ὡς πρὸ τοῦ ἥλιον λαβεῖν εὔτακτον σφαίρᾳ δρόμον,

ἀτάκτως ἐκεκίνητο τὰ σύμπαντα στοιχεῖα,

τὴν εὐκρασίαν φθείροντα, τὸ πῦρ δὲ πάντων πλέον.

Ἡλίου δρόμον δὲ τακτὸν σχόντος περὶ τὴν σφαῖραν,

65 ὥσπερ δεσμῷ κατέχοντα ταῦτα πρὸς εὐκρασίαν,

τῷ ἀνασπᾶν ὑγρότητα τὸ φλέγον κεραννύντος,

τῷ δὲ θερμῷ καθαίροντος τὸν κάθυγρον ἀέρα.

Αὕτη ἐστὶν ἡ σύμπασα νῦν ἔννοια τοῦ λόγου.

    Νῦν δὲ καὶ κατατμήμασί τισι λεπτολογήσω,

70 τίς Ἀφροδίτη τέ ἐστι καὶ πῶς Διὸς θυγάτηρ,

καὶ πῶς Ἡφαίστου σύνευνος, τίς δ᾽ Ἥφαιστος τυγχάνει,

πῶς Ἄρης ταύτης δὲ μοιχός, καὶ τίς ἐστιν ὁ Ἄρης,

τό τε Ἡλίου μήνυμα καὶ οἱ δεσμοὶ δὲ τίνες,

καὶ τὰ λοιπὰ δὲ σύμπαντα· καὶ δὴ λοιπὸν ἀρκτέον.

75 Ὕλη πρὶν ἦν ἀκίνητος, τὸ Ἔρεβος καὶ Χάος.

at one time the completely moist air prevailed,
while at another the more mild and friendly air did.                50
This the ancient mythographers said was Aphrodite,
the wife of Hephaistos, that is, warmth.
But how did the nature of the air change?
At one time the fire leaped up more fiery
and destroyed the harmonious mixture, Hephaistos's wife.           55
The sun's temperate heat restrained the more disorderly
      impulses,
from where he was appointed to traverse his well-ordered
      circuit;
from this they say that Hephaistos chained Ares.
This I allegorized earlier in iambic meter,
whereas here I have hastily explained the whole idea,            60
how, before the sun took up its well-ordered orbital circuit,
all the elements moved in a disorderly way, destroying
the harmonious mixture, fire more than any other element.
But when the sun acquired a fixed course around the
      sphere,
it was as if they had bound the sun to produce good            65
      weather,
as he, the sun, was tempering the fire by drawing moisture,
purifying the very wet air with warmth.
This is the whole meaning of the story here.
   Now I will explain in detail, section by section,
who Aphrodite is and how she is the daughter of Zeus,          70
how she is Hephaistos's consort, and who Hephaistos is,
how she commits adultery with Ares, and who Ares is,
and what is the Sun's message and what the bonds are,
and all the rest too; and so I must begin.
In the past, matter was immovable, Erebos and Chaos.           75

Ζεὺς δέ, ἀήρ τις κινηθείς, πνεῦμα τῆς εἰδουργίας,
καὶ σὺν αὐτῷ λεπτότερον, ὅπερ ἐστὶν ἡ Ἥρα,
διεῖλον γῆν καὶ θάλασσαν καὶ πρόσγειον ἀέρα,
ὅπερ ἐστὶν ἡ Ἀθηνᾶ. Εἶτα τῇ συγκινήσει
80 ἐς πλέον ἐκαθαίροντο καὶ διηρθροῦντο πλέον,
τοῦτο ἡ Ἀφροδίτη δέ ἐστιν, ἡ εὐθεσία.
Καὶ πῦρ χωλὸν καὶ ἀτελές, ῥαγὲν τῇ συγκινήσει,
τῇ εὐθεσίᾳ τε μιγὲν ἐς πλέον ἤρθρου ταῦτα,
ὅπερ ἐστὶν ὁ Ἥφαιστος, σύζυγος Ἀφροδίτης.
85 Πῦρ δὲ σκιρτῆσαν, ἄτακτον, ἔφθειρε ταῦτα πάλιν,
ὅπερ ὁ Ἄρης ὁ μοιχός ἐστι τῆς Ἀφροδίτης.
Ἡλίου μήνυμά ἐστι τῆς Ἄρεος μοιχείας
ἡ ἐκ θαλάσσης ἄνοδος καὶ τοῦ ἡμισφαιρίου,
καὶ φαῦσις τῶν ἀκτίνων δὲ παρὰ τὸ ἄνω μέρος.
90 Οὕτω γὰρ ἀνερχόμεναι αὗται συγκεκραμέναι,
ὡς τὸ φλογῶδες ὕδασιν αὐτῶν συγκεραννῦσαι,
τῷ δὲ θερμῷ καθαίρουσαι τὸ κάθυγρον ἀέρος
ἔδειξαν νόθον καὶ μοιχὸν ὄντως τὸ πῦρ ἐκεῖνο.
Δεσμοὶ δ᾽ Ἡφαίστου ἄλυτοι δρόμος ὁ περὶ σφαῖραν
95 εὐτάκτως ἄνω κάτω τε πάντα χωρῶν εἰς χρόνον.
Ἥφαιστος δὲ καὶ ἥλιος ἓν κατ᾽ αὐτὸ τυγχάνον,
ὡς μὲν ἰὼν ἐκ τῆς ἁλὸς καὶ δῆλος ὑπηρμένος
ἥλιος κλῆσιν ἔσχηκεν· Ἥφαιστος δὲ καλεῖται,

Zeus, that is, some air that moved, the spirit of speciation,
and with it the spirit, which is Hera,
divided the land and sea and the air near the ground,
which is Athena. Then by commotion
they purified it more and articulated it further,                    80
and this is Aphrodite, being good condition.
And the lame and incomplete fire, cracked by the
    commotion,
mixed in with the good condition, joined them together
    further,
and this is Hephaistos, the husband of Aphrodite.
The fire leaped in disorderly fashion and destroyed              85
    everything again,
which is Ares, who committed adultery with Aphrodite.
The sun's message of Ares's adultery
is his ascent from the sea and the hemisphere,
and the alighting of his rays on its upper part.
For they come up thus tempered,                                  90
as if mixing their flame together with the waters,
and purifying the very wet substance of the air with
    warmth,
they showed that that fire was indeed spurious and an
    adulterer.
And Hephaistos's unbreakable bonds are the course around
    the sphere,
traversing up and down everywhere in an orderly fashion          95
    throughout time.
Hephaistos and the sun happen to be one and the same,
as the sun, coming up out of the sea and clearly rising high
    above
took a name; he is called Hephaistos,

ὡς ὦν θερμὸς πυρώδης τε καὶ ταῖς ἀφαῖς δὲ τόσος,
100 εἴτε καὶ ὡς ἀνάψεων αἴτιος ὢν πυρφόρων.
Ἡφαίστῳ δόμος δέ ἐστι τόπος ὁ πρὸς αἰθέρα.
Λέχος Ἡφαίστου καὶ εὐνὴ τὸ εὔκρατον τυγχάνει.
Ὁ ʽχαλκεὼνʼ Ἡφαίστου δὲ σφοδρότερον γενέσθαι
ʽἄκμωνʼ ἡ σφαῖρα δέ ἐστιν. Ὁ δέ γε ʽἀκμοθέτηςʼ
105 ἐνθέρμου δύναμίς τινος πνεύματος ἐγκειμένου,
ὑφ' οὗ ὁ ἄκμων, οὐρανός, παντὶ κινεῖται χρόνῳ.

Δεσμοὶ δὲ ʽἄρρηκτοίʼ εἰσιν, ὥσπερ καὶ πρὶν εἰρήκειν,
ἡ τοῦ ἡλίου εὔτακτος κίνησις περὶ σφαῖραν,
τὰ πρὸς αἰθέρα ʽθάλαμοςʼ καὶ κοίτη τοῦ Ἡφαίστου.
110 ʽἙρμῖνεςʼ καὶ κλινόποδες τὸ κάτω μέρος σφαίρας,
τὸ δ' ἄνω ἡμισφαίριον τὸ ʽμέλαθρονʼ ὑπάρχει.

Τὸ ὡς ʽἀράχνᾳʼ δὲ ʽλεπτά,ʼ ἃ δ' ʽοὐʼ θεός ʽτιςʼ ἴδοι,
τὴν συγκινοῦσαν εἰσαεὶ δύναμιν σφαίρας λέγει,
ἄρρηκτον οὖσαν καὶ λεπτὴν καὶ ὑπὲρ νοῦν ἀνθρώπων.

115 Μετὰ δεσμῶν δὲ συσκευὴν τίς ἡ ὁρμὴ πρὸς ʽΛῆμνονʼ;
Μετὰ πυρὸς τὴν δύναμιν, τὴν ἄρρητον ἐκείνην,
τὴν τέχνην λεπτουργήσασαν πᾶσαν ἁπλῶς τὴν σφαῖραν,
εἰς Λῆμνον, κόσμον, ἤρξατο θέρμη χωρεῖν ἡλίου.
Εὐκράτῳ θέρμη γὰρ τὸ πῦρ, τὸ ἄτακτον ἐκεῖνο,

as he is warm and fiery and so fiery in his kindling of flames,
or even because he is responsible for kindling torches. 100
Hephaistos's house is a place up in the ether.
Hephaistos's marriage couch and bedstead is the temperate
 weather.
 The 'smithy' of Hephaistos means that it became more
  violent;
the 'anvil' is the sphere. And the 'anvil block'
is the power of some hot wind that was there, 105
which moves the anvil, that is the sky, throughout time.
 The 'unbreakable bonds,' as I said earlier,
are the orderly movement of the sun around the sphere,
and Hephaistos's 'bedroom' and bedstead pertain to the
 ether.
The 'bedposts' and feet of the bed are the sphere's lower 110
 part,
while the 'roof' is the upper hemisphere.
 '*Fine*' as 'spider's webs,' which '*not*' even '*some*' god could
  see,
means the power of the sphere which is always creating
 excitement,
as it is unbreakable and fine and beyond human
 comprehension.
 And after the intrigue of the bonds, why does he rush to 115
  '*Lemnos*'?
After that ineffable power of fire,
and the unalloyed skill that created in detail the whole
 sphere,
the heat of the sun began moving toward Lemnos, that is,
 the world.
For the fire, that unruly element

120 ὃ μοιχικῶς ἐμίγνυτο τῇ νέᾳ διαρθρώσει,

τῇ γινομένῃ ἐκ Διὸς πνεύματος εἰδουργίας,

ἐδέθη καὶ κεκράτηται τῇ συστροφῇ τῆς σφαίρας,

εὐκρατωθὲν καὶ εὐκρατοῦν ὑδάτων ἀνιμήσει.

Λῆμνον, μοιχείας καὶ δεσμοὺς ἔχεις λεπτῶς ῥηθέντας.

125 Ἡ 'αὖτις' τοῦ Ἡφαίστου δὲ ὑποστροφὴ ἐκ 'Λήμνου'

τῆς σφαίρας ἡ ἀνέλευσις, ἡ ἐκ τοῦ ὑπογείου,

σὺν ᾗ θερμότης ἄνεισιν ἡλιακαῖς ἀκτῖσι.

Τὴν περὶ 'πρόθυρα' 'βοὴν' νῦν τοῦ Ἡφαίστου μάθε.

Ἡ τοῦ ἡλίου πρώτη μὲν ἀνέλευσις σὺν σφαίρᾳ

130 τὰ πρόθυρα τυγχάνουσιν, ἅπερ ἐνθάδε λέγει.

Ἡ εὔτακτος δὲ κίνησις 'βοὴ ἡ σμερδαλέα'·

ἡ εὔτακτος πορεία γὰρ ἡλίου βοᾷ μέγα

ἤτοι δεικνύει προφανῶς τῇ τεταγμένῃ βάσει,

ὅτι τὸ πῦρ τὸ μοιχικὸν ἐκεῖνο κατεσχέθη.

135 Χωλὸν τὸ πῦρ ἡλίου δέ, ὁ Ἥφαιστος τυγχάνει,

ὅτι λοξὴν ὁ ἥλιος ποιεῖται τὴν πορείαν,

καὶ βραδυτέραν δὲ πολὺ πυρὸς τοῦ κεραυνίου

καὶ ἀερίου δὲ παντὸς πυρὸς ἀτακτοτέρου,

ἃ Ἄρης κατωνόμασται τοῖς πάλαι μυθογράφοις.

140 'Ἠπεδανὸς' ὁ ἀσθενὴς καὶ ὁ χωλὸς τυγχάνει.

Πῶς δὲ χωλὸς εἰρήκαμεν ὁ Ἥφαιστος τυγχάνει.

Ἡφαίστου λόγοι δὲ λοιπὸν νῦν προσωποποιία.

Τὴν τῶν θεῶν συνέλευσιν εἰς οὐρανὸν νῦν μάθε,

τοῦ Ποσειδῶνος, τοῦ Ἑρμοῦ, Ἀπόλλωνος σὺν τούτοις,

145 καὶ τὴν αἰδὼ τῶν θεαινῶν, μέχρι τοῦ τέλους πάντα.

Μετὰ τὸ σφαῖραν εὔτακτον δρόμον λαβεῖν, ὡς ἔφην,

ὅπερ βοὴν ἐκάλεσεν ὁ ποιητὴς Ἡφαίστου,

that mingled in adultery with the new articulation,        120
emerging from the speciation caused by the spirit of Zeus,
was bound with the temperate heat and mixed by the
      twisting of the sphere,
becoming temperate and moderate, by drawing up the
      waters.
Now you know in detail the meaning of Lemnos, adultery,
      and the aforementioned bonds.

    The return '*again*' of Hephaistos from '*Lemnos*'        125
is the ascent of the sphere from beneath the earth,
with which heat comes up on the rays of the sun.

    Now learn about Hephaistos's 'cry' on the 'threshold.'
The first ascent of the sun with the sphere
is the threshold, of which he speaks here.        130
The 'terrible cry' is the orderly movement;
the orderly journey of the sun cries out loudly,
that is, it shows clearly through its appointed position
that that adulterous fire was restrained.

    And Hephaistos is the lame fire of the sun,        135
because the sun follows an ecliptic course,
much slower than the fire of the thunderbolt
and every other disorderly aerial fire,
which were called Ares by the mythographers of old.

    '*Halting*' means the weak and lame man.        140
We have explained how Hephaistos was lame.
So the words of Hephaistos here are a personification.

    Now learn about the assembly in the sky of the gods,
of Poseidon and Hermes, together with Apollo,
and the modesty of the goddesses, everything to the end.        145
After the sphere took up an orderly course, as I said,
which the poet called the cry of Hephaistos,

τρανῶς δοκοῦσαν, ὡς τὸ πῦρ, τὸ μοιχικὸν ἐδέθη,
ἦλθον θεοί, ὁ Ποσειδῶν, Ἑρμῆς καὶ ὁ Ἀπόλλων.

150 Τουτέστι κατηυκράτωται τὸ πᾶν καὶ ηὐθετήθη
ἀνασπωμένων κάτωθε κεραστικῶν ἰκμάδων,
Ἑρμοῦ, πυρφορημάτων τε καθαρτικῶν ᾀττόντων,
ἃ πνεύματι γινόμενα καθαίρει τὸν ἀέρα.
Ἀπόλλων τε καὶ ἥλιος λαμπρότερος ἐφάνη,

155 ὅπερ λαμπρὸν καὶ γένος νῦν λαμπρότερον στοιχεῖον.
Αἱ δι'αἰδὼ δὲ θήλειαι 'θεαὶ' τοῖς οἴκοις οὖσαι
ὕδωρ τὸ γεωδέστερον, τὸ κάθυγρον ἀέρος.
Τὰ τούτων ἀνιμήθη γὰρ λεπτότερα τοῖς ἄνω
καὶ εὐκρασίας αἴτια γεγόνασιν, ὡς ἔφην.

160 Ταῦτα δέ, ὡς βαρύτερα, τοῖς κάτωθεν ἐλείφθη.
Τῷ πλάσματι δ' ὁ Ὅμηρος προσφυεστάτως λέγει
θηλείας ταύτας σοὶ θεάς, ἤτοι ἀσθενεστέρας,
καὶ ὑπ' αἰδοῦς μὴ ἀνελθεῖν, τοῖς οἴκοις δὲ λειφθῆναι.

Ὁ πρὸς Ἑρμῆν δ' Ἀπόλλωνος δι' Ἀφροδίτην λόγος

165 κἀκείνου συγκατάνευσις, ἐκείνη συγκαθεύδειν
ἔν γε δεσμοῖς τριστοσαπλοῖς, πάντας θεοὺς δὲ βλέπειν,
σαφὲς καὶ προφανές ἐστιν. Ὡς δὲ μετ' ἀκρασίαν
καὶ δέσιν τὴν πρὶν ἄτακτον πυρὸς περὶ τὴν σφαῖραν,
νῦν δ' εὔκρατον καὶ εὔτακτον ἡλιακὴν λαμπάδα

clearly meaning that the adulterous fire was bound,
the gods came, Poseidon, Hermes, and Apollo.
That is, everything became well tempered and was 150
    regulated
as the moist mixture was being pulled down from below,
that is, Hermes, and the purifying flames were darting
    across,
which, coming to existence through the breath of air, purify
    the air.
Apollo, the sun, which is the bright element
and the brighter kind here, appeared brighter. 155
And the female *'goddesses'* who dwelled in their own houses
    out of modesty
are the earthier water, the very wet element of the air.
For some of those were drawn up more finely by the
    elements above
and they became the causes of harmonious mixture, as I
    said.
But others, as they are heavier, were taken by those below. 160
Through this image Homer reveals very fittingly
to you that these female goddesses, that is, the weaker ones,
did not ascend due to modesty but were left behind in their
    homes.

    As for Apollo's speech to Hermes about Aphrodite
and Hermes's agreement, that he would sleep with her 165
in three times as many bonds, even while all the gods
    watched,
its meaning is clear and obvious. As after the disarray
and the previous disorderly binding together of fire around
    the sphere,
here the temperate and well-ordered solar torch

170 καὶ ἁρμογὴν τοῦ σύμπαντος τόσην ἠκριβωμένην,
Ἑρμαϊκὰ διάττουσιν ὅμως καὶ πάλιν σέλα,
καὶ εὐκρασίας αἴτια μᾶλλον εἰσὶν ἐκεῖνα,
πνεύμασι μὲν κινούμενα καὶ πνεύματα δηλοῦντα
καὶ κάθαρσιν ἀέρος δέ. Τυγχάνει γὰρ ἐκεῖνα
175 τί πῦρ ὑγρομενέστερον, περίττωμα ἀέρος.
    Ἡ Ποσειδῶνος αἴτησις, λυθῆναι δὲ τὸν Ἄρην,
ἡ λύσις τε καὶ ἄφιξις ἐκείνου πρὸς τὴν Θράκην.
    Τῆς δ᾽ Ἀφροδίτης ἄφιξις πρὸς ‘Κύπρον’ καὶ τὴν ‘Πάφον’
καὶ τὰ λουτρὰ Χαρίτων δὲ καὶ ἔνδυσις εἱμάτων
180 ἔχουσιν ἀλληγόρημα, ὅπερ τανῦν μοι μάθε.
    Ἀτάκτως πρὶν ἐφέρετο τὸ πῦρ, ὡς ἠκηκόεις,
μετὰ δὲ σφαίρας κίνησιν τὴν εὔτακτον οὐκέτι,
ἀλλ᾽ ἦν κρατοῦν καὶ εὐκρατοῦν τῇ θέσει τῇ τῆς σφαίρας,
ἀνιμωμένων καὶ ὑγρῶν νεφῶν πεπαχυσμένων,
185 καὶ ῥηγνυμένων τῶν νεφῶν, βροντὰς ἀποτελούντων,
πῦρ κεραυνῶν ἐφέρετο, θρασέως ἀναθρῶσκον,
καὶ ὄμβροι ῥέειν ἤρξαντο τὴν γῆν ἐγκυμονοῦντες,
ὃ λύσις ἐστὶν Ἄρεος καὶ ἔλευσις εἰς Θράκην,
καὶ Ἀφροδίτης ἄφιξις εἰς Κύπρον τε καὶ Πάφον,
190 λουτρά τε Χαριτήσια καὶ ἐσθημάτων κόσμος.
    Οἷον ἵνα σαφέστερον ἐρῶ σοί πάλιν τοῦτο,
μετὰ τὴν σφαίρας κίνησιν καὶ κεραυνοὶ καὶ ὄμβροι
καὶ τῶν καιρῶν διαίρεσις ἐφάνη σαφεστέρα,
χειμῶνός τε καὶ ἔαρος, θέρους καὶ μετοπώρου.
195 Καὶ τῷ ὑγρῷ μὲν λύεται πάλιν τὸ πῦρ χειμῶνι,

and the fitting together of the universe in so accurate a way,     170
nevertheless the lights of Hermes dart across again,
and these are rather the causes of good weather,
moving by the blasts of wind, which they thereby reveal
along with the purification of the air. For all this is
some fire resistant to water, the sediment of the air.     175
    Poseidon's request for Ares to be released
is his release and his coming to Thrace.
    The arrival of Aphrodite at '*Cyprus*' and '*Paphos*'
and the baths of the Graces and the donning of clothes
have an allegorical meaning, which you should now learn     180
      from me.
Previously the fire was carried around in a disorderly
      manner, as you have heard,
no longer after the well-ordered movement of the sphere,
but it was in force and being tempered by the sphere's
      position,
as the wet clouds were drawn up and had become thicker,
and as the clouds were bursting, creating thunder,     185
the fire of the thunderbolts was being conveyed, leaping up
      boldly,
and rains started to fall, impregnating the earth,
which is the release of Ares and his coming to Thrace,
and the arrival of Aphrodite at Cyprus and Paphos,
and the baths of the Graces and the decoration of the     190
      garments.
I will say this in order to make this clearer for you again,
after the movement of the sphere thunderbolts and rains
and the division of seasons could be seen more clearly,
of winter and spring, summer and autumn.
And the fire is released again by the wet winter,     195

πῦρ κεραυνῶν καὶ Ἄρεος ταχέως ἀναθρῶσκον,
τῇ εὐκρασίᾳ πᾶσι δὲ τὸ κύειν ἐπορίσθη,
καὶ πάντα φύειν ἤρξατο καὶ χάρισι κοσμεῖσθαι.
Ἔχεις τὸ ἀλληγόρημα πᾶν λεπτοτομηθέν σοι.

200 'Θεοὶ δὲ νῦν παράσχοιέν' ἐστιν ἡ Εἱμαρμένη.
'Διὶ' καὶ 'ἄλλοισι θεοῖς' τῷ οὐρανῷ ἡλίῳ
καὶ τοῖς λοιποῖς στοιχείοις δέ, αὐτῇ τῇ Εἱμαρμένη.
'Θεῶν' δὲ 'κάλλος ἔχουσα' σημαίνει τῶν ἀστέρων.
'Ζεὺς' ὁ 'ἐρίγδουπος' ἀήρ, εὔδιον 'θείη' πλοῦν μοι.

205 Ὥσπερ 'θεῷ' στοιχείῳ νῦν, ἡλίῳ καὶ σελήνῃ.
'Διὸς' θυγάτηρ νῦν νοός, ὁ ἥλιος 'Ἀπόλλων.'
'Θεὸς' παρέσχε σοὶ ᾠδήν, νοῦς ἢ ἡ Εἱμαρμένη·
θεῷ, τῷ νῷ καὶ λογισμῷ, κεκινημένος ἥδε.
Τὸν 'ἵππον,' 'ἄγαλμα θεῶν,' ἡλίου καὶ στοιχείων,

210 ἤτοι ἵνα μνημόσυνον αἰώνιον ὑπάρχῃ,
ἡλίου καθορώμενον κύκλοις μακροῖς καὶ χρόνοις.
'Ἀθήνην' νῦν 'μεγάθυμον' τὴν φρόνησιν εἰρήκειν.
Τὸν 'ἀοιδὸν' τὸν 'θεῖον' δὲ σοφὸν νοεῖν σε δέον.
'Φρένας' τὰς νῆας εἴρηκε τὰς τῶν Φαιάκων ἔχειν,

215 ἐν ναυτικῇ τοὺς Φαίακας ὑπερβολαῖς ἐξαίρων.
Τὸν 'Ποσειδῶ,' τὴν θάλασσαν, φθονῆσαι τούτοις λέγων

the fire of the thunderbolts, of Ares, moves upward quickly,
and impregnation is achieved by the harmonious mixture of
    all,
and everything began to grow and be adorned with graces.
You now have all the allegory finely analyzed for you.
    'May the *gods* grant you' here means Destiny.        200
    '*To Zeus*' and '*to the other* gods' means to the sun in heaven
and to the rest of the elements, to Destiny itself.
    '*Gifted with beauty by the gods*' means by the stars.
    '*Zeus the loud thundering*' means the air, '*may he grant*' me
    fine sailing.
    As '*to a god*' here means to an element, to the sun and    205
    moon.
    The daughter '*of Zeus*' here means of the mind; '*Apollo*' is
    the sun.
    '*God*' provided you with song means mind or Destiny;
by the god, that is by the mind and reason, he had been
    moved in this way.
    'The *horse*,' an '*offering to the gods,*' means to the sun and
    elements,
that is, so that it may be an eternal memorial,    210
looking down on the long cycles and the ages of the sun.
    '*Greathearted Athena*' I have said here means wisdom.
    You should understand that the 'divine singer' is a wise
    man.
He says that the ships of the Phaiakians have '*minds,*'
exalting the Phaiakians for their naval skill with    215
    exaggerations.
Saying that 'Poseidon,' that is, the sea, begrudged them
    means that

τῷ ἄριστα ναυτίλλεσθαι ὑπερβολαῖς ὁμοίως.

Τὸ προειδέναι δὲ χρησμοῖς, 'νῆα ῥαισθῆναι' τούτων,
τῶν ἀπεικότων οὐδαμῶς, οὐδὲ τῇ φύσει ξένον.

220   'Θεὸς' δ' εἴ κε 'τελέσειέν' ἐστιν ἡ Εἱμαρμένη.

'Θεοειδὴς ὁ νοῦς' ἐστιν ὁ δίκαιος ἐνθάδε.

'Θεοὶ' ἡ Εἱμαρμένη δὲ οἱ τεύξαντες ὀλέθρους.

he begrudged their excellent nautical skills, also with
    exaggerations.
    Foreseeing with oracles that their '*ship* would be
     smashed'
is in no way unlikely, nor strange by nature.
    If '*the god will bring to pass*' — this is Destiny.         220
    The 'godlike mind' is here the just man.
    '*The gods*' who prepared destruction means Destiny.

## Ι΄

Αὕτη ἡ ὑπόθεσις τῆς Ἰῶτα Ὀδυσσείας.

Ὁ Ὀδυσσεὺς ἀπάρχεται νῦν σφῶν διηγημάτων
πῶς πρῶτα μὲν τοῖς Κίκοσι πόλεμον συνταράττει,
εἶτα δ᾽ ἀνέμοις ἐξωσθεὶς ἦλθεν εἰς Λωτοφάγους,
μετέπειτα πρὸς Κύκλωπα, Πολύφημον τῇ κλήσει,
5 τὸν ὃν καὶ ἀπετύφλωσεν ἀντάποινα τῶν φίλων,
ἐκ τούτων γὰρ ἓξ βέβρωκε δώδεκα συνελθόντων.

‘Θεοῖς ἀλίγκιος αὐδὴν’ ὁ ἀοιδὸς τυγχάνει·
τοιάδε ᾄδει εὔφθογγα ὡς μουσικὴ ἀστέρων.
‘Θεοὺς’ νῦν ‘οὐρανίωνας’ τὴν Εἰμαρμένην λέγει.
10 ‘Θεάων’ βασιλίδων τε καὶ ἀρχουσῶν γυναικῶν.
‘Ὃν μοι Ζεὺς προέηκεν ἀπὸ Τροίηθεν ἰόντι.’
Ζεὺς καὶ ἡ Εἰμαρμένη νῦν, ὁ δὲ ἀὴρ ἐς πλέον,
φησὶ γάρ· ‘Ἰλιόθεν με ὁ ἄνεμος ἐφόρει.’
‘Διὸς αἶσα’ κατάλληλόν ἐστιν ἡ Εἰμαρμένη.
15 ‘Ἄνεμος’ νῦν ἐκ τοῦ ‘Διὸς’ ἐφώρμησεν ἀέρος.
‘Τῶν δ᾽ ὅς τις λωτοῖο φάγοι μελιηδέα καρπόν,
οὐκέτ᾽ ἀπαγγεῖλαι πάλιν ἤθελεν οὐδὲ νέεσθαι.’
Λωτὸν καὶ τὴν ἀγρίαν μὲν καλοῦσι τὴν βοτάνην,
καὶ δένδρον τι καθέστηκε Γαδείροις καὶ Αἰγύπτῳ,
20 φέρον καρπὸν ὡς κύαμον, ἐξ οὗ ποιοῦσιν ἄρτους.
Τινὲς λωτὸν δὲ λέγουσί τι καλαμῶδες Νείλῳ.

# Book 9

The subject matter of the ninth book of the *Odyssey*.

Here Odysseus begins his own stories,
how first he stirred up war with the Kikonians,
then, blown off course by the winds, he came to the Lotus-
    Eaters,
after that to the Cyclops, called Polyphemos,
whom he blinded in revenge for his friends,          5
for he had eaten six of his twelve companions.

  'Like unto the *gods in voice*' is the singer;
he sings melodious songs like the music of the stars.
By 'the heavenly gods' here he means Destiny.
    By the '*goddesses*' he means queens and ruling women.    10
    '*Which Zeus* laid upon *me as I came from Troy.*'
Zeus here is Destiny and, moreover, the air,
for he says: 'The wind carried me from Troy.'
    '*The evil fate from Zeus*' is appropriately called Destiny.
    Here the 'wind' rushed out from 'Zeus,' that is, from the    15
    air.
    '*And whosoever ate of the honey-sweet fruit of the lotus*
*had no longer any wish to bring back tidings or return.*'
They also call the wild plant lotus,
and it was a tree in Gadeira and Egypt,
bearing a fruit like a bean, from which they make bread.    20
Some say the lotus is a reed by the Nile.

Οὐδεὶς λωτὸς δὲ δύναμιν θέλγειν ἀνθρώπους ἔχει,
ὡς γευσαμένους μὴ ποθεῖν τὴν ἑαυτῶν πατρίδα,
ἐποίκους εἶναι θέλειν δὲ γῆς τῆς λωτοφορούσης.

25 Δεκαετῶς ἐκεῖνοι δὲ πόσα παθόντες Τροίᾳ
καὶ μετὰ τὸν ἀπόπλουν δὲ κύμασιν ἐξωσθέντες
εἰς γῆν μακρὰν ἀλλοδαπήν, πόρρω τῆς σφῶν πατρίδος,
καὶ νῦν προμαντευόμενοι τὰ δυσχερῆ θαλάσσης,
ἰδόντες τὸ φιλόξενον ἀνδρῶν τῶν Λωτοφάγων
30 καὶ γῆν ἐκείνων ἀγαθὴν ἤθελον συνοικῆσαι.
Ὁ Ὅμηρος δ', ὁ πάνσοφος, ἡ θάλασσα τῶν λόγων,
μεταρσιοῖ τὰ εὐτελῆ, τὰ δ' ὑψηλὰ κατάγει,
ἐν τοῖς ἀλληγορήμασι δεινὸς ὢν λογογράφος,
καὶ μυθικῷ τῷ νέκταρι πάντα καταγλυκάζει.

35 'Κυκλώπων δ' ἐς γαῖαν ὑπερφιάλων ἀθεμίστων
ἱκόμεθ', οἵ ῥα θεοῖσι πεποιθότες ἀθανάτοισιν
οὔτε φυτεύουσιν χερσὶν φυτὸν οὔτ' ἀρόωσιν,
ἀλλὰ τὰ γ' ἄσπαρτα καὶ ἀνήροτα πάντα φύονται.'
Θεοὺς τὴν εὐκρασίαν νῦν, τὴν τῶν στοιχείων, λέγει.

40 'Διὸς ὄμβρος ἀέξει' δὲ τοῦ οὐρανοῦ μοι νόει.
'Θεός τις ἡγεμόνευε' τουτέστιν εὐτυχία.

'Ὦρσαν δὲ νύμφαι, κοῦραι Διὸς αἰγιόχοιο,
αἶγας ὀρεσκώους, ἵνα δειπνήσειαν ἑταῖροι.'
Ἐκ τῶν νυμφῶν, τῶν τόπων δὲ νῦν τῶν συνδένδρων λέγει,
45 αἳ θυγατέρες τοῦ Διὸς καὶ οὐρανοῦ τελοῦσιν,
ἀνέμων καταιγίσι τε τρεφόμεναι καὶ ὄμβροις,
ὥρμησαν καὶ ἐξέδραμον αἶγες ἐκ τῶν ἀγρίων.

No lotus has the power to enchant men in such a way that,
having tasted it, they no longer yearn for their homeland
but want to dwell in the lotus-bearing land.
But they, having suffered so much for ten years in Troy,                    25
and having been driven off course by the waves on their
    voyage
to a distant and strange land, far from their own homeland,
and now foreseeing the hardships of the sea,
having seen the hospitality of the Lotus-Eaters,
wanted to live with them in their goodly land.                              30
Homer, the all wise, the sea of speech,
elevates worthless events and draws down lofty ones,
being a clever writer in his allegories,
and with his mythical nectar he makes everything sweeter.
    *'And we came to the land of the Cyclopes, an overweening*        35
*and lawless folk, who, trusting in the immortal gods,*
*plant nothing with their hands nor plow;*
*but everything springs up for them without sowing or plowing.'*
Here he says that the gods are the harmonious mixture of
    the elements.
    Take it from me that *'Zeus's rain gives them increase'* means    40
    of heaven.
    'Some *god guided,'* that is, good fortune.
    *'And the nymphs, the daughters of aegis-bearing Zeus, roused*
*the mountain goats, that my comrades might have their meal.'*
The goats ran from the wild places and rushed from the
    nymphs,
who are here the daughters of Zeus, that is, of heaven,                     45
who here represent densely forested places
and who were nourished by rain and gusts of wind.

'Θεὸς ἔδωκε θήρην' δὲ φρόνησιν, εὐτυχίαν.
'Νοῦς θεουδὴς' ὁ δίκαιος, ὥσπερ καὶ πρώην ἔφην.
50  'Ἀπόλλων' μὲν ὁ ἥλιος· 'ἀκήρατος' δὲ οἶνος,
ὁ κάλλιστος καὶ γέρων δὲ καὶ μὴ φθαρεὶς τῷ χρόνῳ.
'Αὐτὰρ ἔπειτ' ἐπέθηκε θυρεὸν μέγαν ὑψόσ' ἀείρας,
ὄβριμον· οὐκ ἂν τόν γε δύω καὶ εἴκοσ' ἄμαξαι'
τοὺς πυλεῶνας ἔκλεισαν ἐκείνου τοῦ πυλίου,
55  οὓς πόσαι ἀνασπάσειαν ἄμαξαι κεκλεισμένους.
Ἄρτι 'Ζεὺς ἤθελεν' αὐτὸς καὶ οἱ λοιποὶ θεοὶ δέ·
ἀὴρ ἀνέμων συστροφαῖς, σὺν ᾧ ἡ Εἱμαρμένη.
'Αἰδεῖο, φέριστε, θεούς' τὰς παρακλήσεις λέγει·
ψυχῆς δὲ πάθος, ἔλεός εἰσι καὶ παρακλήσεις.
60  'Ζεὺς ὁ ἐπιτιμήτωρ' δὲ τῶν ξένων Εἱμαρμένη.
"Ὅς με θεοὺς κέλεαι ἢ δειδίμεν ἢ ἀλέασθαι·
οὐ γὰρ Κύκλωπες Διὸς αἰγιόχου ἀλέγουσιν
οὐδὲ θεῶν μακάρων, ἐπεὶ ἦ πολὺ φέρτεροί εἰμεν.
Οὐδ' ἂν ἐγὼ Διὸς ἔχθος ἀλευάμενος πεφιδοίμην
65  οὔτε σεῦ οὔθ' ἑτάρων, εἰ μὴ θυμός με κελεύοι.'
Ἢ τῶν ἀφρόνων πέφυκας ἢ ξένος τῶν ἐνθάδε,
ὅστις αἰδεῖσθαί με θεοὺς καὶ παρακλήσεις λέγεις,
μὴ ξενωθεὶς κατασχεθῶ τοιᾷδε Εἱμαρμένη.
Κύκλωπες οὐκ ἐκπλέουσι τῆς ἑαυτῶν πατρίδος,
70  ὅθεν ὑπέρτεροί ἐσμεν τοιᾶσδε Εἱμαρμένης
καὶ φόβου δὲ ξενώσεως καὶ τῶν λιπαρημάτων.
Οὐδὲ ἐγὼ οἰκτεριῶ φόβῳ τοιᾶσδε τύχης
οὐ σοὺς ἑτάρους οὐδὲ σέ, εἰ μὴ αὐτὸς θελήσω.

'*God* gave *game*' means wisdom, good fortune.

The '*God-fearing* mind' is the just one, as I said earlier.

'Apollo' is the sun; 'unmixed' wine 50

is the most handsome old man, not ravaged by time.

    '*Then he lifted on high and set in place the great door stone,*

*a mighty rock; not even twenty-two wagons could pull it*'

means they shut the doors of that gate, which so many
      wagons

would be needed to open after they were closed. 55

    At the same time, '*Zeus*' himself '*was pleased*' and the
      other gods too;

that is, the air with tumultuous winds, and with it Destiny.

    By '*mightiest one, reverence the gods*' he means supplications;

the suffering of the soul is pity and supplication.

    '*Zeus the avenger*' is the Destiny of strangers. 60

    '*Seeing that you bid me either to fear or to shun the gods;*

*for the Cyclopes do not respect Zeus, who bears the aegis,*

*nor the blessed gods, since truly we are better far than they.*

*Nor would I, shunning the wrath of Zeus, spare either you*

*or your comrades, unless my own heart should bid me.*' 65

This means, you are either senseless or a stranger to the
      matters here,

you who say that I should honor the gods and supplication,

lest, after entertaining you as a guest, I might endure such a
      Destiny.

The Cyclopes do not sail out from their own fatherland,

and therefore we are above such a Destiny 70

and the fear of hospitality and supplication.

And I will not pity either you or your companions

out of fear for such fortune, unless I myself wish it.

'Τοὺς δὲ διὰ μελεϊστὶ ταμὼν ὁπλίσσατο δόρπον.'
75 Τῶν φίλων τὴν ἀναίρεσιν κατάβρωσιν νῦν λέγει.
Κύκλωψ γὰρ Εὐρυλέοντα τῆς κόμης ἀναρπάσας,
θατέρᾳ διηντέρευσε κάτω βαλὼν τὸ ξίφος.
'Διὶ χεῖρας' ἀνέσχομεν τῷ οὐρανίῳ ὕψει.
'Εὖχος Ἀθήνη δοίη μου' φρόνησις ἡ οἰκεία.
80 'Ἦ καὶ θεὸς ἐκέλευσεν' αὐτὴ ἡ Εἱμαρμένη.
'Διὸς ὄμβρος ἀέξει' δὲ τοῦ οὐρανοῦ νῦν λέγει.
'Νοῦσον γ' οὔ πως ἔστι Διὸς μεγάλου ἀλέασθαι,'
νόσον, τὴν Εἱμαρμένην δέ, ἀποφυγεῖν οὐκ ἔστιν.
Ὑπέρτεροι ὑπῆρχον δὲ Κύκλωπες Εἱμαρμένης,
85 ἀποδημίας φόβου τε καὶ τῶν λιπαρημάτων.
Τῆς Εἱμαρμένης, νόσου τε, θανάτου καὶ τοιούτων—
Τζέτζης φησίν—ὑπέρτεροι συνόλως οὐχ ὑπῆρχον.
'Ἀλλὰ σύ γ' εὔχεο πατρὶ Ποσειδάωνι ἄνακτι.'
Φέρε δὲ ταύτην καρτερῶς γενναῖος ὑπηργμένος
90 ὁποῖα παῖς θαλάσσης τε εἴτε πετρῶν ἀγρίων.
'Ὁ Ζεὺς καὶ ἄλλοι τε θεοί' οἱ πλάνητες ἀστέρες,
ἤτοι ἡ Εἱμαρμένη γε ἐτίσατο ἀξίως.
'Πομπήν τ' ὀτρύνω δόμεναι κλυτὸν ἐννοσίγαιον·
τοῦ γὰρ ἐγὼ παῖς εἰμί, πατὴρ δ' ἐμὸς εὔχεται εἶναι.'
95 Ἤτοι καὶ εἴπω σοι καιρόν, ὅτε σοὶ πλεῦσαι δέον.
Οἶδα τὰ τῆς θαλάσσης γὰρ τῆς τῇδε σαφεστάτως,
ὡς γεννηθεὶς καὶ ἐντραφεὶς ἐν μέρεσι γῆς τῆσδε.
'Αὐτὸς δ', αἴ κ' ἐθέλῃσ', ἰήσεται, οὐδέ τις ἄλλος.'
Ἰάσεται τὸ θλίβον με ὁ πλοῦς ὁ τῆς θαλάσσης,
100 κατασχεθεὶς ἐνταῦθα γὰρ τὸν ὀφθαλμόν μοι δοίης,
τὴν θυγατέρα τὴν ἐμήν, τὴν Ἕλπην καλουμένην.

'*Then he cut them limb from limb and* made ready *his supper.*'
By the killing of the friends he means here their devouring. 75
For the Cyclops seized Euryleon by the hair and
with the other hand he pierced his guts, thrusting his sword
    below.
We raise up '*our hands to Zeus*' means to high heaven.
'*May Athena grant* me *glory*' means my wisdom.
'*Or a god so bade him*' means Destiny itself. 80
'*Zeus's rain gives them increase*' here means of the sky.
'*You may in no way escape sickness which comes from great
    Zeus*'
means one cannot escape sickness, that is, Destiny.
The Cyclopes prevailed over Destiny,
that is, over the fear of going abroad and of supplications. 85
They did not entirely prevail—Tzetzes says—
over Destiny, disease, death, and the like.
'*But pray to our father, the lord Poseidon.*'
This means bear it patiently, with bravery,
like a child of the sea or of wild rocks. 90
'*Zeus and the other gods*' are wandering stars,
that is, Destiny exacted its vengeance fittingly.
'*And I may speed your sending, that the glorious Earth shaker
    may grant it;*
*for I am his son, and he declares himself my father.*'
That is, I will tell you the time when you must sail. 95
I know the sea here very clearly,
since I was born and reared in parts of this land.
'*And he himself will heal me, if it pleases him, but no other.*'
This means that the sea voyage will heal my distress,
for you, Odysseus, detained here, may give me back my eye, 100
that is, my daughter, called Elpe.

Θάλασσα γὰρ καὶ Ποσειδῶν οὐκ ὀφθαλμοὺς ἰᾶται.
'Οὔτε θεῶν μακάρων οὔτε θνητῶν ἀνθρώπων,'
οὐ βασιλεὺς οὐδὲ σοφός, οὔτε τῆς κάτω τύχης.
105 Πῶς τοῦτο φης, ὦ Ὅμηρε; Καὶ μὴν ὁ Ἀντιφάτης
ὁ Λαιστρυγών, ὁ ἀδελφὸς Κύκλωπος Πολυφήμου,
τὰς Ὀδυσσέως ἔνδεκα κατέαξεν ὁλκάδας,
τὴν Ἕλπην πάλιν δὲ λαβὼν δέδωκε Πολυφήμῳ,
κἄνπερ σὺ τοῦτο σιωπᾷς, θέλων γλυκάζειν μύθοις.
110 Ἀλλ᾽ εἰ καὶ δέδρακεν αὐτὸ τοῦτο ὁ Ἀντιφάτης,
τῇ δυσχερείᾳ, φαίης μοι, θαλάσσης ἐδεδράκει.
Εὔχετο δὲ τῷ ἄνακτι Κύκλωψ τῷ Ποσειδῶνι,
ἤτοι δυσχέρειαν πλοὸς ἐπηύχετο γενέσθαι.
'Ὣς ἔφατ᾽ εὐχόμενος, τοῦ δ᾽ ἔκλυε κυανοχαίτης.'
115 Οὕτω συνέβη Ὀδυσσεῖ περὶ τὸν πλοῦν γενέσθαι.
Εἰς μέρος ἕτερον ἐλθὼν καὶ γὰρ τῆς Σικελίας,
ὡς εἶπον πρίν, ἀπώλεσεν ὁλκάδας Ἀντιφάτης.
'Ζηνὶ κελαινεφέι' δὲ τανῦν τῇ Εἱμαρμένῃ.
Λοιπόν μοι τὸ τοῦ Κύκλωπος πᾶν ἀλληγορητέον.
120 Ὁ Κύκλωψ, ὁ μονόφθαλμος, οὐδὲ ἀνθρώπους ἦσθεν.
Οἱ Ἰσσηδοὶ μονόφθαλμοι, ὡς Ἀριστέας γράφει·
"'Ἰσσηδοὶ χαίτησιν ἀγαλλόμενοι ταναῇσι
καί σφας ἀνθρώπους εἶναι καθύπερθεν ὁμούρους
πρὸς Βορέω, πολλούς τε καὶ ἐσθλοὺς κάρτα μαχητάς,
125 ἀφνειοὺς ἵπποισι, πολύρρηνας, πολυβούτας.
ὀφθαλμὸν δ᾽ ἕν᾽ ἕκαστος ἔχει χαρίεντι μετώπῳ·
χαίτησι λασίῃσι πάντων στιβαρώτεροι ἀνδρῶν."
Οἱ Ἰσσηδοὶ μονόφθαλμοι, οὐ τὰ Κυκλώπων γένη.

For the sea and Poseidon do not heal eyes.

*'No other of the blessed gods or of mortal men can heal me,'*
which means neither a king nor a wise man, nor earthly fate.
How do you say this, O Homer? Indeed Antiphates,       105
the Laistrygonian, the brother of the Cyclops Polyphemos,
destroyed eleven of Odysseus's ships,
then, taking Elpe, gave her to Polyphemos,
although you keep silent about this, wishing to sweeten it
    with myths.
But if Antiphates had done this very thing, you would tell    110
    me
he had done so because of the harshness of the sea.
The Cyclops prayed to lord Poseidon,
that is, he prayed for a difficult voyage.

*'So he spoke in prayer, and the dark-haired god heard him.'*
This is what happened to Odysseus with regard to his    115
    voyage.
For, when he came to another part of Sicily,
as I said previously, Antiphates destroyed their ships.

*'To Zeus, god of the dark clouds'* here means to Destiny.
I must allegorize all the rest about the Cyclops.
The Cyclops, the one eyed, did not eat men.    120
The Issedones have one eye, as Aristeas writes:
"The Issedones delight in their long hair
and they are men sharing a border above
to the north, and they were many and very brave fighters,
rich in horses, rich in lambs, rich in oxen.    125
Each of them has one eye on his beautiful forehead;
with their shaggy hair they are stronger than all men."
The Issedones are one eyed, but not the race of the
    Cyclopes.

Ὅπως δ᾽ ὁ Κύκλωψ λέγεται μονόφθαλμος ὑπάρχειν,
130 καὶ πῶς δαλῷ τετύφλωται, μάνθανε σαφεστάτως.
Οἱ Σικελοί, οἱ Κύκλωπες, πλὴν ὀλιγανθρωποῦντες
ὑπάρχοντες καὶ ἄπειροι τοῦ ναυπηγεῖν ὁλκάδας,
τοὺς ξένους τοὺς καταίροντας πτοούμενοι ἀνήρουν,
μήπως αὐτῶν κρατήσωσι τῆς χώρας ἐπελθόντες.
135 Οὕτω καὶ Ὀδυσσέα δὲ σὺν δώδεκα τῶν φίλων
κατάραντα κατέσχηκε Πολύφημος, ὁ Κύκλωψ·
καθεῖρξε καὶ ἀνεῖλε δὲ καὶ ἓξ ἐκ τῶν ἑταίρων,
Ἄντιφον, Εὐρυλέοντα, Ἀφείδαντα, Κηφέα,
Στράτιόν τε καὶ Μένετον. Τούτους μὲν οὖν ἀνεῖλεν.
140 Οἱ ἓξ περιλειφθέντες δὲ μόνοι μετ᾽ Ὀδυσσέως,
Λυκάων καὶ Ἀμφίαλος, Ἄλκιμος, Ἀμφιδάμας,
Ἀντίλοχος, Εὐρύλοχος βουλαῖς τῶν εὐσυνέτων,
ἢ οἴνῳ ἢ καὶ χρήμασι μεθύσαντες ἐκεῖνον,
τὴν θυγατέρα Κύκλωπος, τὴν Ἔλπην καλουμένην
145 —ὄμμα τελοῦσαν τῷ πατρί τινος αὐτῶν ἐρῶσαν,
οἴξασαν τούτοις τὴν εἰρκτὴν—ἀπέπλεον λαβόντες
κἀκ τῶν ποιμνίων δὲ πολλὰ καὶ ἕτερα τῶν τούτου.
Ἦν δὲ νυκτὸς καιρὸς αὐτοῖς φυγῆς καὶ τοῦ ἀπόπλου.
Ὁ Κύκλωψ, ὄχλος σύμπας τε δραμὼν ἀκρωτηρίοις
150 πολλοὺς ἀμαξιαίους μὲν κάτω κινοῦντες λίθους,
πολλὴν δὲ λίθων χάλαζαν ἐκπέμποντες σφενδόναις·
εἰ μὴ ἡ νὺξ ἐμπόδιος ὁράσεως ὑπῆρχεν,
εἴτ᾽ αὖ κατέκλυσαν αὐτοὺς ὑπερβριθέσι λίθοις,
εἴτε καὶ συγκατήρραξαν αὐτοὺς καὶ τὴν ὁλκάδα.
155 Τοῖς ῥιπτομένοις λίθοις δὲ καὶ τοῖς σφενδονουμένοις
καὶ ὕστερον τὰς ἕνδεκα συνέτριψαν ὁλκάδας

How the Cyclops is said to be one eyed
and how he was blinded with a torch, learn most clearly.          130
The Sicilians, that is, the Cyclopes, for all that they were
few in numbers and inexperienced in shipbuilding,
terrified and killed the foreigners as they arrived,
lest the foreigners attack and prevail over their land.
Thus Polyphemos, the Cyclops, seized Odysseus          135
with twelve of his comrades as he came into port;
he confined and killed six of the comrades,
Antiphon, Euryleon, Apheidas, Kepheus,
Stratios and Menetos. Those were the ones he killed.
The six who survived along with Odysseus,          140
Lykaon, Amphialos, Alkimos, Amphidamas,
Antilochos, and Eurylochos, either through prudent
          planning or
by having made him drunk with wine or even with money,
sailed away after seizing the Cyclops's daughter, called Elpe
—who was her father's eye, and was in love with one of          145
          them,
and opened the prison for them—and moreover they took
many of his sheep and other such things from him.
It was night when they made their escape and sailed away.
The Cyclops and a whole mob ran to the promontory,
rolling down many wagon-sized stones,          150
and hurling a great hail of stones with slings;
if night had not obscured their vision, they would
either have overwhelmed them with enormous stones
or even smashed them and their ship into pieces.
After the stones were hurled and launched with slingshots,          155
and with the Laistrygonians afterward striking

οἱ Λαιστρυγόνες, βάλλοντες ἐκ τῶν ἀκρωτηρίων.
Μετὰ μιᾶς ὁλκάδος δὲ ὁ Ὀδυσσεὺς ἀπέδρα.
Οὕτω μὲν ἡ διήγησις ἔχει τῆς ἱστορίας.

160 Ὅμηρος δέ, τῷ νέκταρι τοὺς λόγους κεραννύων,
τὸ ἄξενον Κυκλώπων τε καὶ ῥώμην αὔξων τούτων,
ὁρῶν ἀκρωτηρίοις τε καὶ γίγασιν εἰκάζει,
τὰς δ᾽ ἀναιρέσεις τὰς αὐτῶν τῶν Ὀδυσσέως φίλων
κατάβρωσιν ἐκ Κύκλωπος λέγει καὶ Λαιστρυγόνων,

165 μέθην δὲ τὴν ἐν χρήμασι χαύνωσιν πρὸς τοὺς φόνους·
τὴν ῥάβδον δὲ τὴν ἀληθῆ τοῦ Κύκλωπος ἐπαύξων
ἴσην 'ἱστῷ' σοι εἴρηκε 'νηὸς ἐεικοσόρου'·
τὴν ἁρπαγὴν τῆς Ἕλπης δέ, τῆς θυγατρὸς ἐκείνου,
τὴν γεγονυῖαν ἔρωτι, πάλιν κατονομάζει

170 τοῦ ὀφθαλμοῦ ἐξαίρεσιν δαλῷ δῆθεν Ἐρώτων.
Τοῦτο τὸ ἀλληγόρημα ξένον οὐχὶ τοῦ Τζέτζου,
πλὴν ὄμματος ἡ τύφλωσις, ἡ ἐν δαλῷ, καὶ μόνον,
ὅτι ἡ Ἕλπη, ὀφθαλμὸς τοῦ Κύκλωπος τελοῦσα,
τοῖς ξένοις συναπέπλευσε λιποῦσα τὸν πατέρα,

175 καὶ ὅτι προμεμέθυστο τοῖς χρήμασιν ὁ Κύκλωψ.
Τὰ δ᾽ ἄλλα σύμπαντα δεινῇ κυμαίνονται τῇ ζάλῃ,
τῶν ὧν τὰ πλείω εἴρηκα καὶ ἠλληγόρηκά σοι.

Ἔχεις μὲν τὴν τοῦ Κύκλωπος πᾶσαν ἀλληγορίαν,
πλὴν βραχυτάτων τῇ φειδοῖ τοῦ χάρτου παρειμένων.

from the promontories, they crushed eleven ships.
Odysseus escaped with one ship.
That is the telling of the basic story.
But Homer, mixing his words with nectar,                        160
exaggerating the Cyclopes's lack of hospitality and their
    strength,
likens them to the promontories of mountains and to
    giants,
and the devouring by the Cyclops and the Laistrygonians
means the slaying of Odysseus's friends;
by the intoxication of money he means the relaxation         165
    before the murders;
magnifying the size of the real staff of the Cyclops,
he said that it was equal to the 'mast *of a twenty-oared ship*';
the seizure of Elpe, his daughter,
which came about because of love, he calls again
the removal of the eye specifically with the torch of          170
    Passions.
This allegory is someone else's, not Tzetzes's own,
except the blinding of the eye, with the torch alone,
namely that Elpe, being the eye of the Cyclops,
sailed away with the foreigners, leaving her father,
and that the Cyclops had been intoxicated by money in      175
    advance.
Everything else is tossed about in terrible confusion,
most of which I have told you and allegorized.
    Here you have the entire allegory of the Cyclops,
except for very brief omissions, to save paper.

# Κ'

Τοῦ Κάππα ἡ ὑπόθεσις τῆς Ὀδυσσείας λέγει.

Αἴολον, τὸν δεσπότην μὲν δεσπότου τῶν ἀνέμων,
ἀσκῷ βοὸς τῷ Ὀδυσσεῖ δεσμῆσαι τοὺς ἀνέμους,
μόνον αὐτῷ πνεῖν Ζέφυρον ὡς οὔριον ἐᾶσαι,
ἔγγιστα τῆς πατρίδος δὲ νυστάξαι Ὀδυσσέα.
5 Τὸν τῶν ἀνέμων δὲ ἀσκὸν λυσάντων τῶν ἑταίρων,
παλινοστῆσαι πρὸς αὐτὰς τὰς νήσους τοῦ Αἰόλου,
καὶ πρὸς τοὺς Λαιστρυγόνας δὲ ἱκέσθαι πλανωμένους,
οὕσπερ οἱ μῦθοι λέγουσιν ἀνθρωποβρῶτας εἶναι,
αὐτάνδρους ἀνθ' ὧν ἔνδεκα συνέτριψαν ὁλκάδας,
10 καὶ μετὰ Λαιστρυγόνας δὲ πρὸς Κίρκην πεπλευκότας,
τοὺς φίλους Ὀδυσσέως μὲν πρῶτον ἐκχοιρωθῆναι,
πάλιν ἀνθρωπωθῆναι δέ· αὐτὸν τὸν Ὀδυσσέα
βουλαῖς Ἑρμοῦ τὸ δυσχερὲς ταυτὶ μὴ πεπονθέναι.

Τζέτζης τὸν Ὀδυσσέα δέ φησιν ἐκχοιρωθῆναι
15 πλέον τῶν φίλων τῶν αὐτοῦ, ἐφ' ὁλοκλήρῳ ἔτει
τῇ Κίρκῃ συγκαθεύδοντα πορνείοις τοῖς ἐκείνης.
Οὕτως ἡ Κίρκη λέγεται καὶ γὰρ χοιροῦν ἀνθρώπους.
Κατάρχουσα τῆς νήσου γὰρ οὔσης ὀλιγανθρώπου
καὶ συρραγὰς πολέμων δὲ τῶν πέριξ πτοουμένη,
20 πορνεῖα συσκευάσασα, πολλοὺς τῶν ἐκπλεόντων

# Book 10

The subject matter of the tenth book of the *Odyssey*.

This book says that Aiolos, lord of the lord of the winds,
imprisoned the winds in a cowhide bag for Odysseus,
allowing only the favorable West Wind to blow for him,
and that Odysseus fell asleep close to his native land.
But when his companions loosened the bag of winds,              5
they returned to Aiolos's islands,
and they came wandering to the Laistrygonians,
who are said by the myths to be man-eaters,
and they destroyed eleven of the ships along with their
    crews.
And after the Laistrygonians they sailed to Kirke;             10
Homer says that Odysseus's friends were first turned into
    pigs
and then turned into men again; but Odysseus himself,
by the wishes of Hermes, did not suffer this misfortune.

But Tzetzes says that Odysseus did turn into a pig
even more than his friends, by sleeping with Kirke             15
for a whole year in her brothels.
For that is how Kirke is said to turn men into pigs.
Ruling over the island which had few inhabitants
and fearing outbreaks of wars among the neighboring
    peoples,
she established brothels and thus made many                    20

οὕτως ἐποίει κατοικεῖν καὶ συμμαχεῖν ἐκείνῃ.
Οἱ τῷ βορβόρῳ γοῦν ἀεὶ κρατούμενοι τοῦ πάθους
καὶ τοῖς πορνείοις μένοντες ἐξεχοιροῦντο τάχα.
Οἱ πρὸς βραχὺ δὲ μείναντες ἔμπαλιν ὑπεχώρουν,
25   λύκοι ὁμοῦ καὶ λέοντες ἐκλήθησαν τοῖς μύθοις.
Οὗπερ συμβάντος καὶ αὐτοῖς τοῖς Ὀδυσσέως φίλοις,
ἐξ ἑρμηνέως Ὀδυσσεύς πως γνοὺς ἠκριβωμένως,
ὅπως ἐν ταῖς πορνείαις τε καὶ γέ τισι φαρμάκοις
τοὺς ξένους πάντας παρ' αὐτῇ χοιροῖ τε καὶ κατέχει·
30   μῶλυ λαβὼν ἀπέρχεται πορνείοις τοῖς Κιρκαίοις.
Τὸ μῶλυ γὰρ καὶ κόνυζα καὶ ῥάμνος καὶ ἰτέα
καὶ ἕτερα μυρία δὲ μαγείαις ἀντιπράττει.
Οὕτως ἐλθὼν ὁ Ὀδυσσεύς, καὶ ὁλοκλήρῳ ἔτει
τῇ Κίρκῃ συμφθειρόμενος, πλέον ἦν πάντων χοῖρος.
35   Ἀλλὰ τὰ Κίρκης ἔφημεν καὶ τὰ τῶν Λαιστρυγόνων.
Τὰ τοῦ Αἰόλου φράσω δὲ ἄρτι σοι σαφεστάτως.
Αἴολος, ἄρχων τῶν ἐκεῖ, δώδεκα παῖδας εἶχεν,
ὧνπερ τὰς κλήσεις μάνθανε—καὶ χρόνον μή μοι νόει·
Περίφας σὺν Ἀγήνορι, Εὐχήνωρ τε ὁ τρίτος,
40   Κλύμενος, Ξοῦθος, Μακαρεύς, κλήσεις ἀρρένων αἵδε.
Κλυμένη καὶ Καλλίθυια σύν γε τῇ Εὐρυγόνῃ
καὶ Λυσιδίκῃ ἄλλη τε σύναμα τῇ Κανάκῃ.
Τηρῶν δὲ τὴν ὁμόνοιαν καὶ τὴν στοργὴν Αἴολος
τὰς ἀδελφὰς τοῖς ἀδελφοῖς συνέζευξεν ἐν γάμοις.
45   Ὃς τὸν Αἴολον χρόνον δὲ καὶ μῆνας ληροῖ τούτους,
ἐκ τῶν μηνῶν λεγέτω μοι τίς Μακαρεὺς νοεῖται,
καὶ ποῖος ἡ Κανάκη δὲ καὶ οἱ λοιποὶ ὁμοίως.

of those who sailed past dwell and make an alliance with
    her.
So those who were always overcome by filthy passions
and stayed in the brothels supposedly turned into pigs.
Those who stayed for a short time and withdrew again
were called wolves and lions in the myths.                      25
When this happened to these friends of Odysseus,
Odysseus learned precisely somehow from the interpreter
how with prostitution and certain potions
she turns all strangers into pigs and keeps them near her;
taking moly he removed himself from Kirke's brothels.       30
Moly is also called inula and buckthorn and willow
and myriad other names; it counteracts magic.
Thus Odysseus came and, after being corrupted by Kirke
for a whole year, was more of a pig than anyone.
But now we are done talking about Kirke and the          35
    Laistrygonians.
   Now I will tell you very clearly about Aiolos.
Aiolos, ruling over the people there, had twelve children,
learn their names—and do not think that I mean the year:
Periphas and Agenor, Euchenor third,
Klymenos, Xouthos and Makareus were the names of the    40
    boys.
Klymene and Kallithyia with Eurygone
and Lysidike and one more along with Kanake.
Aiolos, preserving concord and affection,
yoked in marriage the sisters and the brothers.
He who rants that Aiolos is the year and the children are    45
    the months,
let him tell me which of the months Makareus represents,
and which Kanake and likewise the rest of them.

Πῶς τὸν Αἴολον λέγουσι δεσπότην δὲ ἀνέμων
καὶ Ὀδυσσεῖ τὸν Ζέφυρον μόνον ἐᾶσαι πνέειν,
50  ἀσκῷ δεσμῆσαι δὲ πνοὰς καὶ τῶν λοιπῶν ἀνέμων,
ἄκουε καί μου μάνθανε τὸ πᾶν ἠκριβωμένως.
Οἱ τελεσταὶ μὲν λέγουσι καὶ οἱ θαυματεργάται,
ἂν ἐξ ἰχθύος τις ἀσκὸν ποιήσειε δελφῖνος,
φυσήσας τοῦτον δήσῃ τε, πρὸς ἄνεμον δὲ θείη,
55  ἐκεῖνος μόνος πνεύσειε, σιγήσουσι δ᾽ οἱ ἄλλοι.
Ἴσως δ᾽ ἂν ὑπολάβοι τις, καὶ τὸν Αἴολον τοῦτον
εἶναι τοιοῦτον τελεστὴν καὶ ἔμπειρον τοιούτων
καὶ οὕτω δρᾶσαι, Ζέφυρον τῷ Ὀδυσσεῖ πνεῖν μόνον,
πᾶσαν πνοὴν δὲ τῶν λοιπῶν ἐγκατασχεῖν ἀνέμων,
60  οὐκ ἔστι τοῦτο οὐδαμῶς. Ἦν δ᾽ οὗτος ὁ Αἴολος
ναυτιλλομένων φροντιστὴς καὶ φροντιστὴς ἀνέμων,
ὡς λέγειν πᾶσιν ἀκριβῶς, ποῖος ἀνέμων πνεύσει,
καὶ μέχρι ποίου χρόνου δὲ οὗτος κρατήσει πνέων,
καθάπερ δὴ καὶ Ὀδυσσεῖ ἐκπλέοντι προεῖπεν·
65  "ὁ ἄνεμος, ὁ Ζέφυρος οὗτος, οὐ λήξει πνέων·
ἔστ᾽ ἂν ἀποκομίσηται πρὸς τὴν αὐτοῦ πατρίδα,
εἰ μή που σὺ βραδύνειας καὶ μελλητὴς φανείης."
Οὗ γεγονότος καὶ αὐτοῦ ῥαθύμου γεγονότος,
ἀντίπνους πνεύσας ἄνεμος στρέφει πρὸς Αἰολίαν.
70  Ὅμηρος ὕπνον λέγει δὲ τὴν τούτου ῥαθυμίαν,
τὴν ἐναντίαν πνεῦσιν δὲ πάλιν ἀνέμων λέγει
παρὰ ἑταίρων τοῦ ἀσκοῦ τὴν τῶν ἀνέμων λύσιν.
Ἀλλ᾽ ἤδη μὲν εἰρήκειμεν πάντα τὸν νοῦν τοῦ Κάππα,
ὁπόσος ἦν ἁρμόδιος ἀλληγορεῖσθαι τέως.

As for the tale that Aiolos was lord of the winds
and allowed only the West Wind to blow for Odysseus,
and tied up the remaining winds in the bag,                    50
listen to me and learn everything in detail.
The priests and the miracle workers say that
if someone were to make a bag from a dolphin skin
and should blow into it, tie it, and set it against the wind,
it alone would blow, the others will remain still.             55
Perhaps one might interpret this to mean that Aiolos
is also a priest and experienced in such things, and
he made the West Wind alone blow for Odysseus
and restrained the entire force of the other winds,
but this is not so. This Aiolos was                           60
the protector of navigators and the protector of winds,
telling everyone exactly which wind will blow,
and how long it will keep blowing,
just as he foretold to Odysseus as he sailed away:
"The wind, this West Wind, will not stop blowing;             65
it will carry you to its own fatherland,
unless you somehow are delayed and appear to
    procrastinate."
When this happened and he became lazy,
an adverse wind blew and turned them toward Aiolia.
Homer calls his laziness sleep,                               70
he says again that the adverse blowing of the winds
is the loosening of the bag of winds by his companions.
But we have already told you all the meaning of the tenth
    book,
as much as was fitting to be allegorized up till now.

75  Νῦν δὲ καὶ πᾶν κατάτμημα χρῇζον ἀλληγορίας
ἀλληγορήσω προσφυῶς τοῖς τόποις τοῖς ἑκάστου.
'Θεοῖς' τοῖς 'ἀθανάτοισι' φίλον Αἴολον λέγει,
τὸν φρόνιμον καὶ ἔννουν δὲ καὶ στοχαστὴν μελλόντων.
'Τεῖχος δὲ χάλκεόν' φησιν, ὡς ὂν τῶν στερροτάτων,
80  εἴτε τὸ τειχιζόμενον ὅπλοις καὶ στρατιώταις.
Ταμίαν δὲ ἐποίησεν 'ἀνέμων' ὁ 'Κρονίων,'
ἤγουν προγνώστην τέθεικεν ὑπάρχειν τῶν ἀνέμων,
ἡ σκοτεινὴ καὶ ἄγνωστος τοῖς πᾶσιν Εἱμαρμένη,
εἴτε ὁ νοῦς καὶ λογισμὸς καὶ φρόνησις οἰκεία.
85  'Ἄνδρα τόν, ὅς κε θεοῖσιν ἀπέχθηται μακάρεσσιν.'
Ὃς ἄφρων νῦν ἐστιν, αὐτῇ μισούμενος φρονήσει,
ἢ καὶ τὸ ὃς μεμίσηται αὐτῇ τῇ Εἱμαρμένῃ.
'Γυναῖκα' ἴσην 'κορυφῇ τοῦ ὄρους' δὲ νῦν λέγει
ἀγρίαν, ὑψουμένην τε τῷ τύφῳ καὶ μεγάλην.
90  'Αὐτίχ' ἕνα μάρψας ἑτάρων ὁπλίσσατο δόρπον,'
καὶ μετὰ ἔπη δέ τινα πάλιν φησὶν ὁμοίως.
'Ἰχθῦς δ' ὡς πείροντες ἀτερπέα δαῖτα πένοντο.'
Τὰς ἀναιρέσεις τῶν ἀνδρῶν νῦν καταβρώσεις λέγει.
'Κίρκη ἐϋπλόκαμος, δεινὴ θεὸς αὐδήεσσα'
95  θεὸς φωνῇ ἀνθρώπου δὲ χρωμένη καὶ λαλοῦσα,
ἤτοι σοφὴ ταῖς ἐπῳδαῖς καὶ ἄρχουσα τῶν τόπων.
Οἱ γὰρ ἀστέρες, οἱ θεοὶ στοιχεῖα, καὶ οἱ ἄλλοι
θεοὶ μὲν ὀνομάζονται, αὐδήεντες δὲ οὔκουν.

Now since every section needs allegorization,                    75
I will allegorize suitably each thing in its proper passage.
　He calls Aiolos dear to the *'immortal gods,'*
the prudent, thoughtful one, and diviner of the future.
　He speaks of a *'wall of bronze,'* as it was very sturdy,
or it was fortified by arms and soldiers.                        80
　The *'son of Kronos'* made Aiolos the master *'of winds,'*
that is, he made him have foreknowledge of the winds,
of dark Destiny unknown to everyone,
or this is wisdom and reason and his own sense.
　*'That man, who is hated of the blessed gods.'*                85
This man is here thoughtless, being hateful to wisdom
　　itself,
or it even means that he has been hated by Destiny itself.
　Here he says *'his wife'* was tall 'as a mountain peak,'
wild, elevated in arrogance, and tall.
　*'Straightaway he seized one of my comrades and* made ready   90
　　for his meal'
and then he says some more words to the same effect.
　*'And spearing them like fish,* they bore *them home, a loathsome
　　meal.'*
The slaying of the men he here calls their devouring.
　*'Fair-haired Kirke, a dread goddess speaking with human
　　voice,'*
means that the god used human voice and speech,               95
that is, she was wise in spells and ruled over the lands.
For the stars, that is, the gods, are the elements, and the
　　others
are called gods, they certainly do not speak.

Ἥλιον νῦν Ὠκεανὸν ἀκούοντες ἐνθάδε
100  πατέρα Κίρκης, ἄνθρωπον καὶ βασιλέα νόει.
Τὸν 'φαεσίμβροτον' λαμπρὸν ἐν τοῖς ἀνθρώποις νόει.
'Θεός τις ἡγεμόνευε' τύχη τις προηγεῖτο.
'Θεῶν τις ὀλοφύρατο' ᾠκτείρησεν ἡ τύχη.
'Θεᾶς καλλιπλοκάμοιο' ἀρχούσης βασιλίδος.
105  'Θεάων' βασιλίδων νῦν, ὁμοίως τῷ προτέρῳ.
Ἠὲ 'θεὸς' ἢ καὶ 'γυνὴ' πάλιν τουτὶ σημαίνει·
ἢ ἦχος ἔστι τῶν ὀρῶν, ἢ καὶ γυνή τις ᾄδει.
'Φάρμακα' ἦσαν δὲ λυγρὰ τῷ 'σίτῳ' μεμιγμένα.
Αἱ τῶν πορνῶν νῦν ἐπαφαί, αἵπερ ἐχοίρουν τούτους.
110  Ῥάβδος, ἡ πλήττουσα αὐτούς, αἱ ἴυγγες τοῦ πόθου.
'Ἑρμείαν' νῦν 'χρυσόρραπιν,' ὃς εἶπε τὰ τῆς Κίρκης.
'Θεοῦ εὐνήν,' τῆς Κίρκης δέ, τῆς βασιλίδος, λέγει.
'Μῶλυ καλέουσι θεοί' καὶ οἱ ἑξῆς θεοὶ δέ
σοφοὺς τανῦν σημαίνουσιν, οὐχ᾽ ἕτερόν τι πλέον.
115  Ὁ τοῦ Ἑρμοῦ δὲ 'Ὄλυμπος' τὸν οἶκον τὸν ἐκείνου.
Ὁ περὶ 'Ὀδυσσέως' δὲ Ἑρμῆς εἰπὼν τῇ Κίρκῃ
τὶς ἑρμηνεὺς ἡκούετο πλανᾶσθαι γὰρ ἐκ Τροίας.
Αἱ 'τέσσαρες ἀμφίπολοι' τῆς Κίρκης τί δηλοῦσιν;
Ἔχειν ἐκείνην ἄφθονα τὰ ἐξ ὡρῶν τεσσάρων.
120  Σὺ μὴ κιρκαίως Κίρκην δὲ τὸν χρόνον ὀνομάσῃς.
Πῶς γὰρ Τηλέγονον γεννᾷ χρόνος ἐξ Ὀδυσσέως;
Καὶ τὰ λοιπὰ πῶς φαίη τις τῆσδε τῆς ἱστορίας;

Hearing that Helios, who is here Okeanos,
was Kirke's father, you should understand he was a man and     100
    a king.
And that 'bringing light to mortals' means shining among
    men.
    'And *some god guided us*' means some chance led the way.
    '*Some god took pity*' means fate pitied him.
    '*Of the fair-haired goddess*' means of the ruling queen.
    '*Of the goddesses*' here means of the queens, just as before.     105
    '*Goddess*' or '*woman*' again means the same;
it is either a sound of the mountains, or some woman is
    singing.
    Baneful '*drugs*' were mixed in the '*food.*'
Here they are the caresses of prostitutes, who turned them
    into pigs.
    The wand that struck them is the spells of passion.     110
    Here he means 'Hermes with the golden wand,' who
        spoke the words of Kirke.
    '*The bed of the goddess,*' of Kirke, means of the queen.
    '*The gods call it moly*' and the gods in the subsequent
        passage
mean wise men here, nothing more.
    Hermes's 'Olympos' means his house.     115
    Hermes who spoke about 'Odysseus' to Kirke means
a certain interpreter was heard to have wandered from Troy.
    What do the '*four handmaidens*' of Kirke mean?
That she had an abundance of the four seasons.
You should not falsely call Kirke time.     120
For how does time beget Telegonos from Odysseus?
And how might one recount the remaining elements of this
    story?

Ἡ 'ῥάβδος' καὶ τὸ 'φάρμακον' τὸ βροτουργοῦν ἐκ
  χοίρων
ἡ μετ' ὀργῆς παραίνεσίς ἐστι καὶ νουθεσία.

125  Εἰς Ἅιδου δὲ κατέλευσιν καὶ χρῆσιν Τειρεσίου
βουλαῖς τῆς Κίρκης νόησον που τῶν ἐκεῖσε τόπων,
τὸν Ὀδυσσέα χρῆσθαι δὲ ταῖς αἱματομαντείαις
σὺν τοῖς ἐκεῖσε μάντεσι καὶ μάγοις ὑπηργμένοις,
ἀναγαγοῦσιν εἴδωλον ψυχῆς τοῦ Τειρεσίου,
130  ἐξ οὗ πάντα μεμάθηκεν, ὁπόσων χρείαν εἶχε.

'Τίς ἂν θεὸν οὐ θέλοντα ἐν ὀφθαλμοῖσιν ἴδοι;'
Τίς ἂν σοφοῦ μὴ θέλοντος οἰκονομίαν γνοίη;

The 'wand' and the '*drug*' that made pigs into men
are exhortation and advice with anger.
   Understand that the descent into Hades and Teiresias's   125
     prophecy
mean that by Kirke's wishes somewhere in those places
Odysseus made use of blood divinations
with the assistance of the seers and the mages who were
     there,
leading up the shade of Teiresias's soul
from whom he learned everything he needed.   130
   '*Who* could behold with his *eyes a god* against his will?'
Which means, who could understand a wise man's
     dispensation against his will?

## Λ΄

Ἡ Λάμβδα δὲ ὑπόθεσίς ἐστι τῆς Ὀδυσσείας.

Αὐτὸς λαβὼν ὁ Ὀδυσσεὺς τὰς Τειρεσίου χρήσεις,
ἃς κατελθόντι ἔχρησεν αὐτῷ περὶ τὸν Ἅιδην,
καὶ τὴν μητέρα εἶδέ τε καὶ πόσας ἡρωίδας,
τινὰς τῶν ἐν τῇ Τροίᾳ τε καὶ τοὺς κολαζομένους.
5　Πῶς τούτῳ Κίρκη ὄπισθεν ἀγρίας πνοὰς πέμπει;
Πέμπειν ἀνέμους Ὀδυσσεῖ οὐκ εὐσθενὴς ἡ Κίρκη,
πνοὴν δ᾽ ἰδοῦσα ἄγριον, ἐκέλευσε πλεῖν τότε.

᾽Η δ᾽ ἐς πείραθ᾽ ἵκανε βαθυρρόου Ὠκεανοῖο.
Ἔνθα δὲ Κιμμερίων ἀνδρῶν δῆμός τε πόλις τε,
10　ἠέρι καὶ νεφέλῃ κεκαλυμμένοι· οὐδέ ποτ᾽ αὐτοὺς
Ἥλιος φαέθων καταδέρκεται ἀκτίνεσσιν.᾽
Τοὺς Κιμμερίους οἱ πολλοὶ ἔθνος φασὶν ὑπάρχειν
περὶ τοὺς Ταυροσκύθας τε καὶ τὴν Μαιῶτιν λίμνην,
οἵπερ ἀφώτιστοί εἰσιν, ἥλιον οὐχ ὁρῶντες,
15　ἐν σκότει δὲ διάγουσιν ἔν τε νυκτὶ βαθείᾳ.
16　Ἡμέρας τεσσαράκοντα καιρὸς δ᾽αὐτοῖς τοῦ σκότους·
16a　ὅταν ἐν τῷ Καρκίνῳ δὲ ὁ ἥλιος ὑπάρχῃ,
16b　ἡμέρας τεσσαράκοντα ὁλόφωτοι τελοῦσιν.
17　Ἄλλοι δ᾽ ἄλλ᾽ ἀψευδέστατα λέγουσι περὶ τούτων.
Καὶ Θέων ἐν συνόψει δὲ Συντάξεως Μεγάλης

# Book II

This is the subject matter of the eleventh book of
the *Odyssey*.

Odysseus himself received the prophecies of Teiresias
which the latter prophesied to him when he descended to
    Hades,
and saw his mother and so many heroines,
some of whom had been at Troy, and those being punished.
How did Kirke send wild breezes behind him?        5
Kirke was not powerful enough to send winds for Odysseus,
but seeing a savage wind stir up, she ordered him to set sail
    then.

  '*She came to the limits of deep-flowing Okeanos,*
*where is the people and city of the Kimmerians,*
*wrapped in mist and cloud. Never does*        10
*the sun look down on them with his rays.*'
Many say the Kimmerians are a race
near the Tauroskythians and the Maeotic lake,
who are without light, and do not see the sun,
but live in darkness and in the depths of night.        15
The time of darkness lasts forty days for them;        16
whenever the sun is in Cancer,        16a
then they are fully lit for forty days.        16b
And others say other irrefutable things about them.        17
Theon in the synopsis of the *Almagest* says

ἔκμηνον φῶς καὶ σκότος δὲ λέγει τοῖς Κιμμερίοις.

20 Ὅμηρος Κιμμερίους δὲ παρ᾽ Ἰταλίαν λέγει,
καὶ ἀφωτίστους εἰσαεὶ τούτους φησὶν ὑπάρχειν,
καὶ τοῦτο θόρυβον πολὺν τοῖς φυσικοῖς παρέσχεν.
Εἰσὶ δὲ οἱ Κιμμέριοι μέρος βραχὺ καὶ δῆμος
ἔθνους τινὸς Ἰταλικοῦ, αἱ δὲ οἰκήσεις τούτων
25 ἐν φάραγξι καὶ κοίλοις τε καὶ βαθυτάτοις τόποις,
καὶ οὕτως ἥλιος αὐτοῖς οὐδ᾽ ὅλως ἐπιλάμπει.
Ἐκεῖ καὶ λίμνη τίς ἐστι Σιάχα καλουμένη,
ἣ καὶ τὰ φύλλα πίπτοντα βυθίζεται τῶν δένδρων.
Ἐκεῖ δὲ καὶ μαντεῖον ἦν ψυχαγωγῶν ἀνθρώπων,
30 οἳ Ὀδυσσεῖ, <καθαίροντες αὐτοῦ> τὴν ἁμαρτίαν,
ἀναγαγόντες δῆθε τε ψυχὴν τοῦ Τειρεσίου·
δι᾽ αὐτοῦ μὲν μαντεύονται πάντα τῷ τοῦ Λαέρτου,
καὶ πάντα δὲ δεικνύουσι τὰ τῶν νεκρῶν καὶ ζώντων,
ὅθεν εἰς Ἅιδου λέγουσιν ἐλθεῖν τὸν Ὀδυσσέα.
35 'Θεῶν' δὲ 'μήνιμα' δηλοῖ ὀργὴν ἐξ Εἱμαρμένης.
'Θεὸς' δὲ 'νόστον' χαλεπὸν 'θήσει' ἡ Εἱμαρμένη,
ἣ καὶ ἡ θάλασσα αὐτή, ὡς κατωτέρω λέγει.
'Χωόμενος, ὅτι οἱ υἱὸν φίλον ἐξαλάωσας,'
ἡ θάλασσα φρουρεῖται γὰρ παρὰ τῶν ὁμορούντων,
40 ἁρπασάντων τὴν Κύκλωπος παῖδα καὶ σχεῖν ζητούντων.
'Ὁππότε κε πρῶτον πελάσῃς εὐεργέα νῆα
Θρινακίῃ νήσῳ, προφυγὼν ἰοειδέα πόντον,
βοσκομένας δ᾽ εὕρητε βόας καὶ ἴφια μῆλα
Ἡελίου, ὃς πάντ᾽ ἐφορᾷ καὶ πάντ᾽ ἐπακούει.'
45 Βοῦς ἱεροὺς ἡλίου νῦν τοὺς ἀροτῆρας λέγει,

that the Kimmerians have six months each of light and
    darkness.
Homer says the Kimmerians are in Italy,                                20
and he says that they are constantly without light,
and this caused much confusion for natural philosophers.
The Kimmerians are a small part and a people
of a certain Italian race, and their settlements
are in ravines and hollows and in very deep locations,                 25
and thus the sun does not shine upon them at all.
There is found a lake called Siacha,
where falling tree leaves sink.
Also found there was an oracle of necromancers,
who, purifying Odysseus from sin,                                      30
supposedly conjured up for him Teiresias's soul;
through him they prophesied everything to the son of
    Laertes,
and they showed him everything pertaining to the dead and
    the living,
because of which they say Odysseus went into Hades.
    'The wrath of the gods' denotes rage sent from Destiny.            35
    'God will make' a harsh 'return' is Destiny,
or also the sea itself, as he says below.
    'Angered that you blinded his dear son'
means that the sea is guarded by those on the borders,
who seized the Cyclops's daughter and asked to keep her.              40
    'As soon as you shall bring your well-built ship
to the island of Thrinakia, escaping from the violet sea,
and you find grazing there the oxen and the fat flocks
of Helios, who oversees and overhears all things.'
Here he calls the sacred Cattle of the Sun plow oxen,                 45

ὡς καὶ ἀρχῇ προείπομεν τῆς Ἄλφα Ὀδυσσείας
καὶ πάλιν δὲ πλατύτερον, οὗ δέον, γράφω ταῦτα.
   Τοῖς 'ἀθανάτοις' δὲ 'θεοῖς,' τῇ Εἱμαρμένῃ λέγει
καὶ τοῖς στοιχείοις δὲ αὐτοῖς, τοῖς οὐρανίοις μόνον,
50 Διὶ καὶ τῷ Ἡλίῳ τε, ἤτοι πυρί, ἀέρι.
   Ταῦτα που 'ἐπεκλώσαντο θεοὶ' ἡ Εἱμαρμένη.
   'Ἡ δολιχὴ νοῦσος; ἢ Ἄρτεμις ἰοχέαιρα;'
'Ἄρτεμις ἰοχέαιρα' ἡ νόσος ἡ ὀξεῖα,
ὡς γὰρ πολλάκις ἔφημεν, τὰς νόσους τὰς ὀξείας
55 σελήνῃ τῷ ἡλίῳ τε οἱ παλαιοὶ προσῆπτον.
   Ὡς κἂν τῷ ἐπιδείκνυται τόδε συμφανεστέρως,
μᾶλλον τῶν ἄλλων πλέον δὲ ὀξέων νοσημάτων
τὰ ἐκ λοιμοῦ νοσήματα προσῆπτον τοῖς ῥηθεῖσιν.
   Ἡ Περσεφόνη, μοῖρα τε καὶ θάνατος ἑκάστου,
60 παῖς εἶναι λέγεται 'Διός,' αὐτῆς τῆς Εἱμαρμένης.
   Ἡ Περσεφόνη πάλιν δὲ ὁ τόπος ὁ τοῦ Ἅιδου·
παῖς εἶναι λέγεται 'Διός,' τοῦ εἰδουργοῦ ἀέρος,
ὃς πρὶν ἐξ ὕλης κινηθεὶς διήρθρωσε τὰ πάντα,
ὥσπερ νεανιεύονται δόξαι σοφῶν Ἑλλήνων.
65 'Τυρὼ' τοῦ Ἐνιπέως μέν, ἀνθρώπου τινός, ἤρα,
ἐξ οὗ τὴν κλῆσιν Ἐνιπεὺς ὁ ποταμὸς ἐσχήκει.
   Ἀντὶ τοῦ Ἐνιπέως δέ τις ποταμὸς τὴν κλῆσιν
ἐμίγη ταύτῃ τῇ Τυροῖ ἤ τις τῶν ἐκ θαλάσσης.
   'Διὸς ἐν ταῖς ἀγκοίνῃσι,' τουτέστι βασιλέως.
70 'Θεοὶ θέσαν ἀνάπυστα' θεῶν βουλάς τε πάλιν.
   Τὴν Εἱμαρμένην νόει μοι τῇδε τὰ ἔπη λέγειν.

as we previously said at the beginning of Book One of the
    *Odyssey,*
and here I write this more expansively, as is necessary.
    By 'to the immortal gods' he means to Destiny
and to the elements themselves, the celestial ones alone,
to Zeus and to the Sun, that is, to fire, to air.      50
    The '*gods* spun' these, that is, Destiny.
    '*Was it a long disease, or did Artemis the archer?*'
'*Artemis the archer*' is the acute disease,
for as we have said many times, people of old
attributed acute diseases to the moon and the sun.      55
Just as if this is even revealed to him more manifestly,
much more than the other acute diseases,
they ascribed the diseases that come from plague to the
    aforementioned.
    Persephone, the fate and death of each man,
is said to be the child of '*Zeus,*' that is, of Destiny itself.      60
Again Persephone is the location of Hades;
she is said to be the child '*of Zeus,*' that is, of the air that
    speciates,
which, having previously been moved from matter,
    articulated everything,
as the beliefs of the wise Greeks insolently say.
    '*Tyro*' was in love with Enipeus, a man,      65
after whom the river Enipeus received its name.
Instead of Enipeus, a river of the same name
or someone from the sea lay with this Tyro.
    '*In the arms of Zeus,*' that is, of the king.
    '*The gods made these things known*' again means the gods'      70
    counsel.
Understand that the words here mean Destiny.

Καὶ 'χαλεπὴ' κατέδησε 'μοῖρα' 'θεοῦ' ὁμοίως.
"Ἥ ῥ' ὑπὸ Τυνδαρέῳ κρατερόφρονε γείνατο παῖδε,
Κάστορά θ' ἱππόδαμον καὶ πὺξ ἀγαθὸν Πολυδεύκην.
75  Τοὺς ἄμφω ζωοὺς κατέχει φυσίζοος αἶα,
οἳ καὶ νέρθεν γῆς τιμὴν πρὸς Ζηνὸς ἔχοντες.
Ἄλλοτε μὲν ζώουσ' ἑτερήμεροι, ἄλλοτε δ' αὖτε
τεθνᾶσιν· τιμὴν δὲ λελόγχασιν ἶσα θεοῖσι.'
Γῆν ζῶντας ἔχειν λέγουσι Κάστορα, Πολυδεύκην,
80  διὰ τὸ δίκαιον αὐτῶν καὶ ἀρετὰς τὰς ἄλλας.
Οἱ ἀρεταῖς βιοῦντες γὰρ ζῶσι καὶ τεθνηκότες.
Διὰ Θησέα γὰρ αὐτοὶ στρατεύσαντες Ἀθήναις,
τὴν ἀδελφὴν τὴν ἑαυτῶν ἀπέλαβον Ἑλένην,
καὶ μόνην ἠχμαλώτισαν μητέρα τοῦ Θησέως.
85  Τῶν δ' ἄλλων πάντων οὐδὲ εἷς ἄχρι τριχὸς ἐβλάβη,
δι' ἃ καὶ νέρθεν ὄντες γῆς τιμαῖς τῆς Εἱμαρμένης,
ἡμέραν παρ' ἡμέραν μέν, τοῖς εὐηργετημένοις
ὥσπερ θεοὶ τετίμηνται, ἀστέρες καὶ στοιχεῖα,
καὶ ψυχικαὶ δυνάμεις δέ, δίκαιον σὺν φρονήσει,
90  ἐν τῇ μιᾷ ἡμέρᾳ μὲν ὑμνούμενοι ὡς ζῶντες,
ἐν τῇ ἑτέρᾳ πάλιν δὲ τρόπῳ τῶν τεθνηκότων.
Ἰφιμεδείας καί τινος γενναίου Ποσειδῶνος,
γίγαντες νέοι ἄθεοι γεννῶνται τῶν ἀφρόνων,
ὧνπερ αἱ κλήσεις Ὤτος τε καὶ Ἐπιάλτης ἦσαν,
95  οὓς ψυχικῶς, στοιχειακῶς ἐν στίχοις ἰαμβείοις
πρότερον ἠλληγόρησα, νῦν δὲ πραγματικῶς σοι.
Τὰς ἀφροσύνας Ὅμηρος ἐκείνων παρεισφέρει,
καὶ πῶς λοιμῷ τεθνήκασιν, Ἀπόλλωνος τοξείᾳ·
ζῶντες δὲ καὶ τὸν Ἄρεα μυθεύονται δεσμῆσαι,

And '*a grievous fate of the god*' put him in bonds likewise.
  '*Who bore to Tyndareus two sons, stout of heart,*
*Kastor the tamer of horses, and the good boxer* Polydeukes.
*These two the earth, the giver of life, covers, albeit alive,*                    75
*and even in the world below they have honor from Zeus.*
*One day they live in turn, and one day they are*
*dead; and they have won honor similar to that of the gods.*'
They say that the earth holds Kastor and Polydeukes,
       although still alive,
because they are just and have other virtues.                                    80
Those who live in virtue live even when they are dead.
For they marched against Athens because of Theseus,
and took away their sister Helen,
and captured only Theseus's mother.
Not even one hair of any other was harmed, wherefore,                            85
although below the earth, they are honored by Destiny,
that is, day after day they are honored like gods
by those whom they benefited, that is, like stars and
       elements,
and the powers of the soul, justice along with prudence,
are celebrated as if living one day,                                             90
and on the next again in the manner of the dead.
   From Iphimedeia and a certain brave Poseidon
are born young foolish giants who denied the gods,
whose names were Otos and Epialtes,
whom I formerly allegorized spiritually, elementally                             95
in iambic lines; here I do so for you historically.
Homer also relates, along with their foolishness,
how they died from the plague, from the archery of Apollo.
While still alive they were said to have put Ares in chains

100 ὅτι πάντας κατέπαυσαν σφῶν ῥώμῃ τοὺς πολέμους.

Τὴν 'Ἀριάδνην,' 'Μίνωος' τελοῦσαν θυγατέρα,
Θησέως ἄγοντος αὐτὴν Ἄρτεμις Νάξῳ κτείνει.
Οἱ δέ φασι, Διόνυσον ταύτην ἁρπάξαι Νάξῳ.
Ὁ Τζέτζης, εἰρηνεύων δὲ καὶ διαλύων μάχας,

105 ἕν σοι τὰ δύο καὶ ταὐτὸν νῦν λέγω πεφυκέναι,
οἴνου πόσει θανοῦσα γὰρ ἡρπάγη Διονύσῳ.
Ἐπεὶ τῶν νοσημάτων δὲ τῶν ὀξυτάτων πάντων
αἴτιος εἶναι λέγεται ἥλιος καὶ σελήνη,
εὐλόγως γράφει νῦν, αὐτὴν τὴν Ἄρτεμιν τοξεῦσαι.

110 Καὶ τὸν ἐξ οἴνου θάνατον σεμνῶς σοι παρεμφαίνει,
ταῖς 'Διονύσου' ἐκβοῶν κτεῖναι δὲ 'μαρτυρίαις,'
ἤγουν ὀξέως τέθνηκεν οἴνου ἀμέτρῳ πόσει.

'Θεῶν ἰότητ'' φησι βουλαῖς τῆς Εἰμαρμένης.

'Ζεὺς' νῦν 'εὐρύοπά' ἐστιν αὐτὴ ἡ Εἰμαρμένη,

115 ἥ ἐστι μεγαλόφωνος καὶ περιθρυλλουμένη.

'Τεύχεσιν ἀμφ' Ἀχιλῆος· ἔθηκε δὲ πότνια μήτηρ·
παῖδες δὲ Τρώων δίκασαν καὶ Παλλὰς Ἀθήνη.'
Ἡ περὶ ὅπλων γέγονε κρίσις ἐγγὺς θαλάσσης.
Τὴν θάλασσαν γινώσκεις δέ, πῶς μήτηρ Ἀχιλλέως.

120 Παῖδες δὲ Τρώων δίκασαν αἰχμάλωτοι τὴν κρίσιν,
καὶ ἡ Παλλὰς Ἀθήνη δέ, οἱ φρόνιμοι Ἑλλήνων.

'Πῆμα θεοὶ' δὲ ἔθεσαν αὐτὴ ἡ Εἰμαρμένη,
καὶ 'Ζεὺς' ὁμοίως τὸν 'στρατὸν ἤχθηρεν' Εἰμαρμένη.

because they ended all wars through their strength.                    100
   Artemis killed '*Ariadne,*' the daughter of '*Minos,*'
on Naxos, after Theseus led her there.
Some, however, say that Dionysos snatched her on Naxos.
I, Tzetzes, making peace and breaking up battles,
tell you here that those two are one and the same,                     105
for after dying from drinking wine, she was seized by
      Dionysos.
Since the sun and the moon are said to be responsible
for all the very acute diseases,
here Homer writes sensibly that Artemis shot her with her
      arrows.
And he solemnly suggests to you that it was death from        110
      wine,
exclaiming that Artemis killed her by the 'testimonies *of*
      *Dionysos,*'
that is, she died of acute illness from immoderate wine
      consumption.
   '*By the favor of the gods*' means by the wishes of Destiny.
   '*Zeus, the far sounding,*' is here Destiny itself,
which is loudmouthed and talked about by everyone.              115
   '*For the arms of Achilles; his honored mother had set them;*
*and the judges were the sons of the Trojans and Pallas Athena.*'
The decision about the arms happened near the sea.
You know the sea, how it is Achilles's mother.
The captive sons of the Trojans made the decision             120
along with Pallas Athena, the wisdom of the Greeks.
   '*The gods*' set before them '*misery*' means Destiny itself
and, similarly, '*Zeus who bore hatred against the army*' is
      Destiny.

'Καὶ Τιτυὸν εἶδον, Γαίης ἐρικυδέος υἱόν.'

125 Ὁ Τιτυὸς παῖς θυγατρὸς Ὀρχομενοῦ, Ἐλάρας,
τὴν ἣν ταφεῖσαν, ἔγκυον οὖσαν, ἀνατεμόντες
Καισάρων πάντων πρώτιστον τὸν Τιτυὸν ἐξῆξαν.
Ὅθε καὶ λέγουσιν, αὐτὸν γῆς παῖδα πεφυκέναι.
'Λητὼ γὰρ ἥλκησε, Διὸς κυδρὴν παράκοιτιν.'

130 Λητὼ καὶ νὺξ καὶ ὁ αἰθὴρ ἕν, σύνευνος ἀέρος.

131 Τὴν νύκτα πῶς δὲ Τιτυὸς ἦν τραυματίζων μάθε.

131a Ἐν ταῖς νυξί, τοῖς μέρεσιν ἐστὼς τοῦ Πανοπέως,

131b τοὺς ἐρχομένους εἰς Δελφοὺς ὑπῆρχε τραυματίζων.

132 Πάντας γοῦν ἁμαρτήσαντας ἀνθρώπους ἐν τῷ βίῳ
καὶ Ἕλληνες ἐδόξαζον ἐν Ἅιδου τιμωρεῖσθαι,
ὡς τοῦτόν τε καὶ Τάνταλον καὶ Σίσυφον σὺν τούτοις,

135 οὓς αἱμαντομαντείαις νῦν καὶ οὗτος ἰδεῖν λέγει.
Ἀρχιερεὺς καὶ ἄρχων δὲ ὁ Τάνταλος ὑπάρχων,
ζῶν τὰ θεῶν μυστήρια εἰπὼν ἐτιμωρήθη,
ἃ καὶ ἠλληγορήσαμεν, ὅπου ὑπῆρχε δέον.
Ἐν Ἅιδου δὲ κολάζεσθαι τοῦτόν φασι τοιῶσδε.

140 'Ζηνὸς μὲν παῖς' ὁ Ἡρακλῆς ὑπῆρχε, βασιλέως
καὶ ἀστρολόγου, μάντεως, μάγου, σοφοῦ τοῖς πᾶσι.
Πλείστους δεδμῆσθαι Εὐρυσθεῖ, κελεύει δ' ὁ Κρονίων,
ἡ Εἱμαρμένη προφανῶς, καὶ τοῦτο ἐατέον.
Τὸν Ἡρακλέος "Ἅιδην" δὲ νῦν ἀλληγορητέον.

145 Ἅιδης ὑπῆρχε βασιλεὺς τῆς Μολοσσίας χώρας.
Τούτῳ τὴν κλῆσιν Κέρβερος μέγας ὑπῆρχε κύων,
θυγάτηρ τε ὡραῖά τις ἦν, καλουμένη Κόρη,
ἣν ὁ Πειρίθους καὶ Θησεὺς μέλλοντες ἐφαρπάσαι.

'*And I saw Tityos, son of glorious Gaia.*'

Tityos was the son of Orchomenos's daughter, Elara,   125

whom, after he buried her while she was pregnant, they cut open

and took out the very first of all the "Caesarians," Tityos.

From which they say that he was the son of the earth.

'*For he had dragged about Leto, Zeus's glorious bedfellow.*'

Leto is one with the night and ether, bedfellow of air.   130

Learn how Tityos wounded the night.   131

At night, standing in the region of Panopeus,   131a

he used to wound those coming to Delphi.   131b

So the Greeks believed that all men who had sinned in life  132

would be punished in Hades,

such as him and Tantalos and with them Sisyphos, all of whom

he claims here that he saw himself through blood divination.  135

Tantalos, being the high priest and ruler, was punished

for revealing the mysteries of the gods while he was alive,

which we have allegorized, where it was necessary.

They say that he was punished in Hades in such a way.

'*The son of Zeus*' was Herakles, the son of a king   140

and an astrologer, a diviner, a mage, wise in all things.

Kronos's son ordered that many were to be enslaved to Eurystheus;

the son of Kronos is obviously Destiny, and this should be left alone.

Here the "Hades" of Herakles needs to be allegorized.

Hades was the king of the land of the Molossians.   145

He had a great dog called Kerberos;

he had a beautiful daughter, called Kore,

whom Peirithous and Theseus intended to snatch away.

Ὁ μὲν Πειρίθους βέβρωτο Κερβέρῳ τῷ ῥηθέντι·
150 Θησεύς, δεσμοῖς δὲ κρατηθείς, ἦν ἐν τοῖς Ἅιδου δόμοις.
Ὁ Ἡρακλῆς δέ, Εὐρυσθεῖ πρὸς Ἅιδην σταλεὶς τοῦτον,
σὺν ἑρμηνεῖ φρονήσει τε, ἃ ὁ "Ἑρμῆς,' 'Ἀθήνη,'
ἀνάγει καὶ τὸν Κέρβερον, ἀνάγει καὶ Θησέα.
Πρὸς τὴν ὁμωνυμίαν δὲ ὁ Ὅμηρος νῦν παίζων,
155 ταῖς Εὐρυσθέως προσταγαῖς τὸν Ἡρακλῆ τὸν μέγαν
πρὸς Ἅιδην ἀνυπόστροφον νῦν κατελθεῖν σοι λέγει.
  'Μὴ κεφαλήν μοι' τῆς Γοργοῦς ἡ Περσεφόνη πέμψῃ,
μὴ φόβον καὶ κατάπληξιν, καὶ τῶν φρενῶν ἐκσταίην.

Peirithous was devoured by the aforementioned Kerberos;
Theseus, bound in chains, was in the house of Hades.           150
Herakles, sent by Eurystheus to this Hades,
with his interpreter and his prudence, which are 'Hermes'
    and '*Athena,*'
led out Kerberos and led out Theseus as well.
Homer, here playing with homonymy, tells you
that by Eurystheus's commands the great Herakles           155
descended into Hades and did not come back.

   '*Lest*' Persephone send '*upon me the head*' of the Gorgon
means lest she send me fear and shock and I lose my mind.

# Μ′

Τῆς Μῦ δὲ ἡ ὑπόθεσις καὶ νοῦς ἐστι τοιόσδε.


Πρὸς Κίρκην Ὀδυσσεύς φησιν, ἃ κατεῖδεν εἰς Ἅιδην·
αὐτὴ προλέγει τούτῳ δέ, πῶς πλεύσει τὰς Σειρῆνας,
καὶ Σκύλλαν καὶ τὴν Χάρυβδιν καὶ τὰ βοῶν Ἡλίου,
ἀπώλειαν τῶν φίλων τε νηὸς κεραυνωθείσης,
5  πῶς τε σωθῇ πρὸς Καλυψῶ μόνος νηὸς ἐν ξύλῳ.

'Νῆσόν τ' Αἰαίην, ὅθι τ' Ἠοῦς ἠριγενείης
οἰκία καὶ χοροί εἰσι καὶ ἀντολαὶ Ἠελίοιο,'
ἤγουν οὗ φῶς καὶ ἥλιος, οὗ σκότος Κιμμερίων.
"Ὡς τοι ἐγὼν ἐρέω· μνήσει δέ σε καὶ θεὸς αὐτός,'
10  καὶ ἡ ψυχή σου δὲ αὐτὴ σέ ἀναμνήσει τούτων.
'Σειρῆνας μὲν πρῶτον ἀφίξεαι, αἵ ῥά τε πάντας.'
Αὗται πόρναι περίφημοι καὶ ᾠδικαὶ ὑπῆρχον,
καὶ πτοηθεὶς ὁ Ὀδυσσεύς, μὴ συσχεθῇ καὶ ταύταις,
τὰς πέντε τῶν αἰσθήσεων ἐμφράττει τὰς καὶ φίλους.
15  Οὐ γὰρ τὰ ὦτα ἔχρισεν ἑταίρων ἐν κηρίῳ,
τὸν νοῦν μετεωρίσας τε οὐκ ἐν ἱστῷ νηὸς δέ,
κρίσει δ' ἀρίστου λογισμοῦ παρέπλευσεν ἐκείνας.
'Πλαγκτὰς καλέουσι θεοί' νῦν τοὺς σοφούς μοι νόει.

# Book 12

The subject matter and the meaning of the
twelfth book is this.

Odysseus tells Kirke what he saw in Hades,
and she foretells to him how he will sail past the Sirens
and Skylla and Charybdis, and the events concerning the
      Cattle of the Sun,
the death of his friends when their ship is struck by
      lightning,
and how he will be saved by Kalypso, on a ship's timber.          5

   *The island of Aiaia, the abode of early Dawn*
*and her dancing lawns and the risings of the Sun*' means
where the light and sun are, and the darkness of the
      Kimmerians.
   '*As I shall tell you; and a god shall himself remind you*'
means that your soul itself will remind you of these things.          10
   '*To the Sirens first you shall come, who beguile all men.*'
These were very famous prostitutes, who played music,
and Odysseus, terrified lest he be detained by them,
blocked his five senses that are dear to him.
For he did not anoint his companions' ears with wax,          15
nor did he elevate his mind on the mast of the ship,
but sailed past them using the judgment of his excellent
      reasoning.
   '*The gods call them the Planktai*' means the wise men.

'Τῇ μέν τ' οὐδὲ ποτητὰ παρέρχεται οὐδὲ πέλειαι
20 τρήρωνες, ταί τ' ἀμβροσίην Διὶ πατρὶ φέρουσιν.'
Δοκῶ λέγειν τὸν Ὅμηρον ἐν τῷδε τῷ χωρίῳ,
μηδὲ τὸ ἄστρον φαίνεσθαι ἐκεῖσε τῶν Πλειάδων,
ὡς ἐν τῇ Ἐρυθρᾷ φησι πάλιν ὁ Ἀνταγόρας
αὐτῆς τῆς ἄρκτου μηδαμῶς τὸ ἄστρον καθορᾶσθαι.
25 Αἱ δὲ Πλειάδες σφῶν 'πατρὶ Διί,' τῷ οὐρανῷ δέ,
φέρουσιν ἤτοι ἔχουσι τήνδε τὴν 'ἀμβροσίαν,'
[ἢ φέρουσι παρέχουσι τήνδε τὴν ἀμβροσίαν]
σφῶν ἑσπερίᾳ δύσει μὲν σπόρου καιρὸν σημαίνειν,
ἀνατολαῖς ἑῴαις δὲ τὸ θέρος καταγγέλλειν.
30 Ἄλλην ἐνίησι πατήρ' ἤτοι ἡ Εἱμαρμένη.
'Ἀλλ' Ἥρη παρέπεμψεν, ἐπεὶ φίλος ἦεν Ἰήσων.'
Ἀὴρ δὲ τῷ Ἰάσωνι φίλος ἦν πνεύσας τότε.
'Ἔνθα δ' ἐνὶ Σκύλλῃ ναίει δεινὸν λελακυῖα.'
Σκύλλα δὲ ἀκρωτήριον περὶ τὴν Σικελίαν,
35 δύσπλουν τε καὶ ὀλέθριον τοῖς πλέουσιν ἐκεῖσε,
καὶ μιλιαίας ἓξ δειρὰς ἔχον ἐκτεταμένας,
ὑφάλους πέτρας τε πολλὰς καὶ συστροφὰς ῥευμάτων,
καὶ σάλον πρὸς αὐτὰς <ἀκτὰς> καὶ ῥόχθον τῶν κυμάτων.
Θηρία τε θαλάττια ἐκεῖσε περιπλέει,
40 ἃ φθειρομένων τῶν νηῶν τοὺς ἄνδρας κατεσθίει,
κἀκ τῶν ὁλκάδων δέ τινας πολλάκις ἁρπάζει.
Ἀνάγκη γοῦν τοὺς πλέοντας πρὸς τόσους τοὺς κινδύνους
ἢ προφανῶς καὶ καρτερῶς χρωμένους εἰρεσίαις,
τρεῖς μόνους ἢ καὶ τέσσαρας λιπεῖν ἐκ τῶν ἑταίρων,
45 ἐκπεπτωκότας τῷ σφοδρῷ, τῇ ῥύμῃ τῶν κυμάτων
βορὰν γενέσθαι τοῖς θηρσί, τοὺς δὲ λοιποὺς σωθῆναι,

'*Thereby not even birds may pass, no, not the timorous*
*doves that bear ambrosia to father Zeus.*'                                    20
I think that Homer is saying in this passage
that neither the constellation of the Pleiades appears there,
as Antagoras says again that in the Red Sea
the constellation of the bear can in no way be seen.
'The Pleiades bring,' that means they provide                               25
'to their father Zeus,' that is, to the sky, 'this ambrosia'
[or they bring 'this ambrosia' to those present]
to mark, by setting in the evening, the time for sowing
          seeds,
and to announce the harvest by rising at dawn.
     '*And the father Zeus sent in another one,*' that is, Destiny.    30
     '*But Hera sent her through, for Jason was dear to her.*'
The air was a friend to Jason, having blown then.
     '*Therein dwells Skylla, yelping terribly.*'
Skylla is a promontory in Sicily, dangerous
for ships and destructive to those sailing there,                           35
with mountain glens stretching for six miles,
and many submerged rocks and swirling currents,
swells rolling toward those <shores> and roaring waves.
Sea creatures swim around there, and devour
the crews, after their ships are destroyed,                                  40
and often snatch some of them from the ships.
So those who sailed toward so many dangers,
either clearly had to row with all their might,
and leave only three or four of their comrades behind,
who had fallen overboard in the ferocity and force of the            45
          waves,
to be devoured by the beasts, and for the rest to be saved,

ἢ ῥαθυμίᾳ σύμπαντας φθαρῆναι σὺν ὀλκάδι.
Τὰ τοῦ Σκυλλαίου τοιαδὶ μετέπεσε δ᾽ εἰς μῦθον.

Τῇ Σκύλλῃ οὐ 'γηθήσειεν' οὐδὲ 'θεὸς' ἀντήσει,
50 μεγάλως πτοηθείη τις οὐδ᾽ ἀβλαβῶς παρέλθοι
Σκύλλης τὸν πλοῦν, κἄνπερ σοφός, ὥς τέ φησι, τυγχάνῃ,
ἤτοι σοφὸς καὶ τελεστὴς καὶ ἐπῳδὸς καὶ μάγος.
'Οὐδὲ θεοῖς ὑπείξεαι·' Θεοὶ νῦν τὰ στοιχεῖα.
'Ἡ δέ τοι οὐ θνητή, ἀλλ᾽ ἀθάνατον κακόν ἐστι.'
55 Ἡ Σκύλλα ζῶον, Ὀδυσσεῦ, κύων θνητὸς οὐκ ἔστιν,
ἀλλὰ θαλάσσης μέρος τι ναυτιλλομένοις οἷον.
'Ἀλλὰ μάλα σφοδρῶς ἐλάαν, βωστρεῖν δὲ Κράταιιν,
μητέρα τῆς Σκύλλης, ἥ μιν τέκε πῆμα βροτοῖσιν.
Ἥ μιν ἔπειτ᾽ ἀποπαύσει ἐς ὕστερον ὁρμηθῆναι.'
60 Βλέπε νῦν γέροντος χρυσοῦ καὶ μελιχρὴν καρδίαν
καὶ ὀνομάτων πλάσματα. Θέλων εἰπεῖν γὰρ τῇδε,
ὡς "πρὸς τὴν Σκύλλαν πολεμεῖν, ὦ Ὀδυσσεῦ, οὐ δέον,
ἐν κραταιᾷ δυνάμει δὲ ναύταις βοᾶν, ἐλαύνειν,
οὕτω γὰρ ἂν ἐκφύγητε καὶ δεύτερον βλαβῆναι"
65 (ἡ κραταιὰ γὰρ δύναμις ἐτέκνωσε τὸ ῥεῦμα),
Σκύλλαν καὶ Κράταιίν φησι καὶ ταύτης παρακλήσεις,
καὶ ἐξ αὐτῆς ἀπόπαυσιν παιδὸς αὐτῆς, τῆς Σκύλλας.
'Θρινακίην δ᾽ ἐς νῆσον ἀφίξεαι· ἔνθα δὲ πολλαὶ
βόσκοντ᾽ Ἠελίοιο βόες καὶ ἴφια μῆλα,
70 ἑπτὰ βοῶν ἀγέλαι, τόσα δ᾽ οἰῶν πώεα καλά,
πεντήκοντα δ᾽ ἕκαστα· γόνος δ᾽ οὐ γίνεται αὐτῶν,
οὐδέ ποτε φθινύθουσι. Θεαὶ δ᾽ ἐπιποιμένες εἰσί.'

or all of them would have been lost along with the ship due
    to lack of effort.
Thus did the stories about the promontory of Skylla change
    into myth.
  Not even '*a god would rejoice*' if he were to meet Skylla
    face to face
means he would be terrified and would not sail around       50
Skylla unhurt, even if he were a wise man, as he says,
that is, a wise man, an initiate, an enchanter, and a mage.
  '*Will you not yield even to the gods?*' The gods here are the
    elements.
  '*She is not mortal, but an immortal bane.*'
Skylla is not an animal, O Odysseus, she is not a mortal dog,   55
but some place in the sea dangerous for seafarers.
  '*But row past with all your might, and call upon Krataiïs,*
*the mother of Skylla, who bore her as a bane to mortals.*
*Then she will keep her from darting forth again.*'
See here the honey-sweet heart of the golden old man      60
and the invention of names. For wishing to say in this way
that "one should not, O Odysseus, fight against Skylla,
but the sailors should shout forcefully and forge ahead,
for thus you would escape being harmed a second time"
(for the powerful force created the current),       65
he speaks of Skylla and Krataiïs and how to supplicate her,
and how she calms her daughter Skylla.
  '*And you will come to the isle Thrinakia. There in great*
    *numbers*
*graze the Cattle of the Sun and his fat flocks,*
*seven herds of cattle, and as many fair flocks of sheep,*   70
*and fifty in each. These bear no young,*
*nor do they ever die, and goddesses are their shepherds.*'

Τῇ Ἄλφα τῆς παρούσης νῦν βίβλου, τῆς Ὀδυσσείας,
τοὺς ἀροτῆρας ἔφημεν βόας Ἡλίου εἶναι.
75 Ἰστέον, ὡς καὶ βόας δὲ καὶ πρόβατα καὶ ἵππους
καὶ ἄπαν ζῷον ἕτερον καὶ ἄλση καὶ φυτὰ δέ
ἡλίῳ ἀνετίθεντο, ἀέρι καὶ τοῖς ἄλλοις.
Οὐδὲν τοιοῦτον ζῷον δέ τις ἀνελεῖν ἐτόλμα,
οὔτε τὸ ἄλσος δὲ τεμεῖν, ἀεὶ δὲ ἐτηροῦντο,
80 ἐν τῇ αὐτῇ ποσότητι τῶν στείρων πεφυκότα,
κἂν ἐτεθνήκει τι αὐτῶν, πάλιν ἀπεπληροῦτο.
Αἱ τῶν βοῶν ἀγέλαι δὲ Ἡλίου καὶ προβάτων
ἑπτὰ μὲν ἦσαν ἔχουσαι ἀνὰ πεντηκοντάδος,
καὶ φύλακα Φαέθουσαν ὁμοῦ καὶ Λαμπετίην,
85 εὐλόγῳ λόγῳ προσφυεῖ καὶ χρόνῳ καὶ ἡλίῳ.
Πεντήκοντα καὶ δύο γὰρ ἔτους αἱ ἑβδομάδες,
ποιητικοὶ δὲ ἀριθμοῖς ἀπηρτισμένοις χρῶνται.
Ἡμέραι δὲ πεφύκασι φρουρεῖν τὰς ἑβδομάδας,
αἱ ἑβδομάδες μῆνας δέ, μῆνες δὲ πληροῦν χρόνον,
90 κἂν μῆνας παραλέλοιπεν εἰπεῖν τῇ συντομίᾳ,
καὶ τῷ μὴ θέλειν φανερῶς δεῖξαι γυμνὸν τὸν μῦθον.
Ἐπεὶ τοῖς Ὀδυσσέως δὲ συμπέπτωκεν ἑταίροις
φαγοῦσι τούτων τῶν βοῶν, πάντας θανεῖν θαλάσσῃ,
ἐκτρέπων πάντας Ὅμηρος πράξεων τῶν ἀθέσμων,
95 τί οὐ ποιεῖ, τί οὐ λαλεῖ κινοῦν εἰς νουθεσίαν;
Φέρει καὶ γὰρ τὸν ἥλιον ἐν προσωποποιίᾳ,
ἀγανακτοῦντα περιττῶς, ζητοῦντα τιμωρίαν,
καὶ τῶν βοῶν τοῖς 'ὀβελοῖς μυκώμενα' 'τὰ κρέα,'

In the first book of the present volume, on the *Odyssey*,
we said that the cattle of the Sun are plow oxen.
It should be known that oxen, sheep, and horses          75
and every other animal and groves and plants
were dedicated to the sun, to the air, and the rest.
Nor did anyone dare to kill such an animal,
nor to chop down the groves, but always they were
      maintained,
as they grew in equal number to those without issue,      80
and should any of them die, it was always replaced again.
The herds of the oxen and sheep of the Sun
were seven, having fifty animals in each,
and had Phaethousa and Lampetie as guards,
in an eloquent story suitable to time and the sun.        85
For the weeks of the year are fifty-two,
and the poets use rounded numbers.
The days were formed to watch over the weeks,
the weeks to watch over the months, the months to
      complete the year,
even if he omitted to speak of the months due to          90
      conciseness,
and because he did not wish to manifestly lay bare the
      myth.
Since it happened that the companions of Odysseus
who ate these oxen all died at sea,
to avert everyone from unlawful deeds,
what did Homer not do or say to instruct and to warn      95
      them?
For he even introduces the sun in a personification,
as being exceedingly displeased and seeking punishment,
as '*the flesh*' of the oxen 'bellowed *on the spits*,'

καὶ 'καθερπούσας' βύρσας δὲ καὶ ἕτερα μυρία,
100 ἅπερ κολαστικώτερον ἂν εἶπε ῥήτωρ γράφων.
[Τοῖς ὀβελοῖς ἂν εἶπε τις μυκᾶσθαι τότε κρέα.]
'Ζεὺς' ὦσεν 'ἄνεμον' ζωὴν ὁ οὐρανὸς ἐνθάδε.
Σπηλαίῳ ἦσαν τὰ Νυμφῶν γλυφαὶ τῶν Νηρηΐδων.
'Ἡρώμην πάντεσσι θεοῖς' ἀέρι καὶ στοιχείοις.
105 'Ῥέξομεν ἀθανάτοισι' στοιχείοις, Εἱμαρμένῃ.
Ἕψονται 'ἄλλοι' δὲ 'θεοὶ' ἀστέρες ἢ στοιχεῖα.
'Ζεῦ πάτερ' ἤγουν ὦ ἀὴρ καὶ τὰ λοιπὰ στοιχεῖα·
ὁ γὰρ ἀὴρ καὶ τὸ ὑγρὸν εἴωθεν ὑποφέρειν.
Ἡ 'Λαμπετίη ἄγγελος' ἀπέρχεται Ἡλίῳ.
110 Ἑβδόμην 'Ζεὺς' ἐποίησεν, ὁ οὐρανός, ἡμέραν,
ἀποκατάστασις καὶ γὰρ τοῦ οὐρανοῦ ἡμέρα.
'Διὸς πληγεῖσα κεραυνῷ' νεφῶν τε καὶ ἀέρος.
Θεός, ἡ Εἱμαρμένη δέ, τὸν νόστον ἀφῃρεῖτο.
'Σκύλλην' ἐμὲ δὲ ὁ 'πατήρ,' ἤγουν ἡ Εἱμαρμένη,
115 'οὐκ εἴασε' θεάσασθαι· τί δὲ ἂν ἐθεάθης;
Ὁ πᾶς φόβος ἐν Σκύλλῃ γάρ, μὴ καταχθῇ τὸ πλοῖον,
καὶ οἱ πλωτῆρες ὕδασιν ἐμπέσωσι θαλάσσης.
Σὺ δὲ πεσὼν τί δέδοικας ἔτι λοιπὸν τὴν Σκύλλαν,
εἰ μή που φῇς πτοούμενος μὴ ἐντυχεῖν θηρίῳ;
120 Καὶ τὸ πεσεῖν εἰς θάλασσαν πᾶς φαίη δεινὸν λέγει.
Πρὸς τοῦτο τοῦτο δέ φημι· ὁ παίζων τῇδε γράφει,
ὅτι μετὰ τὴν ἔκπτωσιν, ἣν πέπτωκε θαλάσσῃ,
ὁ Ζεὺς ἐκεῖνον κατιδεῖν οὐκ εἴασε τὴν Σκύλλαν.
'Θεοὶ ἐς νῆσον πέλασαν ἤδη τὴν Ὠγυγίαν.'
125 Στοιχεῖα, θάλασσα αὐτὴ καὶ αἱ πνοαὶ ἀνέμων,
θεοὶ καὶ Εἱμαρμένη δὲ νοεῖται τοῖς ἐνθάδε.

and their hides 'crawled' and countless other such things,
which an orator would say while writing in a more minatory    100
    way.
[One would say that the flesh then bellowed on the spits.]
   '*Zeus*' roused the '*wind*' here means the sky roused life.
   In the cave were the carved seats of the Nereid Nymphs.
   '*I prayed to all the gods*' means to the air and the elements.
   '*Let us offer sacrifice to the immortals*' means to the    105
    elements, to Destiny.
   '*The other gods*' consent means the stars or the elements.
   '*Father Zeus,*' that is, O air and the other elements;
for the air and moisture are accustomed to provide support.
   '*Lampetie, a messenger,*' went away to the Sun.
   '*Zeus,*' the sky, created the seventh day,    110
for day is the restoration of the sky.
   '*Smitten by Zeus's bolt*' means by the clouds and the air.
God, that is, Destiny, hindered his homecoming.
   'My *father*' Zeus, that is, Destiny, 'did not allow *Skylla*'
to look at me: Why would you be seen?    115
For every fear is in Skylla, lest the ship be shattered,
and the sailors fall into the waters of the sea.
But after you fell, why then did you still fear Skylla,
unless you mean you are afraid to encounter a beast?
And to fall into the sea, everyone would say, he calls it    120
    terrible.
To this I say: Homer playfully writes in this way,
that after the shipwreck, when he fell in the sea,
Zeus did not allow Skylla to look upon him.
   '*The gods brought me to* the *island* of Ogygia.'
The elements, the sea itself, and the breezes of the winds,    125
mean the gods and Destiny here.

# N′

Αὕτη ἐστὶν ὑπόθεσις τοῦ Νῦ τῆς Ὀδυσσείας.

Μετὰ τῶν δώρων Φαίακες τὸν Ὀδυσσέα τῇδε
κοιμώμενον ἐξάγουσιν εἰς γῆν τὴν τῆς Ἰθάκης.
Τῷ δ᾽ ὑποστρέφειν Ποσειδῶν τούτων λιθοῖ τὴν νῆα.
Τῷ Ὀδυσσεῖ δὲ Ἀθηνᾶ κτεῖναι μνηστῆρας λέγει,
5   τὰ δ᾽ ἐκ Φαιάκων χρήματα τούτου σπηλαίῳ κρύπτει.
Αὐτὸν δὲ μετεμόρφωσεν ὥσπερ μορφὴν γερόντων.

   ‘Ζηνὶ κελαινεφέϊ᾽ δὲ ἄρτι τῇ Εἱμαρμένῃ.
   ‘Θεοὶ οἱ Οὐρανίωνες᾽ ὁμοίως Εἱμαρμένη
   καὶ τὸ ‘θεοὶ δὲ ἀρετὴν ὀπάσειαν᾽ ὡσαύτως.
10   ‘Διὶ πατρὶ᾽ ὁμοίως δέ· οἱ οὐρανοῦ θεοὶ δὲ
   δηλοῦσιν Εἱμαρμένην τε δηλοῦσι καὶ στοιχεῖα.
   ‘Ἄνδρα φέρουσα θεοῖς ἐναλίγκια μήδε᾽ ἔχοντα᾽
   ταῖς ψυχικαῖς δυνάμεσιν ὅμοιον καὶ ἀγχίνουν.
   ‘Ἱρὸν Νυμφάων αἳ Νηϊάδες καλέονται᾽
15   ὅσα φησὶν ἐν ἱερῷ τῷ τῶν νυμφῶν ᾧ λέγει.
   ‘Κρητῆρές τε καὶ ἀμφορεῖς, ἱστοί,᾽ πορφύρας φάρη,
   λιθόξεστα μιμήματα ἦσαν καὶ εἰκασίαι.
   ‘Αἱ μὲν πρὸς Βορέαο καταιβαταὶ ἀνθρώποισιν,
   αἱ δ᾽ αὖ πρὸς Νότου εἰσὶ θεώτεραι· οὐδέ τι κείνῃ
20   ἄνδρες ἐσέρχονται, ἀλλ᾽ ἀθανάτων ὁδός ἐστιν.᾽

# Book 13

This is the subject matter of the thirteenth book of
the *Odyssey.*

The Phaiakians send Odysseus off along with the gifts in
    this way,
as he was sleeping, to the land of Ithake.
On their return, Poseidon turns their ship to stone.
Athena tells Odysseus to kill the suitors,
and she hides his treasures from the Phaiakians in a cave.    5
She changed his appearance to make him look like an old
    man.

    '*To Zeus, god of the dark clouds*' here means to Destiny.
    '*The gods of heaven*' similarly means Destiny,
and so too '*may the gods grant you prosperity.*'
    '*To father Zeus*' similarly; the gods of heaven    10
signify Destiny and they signify the elements as well.
    '*Bearing a man the peer of the gods in counsel*'
means similar to them in spiritual powers and intelligent.
    '*Sacred to the Nymphs that are called Naiads*'
means everything in the nymph sanctuary of which he    15
    speaks.
There were '*mixing bowls and* jars, *looms,*' purple clothes,
stone-carved representations and likenesses.
    '*One entrance toward the North Wind, by which men go down,*
*while the other toward the South Wind is more sacred; nor do*
*men enter through it, for it is the way of the immortals.*'    20

Αἱ μὲν βαταὶ τυγχάνουσι τοῖς σύμπασιν ἀνθρώποις,
αἱ δέ εἰσι θεώτεραι καὶ ἱερέων μόνων.
῾Ὥπασαν οἴκαδ᾽ ἰόντι διὰ μεγάθυμον Ἀθήνην᾽
διὰ τὴν φρόνησιν αὐτοῦ δεδώκασι τὰ δῶρα.

25  ᾽Αὐτοὶ δ᾽ αὖτ᾽ οἰκόνδε πάλιν κίον· οὐδ᾽ ἐνοσίχθων
λήθετ᾽ ἀπειλάων, τὰς ἀντιθέῳ Ὀδυσῆϊ…᾽
Φαίακες δ᾽ ὑπεστρέφοντο δεινῇ τῇ τρικυμίᾳ,
ἐν πέτραις διεφθάρησαν ῥαγείσης τῆς ὁλκάδος.
Τὴν τρικυμίαν Ὅμηρος πλάττει δὲ Ποσειδῶνα

30  ὡς πρὸς τὸν Δία οὐρανόν, ἅπερ φησί, λαλοῦντα
καὶ Δία πάλιν πρὸς αὐτόν. Ἃ Ποσειδῶν δὲ λέγει·
"'ἀλλὰ σὸν αἰεὶ θυμὸν ὀπίζομαι ἠδ᾽ ἀλεείνω,'"
καλῶς φησιν· ἡ θάλασσα κλύδωνας γὰρ οὐκ ἔχει,
ἂν οὐρανός τε καὶ ἀὴρ τελῶσι τῶν νηνέμων.

35  Τὴν τῆς νηὸς ἀπώλειαν, ἣν ἔφη περὶ πέτρας,
καὶ πρὸς τοὺς Φαίακάς φησι φθόνον ἐκ Ποσειδῶνος,
ἀνθ᾽ ὧν ἐτέλουν ἄριστοι φθόνον ναυτιλλομένων.
Τὸ τῇ θαλάσσῃ νῆα δὲ ῥαισθῆναι τῶν Φαιάκων
καὶ μέγα ὄρος τούτων δὲ τὴν πόλιν γεγονέναι,

40  ἐκ παλαιῶν τοῖς Φαίαξιν ἠκούετο τῶν χρόνων.
Ἡ Ἀθηνᾶ τῷ Ὀδυσσεῖ ποιεῖ ἀορασίαν,
καὶ τὴν Ἰθάκην ἀγνοεῖ τὴν ἑαυτοῦ πατρίδα.
Τουτέστι χρόνον ἐς μακρὸν ἔκδημος ὢν Ἰθάκης
γνῶναι αὐτὴν οὐκ ἴσχυε φρονήσει τῇ οἰκείᾳ,

45  ἐζυγομάχει δὲ πολλά· διὸ καὶ κατηρᾶτο.
Ὁ ῾Ζεὺς ὁ ἱκετήσιος,᾽ ἤγουν ἡ Εἱμαρμένη,
ἣ τοῖς ἱκέταις βοηθεῖ, Φαίαξι δοίη βλάβας.
Ἦλθε σχεδὸν ἡ Ἀθηνᾶ δέμας ὁμοιωθεῖσα

The first entrance is for all people,
the other is more sacred and for priests alone.
   '*As he set out for home, thanks to greathearted Athena*'
means they gave him gifts on account of his prudence.
   '*Then they themselves returned home again. But the earth*        25
       *shaker*
*did not forget his threats against godlike Odysseus . . .*'
The Phaiakians were turned away by a terrible tempest,
they were killed when their ship shattered on the rocks.
Homer fashions the tempest into Poseidon,
speaking the words that Homer says to Zeus, that is, the        30
       sky,
and Zeus responding to him. This is what Poseidon says:
"'*but I ever dread and avoid your wrath,*'"
which is well said, for the sea does not have billows
if the sky and the air are calm and windless.
As for the ship's destruction, which he said happened on        35
       the rocks,
he calls it Poseidon's malice toward the Phaiakians,
meaning the nobles felt malice against them as they sailed.
   That the Phaiakian ship would be destroyed at sea
and their city would be turned into a great mountain,
had been known among the Phaiakians since ancient times.        40
Athena impaired Odysseus's vision
and he could not recognize his native land of Ithake.
That is, having been away from Ithake for a long time,
he was unable to recognize it through his own senses,
but struggled a lot; this is why he was cursing.        45
   'May *Zeus, the suppliant's god,*' that is, Destiny,
which helps suppliants, harm the Phaiakians.
Athena drew near, in form resembling

νέῳ παιδὶ καὶ τρυφερῷ ποιμνίων ἐπιστάτῃ.
50  Νῦν Ἀθηνᾶν καὶ φρόνησιν ὁ Ὅμηρός σοι λέγει
ἐκεῖνο τὸ παιδάριον, ὃ ἔνεμε τὴν ποίμνην.
Ἐκεῖνο πάντα γὰρ λεπτῶς εἰπὸν πρὸς Ὀδυσσέα
τὴν ἄνοιαν ἐσκέδασεν, ἣν εἶχε τῆς πατρίδος,
καὶ ὥσπερ κατεφρένωσε τὸν πρὶν ἠγνοηκότα.
55  ‛Ὣς φατο, μείδησεν δὲ θεὰ γλαυκῶπις Ἀθήνη,
χειρί τέ μιν κατέρεξε· δέμας δ᾽ ἤϊκτο γυναικί.’
Ὡς ἀκριβῶς ἐπέγνωκεν ἅπαν ἐκ τοῦ ποιμένος,
ἐμμειδιᾷ ἐν τῇ φρενὶ τῇ ἑαυτοῦ, Ἀθήνῃ·
ὁμαλισθεὶς μὲν τῇ ᾽χειρί᾽ καὶ πρακτικῶς νοήσας,
60  ὁπόσον ἔχρῃζε μαθεῖν, ἵνα διττολογήσω
χρήζων Ὁμήρου παίγνια σαφῶς σοι παρεστάναι.
Τὸ ᾽γυναικί᾽ δὲ ᾽ἤϊκτο᾽ ᾽καλῇ τε καὶ μεγάλῃ᾽
᾽καὶ ἀγλαὰ᾽ δὲ καὶ λαμπρὰ ἐπισταμένη ᾽ἔργα᾽
τοῦτο σημαίνει προφανῶς, ὡς ἀγνοῶν ἦν πρῶτον.
65  Ἐκ τοῦ παιδὸς δὲ διδαχθεὶς ἠκριβωμένως ἔγνω
καὶ σφῶν εἴκασε φρόνησιν τῷ συνεργῷ γυναίῳ,
ἤτοι πάλιν κατήρξατο πανουργιῶν ὡς πρώην.
Ὅσα δὲ πλάττει Ἀθηνᾶν λέγουσαν Ὀδυσσῇϊ,
αὐτὸς αὑτῷ ὁ Ὀδυσσεὺς νῷ τῷ οἰκείῳ λέγει.
70  “Πανοῦργος καὶ ᾽ἐπίκλοπος,᾽ ὅς με νικήσει δόλοις,
κἄνπερ θεός τις καὶ σοφός, ὃς ἀντιστάς μοι εἴη·
ἐγὼ γὰρ πράξεσι χειρῶν ἀνθρώπους ὑπερτρέχω,
φρόνησις δέ μου συμβουλαῖς φρονήσεις τὰς τῶν ἄλλων.
Ἀλλά γε δὴ βουλεύσομαι κρύψιν ἐμῶν χρημάτων·”
75  καὶ τὰ λοιπὰ δὲ σύμπαντα τί δεῖ λεπτολογεῖν με;

a young, delicate boy, keeper of the flocks.
Here Homer tells you that that young boy who grazed          50
the flock was Athena, that is, wisdom.
For he, having told Odysseus everything in detail,
dispelled his ignorance of his native land, as if
instilling wisdom in the man who was previously ignorant.

   '*So he spoke, and the goddess, flashing-eyed Athena, smiled,*          55
*and stroked him with her hand and changed her form to a*
      *woman.*'
This means that when he accurately learned everything
      from the shepherd,
he smiled in his own mind, that is, Athena;
caressed by '*her hand*' means having thought practically
as much as he needed to understand, that I may say it twice,          60
because I need to show you clearly Homer's ploys.

   '*She changed herself into a woman, beautiful and tall*'
'*and*' skilled in '*splendid*' and radiant '*handiwork*'
clearly means this, that he was formerly ignorant.
Having been instructed by the boy, he learned accurately          65
and he guessed the purpose of these things with the
      woman's help,
that is, he started again his scheming as before.
The things Homer makes Athena tell Odysseus,
Odysseus himself tells to his own mind.

   "He is clever and '*wily*' who will beat me with cunning,          70
even if it is some god, that is, a wise man, who would oppose
      me;
for I surpass men in the deeds done by hand,
and my wisdom surpasses the wisdom of others in counsel.
But I will devise the concealment of my treasure";
and what need is there for me to speak about all the rest in          75
      detail?

'Ἀλλά τοι οὐκ ἐθέλησα Ποσειδάωνι μάχεσθαι
πατροκασιγνήτῳ, ὅς τοι κότον ἔνθετο θυμῷ,
χωόμενος ὅτι οἱ υἱὸν φίλον ἐξαλάωσας.'
Οὐκ ἐβοήθησε, φησί, φρόνησίς μοι θαλάσσῃ,
80 ἥσπερ θαλάσσης, τῆς ὀργῆς, πεῖραν ἐσχήκειν πόσην
τοῦ νησιώτου καὶ παιδὸς Κύκλωπος τῆς θαλάσσης
τὸν ὀφθαλμὸν τετυφλωκώς, ἀφῃρηκὼς τὴν παῖδα
καὶ ἐμβραδύνων δι' αὐτὴν παρὰ καιρόν τε πλεύσα
καὶ τὰς μυρίας ὑποστὰς ἐκείνας περιστάσεις.
85 Σικελικὸν γὰρ πέλαγος παρὰ καιρὸν οὐ πλεῖται,
ὡς σύμπαν ἄλλο πέλαγος, πάντων δὲ τοῦτο πλέον.
Πῶς δὲ πατροκασίγνητον λέγει τὸν Ποσειδῶνα
τῆς Ἀθηνᾶς φρονήσεως, τοῦτο τανῦν λεκτέον.
Μετάβασις ὀνόματος τοῦτο ἐστὶ τὸ σχῆμα.
90 Ζεὺς γὰρ ὁ Κρήτης βασιλεύς, ὁ οὐρανὸς ὁ νοῦς τε
καὶ ἕτερα μυρία δέ· ἀλλ' οὐρανοῦ Διὸς μέν,
ὃς Ζεὺς θαλάσσης ἀδελφός, ἀὴρ Ἀθήνη τέκνον.
Διὸς νοὸς θυγάτηρ δὲ ἡ φρόνησις Ἀθήνη
καὶ ταύτης δὲ πατράδελφος ὁ Ποσειδῶν θυμός τε.
95 Νῦν δὲ τὴν θάλασσάν φησι πατράδελφον φρονήσει
ὀνόματος, ὡς ἔφημεν, χρώμενος μεταβάσει.
    'Ἀλλ' ἄγε τοι δείξω Ἰθάκης ἔδος, ὄφρα πεποίθῃς.
Φόρκυνος μὲν ὅδ' ἐστὶ λιμήν, ἁλίοιο γέροντος.'
Ὁ Ὀδυσσεὺς τῷ λογισμῷ ἔτι παρυποσκάζων
100 καὶ μὴ δοκῶν ἐν τῇ αὐτοῦ πατρίδι πεφυκέναι,
ἀπὸ λιμένος, δένδρων τε σπηλαίων καὶ Νηρίτου
πᾶν ἐπιγνοὺς ἀπέβαλε τὴν πρὶν ἀγνοησίαν.

'*Yet, you must know, I did not wish to strive against Poseidon,*
*my father's brother, who laid up wrath in his heart against you,*
*angered that you blinded his dear son.*'
He means, my wisdom did not help me at sea,
of which sea, that is, of wrath, I have had so much                    80
    experience,
having blinded the eye of Cyclops, the islander and son
of the sea, having snatched his daughter
and, because of her, moving slowly and sailing out of season,
having endured those countless circumstances.
For the Sicilian sea cannot be sailed out of season,                   85
just like every other sea, but this one more than all the
    others.
Why he calls Poseidon the paternal uncle
of Athena, that is, of wisdom, needs to be explained here.
This figure of speech is name transition.
For Zeus is the king of Crete, the sky and mind,                       90
and countless other things; but the air, that is Athena, is the
    child
of the sky, that is Zeus, and Zeus is the brother of the sea.
The daughter of Zeus, that is, mind, is Athena, that is,
    wisdom,
and her paternal uncle is Poseidon, that is, anger.
Here he calls the sea wisdom's paternal uncle,                         95
using, as we said, name transition.
  '*But come, I will show you the land of Ithake, that you may be*
    *sure.*
*This is the harbor of Phorkys, the old man of the sea.*'
Odysseus was still lagging behind in his reasoning
and not realizing that he was in his own fatherland,                   100
but recognizing everything from the harbor, the trees,
the caves, and Neriton, he shed his previous ignorance.

'Ὣς εἰποῦσα θεὰ δῦνε σπέος ἠεροειδές,
μαιομένη κευθμῶνας ἀνὰ σπέος· αὐτὰρ Ὀδυσσεὺς
105 ἆσσον πάντ᾽ ἐφόρει, χρυσὸν καὶ ἀτειρέα χαλκόν…'
Ἡ Ὀδυσσέως φρόνησις ἐφεῦρε τοῦς κευθμῶνας,
αὐτὸς δ᾽αὑτοῦ τῷ σώματι φέρων ἐτίθει ταῦτα.
'Οἳ δή τοι τρίετες μέγαρον κάτα κοιρανέουσι'
ταῦτα ἠκούετο γραφαῖς ἢ ὁ ποιμὴν εἰρήκει.
110 'Ὤ πόποι, ἦ μάλα δὴ Ἀγαμέμνονος Ἀτρεΐδαο'
ταῦτα εἰς νοῦν βαλλόμενος δεινοπαθεῖ καὶ λέγει·
"θάνατον Ἀγαμέμνονος κἀγὼ ἂν ἐτεθνήκειν,
εἰ μὴ φρονήσει τῇ ἐμῇ πᾶν ἐρωτήσας ἔγνων."
Ταῦτα εἰπὼν καὶ συγκαμφθεὶς ἐπενδυθείς τε ῥάκη
115 εἰς τὸ συβώσιον αὐτοῦ πρὸς Εὔμαιον ἱκνεῖται,
ἔστ᾽ ἂν καὶ ὁ Τηλέμαχος ὑπέστρεψεν ἐκ Σπάρτης
φρονήσει καὶ μηνύμασι Μέντορος καὶ τῶν ἄλλων.

'*So saying, the goddess entered the shadowy cave*
*and searched out its hiding places. And Odysseus brought*
*all the treasure there, the gold and the stubborn bronze . . .*'     105
Odysseus's wisdom found the hiding place,
himself carrying these with his own body, he placed them
    there.
  '*Who now for three years have been lording it in your halls*'
means he learned this from letters or the shepherd told
    him.
  '*Alas, surely Agamemnon, son of Atreus*'     110
means tossing these things about in his mind, he suffers
    terribly and says:
"I would have suffered the death of Agamemnon as well,
if I had not learned everything, having asked my own
    wisdom."
So saying and bending his knees, he put on rags
and went to Eumaios, to his own pigsty,     115
and it would be there that Telemachos also returned from
    Sparta
because of the wisdom and messages of Mentor and the
    others.

Ξ′

Αὕτη τῆς Ξῑ ὑπόθεσις Ὁμήρου Ὀδυσσείας.

Ὁ Ὀδυσσεὺς ῥακενδυτῶν ὡς πένης ἀφικνεῖται
τοῖς συβωσίοις ἑαυτοῦ πρὸς Εὔμαιον συβώτην
καὶ Κρὴς εἶναι πλασάμενος πόσους ἐνείρει λόγους
διήγησιν τῶν πράξεων δῆθεν αὐτοῦ τελοῦντας.

5   'Αὐτὰρ ὁ ἐκ λιμένος προσέβη τρηχεῖαν ἀταρπὸν
χῶρον ἀν' ὑλήεντα δι' ἀκρίας, ᾗ οἱ Ἀθήνη,'
ὅπου αὐτὸν τὸ φρόνημα προὔτρεψε τὸ οἰκεῖον.
'Ἀντίθεοι μνηστῆρες' δὲ θεοῖς μεμισημένοι.
'Ἄλγεα δόσαν οἱ θεοὶ' ἀστέρες, Εἱμαρμένη.

10  'Ζεύς τοι δοίη, ξεῖνε, καὶ ἀθάνατοι θεοὶ ἄλλοι.'
Ὁ Ζεύς, ὁ πλάνης δὲ ἀστήρ, καὶ οἱ λοιποὶ ἀστέρες,
ἤγουν ἡ Εἱμαρμένη σοι πᾶν, ὅπερ θέλεις, δοίη.
Τὸ 'πρὸς Διὸς' δὲ ὁμοίως τῆς Εἱμαρμένης λέγει.
'Θεοὶ νόστον κατέδησαν,' 'θεὸς ἔργον αὐξάνει'

15  τὴν Εἱμαρμένην νόησον ἀμφότερα νῦν λέγειν.
Θεοὶ καὶ Ζεὺς ὡς τὰ λοιπὰ φασιν τὴν Εἱμαρμένην.
'Θεοῦ δὲ ἔκλυον αὐδὴν' ὡς ἐν τῇ συνηθείᾳ
οὐδὲ τό, τί ἐστι θεός, ἴσασι κἂν ἐν λόγῳ.

# Book 14

This is the subject matter of the fourteenth book of
Homer's *Odyssey.*

Odysseus, dressed in rags like a beggar, arrives
at his own pigsty, at the house of Eumaios his swineherd
and, pretending to be a Cretan, he strings together many
    tales,
which are supposedly the narration of his deeds.

   *'But Odysseus went forth from the harbor by the rough path*     5
*up over the woodland and through the heights to the place where*
    *Athena,'*
that is, his own wisdom, urged him to go.
    The *'suitors, hostile to the gods'* means those hated by the
    gods.
    'The *gods have given much grief'* means the stars, Destiny.
    *'Stranger, may Zeus and the other immortal gods grant you.'*     10
May Zeus, the wandering star, and the rest of the stars,
that is, Destiny, grant you everything you wish.
    With *'from Zeus'* he similarly means from Destiny.
    'The *gods* have hindered the *return,'* 'the *god* makes the
    *labor* to prosper,'
you should understand that here both mean Destiny.     15
The gods and Zeus mean Destiny, like all the rest.
    *'They heard some voice of a god'* means what it normally
    means
but they did not even know what a god is logically.

Νῦν τὸ 'θεοῦ' πλὴν τοῦ σοφοῦ καὶ βασιλέως μόνου
20 τὰς σημασίας τοῦ 'θεὸς' τὰς τρεῖς δηλοῖ τὰς ἄλλας,
στοιχεῖα καὶ ἀστέρας δὲ αὐτῆς τῆς Εἱμαρμένης,
τὰς ψυχικὰς δυνάμεις τε, τὸ δίκαιον καὶ τἄλλα.
'Ζεὺς οἶδεν ἄλλοι τε θεοὶ' πάλιν ἡ Εἱμαρμένη.
'Ἴστω νῦν Ζεὺς πρῶτα θεῶν ξενίη τε τράπεζα.'
25 Ζεὺς οὐρανὸς ἢ ἥλιος, θεῶν δὲ τῶν στοιχείων.
'Τὸν ὂν ἐθρέψαντο θεοὶ' στοιχεῖα, Εἱμαρμένη.
'Τῶν ἀθανάτων ἔβλαψέ τις δὲ τὰς φρένας' πάλιν
ἡ Εἱμαρμένη δυστυχὴς ἢ καὶ κακοβουλία.
'Χεῖρα Κρονίων' δὲ διδοὺς ἄδηλος Εἱμαρμένη.
30 Καὶ τὸ 'θεῶν ἰότητι' βουλῇ τῆς Εἱμαρμένης
ἢ βλάβη καὶ τοξεύμασιν αὐτῆς τῆς Εἱμαρμένης.
Τὸ δὲ 'θεὸς ὣς τίετο' ὡς ἥλιος ἀὴρ τε.
'Θάρσος,' φησί, 'μοὶ ἔδοσαν ὁ Ἄρης καὶ Ἀθήνη,'
θυμός τε καὶ ἡ φρόνησις, δόλοι καὶ πανουργίαι,
35 εἴτ' οὖν πολέμων ἄσκησις σὺν ἅμα τῇ φρονήσει
φίλα φρεσὶν ἐποίησαν· θεοὶ ἡ Εἱμαρμένη.
Ὁ 'Ζεύς' τε ὁ 'εὐρύοπα' ὁμοίως Εἱμαρμένη,
ἡ πᾶσι περιθρύλλητος καὶ πᾶσι βοωμένη.
Τίς δ' ὁ ἐν νήεσι 'θεὸς' τοὺς Ἀχαιοὺς σκεδάσας;
40 Ἀὴρ ἀνέμους χαλεποὺς ἐκείνοις ἐπιπνεύσας.
'Ζεὺς' δὲ 'μητίετα' ὁ νοῦς ἢ καὶ ἡ Εἱμαρμένη.
'Ῥέζειν θεοῖς' στοιχείοις τε καί γε τῇ Εἱμαρμένῃ.
Ὁ 'Ζεὺς' ὁ 'τερπικέραυνος,' 'Ζεὺς' δὲ 'φρεσὶ ποιήσας'
καὶ Ζεὺς ὁ 'ξείνιος' ὁμοῦ εἰσιν ἡ Εἱμαρμένη.

Here '*of a god,*' apart from the wise man and the king alone,
signifies the other three meanings of 'god':                           20
the elements and the stars of Destiny itself,
the powers of the soul, justice, and the like.
   'Zeus and *the other gods know*' is Destiny again.
   '*Let Zeus above all the gods now be my witness, and this
      hospitable board.*'
Zeus is the sky or the sun, the gods means the elements.               25
   'The *gods* nourished him,' that is, the elements, Destiny.
   '*Some one of* the *immortals* harmed his *mind*' again
means a Destiny of misfortune or evil counsel.
   '*The son of Kronos*' giving '*his hand*' means an unknowable
      Destiny.
And '*by the gods' will*' means by Destiny's counsel                   30
or by the harm and the arrows of Destiny itself.
   '*Honored as a god*' means as the sun and the air.
   '*Courage,*' he says, '*Ares and Athena gave me,*'
that is, anger and wisdom, cunning and scheming,
or the practice of war together with wisdom                           35
did things pleasing to the heart; the gods are Destiny.
   '*Zeus*' the '*far sounding*' similarly is Destiny,
which is famous to all and acclaimed by everyone.
   But who is the '*god*' who scattered the '*Achaians*' in their
      ships?
The air that blew harsh winds upon them.                              40
   '*Zeus, the counselor,*' is the mind or even Destiny.
   '*To sacrifice to the gods*' means to the elements and to
      Destiny.
   '*Zeus who hurls thunderbolts,*' '*Zeus*' who 'put it in his
      thoughts'
and Zeus the protector of 'strangers' similarly is Destiny.

45 Καὶ 'Ζεὺς' ἐβούλετ' 'ὄλεθρον' ὁμοίως Εἱμαρμένη.

'Κρονίων' ἐστιν οὐρανὸς ὁ στήσας τὴν 'νεφέλην'

καὶ 'Ζεὺς' ὁμοίως οὐρανὸς ὁ 'ἄμυδις βροντήσας.'

'Θεὸς' δ' ὃς 'νόστον' αἴνυτο καὶ 'Ζεὺς ἱστὸν' ὁ δοὺς δὲ

ἕτερον οὐ δηλοῦσι τι, ἀλλὰ τὴν Εἱμαρμένην.

50 'Τὸν δ' ἐς Δωδώνην φάτο βήμεναι, ὄφρα θεοῖο

ἐκ δρυὸς ὑψικόμοιο Διὸς βουλὴν ἐπακούσῃ'

ὄφρα βουλὴν <ἀκούσειεν> Διός, τῆς Εἱμαρμένης,

ἢ ὄφρα ἔκ τινος θεοῦ σοφοῦ καὶ χρησμολόγου

Διὸς βουλὴν ἀκούσειεν, ἤτοι τῆς Εἱμαρμένης.

55 'Δεσμὸν ἀνέγναμψαν θεοὶ' καὶ 'ἔκρυψαν θεοί' με

καὶ 'ἤχθετο θεοῖσί' τε καὶ 'ἤγαγεν ὁ δαίμων'

ὁμοίως πάντα νόει μοι δηλοῦν τὴν Εἱμαρμένην.

'Μάρτυροι ἀμφοτέροις δὲ θεοὶ' οἱ τοῦ Ὀλύμπου

ὁ Οὐρανός, ὁ Ἥλιος, ἡ φύσις τῶν ἀστέρων.

60 Τὸ 'Δία δὲ Κρονίωνα προφρόνως ἱκετεύσω'

τὴν Εἱμαρμένην δὲ δηλοῖ, ἥλιον οὐρανόν τε,

ἤτοι "πῶς ἀνατείνοιμι εἰς οὐρανὸν τὰς χεῖρας

πᾶσι θεοῖς," στοιχείοις τε, φησί, καὶ Εἱμαρμένη.

'Τὴν μὲν ἴαν νύμφῃσι καὶ Ἑρμῇ, Μαιάδος υἱεῖ.'

65 Νύμφαι τὰ ὕδατά εἰσι καὶ δένδρων εὐκαρπίαι,

Ἑρμῆς ἀστὴρ λυσιτελῶν ζώοις καὶ ἐμπορίαις.

'Φίλος' ἀκούων δὲ 'Διι' καὶ τὸ 'θεός' σοι 'δώσει'

τὴν Εἱμαρμένην λέγουσι, 'θεοῖς' δ' αἰειγενέταις

τὴν Εἱμαρμένην δὲ δηλοῖ καὶ τὰ στοιχεῖα πάντα.

70 Ὁ 'Ζεὺς' ὁ βρέχων 'πάννυχος' ὁ οὐρανὸς τυγχάνει.

And 'Zeus' devised 'destruction' similarly is Destiny.                45
  'The son of Kronos' is the sky, the maker of 'cloud,'
and 'Zeus' who 'thundered at the same time' is likewise the
      sky.
  'The god' who took away their 'homecoming' and 'Zeus' who
      gave 'the mast'
mean nothing else except Destiny.
  'He said he had gone to Dodona, to hear                            50
the will of Zeus from the high-crested oak of the god'
means, so that <he may hear> the will of Zeus, of Destiny,
or hear the will of Zeus, that is, of Destiny,
from some god, that is, some wise man and diviner.
  'The gods undid my bonds' and 'the gods hid me'                    55
and 'he was hated by the gods' and 'a god has brought'
likewise you should understand from me that they all mean
      Destiny.
  'The gods' on Olympos shall be 'witnesses for us both'
means the Sky, the Sun, the nature of the stars.
  "I will supplicate 'Zeus, the son of Kronos' willingly"           60
means Destiny, the sun and the sky,
that is, "how I might stretch my hands up to the sky
to all the gods," means to the elements and to Destiny.
  'For the Nymphs and for Hermes, son of Maia.'
The Nymphs are the waters and the fruitfulness of the               65
      trees,
Mercury is the star advantageous to animals and commerce.
  Hearing 'dear to Zeus' and the 'god will give' you,
they mean Destiny; 'to the gods that are forever,'
signifies Destiny and all the elements.
  'Zeus' raining 'the whole night through' is the sky.              70

# Ο′

Τοῦ Ο′ νῦν τὴν ὑπόθεσιν μάθε τῆς Ὀδυσσείας.

Παρὰ τὴν Λακεδαίμονα ἡ Ἀθηνᾶ ἐλθοῦσα
προτρέπει τὸν Τηλέμαχον ἀπάραι πρὸς Ἰθάκην.
Καὶ δὴ δῶρα δεξάμενος παρὰ τοῦ Μενελάου
σὺν τῷ υἱῷ τοῦ Νέστορος ἄπεισι Πεισιστράτῳ.
5  Καὶ δὴ Πεισίστρατος αὐτὸς περὶ τὴν ναῦν κομίσας
ἄγει τὸ ἅρμα τῷ πατρί, Τηλέμαχος δ᾽ εὐθέως
λαβὼν καὶ Θεοκλύμενον τὸν μάντιν ἀποπλέει·
ἦν δ᾽ οὗτος φόνον δεδρακὼς καὶ ἱκετεύσας τοῦτον.
Τῷ Ὀδυσσεῖ δ᾽ ὁ Εὔμαιος ἀνερωτῶντι λέγει
10  πατρίδα, γένος καὶ γονεῖς καὶ πῶς ἠνδραποδίσθη.

*'Η δ᾽ εἰς εὐρύχορον Λακεδαίμονα Παλλὰς Ἀθήνη*
*ᾤχετ᾽, Ὀδυσσῆος μεγαθύμου φαίδιμον υἱὸν*
*νόστου ὑπομνήσουσα καὶ ὀτρυνέουσα νέεσθαι.'*
Μέντωρ ὁ φρονιμώτατος μήνυμα ἢ καὶ γράμμα
15  στείλας εἰς Λακεδαίμονα Τηλέμαχον προτρέπει
παλινδρομῆσαι τάχιστα πρὸς τὴν αὐτοῦ πατρίδα,
πῶς τε καὶ ποίῳ τρόπῳ δὲ πάντα λεπτολογήσας.
*'Θεοὶ κυδρὴν παράκοιτιν' τανῦν ἡ Εἰμαρμένη.*

# Book 15

Learn the subject matter of the fifteenth book of
the *Odyssey*.

Athena, coming to Lakedaimon,
urges Telemachos to sail away to Ithake.
And having received gifts from Menelaos,
he departs with Nestor's son, Peisistratos.
Indeed Peisistratos, having brought them to the ship     5
    himself,
drives the chariot to his father; Telemachos, immediately
receiving Theoklymenos the seer, sails away;
he had committed murder and had supplicated him.
Eumaios answers Odysseus, who had asked him
about his fatherland, his family, and parents, and how he     10
    was enslaved.

   *'But Pallas Athena went to spacious Lakedaimon*
*to remind the glorious son of greathearted Odysseus*
*of his need to return, and to hasten his coming.'*
That is, Mentor, the most wise, having sent a message or a
    letter
to Lakedaimon, urged Telemachos     15
to return as quickly as possible to his fatherland,
explaining everything in detail, how and in what way.
   *'The gods* send you *a noble bride'* here means Destiny.

"'Πέμψει δὲ οὖρον ὄπισθέ τις ἐκ τῶν ἀθανάτων,'
20 ὅστις ἐστὶ φυλάττων· δέ, ἤτοι τῇ εὐμοιρίᾳ,
ἀνέμου οὔρου πνεύσαντος πλέων ἐνταῦθα χώρει."
'Ἡ μὲν ἄρ' ὣς εἰποῦσ' ἀπέβη πρὸς μακρὸν Ὄλυμπον'
ὁ ἐκ τοῦ Μέντορος αὐτοῦ σταλεὶς τῷ Τηλεμάχῳ
τὸ γράμμα δοὺς ἢ καὶ εἰπὼν ὅσαπερ παρηγγέλθη,
25 ἀπέδραμε πρὸς Ὄλυμπον καὶ λογισμὸν οἰκεῖον
ἤτοι Τηλέμαχον, παρεὶς ἐσκόπει τὰ οἰκεῖα.
'Τηλέμαχ', ἤ τοι νόστον, ὅπως φρεσὶ σῇσι μενοινᾷς,
ὥς τοι Ζεὺς τελέσειεν, ἐρίγδουπος πόσις Ἥρης.'
Ζεὺς νῦν ὁ οὐρανός ἐστιν, ὁ σύζυγος αἰθέρος,
30 ἀντὶ τοῦ "εἴθε πνεύσειέ σοι προσφιλὴς ἀήτης."
'Ἦ νῶϊν τόδ' ἔφηνε θεὸς τέρας ἦε σοὶ αὐτῷ·'
θεὸς στοιχεῖον, οὐρανὸς εἴτε καὶ Εἰμαρμένη.
'Κλῦτέ μευ· αὐτὰρ ἐγὼ μαντεύσομαι, ὡς ἐνὶ θυμῷ
ἀθάνατοι βάλλουσι καὶ ὡς τελέεσθαι ὀΐω.'
35 Ἀθάνατοι μὲν νῦν εἰσιν αἱ ψυχικαὶ δυνάμεις,
ὁ νοῦς καὶ ἡ διάνοια καὶ λογισμὸς σὺν τούτοις.
'Οὕτω νῦν Ζεὺς θείη, ἐρίγδουπος πόσις Ἥρης·
τῷ κέν τοι καὶ κεῖθι θεῷ ὣς εὐχετοῴμην.'
Ὁ Ζεύς ἐστιν ὁ οὐρανός, ὁ σύζυγος αἰθέρος,
40 'θεῷ δὲ ὣς' ὡς οὐρανῷ εἴτε μὴν τῷ ἡλίῳ.
'Υἱέος Ὀρτιλόχοιο, τὸν Ἀλφειὸς τέκε παῖδα.'
Ἄνθρωπός τις ὁ Ἀλφειὸς πατὴρ ἦν Ὀρτιλόχου·
ἐκ τούτου δὲ καὶ ποταμὸς Ἀλφειὸς ἐκλήθη.
'Ἦ τοι ὁ μὲν τὰ πονεῖτο καὶ εὔχετο, θῦε δ' Ἀθήνῃ'
45 εὔχετο τῇ Ἀθήνῃ δέ, τοῦτ' ἔστι τῷ ἀέρι,
ἄνεμον οὔριον νηΐ εὐχόμενος γενέσθαι.

"'*One*' of the '*immortals* who protects you,' that is, with
   good fate
'*will send a fair breeze behind you,*'                                     20
and with a favorable wind blowing, sail forth thither."
   '*So saying, she departed to high Olympos*'
means the man sent to Telemachos from Mentor,
after giving the letter or just saying what he was instructed,
ran back up to Olympos, and his own reasoning,                              25
that is, Telemachos, standing by, considered his
   circumstances.
   '*Telemachos, may Zeus, the loud-thundering lord of Hera,*
*bring to pass for you your return, as your heart desires.*'
Zeus here is the sky, the husband of ether,
instead of saying "may a well-disposed wind blow for you."                  30
   '*Whether it was for us two that the god showed this sign, or for*
      *yourself*'
here the god is an element, the sky or even Destiny.
   '*Hear me, and I will prophesy as the immortals put it*
*into my heart, and as I think it will be brought to pass.*'
The immortals here are the powers of the soul,                              35
intelligence, thoughtfulness, and reason alongside them.
   '*So may Zeus grant, the loud-thundering lord of Hera;*
*then will I even there ever pray to you, as to a god.*'
Zeus is the sky, the husband of ether;
'*as to a god*' means as to the sky or indeed to the sun.                   40
   '*Of the son of Ortilochos, whom Alpheios begot.*'
Alpheios was a man, the father of Ortilochos;
the river Alpheios was named after him.
   '*He verily was busied thus, and was praying and sacrificing to*
      *Athena*';
he was praying to Athena, that is, to the air,                             45
praying for a favorable wind for his ship.

Ὃν περὶ κῆρι φίλει Ζεύς τ᾽ αἰγίοχος καὶ Ἀπόλλων
παντοίην φιλότητ᾽· οὐ δ᾽ ἵκετο γήραος οὐδόν,'
ὃν ὅτε Ζεὺς καὶ Οὐρανὸς καὶ Ἥλιος ἐφίλει
50 παντοίην δὴ φιλότητα, καὶ γὰρ ὑπῆρχεν οὗτος
καὶ ἀστρολόγος ἄριστος καί γε οἰωνοσκόπος,
ἀεροσκόπος τε ὁμοῦ καὶ ἕτερα μυρία.
    'Ἀλλ᾽ ἦ τοι Κλεῖτον χρυσόθρονος ἥρπασεν Ἠὼς
    κάλλεος εἵνεκα οἷο, ἵν᾽ ἀθανάτοισι μετείη.'
55 Ὁ Κλεῖτος ὡραιότατος εἰς κάλλος ὑπηργμένος
ἡμέρᾳ τε λαμπρότατος καὶ τῷ παρόντι βίῳ
ἀναρπασθῆναι τῇ Ἠοῖ μυθεύεται τῷ κάλλει,
ὡς συμπαρείη καὶ αὐτὸς στοιχείοις ἀθανάτοις.
    'Μάντιν Ἀπόλλων ἔθηκεν' ἐν τῷ ναῷ Ἡλίου
60 χρησμολογῶν καὶ μάντις ἦν τὰ μέλλοντα προλέγων
ἢ ἐξ ἡλίου καὶ λοιπῶν ἀστέρων καὶ τῶν ἄστρων
ὡροσκοπῶν προὔφθέγγετο πᾶν μέλλον γεγονέναι.
    'Τοῖσιν δ᾽ ἵκμενον οὖρον ἵει γλαυκῶπις Ἀθήνη,'
    ἀὴρ δ᾽ ὁ ἔκλαμπρος αὐτοῖς ἧκε φορ��ὺς ἀνέμους.
65 Ἑρμείαο ἕκητι διακτόρου, ὅς ῥά τε πάντων
    ἀνθρώπων ἔργοισι χάριν καὶ κῦδος ὀπάζει,'
    Ἑρμείου τοῦ ἀστέρος νῦν· λυσιτελεῖ γὰρ πόσοις.
    'Φίλος Διὶ δὲ γένοιο πατρί,' τῇ Εἱμαρμένῃ.
    'Διὶ δὲ εὔχεται' θανεῖν πάλιν τῇ Εἱμαρμένῃ.
70 Ἔργον ἀέξουσιν μάκαρες θεοί, ᾧ ἐπιμίμνω·'
    τανῦν οἱ μάκαρες θεοὶ ἀστέρες Εἱμαρμένης.
    'Ἀλλ᾽ ὅτε γηράσκωσι πόλιν κάτα φῦλ᾽ ἀνθρώπων,
    ἐλθὼν ἀργυρότοξος Ἀπόλλων Ἀρτέμιδι ξὺν

'*Whom Zeus, who bears the aegis, and Apollo heartily loved
with all manner of love; yet he did not reach the threshold of old
    age,*'
means when Zeus, that is the Heaven and Sun, loved him
with all manner of love, for he was                                    50
the best astrologer and diviner of omens,
and air diviner, and, moreover, a myriad other things.
    '*Now golden-throned Dawn snatched away Kleitos
on account of his beauty, to dwell with the immortals.*'
That is, Kleitos was very handsome in his looks                        55
and very radiant in the daylight, and in his youth he is said
in myth to have been snatched by Dawn because of his
        beauty,
so that he too may coexist with the immortal elements.
    '*Apollo* made *him a seer*' in the temple of the Sun
means that he was a seer, delivering oracles and foretelling           60
        the future,
or that using the sun and the other stars and planets,
he was predicting through horoscopes all that would
        happen.
    '*And flashing-eyed Athena sent them a favorable wind*'
means the radiant air brought them favorable winds.
    '*By the favor of Hermes, the messenger,*                          65
*who lends grace and glory to the deeds of all men*'
here means the star Mercury; for it benefits so many things.
    '*Might you be as dear to father Zeus*' means to Destiny.
    '*He prays to Zeus*' to die again means to Destiny.
    '*The blessed gods favor the work I pursue;*'                      70
here the blessed gods are the stars of Destiny.
    '*But when the tribes of men grow old throughout the city,
Apollo, of the silver bow, comes with Artemis*

οἷς ἀγανοῖς βελέεσσιν ἐποιχόμενος κατέπεφνεν.'
75  Φησὶ μηδέποτε νοσεῖν ἀνθρώπους τοὺς ἐκεῖσε.
Ὅταν δ'ἐκείνοις ἐπιστῇ γηράσασι τὸ τέλος,
νόσοις ὀξείαις θνήσκουσιν, αἵ Ἄρτεμις, Ἀπόλλων.
Νόσους ὀξείας γάρ φησιν ἡλίου καὶ σελήνης.
Ἴκελος 'ἀθανάτοισι,' τοῖς ἄστρασιν, ἡλίῳ
80  ἢ ψυχικαῖς δυνάμεσι, φρονήσει καὶ δικαίῳ.
Ζεὺς οὖρον ἴαλλε' τανῦν ὁ οὐρανὸς ἀήρ τε.
Ἕβδομον ἦμαρ θῆκε Ζεὺς' ὁ οὐρανὸς νῦν μόνος.
Ἀποκατάστασίς ἐστι τοῦ οὐρανοῦ ἡμέρα.
Ἡ δὲ βαλοῦσα 'Ἄρτεμις' ἡ νόσος ἡ ὀξεία.
85  Ὁ θεὶς 'ἐσθλὸν' δὲ σὺν 'κακῷ' 'Ζεὺς' νῦν ἡ Εἱμαρμένη.
Ἴσα θεῷ' ὁρόωσιν ἀστέρι, βασιλῆι.
Ζεὺς οἶδεν ὁ Ὀλύμπιος' ἡ ἄνω Εἱμαρμένη.
Κίρκος' ἐστὶν 'Ἀπόλλωνος' 'ἄγγελος' ὁ ἱέραξ·
ζῷον ἐστὶ γὰρ ἱερὸν ἱέραξ τοῦ Ἡλίου,
90  Αἰγύπτιοι ὡς λέγουσι καὶ ὁ Χαιρήμων γράφει.
Οὔ τοι ἄνευ θεοῦ,' τοδὶ τουτέστιν Εἱμαρμένης.

*and assails them with his gentle shafts and slays them.'*
He means that men who live there never get sick.            75
Whenever the end comes for them after they get old,
they die of acute diseases, which are Artemis and Apollo.
For he says that acute diseases come from the sun and the
     moon.
  A man similar *'to the immortals'* means to the stars, to the
     sun
or to the powers of the soul, to wisdom and to justice.     80
  *'Zeus sent them a favorable wind'* here means the sky and
     the air.
  *'Zeus brought upon us the seventh day'* here means the sky
     alone.
Day is the restoration of the sky.
  *'Artemis'* shooting is acute disease.
  *'Zeus'* who gave *'good'* along with *'evil'* here means Destiny.   85
They look upon him *'as a god'* means as a star, a king.
  *'Olympian Zeus knows'* means a higher Destiny.
  *'The hawk messenger of Apollo'* is the falcon;
for the hawk is the sacred animal of the Sun,
as the Egyptians say and Chairemon writes.                  90
  *'Surely not without a god's warrant,'* that is, Destiny's.

## Π′

Οὗτος σκοπὸς τυγχάνει δὲ τοῦ Πῖ τῆς Ὀδυσσείας.

Εἰς σφοὺς ἀγροὺς Τηλέμαχος ἐκ τῆς νηὸς ἀνῆλθε.
Τὸν Εὔμαιον εἰς πόλιν δὲ πέμπει πρὸς Πηνελόπην
δηλῶσαι ταύτῃ μέλλοντα τὴν τούτου παρουσίαν.
Τῷ Τηλεμάχῳ δ᾽ Ὀδυσσεὺς αὐτὸν ἀναγνωρίζει.
5 Κενοὶ δὲ ὑποστρέφουσιν οἱ σὺν νηῒ σταλέντες
ὡς κτείνοντες Τηλέμαχον ἀντήσαντες θαλάσσῃ.

'Ἐπέκλωσεν' ὁ 'δαίμων' δὲ τανῦν ἡ Εἱμαρμένη,
καὶ τὸ 'θεοῦ ὀμφῇ' δηλοῖ χρησμοῖς τῆς Εἱμαρμένης,
καὶ τὸ 'θεῶν ἐν γούνασιν' ὁμοίως Εἱμαρμένης.
10 Ἡ Ἀθηνᾶ ἡ φρόνησίς ἐστι νῦν Ὀδυσσέως,
ἡ 'γυναικὶ' ποικιλουργῷ 'δέμας' ὁμοιωθεῖσα.
Καὶ πάντα προειρήκειμεν τῷ Νῦ σοι σαφεστάτως.
Οὐκ 'ἐναργεῖς' γὰρ 'οἱ θεοὶ' τοῖς σύμπασιν ὁρῶνται,
τὰ γὰρ ψυχῆς βουλεύματα ἑτέροις οὐχ ὁρῶνται,
15 μόνοις δὲ τοῖς βουλεύμασι καὶ τοῖς ἐνθυμουμένοις.
'Ἀλλ᾽ Ὀδυσσεύς τε κύνες τε ἴδον, καὶ ῥ᾽ οὐχ ὑλάοντο,'
αὐτὸς αὐτὸν μεταβαλὼν ἐμπεπλασμένου γήρως
καὶ τῶν ῥικνῶν ῥακέων δὲ καὶ κατεκλελυμένων,
ὃ ἔπραττεν, ἐγίνωσκεν. Οἱ κύνες δὲ ὁμοίως

# Book 16

This is the scope of the sixteenth book of the *Odyssey*.

Telemachos disembarked from his ship in his own fields.
He sends Eumaios into the city, to Penelope,
intending to inform her of his presence there.
Odysseus makes himself known to Telemachos.
The men return empty-handed who had been sent with a     5
    ship,
to ambush and kill Telemachos at sea.

  '*So has a god spun*' here means Destiny,
and '*because of a god's prophecy*' means because of Destiny's
    oracles,
and '*on the knees of the gods*' similarly means of Destiny.
  Athena here is Odysseus's wisdom,     10
who similarly appears '*in the form*' of a skilled '*woman.*'
And we have told you everything in advance most clearly in
    the Thirteenth Book.
  For the '*gods*' are not '*manifestly*' visible to everyone,
means, for the counsels of the soul are not visible to others,
but only to one's own resolutions and recollections.     15
'*But Odysseus saw* her, *as did the hounds, and they barked not*'
means, having changed his appearance with fabricated old
    age
and tattered rags completely frayed,
he understood what he was doing. The dogs likewise

20  ἄπαξ γνωρίσαντες αὐτὸν καὶ μεταβεβλημένον,
    πάλιν καλῶς ἐγίνωσκον οὐδ' ὅλως δὲ ὑλάκτουν.
    Τῆς Ἀθηνᾶς τὴν ῥάβδον νῦν εἰρήκειν σὺν τοῖς ἄλλοις.
    'Ετέρωσε βαλ' ὄμματα,' μήπως 'θεός' τις 'εἴη,'
    ἤτοι σοφὸς καὶ τελεστὴς καὶ μάγος δὲ τὴν τέχνην.
25  'Ἦ μάλα τις θεός ἐσσι, τοὶ οὐρανὸν εὐρὺν ἔχουσιν.'
    Ὄντως σοφὸς καὶ μάγος τις καὶ τελεστὴς ὑπάρχεις.
    Οἳ 'οὐρανόν περ ἔχουσι,' τὰ οὐρανοῦ τελοῦσιν
    ἢ ὑψηλοὶ οὐράνιοι τελοῦσι τῇ φρονήσει.
    'Ἀλλ' ἵληθ', ἵνα τοι κεχαρισμένα δώομεν ἱρά'
30  ἀλλ' ἵληθι καὶ ἵλεως γενοῦ ἤτοι βοήθει
    καὶ τοὺς μνηστῆρας ἄνελε καὶ δῶρα λαμπρὰ δέχου.
    'Οὐ σύ γ' Ὀδυσσεύς ἐσσι, πατὴρ ἐμός, ἀλλά με δαίμων'
    δαίμων τὰ σὰ τεχνάσματα τὰ μαγικά μοι θέλγει,
    εἴτ' οὖν ὁ δαίμων ὁ ἐμὸς καὶ λογισμός με σφάλλει.
35  'Ἦ γάρ τοι νέον ἦσθα γέρων καὶ ἀεικέα ἔσσο·
    νῦν δὲ θεοῖσιν ἔοικας, οἳ οὐρανὸν εὐρὺν ἔχουσι.'
    Ὡραῖος εἶ καὶ εὐειδὴς δίκην λαμπρῶν ἀστέρων.
    'Αὐτάρ τοι τόδε ἔργον Ἀθηναίης ἀγελείης,'
    τοῦτο ἐξειργασάμην δὲ φρονήσει τῇ οἰκείᾳ.
40  'Ῥηΐδιον δὲ θεοῖσι, τοὶ οὐρανὸν εὐρὺν ἔχουσι,'
    θεοῖς ψυχῆς δυνάμεσι, φρονήσει τε καὶ τέχνη.
    'Θεῶν ἰότητι' βουλῇ ἐμῶν πανουργημάτων.
    'Καὶ φράσαι, ἥ κεν νῶϊν Ἀθήνη σὺν Διὶ πατρὶ'
    σκόπει, εἰ νοῦς καὶ φρόνησις ἡμῖν οὐκ ἐπαρκέσει.

immediately recognized him even with a changed      20
    appearance;
again they knew him well and did not bark at all.
  I have already spoken of Athena's staff, among other
    things.
  *'He turned his eyes aside,'* in case he *'should be a god,'*
that is, a wise man and a priest and a mage in skill.
  *'Verily you are a god, one of those who hold broad heaven.'*     25
This means, you are indeed a wise man and mage and priest.
Those who *'hold heaven'* accomplish heavenly things
or they are lofty, heavenly in their wisdom.
  *'But, be gracious, that we may offer you acceptable sacrifices'*
means be gracious and graceful, that is, help     30
and kill the suitors and receive radiant gifts.
  *'You are not my father Odysseus, but some god'*
means you, a god, cast your magic tricks on me,
or the god, that is, my reason, confuses me.
  *'For just now you were an old man and meanly clad,*     35
*whereas now you are like the gods, who hold broad heaven.'*
This means you are handsome and comely as bright stars.
  *'But this, you must know, is the work of Athena, the forager,'*
which means I accomplished this with my own wisdom.
  *'Easy it is for the gods, who hold broad heaven,'*     40
means for the divine powers of the soul, that is, for wisdom
    and skill.
  *'By favor of the gods'* means by the will of my scheming.
  *'And tell me whether for us two Athena, with father Zeus'*
means you should consider if intelligence and wisdom will
    not suffice for us.

45 ‘Ἐσθλὼ τούτω ἀμύντορε,’ οὓς ‘ἀγορεύεις,’ πάτερ,
‘ὕψι περ ἐν νεφέεσσι καθημένω· ὥ τε καὶ ἄλλοις’
ἐν ὕψει τῷ τῆς κεφαλῆς ὄντες ἐγκεκρυμμένοι.
‘Παλλὰς Ἀθηναίη θέλξει καὶ μητίετα Ζεύς,’
ὁ νοῦς ἐμοῦ καὶ φρόνησις τούτους ἐξαπατήσει.
50 ‘Τέρας Διὸς’ φρονήσεως καὶ λογισμοῦ σημεῖα.
‘Θεοὶ’ κακῶν ἐκλύσαντες αὐτὴ ἡ Εἱμαρμένη,
καὶ ‘οἴκαδε ἀπήγαγεν ὁ δαίμων’ Εἱμαρμένη.
‘Θεῶν εἰρώμεθα βουλάς,’ τίς νῦν ὁ νοῦς τοῦ λόγου;
Βουλὴν ἀναζητήσωμεν μαθεῖν τῆς Εἱμαρμένης·
55 ἐκ μαντειῶν δὲ καὶ χρησμῶν ἅπας μανθάνει τάδε.
‘Διὸς’ τῆς Εἱμαρμένης δὲ ‘θέμιστες’ αἱ μαντεῖαι.
‘Ζεὺς μάρτυς’ δὲ τανῦν ἐστιν Ἥλιος Οὐρανός τε·
ἡ Εἱμαρμένη τε αὐτὴ νοεῖται Ζεὺς ἐνθάδε.
‘Θάνατον’ τὸν ‘θεόθεν’ δὲ καὶ τὸν τῆς Εἱμαρμένης
60 φυγεῖν τε καὶ ‘ἀλέασθαι’ οὐ δυνατὸν ἀνθρώποις.
‘Ὕπνον βλεφάροις Ἀθηνᾶ’ τῇ Πηνελόπῃ βάλλει·
εἴτ’ οὖν φρονήσει ἑαυτῆς εἰς ὕπνον κατεκλίθη,
ἢ Ἀθηνᾶ καὶ ὁ ἀὴρ ὑγρότερος ὑπάρχων
καθείλκυσε καὶ ἄκουσαν ἐκείνην ὡς πρὸς ὕπνον.
65 Ἡ Ἀθηνᾶ δὲ πλήξασα ‘ῥάβδῳ’ τὸν Ὀδυσσέα
εἰς γέροντα μετέστρεψε πάλιν αὐτὸν ὡς πρώην.
Αὐτὸς αὐτὸν μεμψάμενος φρονήσει τῇ οἰκείᾳ,
μήπως νοήσῃ Εὔμαιος, ὡς Ὀδυσσεὺς ὑπάρχει,
πάλιν αὐτὸν τῷ πένητι τῷ πεπλασμένῳ κρύπτει.

'*These good* helpers' whom '*you mention,*' father,                    45
'*though high in the clouds they abide, and above others,*'
means hidden in the top of the head.
   '*Pallas Athena and Zeus, the counselor, will beguile them,*'
that is, my mind and wisdom will deceive them.
   '*Sign from Zeus*' means signs of wisdom and reason.                    50
   '*The gods* have delivered him from evil' means Destiny
      itself,
   and the '*god has brought him home*' means Destiny.
   '*Let us seek to learn the will of the gods,*' means what is here
      the will of reason?
It means, let us seek to learn the will of Destiny;
everyone learns these from divinations and oracles.                    55
   '*The oracles of Zeus*' are the divinations of Destiny.
   '*Zeus* the witness' here is the Sun and the Sky.
Zeus here is also understood to be Destiny itself.
   '*Death from the gods*' means also that it is not possible
for men to escape and '*to avoid*' death from Destiny.                    60
   'Athena' cast '*sleep*' upon Penelope's 'eyelids';
she was either put to sleep by her own wisdom
or Athena, which is the moister air,
dragged her into sleep against her will.
   Athena smote Odysseus '*with her wand*'                    65
and changed him again into an old man as before.
Blaming himself through his own wisdom,
in case Eumaios understood that he was Odysseus,
again he hid by disguising himself as a poor man.

## Ρ'

Τοῦ Ῥῶ τῆς Ὀδυσσείας δὲ τοῦτον σκοπόν μοι νόει.

Ἐκ σφῶν ἀγρῶν Τηλέμαχος ἐλθὼν πρὸς τὴν μητέρα
τὴν ἐκδημίαν τὴν αὑτοῦ φησιν ἐν κεφαλαίῳ.
Ὁ μάντις Θεοκλύμενος ἔφη δὲ Πηνελόπῃ,
ὡς ἔστιν ἔνδον Ὀδυσσεύς, κτενεῖ δὲ τοὺς μνηστῆρας.
5  Μετὰ βραχὺ καὶ Ὀδυσσεὺς ὡς πένης σὺν Εὐμαίῳ
ἱκνεῖται καὶ γνωρίζεται τῷ σφῷ κυνὶ τῷ Ἄργῳ.
Εἶτα πάλιν ὁ Εὔμαιος ἀγροῖς ἀνθυποστρέφει,
αὐτὸς δ' ὡς ξένος καὶ πτωχὸς οἴκοις οἰκείοις μένει.

'Ἀρτέμιδι ἰκέλη ἠὲ χρυσῇ Ἀφροδίτῃ'
10  Σελήνη κάλλει ὅμοιος ἢ τῇ ἐπιθυμίᾳ·
τὸ δὲ 'χρυσῇ' μεταφορὰ ἐκ τοῦ χρυσοῦ, τιμία.
'Εὔχεο πᾶσι θεοῖσι τελήεσσας ἑκατόμβας'
στοιχείοις, Εἱμαρμένη τε δυνάμει τε ψυχῆς τε.
Ὁ 'Ζεὺς' ἢ Εἱμαρμένη δὲ τοῖς τόποις τοῖς ἐνθάδε.
15  Ἡ Ἀθηνᾶ καὶ φρόνησις 'κατέχευε' δὲ 'χάριν.'
Τὸ δὲ 'θεῶν ἰότητι' βουλῇ τῆς Εἱμαρμένης.
'Αἲ γάρ, Ζεῦ τε πάτερ καὶ Ἀθηναίη καὶ Ἄπολλον,'
ὦ οὐρανὲ καὶ ἥλιε καὶ φῶς λαμπρὸν ἡλίου.
'Νύμφην' φησὶ τὴν 'Καλυψὼ' τοιουτοτρόπῳ τρόπῳ·
20  τὰ νεωστὶ φαινόμενα πάντα καλοῦνται νύμφαι,

# Book 17

Understand from me the scope of the seventeenth
book of the *Odyssey*.

Telemachos, coming to his mother from his own fields,
gave her a summary account of his trip abroad.
The seer Theoklymenos said to Penelope that
when Odysseus came inside, he would kill the suitors.
A short time later, Odysseus comes with Eumaios          5
in the guise of a poor man and is recognized by his own dog
  Argos.
Afterward, Eumaios returns to the fields,
while Odysseus himself remains in his own house as a
  stranger and beggar.

 '*Like unto Artemis or golden Aphrodite*'
means equal in beauty to the Moon or desire;                10
'*golden*' is a metaphor from gold, that is, valuable.
 '*Pray to all the gods that you will offer hecatombs,*'
means to the elements, to Destiny, to the power of the soul.
 '*Zeus*' is Destiny in these passages.
 Athena, that is, wisdom, 'shed grace upon him.'          15
 '*By the will of the gods*' means by the will of Destiny.
 '*I would, O father Zeus, and Athena, and Apollo,*'
means O sky and sun and bright light of the sun.
He means the 'Nymph Kalypso' in such a way:
all things that newly appear are called nymphs,              20

δένδρα καὶ ζῷα νεαρά, συγγράμματα τὰ νέα.
Ὅθε Δρυάδες λέγονται Νύμφαι ἐπιμηλίδες,
καὶ Νύμφαι Μοῦσαι καὶ λοιπὰ καὶ νύμφαι δὲ γυναῖκες
παρὰ τὸ νέον φαίνεσθαι, πρότερον κεκρυμμέναι.
25 Κατ' ἐξοχὴν τὰ ὕδατα Νύμφας καλοῦσι μᾶλλον
Νηΐδας Νηρηΐδας τε, ἐξ ὧν καὶ Καλυψὼ δέ·
ὡς οὖσαν νησιώτιδα καὶ μέσον τῶν ὑδάτων,
Νύμφην κατονομάζουσιν ὡς δῆθε Νηρηΐδα.
'Οὖρον' δὲ οἱ 'ἀθάνατοι' 'ἔδοσαν' τὰ στοιχεῖα,
30 ὁ οὐρανὸς καὶ ὁ ἀήρ, ἐξ ὧν πνοαὶ ἀνέμων.
'Ἴστω νῦν Ζεὺς πρῶτα θεῶν ξενίη τε τράπεζα'
Ζεὺς οὐρανὸς καὶ ἥλιος ἐκ τῶν στοιχείων ἴστω.
'Νυμφάων' Νηρηΐδων νῦν τουτέστιν Ὑδριάδων.
'Θεὸς ἄγει τὸν ὅμοιον ὁμοίῳ' Εἱμαρμένη.
35 'Νύμφαι κρηναῖαι' τοῦ 'Διὸς' καὶ Οὐρανοῦ δὲ 'κόραι.'
'Ἀγάγη δαίμων' δὲ αὐτόν, τουτέστιν Εἱμαρμένη.
'Αἴθε Ἀπόλλων βάλλοιεν' ἐξ ὀξειῶν τις νόσος.
'Φίλην δαιτὶ τὴν φόρμιγγα ἐποίησαν θεοὶ δέ,'
ἡ Εἱμαρμένη ἢ σοφοὶ καὶ φρόνιμοι δὲ ἄνδρες.
40 'Ἥμισυ γάρ τ' ἀρετῆς ἀποαίνυται εὐρύοπα Ζεὺς'
ἡ Εἱμαρμένη νῦν ὁ Ζεὺς ὁ ἀρετὴν διχάζων.
Τὸ 'Ζεῦ ἄνα, Τηλέμαχον' ὁμοίως Εἱμαρμένη.
'Ἀθήνη' δὲ καὶ φρόνησις 'ὤτρυνεν' Ὀδυσσέα.
'Μὴ τὸ θεὸς τελέσειεν' αὐτὴ ἡ Εἱμαρμένη.
45 Καὶ 'Ζεὺς' ὁ ἀλαπάζων τὲ ὁμοίως Εἱμαρμένη.

the young trees and animals, new books.
From this, the Nymph shepherdesses are called Dryads,
and the Muses are called Nymphs and the like, as are
    women too
as they first appear, having been hidden before.
As a general rule they call the waters Nymphs and Naiads     25
and Nereids, from among whom Kalypso comes as well;
since she was an islander and the midst of the sea,
they call her a Nymph, as she was supposedly a Nereid.
   'The *immortals gave me a fair wind*' means the elements,
the sky and the air, from which the gusts of winds come.     30
   '*Let Zeus be my witness above all gods, and this hospitable*
    *board*'
means let it be Zeus, that is the sky and the sun among the
    elements.
   '*Of the nymphs,*' of the Nereids, which means here of the
    Water Nymphs.
   '*The god is bringing like* to like' means Destiny.
   '*The Nymphs of the fountain*' are the 'daughters of *Zeus,*'     35
    that is, the Sky.
   'That some *god* may guide' him, that is, Destiny.
   'Would that *Apollo* shoot,' means some acute disease.
   '*The gods* have made the dear lyre *for the feast,*'
means Destiny or wise and prudent men.
   'For Zeus, *the far sounding, takes away half his worth.*'     40
Zeus, who divides virtue in half here, is Destiny.
   '*King Zeus, grant that Telemachos*' likewise means Destiny.
   '*Athena,*' that is, wisdom, 'urged on' Odysseus.
   '*May the god never bring such a thing to pass*' means Destiny
    itself.
   And '*Zeus*' the ravager similarly means Destiny.     45

Καὶ 'Ζεὺς ὁ τερπικέραυνος' τανῦν ἡ Εἱμαρμένη,
ἣ φλέγει πλέον κεραυνοῦ πάντας ἠτυχηκότας.

'Ἀλλ' εἴ που πτωχῶν γε θεοὶ καὶ Ἐρινύες εἰσίν,'
εἰ βλέπει ταῦτα Ἥλιος, εἰσὶ καὶ τιμωρίαι
50 ἐξ Εἱμαρμένης δηλαδὴ πτωχοῖς προσβοηθοῦσαι.

'Θεός τις ἐπουράνιός' τις ἐν σοφίᾳ μέγας
εἴτε καὶ μέγας βασιλεὺς καὶ ὑψηλὸς ἐν βίῳ.

Βολαί εἰσιν Ἀπόλλωνος θάνατοι τῶν ὀξέων.

'Ἐκδεδαὼς ἐκ τῶν θεῶν ὁ ἀοιδὸς δὲ ᾄδει'
55 ἢ ἐκ τῆς Εἱμαρμένης γε ἢ ἐξ αὐτῶν ἀστέρων
ἢ ἐκ σοφῶν ἢ καὶ φρενὸς οἰκείης σοφωτάτης.

Οὕσπερ ὁ 'Ζεὺς' 'ὀλέσειεν' αὐτὴ ἡ Εἱμαρμένη.

'Ἐμοὶ καὶ ἀθανάτοισιν' ὁμοίως Εἱμαρμένη.

And '*Zeus who delights in thunderbolts*' here is Destiny,
which burns all unfortunate men more than lightning.
  '*But, if for beggars there are gods and Furies*'
means if the Sun sees this, there are also punishments
from Destiny that clearly help the beggars.                          50
  '*Some heavenly god*' means someone great in wisdom
or even a great king lofty in life.
  The arrows of Apollo are deaths from acute illness.
  'The singer taught by the gods sings'
means either by Destiny, or by the stars themselves             55
or by wise men or even by his own very wise mind.
  May '*Zeus,*' that is, Destiny itself, 'destroy' those men.
  '*To me and to the immortals*' similarly means Destiny.

## Σ′

Τοιάδε ἡ ὑπόθεσις τῆς Σίγμα Ὀδυσσείας.


Τοῦ Ὀδυσσέως ὡς πτωχοῦ σφοῖς οἴκοις προσαιτοῦντος,
'πτωχὸς πανδήμιος' ἐλθὼν Ἀρναῖος, Ἴρος κλῆσιν,
ἐκεῖνον ἐξεδίωκε· βουλῇ δὲ τῶν μνηστήρων
πάλην συνάψας Ὀδυσσεὺς κατέαξεν ἐκεῖνον.
5 Οὗ ἕνεκα Τηλέμαχον μέμφεται Πηνελόπη.
Μνηστῆρσι θαυμασθεῖσα δὲ καὶ αἰνουμένη κάλλει
πείθει τοὺς πάντας ἡ ὀργὰς καὶ φέρουσίν οἱ δῶρα.
Ὁ Καλυψοῦς δὲ σύνευνος καὶ θεαινῶν τῶν ἄλλων
τρίχας ἔχων οὐδ' ἡβαιάς, καυσίαν ἐρυθρὰν δέ,
10 ἀνάπτων πῦρ ἐν τῇ νυκτὶ μνηστῆρσι καιρῷ δείπνου
πείθει γελᾶν Εὐρύμαχον καὶ τοὺς λοιποὺς μνηστῆρας.
Φθέγγεται δὲ καὶ Ὀδυσσεὺς Εὐρύμαχόν τι δάκνον·
ὅτι δοκεῖν εἶπε τὸ πῦρ ἅπτειν ἐκ κάρας τούτου,
καὶ '"ἆρα μοι θελήσειας, ὦ ξένε, θητευέμεν;"'

15 "Ὄλβον θεοὶ' ὀπάζουσιν ἀστέρες, Εἱμαρμένη.
Καὶ 'τερπωλὴν δὲ ἤγαγε θεὸς' <ἡ> Εἱμαρμένη.
Ἡ 'Ἀθηνᾶ' καὶ φρόνησις 'ἤλδανε δὲ τὰ μέλη'·
τεθαρρηκὼς οἷς ἔλεξε φρονίμως πρὸς μνηστῆρας,
οὐκέτι συγκαμπτόμενος μείζων πολὺ ἐφάνη.

216

# Book 18

This is the subject matter of the eighteenth book of
the *Odyssey*.

While Odysseus was pleading like a beggar in his own
    home,
a *'public beggar'* came, Arnaios, called Iros,
and tried to drive him away; at the wish of the suitors
Odysseus fought with him and crushed him.
Penelope blames Telemachos for this.        5
Admired by the suitors and praised for her beauty
she in her bloom persuades them all and they bring her
    gifts.
The bedfellow of Kalypso and of the other goddesses,
with no hair at all on his head and wearing a red hat,
lighting the fire at night for the suitors at dinner time,    10
persuades Eurymachos and the other suitors to laugh.
Odysseus spoke hurtful words to Eurymachos, because
Eurymachos said that the fire seemed to shine from
    Odysseus's head,
and "'Would you wish, stranger, *to serve*' me *'for hire'*?"

    The *'gods* give *happiness'* means the stars, Destiny.    15
    And a 'god has brought sport' means Destiny.
    'Athena,' that is, wisdom, *'filled out* his limbs,'
which means that, feeling confident, he spoke wisely to the
    suitors;
no longer being bent over, he appeared much larger.

20 'Ζεύς τοι δοίη, ξεῖνε, καὶ ἀθάνατοι θεοὶ ἄλλοι,'
ὁ Ζεὺς ὁ πλάνης νῦν ἀστὴρ καὶ οἱ λοιποὶ ἀστέρες.
 Οἱ 'ἀρετὴν παρέχοντες θεοὶ' ἡ Εἱμαρμένη
καὶ οἱ 'θεοὶ οἱ μάκαρες' 'πατὴρ ἀνδρῶν θεῶν τε.'
 Καὶ 'δῶρα' δ' ἅ φησι 'θεῶν,' πάντα ἡ Εἱμαρμένη.
25 'Ἀθήνη' δὲ ἡ φρόνησις δῆλον τοῦ Ὀδυσσέως.
 Ἡ 'Ἀθηνᾶ' ἡ φρόνησις πάλιν δὲ Πηνελόπης.
 'Ἡρῶ τοῖς ἀθανάτοισι' στοιχείοις, Εἱμαρμένη.
 'Θεοὶ Ὄλυμπον ἔχοντες' πάλιν ἡ Εἱμαρμένη.
 Ἡ Πηνελόπην 'Ἀθηνᾶ' καλλύνουσα ἀὴρ δέ.
30 Τῷ ὕπνῳ κρατηθεῖσα γάρ, ἀέρι τῷ ἐνύγρῳ,
τὸ πρὶν σύννουν διέλυσε χροιὰν λαβοῦσα κάλλος.
 'Αἴ γάρ, Ζεῦ τε πάτερ καὶ Ἀθηναίη καὶ Ἄπολλον,'
ὦ οὐρανέ τε καὶ ἀὴρ σὺν ἅμα τῷ ἡλίῳ.
 'Ὤλεσαν οἱ ἀθάνατοι,' 'σεῦε κακά τε δαίμων,'
35 'εἴ κεν ἐάσῃ με θεὸς' καὶ 'Ζεὺς ὄλβον ἀπηύρα'·
τὰ τέσσαρα σημαίνουσιν ὁμοῦ τὴν Εἱμαρμένην.
 'Μνηστῆρας ἡ Ἀθήνη δὲ οὐκ εἴα' Ὀδυσσέως,
'οὐκ ἀθεεὶ' καὶ ἄνευθε καλλίστης Εἱμαρμένης.
 'Κρονίων' ὄρσει 'πόλεμον' πάλιν ἡ Εἱμαρμένη.
40 Καὶ τὸ 'θεῶν τις ὀροθύνει' ταὐτὸν σημαίνει.
 'Θεοῖσι σπείσαντες' αὐτοῖς στοιχείοις, Εἱμαρμένη.

'*May Zeus grant your wish, stranger, and the other immortal*    20
   *gods*';
Zeus here means the wandering star and the other stars.
   '*The gods* giving him *prosperity*' means Destiny,
as do 'the *blessed gods*' and '*the father of men and gods.*'
   And all that he calls '*gifts of the gods*' are Destiny.
   '*Athena*' is clearly Odysseus's wisdom.    25
   'Athena' is again the wisdom of Penelope.
   '*Prayer to* the *immortals*' means to the elements, to
      Destiny.
   '*The gods* who hold *Olympos*' is Destiny again.
   'Athena' making Penelope beautiful is the air.
For overpowered by sleep, by moist air,    30
she dissolved her prior worry and became beautiful in
      appearance.
   '*I would, O father Zeus, and Athena, and Apollo*'
means O sky and air and, along with them, the sun.
   'The *immortals destroyed,*' '*woes has some god* brought me,'
'if the *god* will bring *me* back' and '*Zeus has taken away my*    35
   *happiness*';
these four all mean Destiny.
   '*Athena* would in no wise *suffer* the *suitors*' of Odysseus
   and
'*nor without the gods' will*' means without the will of most
      beautiful Destiny.
   '*The son of Kronos*' brings '*war*' again means Destiny.
   And '*some god is urging on*' means the same.    40
   '*Having made libations to the gods*' means to the elements,
      to Destiny.

# Τ′

Αὕτη τῆς Ταῦ ὑπόθεσις Ὁμήρου Ὀδυσσείας.


Σὺν Τηλεμάχῳ Ὀδυσσεὺς μετατιθεῖ τὰ ὅπλα.
Εἶτα δ᾽ ἀνερωτώμενος παρὰ τῆς Πηνελόπης
λέγει Κρὴς εἶναι καὶ ἰδεῖν ἐκεῖ τὸν Ὀδυσσέα
τοιάδε εἵματ᾽ ἔχοντα καὶ Εὐρυβάτην φίλον.
5 Τέλος ὑπ᾽ Εὐρυκλείας δὲ νιπτόμενος τοὺς πόδας
ἐκ τῆς οὐλῆς γνωρίζεται, ἥνπερ συὶ ἐτρώθη.
Ταύτην δὲ πείθει σιωπᾶν καὶ πρὸς μηδένα λέγειν.

'Ἀθήνη' τῇ φρονήσει νῦν ἀντὶ τοῦ Ὀδυσσέως.
'Ἔμβαλε δαίμων ἐν φρεσὶν' ἐν τῇ ψυχῇ ἐπέγνω.
10 Ἡ Ἀθηνᾶ δ᾽ ἡ φαίνουσα ἐν τῷ 'χρυσέῳ λύχνῳ'
οὐκ ἄλλη τίς ἐστι τανῦν, αὐτὴ δὲ ἡ σελήνη.
'Θεός τις ἔνδον' οὐρανοῦ τουτέστιν εὐμοιρία.
'Αὕτη δίκη ἐστὶ θεῶν' κρίσις ἐξ Εἱμαρμένης.
'Ἀρτέμιδι ἰκέλη ἠὲ χρυσῇ Ἀφροδίτῃ'
15 σελήνη κάλλει ὅμοιος ἢ τῇ ἐπιθυμίᾳ.
Ὁ 'Ζεὺς Κρονίων' — ἔφημεν πολλάκις — Εἱμαρμένη.
'Ἀλλ᾽ ἤδη παῖς τοῖος Ἀπόλλωνός γε ἔκητι,'
ἀλλ᾽ ὁ Τηλέμαχος ἀνὴρ ἐτράφη τῷ ἡλίῳ,
ἢ ὅτι θρεπτικός ἐστιν ὁ ἥλιος ἁπάντων,

# Book 19

This is the subject matter of the nineteenth book of
the *Odyssey*.

Odysseus moves the weapons with Telemachos.
Then, after being questioned by Penelope,
he says that he is from Crete and saw Odysseus there
wearing such-and-such clothing, with his friend Eurybates.
Finally, as his feet are washed by Eurykleia,                    5
he is recognized by the scar where he was wounded by a
    boar.
He persuades her to remain silent and not tell anyone.

He says '*with Athena's aid*' here instead of with Odysseus's
    wisdom.
'*Has a god put* in my heart' means he knew it in his soul.
Athena appearing in the 'golden lamp'                            10
is nothing else here but the moon itself.
'*Some god is within*' means a good fate from heaven.
'*This is the gods' justice*' means a judgment from Destiny.
'*Like unto Artemis or golden Aphrodite*'
means like the moon in beauty or in desire.                      15
'*Zeus, son of Kronos*'—we have said many times—means
    Destiny.
'*Yet now is his son by the favor of Apollo such as he was,*'
means yet Telemachos is a man nurtured by the sun,
or since the sun nurtures everything,

20 ὥς πού φησι καὶ Σοφοκλῆς τοῦτο τρανῶς δεικνύων,
'τὴν πάντα γοῦν βόσκουσαν ἡλίου φλόγα,'
ἢ ὅτι ἀνὴρ γέγονεν ἡλιοδρόμοις χρόνοις.
Θεοὶ καὶ 'δαίμων' πάλιν τε 'δαίμων' ἡ Εἱμαρμένη.
Καὶ 'Ζεὺς κῦδος ὀπάζει' δὲ ὁμοίως Εἱμαρμένη.

25 'Τῇσι δ' ἐνὶ Κνωσός, μεγάλη πόλις, ἔνθα τε Μίνως
ἐννέωρος βασίλευε, Διὸς μεγάλου ὀαριστής,'
'ὀαριστὴς' ὁ μηνυτὴς Διὸς τοῦ βασιλέως.
'Ὤρορε δαίμων χαλεπὸς' ἀγρία Εἱμαρμένη.
Τὸν Ὀδυσσέα ὅμοιον 'θεοῖς,' νῷ καὶ φρονήσει.

30 Ὁ 'Ζεὺς' ἡ Εἱμαρμένη νῦν· τὸν '῞Ηλιόν' τε οἶδας
ἐμοῦ λεπτολογήσαντος ὄπισθε σαφεστάτως.
'Ἀγχίθεοι' οἱ δίκαιοι καὶ τῶν φιλοξενούντων.
'Θεὸν δ' ὣς ἐτιμήσαντο,' εἴτ' οὖν ὡς βασιλέα,
εἴθ' ὡς σοφὸν ἢ ἕνα δὲ τῶν κοσμικῶν στοιχείων.

35 Τὸ ὡς θεοῦ 'Διὸς βουλὴν' 'ἐκ τῆς δρυὸς ἀκούσῃ'
ἐλέχθη σοι τοῖς ὄπισθεν ὡς τἆλλα μυριάκις.
'῎Ιστω νῦν Ζεὺς' ὁ οὐρανός, ὁ πρῶτος τῶν στοιχείων,
εἴτ' οὖν ὁ ῞Ηλιος αὐτός, ὁ Γίγας, ὁ πανόπτης.
'Ὁ Ζεύς σε περιήχθηρεν' αὐτὴ ἡ Εἱμαρμένη.

40 'Θυμὸν θεοειδέα' δὲ ψυχὴν φρονιμωτάτην.
'Διὶ τερπικεραύνῳ' δὲ τῷ οὐρανίῳ ὕψει
καὶ Εἱμαρμένη δὲ αὐτῇ, ὥσπερ πολλάκις ἔφην.

as Sophocles says somewhere, indicating this clearly,          20
'*the all-nurturing flame* of the sun,'
or since he became a man as the sun marked the passing
          years.
The gods, '*some god,*' and again '*a god*' again mean Destiny.
And '*Zeus grants honor*' similarly means Destiny.
'*Among their cities is the great city Knossos, where Minos*          25
*reigned when nine years old, the bosom friend of great Zeus*';
'*bosom friend*' means the herald of Zeus the king.
'*For some angry god had roused it*' means wild Destiny.
Odysseus similar '*to the gods*' means similar to understand-
          ing and wisdom.
'*Zeus*' here means Destiny; you know what the 'Sun'          30
          means,
since I have explained previously in detail and most clearly.
'*Near kin to the gods*' means just and hospitable men.
'Showed him honor, *as if he were a god*' means as if a king,
or as a wise man or one of the cosmic elements.
'So that he hears *the will of Zeus from the oak*' as of the god          35
was explained to you previously like the other things
          countless times.
'*Let Zeus be my witness*' means the sky, the first of the
          elements,
or the Sun itself, the Giant, the all-seeing.
'Surely *Zeus* hated *you*' means Destiny itself.
'God-fearing *heart*' means the most wise soul.          40
'*To Zeus, who delights in thunderbolts*' means to the high
          heavens
and Destiny itself, as I have said many times.

Τὴν κλεπτοσύνην δὲ αὐτῷ 'θεὸς Ἑρμείας δῶκεν'
ἀστὴρ Ἑρμοῦ γενέθλιος τούτῳ παρέσχε τάδε.

45 'Τῇ γὰρ Ἀθηναίη νόον ἔτραπεν. Αὐτὰρ Ὀδυσσεὺς'
ἡ Ὀδυσσέως Ἀθηνᾶ, φρόνησις, πανουργίᾳ
τὸν λογισμὸν παρέτρεψεν ἐκείνοις, μὴ νοῆσαι.
'Θεὸς δὲ ἔμβαλε θυμῷ' σὸς νοῦς ἐν τῇ ψυχῇ σου,
εἴτε μὴν τὸ ἀνάπαλιν ἡ σὴ ψυχὴ τῷ νῷ σου.

50 'Ἐμοὶ θεὸς δαμάσειε μνηστῆρας' Εἱμαρμένη,
εἴτ' οὖν ἡ φρόνησις ἐμοῦ, δόλοι καὶ πανουργίαι.
'Τοῖς δὲ θεοῖς ἐπίτρεψον' αὐτῇ τῇ Εἱμαρμένῃ.
Ἀνάθου ταῦτα δέ, φησίν, αὐτῇ τῇ Εἱμαρμένῃ
ἢ τῇ φρονήσει τῇ ἐμῇ καὶ τοῖς ἐμοῖς δὲ δόλοις.

55 'Δοιαὶ γάρ τε πύλαι ἀμενηνῶν εἰσὶν ὀνείρων·
αἱ μὲν γὰρ κεράεσσι τετεύχαται, αἱ δ' ἐλέφαντι.'
Νῦν καὶ περὶ γενέσεως ὀνείρων ἐκδιδάσκει
καὶ λέγει, τίνες ἀληθεῖς καὶ τίνες ἐψευσμένοι.
Τοὺς μὲν ἐκ κέρως κεφαλῆς καὶ νοῦ καὶ τῆς ψυχῆς δὲ

60 λέγει τυγχάνειν ἀληθεῖς καὶ μαντευτὰς μελλόντων.
Ὄνειρος πλάσις γὰρ ψυχῆς τὸ μέλλον προτυπούσης.
Οὕτως ὀνείρους λέγει μὲν τοὺς ἐκ ψυχῆς καὶ νοῦ δὲ
τυγχάνειν ἀληθεύοντας· τοὺς δ' ἐκ τῶν ἐλεφάντων,
τοὺς ἐκ ἁπάσης βλάβης δὲ καὶ λογισμῶν ἀστάτων,

65 ψευδεῖς ὑπάρχειν λέγει σοι καὶ τῶν μὴ συντελούντων.
'Ἀθάνατοι τεθείκασι μοῖραν ἐπὶ ἑκάστῳ'
ἡ Εἱμαρμένη ἕκαστα διένειμεν ἀνθρώποις,
ἢ ἡ ἡμέρα τε καὶ νὺξ διένειμαν ἀνθρώποις.

'It was *a god, Hermes,* who gave' this skill in thievery
means his birth star Mercury provided him with such and
    such.
  '*For Athena had turned her thoughts aside. But Odysseus*'      45
means the Athena of Odysseus, that is, his wisdom, turned
    their mind
with scheming, so as not to understand.
  '*A god has put this in your heart*' means your mind in your
    soul
or indeed the converse, your soul in your mind.
  '*If a god were to* subdue *the suitors to me,*' means Destiny,     50
or my own wisdom, trickery, and scheming.
  '*Leave the issue to* the *gods*' means to Destiny itself.
He means, lay this upon Destiny itself
or to my own wisdom and to my own trickery.
  '*For two are the gates of shadowy dreams,*          55
*one is fashioned of horn and one of ivory.*'
Here he teaches about the origin of dreams
and he says which are true and which false.
Those from the gates of horn are from the head, mind, and
    soul;
he says they happen to be true and prophetic of the future.    60
For a dream is a figment of the soul that foretells the future.
Thus he says that dreams coming from the soul and mind
speak the truth; but those coming from ivory,
those arising from every kind of harm and troubled
    thoughts,
he tells you are false ones that are not fulfilled.    65
  '*The immortals* have appointed *a proper time* for *each* thing,'
means Destiny distributed each thing to men,
or day and night distributed them to men.

Ἡ μὲν ἡμέρα πράξεις τε καὶ ἔργων τὰ μυρία,
70  ἡ νὺξ ὕπνον καὶ παῦσιν δὲ τῶν ἔργων τῆς ἡμέρας.
    ῞Υπνον ἐπὶ βλεφάροισιν᾽ ἡ Ἀθηνᾶ δὲ ᾽βάλε᾽
    τὸ τοῦ ἀέρος ἔνυγρον· ὑπνοποιὸν γὰρ τοῦτο.
    Ὅτι δ᾽ ἦν ἔνυγρος ἀὴρ χειμέριός τε χρόνος,
    ἐκ τῆς χοιροσφαγίας τε τῆς περὶ τοῖς μνηστῆρσι
75  καὶ τοῦ ῥιγῶσαι ἱκανῶς Εὐμαίῳ Ὀδυσσέα
    ἔγνως ἀριδηλότατα· λοιπὸν ἐμοὶ παυστέον.

Day gives deeds and countless activities to men,
but night gives sleep and rest from the activities of the day.    70
  'Athena *cast sleep upon her eyelids*'
means the moist part of the air; for this brings sleep.
That the air was moist and it was winter time
you learned most clearly from the pigs slaughtered
on account of the suitors and that Odysseus shivered    75
    considerably
at Eumaios's hut; so I must stop.

## Υ΄

Τοῦ Υ΄ δὲ ἡ ὑπόθεσις τῆς Ὀδυσσείας ἥδε.

Ἐν τῷ προδόμῳ Ὀδυσσεὺς τοῦ οἴκου τοῦ οἰκείου
βοὸς οἰῶν τε δέρμασι κατέκειτο ἀγρύπνως.
Ἐξερχομένας δὲ δμωὰς πρὸς μίξιν τῶν μνηστήρων
ἰδὼν κτανεῖν ἐβούλετο· ἑκὼν παρεὶς ὑπνεῖ δέ.
5 Κλαιούσης Πηνελόπης δέ, ἀνθ᾽ ὧν ὀνείροις εἶδε
συγκαθευδῆσαι Ὀδυσσεῖ, τῷ δ᾽ ἀληθεῖ ψευσθῆναι,
τέρας καὶ φήμην Ὀδυσσεύς οἱ εὔχεται γενέσθαι
καὶ γίνονται ἀμφότερα, βροντὴ μὲν οὐρανόθεν,
ἐξ ἀλετρίδος φήμη δὲ δεινὴ κατὰ μνηστήρων.
10 Ἡμέρας δὲ ὁ Εὔμαιος ἐκείνῳ καὶ βουκόλος
συνομιλοῦσι φιλικῶς, Κτήσιππος δ᾽ εἷς μνηστήρων
πόδα βοὸς ἐτίναξεν, ὡς Ὀδυσσέα πλήξῃ.
Τὸν μάντιν Θεοκλύμενον εἰπόντα τοῖς μνηστῆρσι,
σκότος ὁρᾶν ταῖς κεφαλαῖς ἐκείνων καὶ τοιαῦτα,
15 ἐκέλευσεν Εὐρύμαχος ἐξάγειν ἔξω δόμων,
καὶ Θεοκλύμενος εὐθὺς εἰς Πείραιον ἀπῆλθε.
Μνηστῆρες δὲ Τηλέμαχον ἐγέλων σὺν τοῖς ξένοις.

# Book 20

This is the subject matter of the twentieth book of
the *Odyssey.*

Odysseus, in the forecourt of his own house,
lay wakefully on skins of oxen and sheep.
Seeing the female slaves coming out to lie with the suitors,
he wanted to kill the women but willed himself to relax and
    sleep.
As Penelope was crying because of what she saw in her     5
    dreams,
that she slept with Odysseus, that she had been deceived
    about the truth,
Odysseus prays for an omen and a prophecy,
and both occur, first thunder from the heavens,
then a terrible prophecy against the suitors uttered by a
    woman grinding grain.
Within the day, Eumaios and the cowherd     10
speak amicably to him, but Ktesippos, one of the suitors,
hurled a cow's foot to strike Odysseus.
Eurymachos ordered the seer Theoklymenos,
who had told the suitors that he saw darkness over their
    heads
and such things, to be led out of the house,     15
and Theoklymenos immediately went away to Peiraios.
The suitors laughed at Telemachos and his guests.

‘Μοῦνος ἐὼν πολέσι. Σχεδόθεν δὲ οἱ ἦλθεν Ἀθήνη
οὐρανόθεν καταβᾶσα· δέμας δ᾽ ἤϊκτο γυναικί.’
20 Ἀθήνη νῦν ἡ φρόνησίς ἐστι τοῦ Ὀδυσσέως.
Ὁ οὐρανὸς ἡ κεφαλή, διὰ δὲ πανουργίαν
καὶ τὰ πυκνὰ νοήματα τὰ τοῦ Ἰθακησίου
γυναίῳ φρόνησιν αὐτοῦ τῷ συνεργῷ εἰκάζει.
Ἃ δέ φησιν ὁ Ὀδυσσεὺς δῆθεν ὡς πρὸς ἐκείνην,
25 αὐτὸς εἰς νοῦν τὸν ἑαυτοῦ λογίζεται καὶ λέγει,
καὶ ἅ φησιν ἡ Ἀθηνᾶ ὡσαύτως πρὸς ἐκεῖνον.
‘Εἴ περ γὰρ κτείναιμι Διός τε σέθεν τε ἕκητι,
πῇ κεν ὑπεκπροφύγοιμι; Τά σε φράζεσθαι ἄνωγα.’
Εἰ τοὺς μνηστῆρας κτείναιμι νῷ τε καὶ τῇ φρονήσει,
30 πῇ κεν ὑπεκπροφύγοιμι; Τοῦτό μοι σκοπητέον.
‘Ὣς φάτο, καί ῥά οἱ ὕπνον ἐπὶ βλεφάροισιν ἔχευεν,
αὐτὴ δ᾽ ἂψ ἐς Ὄλυμπον ἀφίκετο δῖα θεάων.’
Τοιαῦτα λογισάμενος τρέπει αὐτὸν πρὸς ὕπνον.
Ἡ φρόνησις δ᾽ ἀνέδραμε πάλιν αὐτῆς εἰς οἶκον,
35 τὸν οὐρανόν, τὴν κεφαλὴν ὁλολαμπῆ τελοῦσαν,
εἰ τέως Δία νοῦν ἔχει καὶ φρόνησιν Ἀθήνην.
‘Δίαν θεάων’ δέ φησι τὴν φρόνησιν εὐλόγως·
τῶν ψυχικῶν δυνάμεων πασῶν γὰρ ὑπερέχει
καὶ τῶν τεσσάρων ἀρετῶν φρόνησις βασιλεύει.
40 Ἄνευ καὶ γὰρ φρονήσεως ἀνδρεία ἢ καὶ ῥώμη
χωλὸν ἀσυντελέστατον καθέστηκε τὸ ζῷον,
ὡσαύτως σωφροσύνη τε καὶ ἡ δικαιοσύνη.
Ὁ Μελιτίδης σωφρονῶν, φρονήσεως δὲ ἄνευ,
κατάγελως ἦν σύμπασιν τοῖς οὖσιν ἐν τῷ βίῳ.
45 “Πῶς οὐ καθεύδεις” γὰρ τινῶν λεγόντων “τῇ συζύγῳ;”

'*One man as he was against so many. Then Athena came down*
*from heaven and drew near to him in the likeness of a woman.*'
Athena here is the wisdom of Odysseus.                                    20
The sky, that is, the head, because of his scheming
and the crafty thoughts of the Ithakan,
likens his wisdom to a woman collaborating with him.
What Odysseus supposedly says to her
he himself ponders in his own mind and speaks to it,                     25
and likewise what Athena says to him.
　'*Even if I were to slay them by Zeus's will and yours,*
*where then should I flee? Of this I bid you take thought.*'
This means if I should kill the suitors with intelligence and
　　wisdom
how would I escape? I must consider this.                                 30
　'*So she spoke, and shed sleep upon his eyelids,*
*but herself, the fair goddess, went back to Olympos.*'
That is, having pondered these things he turns to sleep.
Wisdom ran up again to her own house,
the sky, the head which is shining all over,                             35
if previously it had Zeus, that is, a mind, and Athena, that is,
　　wisdom.
He reasonably calls wisdom a 'fair *goddess*';
for wisdom is superior to all the powers of the soul,
and rules over the four virtues.
Without wisdom, therefore, courage or even strength                      40
make living beings lame and useless,
as do prudence and justice.
Melitides being prudent, but without wisdom,
was a laughing stock to everyone in the world.
For when some people asked him, "Why don't you sleep                     45
　　with your spouse?",

"Μήπως εἰς δίκην ἕλξῃ με ταύτης ἡ μήτηρ" εἶπε.
Δῖαν θεῶν τὴν φρόνησιν Ὅμηρος ὧδε λέγει,
ὡς ψυχικῶν δυνάμεων πασῶν ὑπερτεροῦσαν.
    Τοῦ οὐρανοῦ 'Διός' ἐστιν Ἄρτεμις' παῖς σελήνη·
50  ὀξεῖς θανάτους δέ φασιν ἡλίου καὶ σελήνης.
    'Θεοὶ' ἡ Εἱμαρμένη νῦν, ἡ Ἀφροδίτη' φίλοι,
φίλοι τινὲς καὶ συγγενεῖς ἐκθρέψαντες τὰς κόρας
'τυρῷ' ἀντὶ τοῦ γάλακτι καὶ 'μέλιτι' καὶ 'οἴνῳ.'
    'Ἡ Ἥρη δῶκεν εἶδός τε καὶ πινυτὴν ἐκείναις.'
55  Ὁ γὰρ ἀὴρ αὐξήσεως αἴτιος καὶ φρενῶν δέ.
Πρὸς τὰς ἀέρων κράσεις γὰρ ἴδοις καὶ ζώων φύσεις
ὠχρούς, ἀώχρους, εὐειδεῖς, ἄφρονας, τῶν εὐφρόνων,
ἄγριά τε καὶ ἥμερα, νωθρὰ καὶ τῶν ὀξέων,
εὐμήκη τε καὶ ταπεινὰ καὶ τοῖς λοιποῖς ὡσαύτως.
60  Καὶ ἡ σελήνη, 'Ἄρτεμις,' αὐξήσεως αἰτία,
αὐξήσεως καὶ θρέψεως, θερμὴ καὶ χλιαρὰ γάρ.
    'Ἡ Ἀθηνᾶ' ἡ φρόνησις, διδάσκει δὲ πᾶν ἔργον.'
    'Εὖτ' Ἀφροδίτη δῖα προσέστιχε μακρὸν Ὄλυμπον
κούρης αἰτήσουσα τέλος θαλεροῖο γάμοιο,
65  ἐς Δία τερπικέραυνον—ὁ γάρ τ' εὖ οἶδεν ἅπαντα,
μοῖράν τ' ἀμμορίην τε καταθνητῶν ἀνθρώπων—,'
ὅτε καιρὸς ἦν ταύταις δὲ γάμου καὶ Ἀφροδίτης
ἐξ οὐρανοῦ καὶ τοῦ Διός, τῆς Εἱμαρμένης, τρέπων.
    'Τόφρα δὲ τὰς κούρας Ἅρπυιαι ἀνηρείψαντο
70  καί ῥ' ἔδοσαν στυγερῇσιν Ἐρινύσιν ἀμφιπολεύειν.'

he said, "In case her mother takes me to court."
Homer here says that wisdom is a fair goddess,
as it surpasses all the powers of the soul.
   'Artemis,' the moon, is the child of 'Zeus,' the heavens;
they say that deaths from acute illness come from the sun     50
     and moon.
   'The gods' here are Destiny, 'Aphrodite' is the friends,
that is, some friends and kinsmen who have nourished the
     girls
'with cheese' instead of milk, and 'with honey' and 'wine.'
   'Hera gave them beauty and wisdom.'
For air is responsible for growth and the mind.     55
You could see the mixing of the air and animal natures,
pale, not pale, beautiful, foolish, sensible,
wild and tame, sluggish and swift,
tall and humble, and likewise for the other characteristics.
And the moon, 'Artemis,' is also the cause of growth,     60
of growth and rearing, for it is hot and warm.
   'Athena,' that is, wisdom, teaches every 'craft.'
   'But while divine Aphrodite was going to high Olympos
to ask for the maidens the accomplishment of gladsome marriage,
going to Zeus who delights in thunderbolts—for he knows all     65
     things well,
both the good and bad fortune of mortal men—'
means when it was their time for marriage, that is, for
     Aphrodite,
the weather turned them away from the heavens and from
     Zeus, that is, Destiny.
   'Meanwhile the Harpies snatched away the maidens
and gave them to the hateful Furies to deal with.'     70

Ἤτοι φρενῶν ἐξώσθησαν τραπεῖσαι πρὸς μανίαν
καὶ ἄφαντοι γεγόνασιν ὥσπερ ἀνηρπαγμέναι
Ἁρπυίαις καὶ ἀνέμοις δὲ ῥαγδαίοις καὶ βιαίοις.
   'Ὀνείρατα ἐπέσσευε δαίμων,' ἡ Εἱμαρμένη,
75 εἴτ' οὖν ὁ ὕπνος εἴτε νὺξ εἴτε νοὸς ἡ πλάσις.
   'Εὔξατο, χεῖρας ἀνασχὼν Διί,' τῷ οὐρανῷ δέ·
   'Ζεῦ πάτερ, εἴ μ' ἐθέλοντες ἐπὶ τραφερήν τε καὶ ὑγρήν.'
   'Ζεῦ πάτερ' Εἱμαρμένης νῦν οἱ σύμπαντες ἀστέρες.
   'Διὸς τέρας φανείη' δὲ ἐξ οὐρανοῦ σημεῖον
80 ἡ Εἱμαρμένη τι δηλοῦν καὶ μέλλον τελεσθῆναι.
   'Ζεῦ πάτερ, ὅς τε θεοῖσι καὶ ἀνθρώποισιν ἀνάσσεις,'
ὦ πνεῦμα ζῳογόνον, σὺ ψυχὴ παντὸς τοῦ κόσμου.
   'Θεοί,' ἡ Εἱμαρμένη δέ, 'τισαίατο τὴν λώβην.'
   Καὶ πάλιν δὲ 'δυόωντες θεοὶ' ἡ Εἱμαρμένη.
85    'Ζεῦ πάτερ, οὔ τις σεῖο θεῶν ὀλοώτερος ἄλλος'
οὐδὲν ὀλεθριώτερόν ἐστι τῆς Εἱμαρμένης·
τῶν ψυχικῶν δυνάμεων, 'θεῶν' ἐνθάδε λέγει.
   'Ὄπιδα' τούτων δὲ τανῦν τὸ δίκαιον σὺ νόει.
   Ἄρτι 'Ζεὺς' ὕπατος 'θεῶν' τὸ ζῳογόνον πνεῦμα.
90    'Κρονίων δὲ τελέσειεν' αὐτὴ ἡ Εἱμαρμένη.
   'Πᾶσι θεοῖς ἐπεύξατο' στοιχείοις, Εἱμαρμένη.
   Ὁ 'Ζεὺς Κρονίων' πάλιν δὲ ἄδηλος Εἱμαρμένη.

That is, they were forced out of their mind, turned to
    madness,
and became invisible as if they had been snatched away
by the Harpies, that is, by the raging, violent winds.
   '*A god sends* evil dreams' means Destiny,
either sleep or night or the figments generated by thought.   75
   '*He prayed, lifting up his hands to Zeus,*' that is, to the
    heavens.
   '*Father Zeus, if you gods have willingly brought me over land
    and sea.*'
'*Father Zeus*' here is all the stars of Destiny.
   'Let *a sign from Zeus* appear' means a heavenly sign,
that is, Destiny, to show something that is about to happen.   80
   '*Father Zeus, who are lord over gods and men*'
means O life-giving spirit, you are the soul of the entire
    universe.
   '*The gods,*' that is, Destiny, '*might take vengeance.*'
   '*The gods* plunging into misery' is again Destiny.
   '*Father Zeus, none of the gods is more baneful than you*'   85
means nothing is more destructive than Destiny;
here by 'the *gods*' he means the powers of the soul.
   With the gods' '*wrath*' here you should understand
    justice.
   Now '*Zeus*' supreme '*among the gods*' is the life-giving
    spirit.
   '*Might the son of Kronos fulfill*' means Destiny itself.   90
   '*He prayed to all* the gods' means to the elements, to
    Destiny.
   '*Zeus, son of Kronos*' again here is unknowable Destiny.

'Οὐ μὰ Ζῆν', Ἀγέλαε, καὶ ἄλγεα πατρὸς ἐμοῖο,'
οὐ, μὰ τὴν Εἱμαρμένην τε καὶ θλίψεις τὰς πατρῷας,
95 ἢ μὰ τοῦ κόσμου τὴν ψυχὴν καὶ θλίψεις τὰς πατρῴας.
'Μὴ τοῦτο δὲ τελέσειε θεὸς' ἡ Εἱμαρμένη,
ἢ ὁ ἐμός τε λογισμὸς εἴθε μὴ δρῴη τοῦτο.
'Ἄσβεστον ὦρσε γέλων δὲ μνηστῆρσιν ἡ Ἀθήνη'
ἡ Τηλεμάχου φρόνησις γέλων αὐτοῖς παρέσχεν.
100 'Οἷον δὴ τάχ' ἔμελλε θεὰ καὶ καρτερὸς ἀνήρ'
ὁ Ὀδυσσεὺς ὁ καρτερὸς μετὰ τῆς πανουργίας.

'*No, by Zeus, Agelaos, and by the woes of my father*'
means no, by Destiny and my father's woes,
or by the soul of the universe and my father's woes.     95
    '*May God never bring such a thing to pass*' means
may Destiny, or my reason, not do this.
    '*Athena roused unquenchable* laughter *among the suitors*'
means Telemachos's wisdom provided them with laughter.
    '*Such as a goddess and a mighty man were soon to spread*'     100
means powerful Odysseus with his cunning.

# Φ'

Αὕτη τῆς Φῖ ὑπόθεσις Ὁμήρου Ὀδυσσείας.

Ἡ Πηνελόπη τίθησιν ἆθλον αὑτῆς τὸν γάμον,
ὃς τῶν μνηστήρων τείνειε τόξον τοῦ Ὀδυσσέως
καὶ διὰ τῶν πελέκεων εὐστόχως ὀϊστεύσει.
Εὔμαιος καὶ βουκόλος δὲ τὰ τοῦ δεσπότου τόξα
5 ἰδόντες κατεδάκρυσαν· ἐκτὸς δ' ἐκβεβλημένοις
τὸ πᾶν αὐτοῖς ὁ Ὀδυσσεὺς λοιπὸν ἀνακαλύπτει
καὶ ὑπισχνεῖται δὲ αὐτοὺς ποιῆσαι Τηλεμάχους
καὶ πᾶν προῳκονόμησε σὺν τῷ υἱῷ καὶ τούτοις.
Τέλος μνηστήρων οὐδενὸς ἐντεῖναι δυνηθέντος,
10 αὐτὸς τὸ τόξον ἔτεινεν ἐκείνων κωλυόντων
καὶ δι' ὀπῶν τῶν δώδεκα πελέκεων τοξεύει.

Νῦν Ἀθηνᾶν γλαυκῶπιδα' τὴν φρόνησιν γινώσκεις.
'Ἴκελος ἀθανάτοισιν' ἄστρασιν ἴσος κάλλει
ἢ ἴσος τῷ Ἡλίῳ δέ, ταῖς τόξων εὐστοχίαις.
15 Καὶ Ἥλιος ὡς τόξῳ γὰρ αὐτοῦ τὰς λαμπηδόνας
εὐστόχως πέμπει δι' ὀπῶν καὶ πάνυ σμικροτάτων.
Ὁ Ἡρακλῆς Διὸς υἱὸς' ὑπῆρχε, βασιλέως,
μάγου καὶ ἀστρολόγου δὲ πάντων ὑπερτεροῦντος.
Τῶν ψυχικῶν δυνάμεων, 'θεῶν,' ἐνθάδε λέγει.
20 'Καί τις θεῶν ἐνέγκοιεν αὐτὸν' ἡ Εἱμαρμένη.

238

# Book 21

This is the subject matter of the twenty-first book of
Homer's Odyssey.

Penelope sets up a competition for her hand,
whoever from among the suitors would string Odysseus's
    bow
and accurately shoot through the axes.
Eumaios and the cowherd, seeing their master's bow,
began to cry; so Odysseus reveals everything to them     5
after they had been thrown out,
and promises to turn them into Telemachoi, and
arranged everything in advance with his son and these men.
Finally, since none of the suitors could string it,
he himself strings the bow as they tried to prevent him,     10
and shoots an arrow through the holes of the twelve axes.

    Here you recognize 'flashing-eyed Athena' as wisdom.
    'Like *the immortals*' means equal in beauty to the stars
or equal to the Sun, because of the accuracy of his arrows.
For the Sun sends his rays accurately as from a bow     15
through even the smallest holes.
    'Herakles' was 'the son *of Zeus*,' of a king,
a mage, and an astrologer preeminent over all.
    With '*of the gods*' he means here of the powers of the soul.
    '*And some one* of the gods should bring *him*' means     20
    Destiny.

Ψυχὴν τοῦ κόσμου σύμπαντος τὸ 'Ζεῦ πάτερ' σημαίνει.
'Αὐτὸν ἀγάγοι δαίμων' δὲ αὐτὴ ἡ Εἱμαρμένη.
'Πᾶσι θεοῖσιν ηὔξατο' στοιχείοις, Εἱμαρμένη.
''Εμοὶ δαμάσειε θεὸς' φρόνησις, Εἱμαρμένη.

25   'Τοῖο θεοῖο ἑορτὴν' ''Ερωτος, Ἀφροδίτης.
Τὸ 'ἐπιτρέψαι δὲ θεοῖς' νῦν τὸ πεισθῆναι λέγει.
Θεοὺς δὲ νῦν τὸν ''Ερωτα καὶ Ἀφροδίτην λέγει.
''Ηῶθε κράτος δὲ θεὸς δώσει' ἡ Εἱμαρμένη.
'Ἀθήνην ὕπνον βάλλουσαν ἐπὶ βλεφάροις' εἶπον

30   τὸν κάθυγρον ἀέρα σοι. Καὶ φρόνησιν νοήσεις,
φρονήσει γὰρ ἠθέλησεν ὕπνῳ κατασχεθῆναι.

'Ἰλήκησιν Ἀπόλλων τε καὶ οἱ θεοὶ οἱ ἄλλοι'
ἂν ἵλεως ὁ ''Ηλιος καὶ τὰ λοιπὰ στοιχεῖα,
ἤτοι ἂν ζῶμεν καί ἐσμεν ἐν τῷ παρόντι κόσμῳ

35   ὁρῶντες μὲν τὸν ''Ηλιον, πνέοντες δὲ ἀέρα
καὶ τοῖς καρποῖς τρεφόμενοι, πίνοντες δὲ καὶ ὕδωρ.
Ὁ 'Ζεὺς' τανῦν ὁ οὐρανὸς 'ἔκτυπε δὲ μεγάλως.'

The '*father Zeus*' signifies the soul of the entire universe.
'*May a god guide* him' means Destiny itself.
'He prayed *to all the gods*' means to the elements, to
    Destiny.
'A *god* shall subdue *unto me*' means wisdom, Destiny.
The 'feast *of the god*' means of Love, of Aphrodite.                    25
With '*leave it* to the gods' here he means to be persuaded.
Here he means that the gods are Love and Aphrodite.
    'In the morning *the god will give* victory' means Destiny.
    'Athena casting *sleep upon* her eyelids' I said
to you is moist air. You will also know it is wisdom,                    30
for, because of her wisdom, she wished sleep to overcome
    her.
    '*Apollo, be gracious, and* the *other gods*'
means if the Sun and the other elements are propitious,
that is, if we live and exist in this present world,
seeing the Sun, breathing the air,                                       35
being nourished with fruits of the earth, and drinking
    water.
    '*Zeus thundered* loudly' here is the sky.

# X′

Τῆς Ὀδυσσείας δὲ τῆς ΧῙ ὑπόθεσις τοιάδε.

Ὁ Ὀδυσσεὺς σὺν τῷ υἱῷ, βουκόλῳ καὶ Εὐμαίῳ
πάντας μνηστῆρας ἀναιρεῖ, τὸν ἀοιδὸν δὲ μόνον
Φήμιον καὶ τὸν Μέδοντα θεράποντα παρῆκε,
τοῦ Τηλεμάχου σφῷ πατρὶ φείσασθαι τούτων φάντος.
5 Διὰ τοῦ Τηλεμάχου δέ, Εὐμαίου καὶ βουκόλου
κτείνει καὶ τὸν Μελάνθιον, τὸν τῶν αἰγῶν βουκόλον,
καὶ θεραπαίνας δώδεκα μνηστῆρσι μιγνυμένας,
ἐξαγαγούσας τοὺς νεκροὺς πρῶτα τοὺς τῶν μνηστήρων,
καὶ καθαράσας ἀκριβῶς πᾶν μίασμα τοῦ οἴκου.
10 Εἶτα τὸν οἶκον θυμιᾷ καὶ Εὐρυκλείᾳ λέγει,
καὶ αἱ λοιπαὶ ἐξέρχονται, ἀσπάζονται δ' ἐκεῖνον.

'Ἀπόλλων εὖχος' πόροι δὲ ὁ Ἥλιος ὑπάρχει,
ἤτοι ἐκπέμψω εὔστοχα ὡς Ἥλιος ἀκτῖνας,
ἢ εἰ ὁ Ἥλιος ἐμοὶ καὶ τῆς ζωῆς ὁ χρόνος
15 ἐξ Εἱμαρμένης μένει μοι τηρῶν τὴν εὐτυχίαν,
κατευστοχήσω καὶ σκοποῦ τοῦ κατὰ τῶν μνηστήρων.
'Θεοὺς' ἀστέρα Ἥλιον νῦν καὶ λοιποὺς ἀστέρας.
Τὰ ἅπερ 'οὐκ ἐτέλεσε Κρονίων' Εἱμαρμένη.
'Τοῖσι δ' ἐπ' ἀγχίμολον θυγάτηρ Διὸς ἦλθεν Ἀθήνη,
20 Μέντορι εἰδομένη ἠμὲν δέμας ἠδὲ καὶ αὐδήν.'
Νῦν Ἀθηνᾶ ἡ φρόνησίς ἐστι τοῦ Ὀδυσσέως·

# Book 22

This is the subject matter of the twenty-second book of
the *Odyssey*.

Odysseus, with his son, the cowherd and Eumaios,
kills all the suitors; he spares only
the singer Phemios and his servant Medon,
as Telemachos told his father to spare them.
Through Telemachos, Eumaios, and the cowherd,                    5
he kills Melanthios, the goatherd,
and twelve slave girls who had lain with suitors,
first making them carry out the corpses of the suitors
and thoroughly clean all the defilement from his house.
Then he fumigates the house and tells Eurykleia,              10
and the other slave girls come out and embrace him.

   May '*Apollo*' grant me '*glory*' is the Sun,
that is, I will accurately send out rays like the Sun,
or if the Sun, that is, the length of my life
given to me by Destiny, maintains my good fortune,           15
I will be quite successful in my aim against the suitors.
   '*The gods*' here are the Sun star and the other stars.
   '*That*' which '*the son of Kronos did not* bring to pass' means
      Destiny.
   '*Then Athena, daughter of Zeus, drew near them,*
*like unto Mentor in form and voice.*'                         20
Athena here is Odysseus's wisdom; but how did it take

πῶς δ᾽ ὡμοιώθη Μέντορι; Δείσας πληθὺν μνηστήρων,
μήπως ἡττήσωσιν αὐτοὺς τέσσαρας ὑπηργμένους,
πλάττεται δῆθε Μέντορα ἐκείνοις συνυπάρχειν.

25 Μετὰ καὶ ἄλλων δηλαδὴ καὶ ὡς πρὸς τοῦτον λέγει.

*'Ως φάτ᾽ ὀϊόμενος λαοσσόον ἔμμεν᾽ Ἀθήνην᾽*
οὕτως εἰρήκει Ὀδυσσεὺς καίπερ σαφῶς γινώσκων,
ὅτι οὐδείς, ᾧ προσφωνεῖ, συμπαρυπάρχει τούτῳ·
τοῦτο δ᾽ αὐτοῦ φρονήσεως ὑπάρχει πανουργία.

30 *'Ως φάτ᾽, Ἀθηναίη δὲ χολώσατο κηρόθι μᾶλλον,*
*νείκεσσεν δ᾽ Ὀδυσσῆα χολωτοῖσιν ἐπέεσσιν·᾽*
αὐτὸς αὐτὸν ἐπέπληξε τάδε κατ᾽ ἔπος λέγων·
"οὐκ εἴην ἂν ὁ Ὀδυσσεὺς ὁ πέρσας ἐγὼ Τροίαν,
ὁ τὰ καὶ τὰ ποιήσας δὲ τῇ τότε Τρώων μάχῃ,

35 εἰ ἐν τοῖς οἴκοις τοῖς ἐμοῖς ἀνάσχωμαι τοιάδε
καὶ μὴ θανάτῳ σύμπαντας πρεπώδει παραπέμψω."

*'Η ῥα, καὶ οὔ πω πάγχυ δίδου ἑτεραλκέα νίκην,*
*ἀλλ᾽ ἔτ᾽ ἄρα σθένεός τε καὶ ἀλκῆς πειρήτιζεν*
*ἠμὲν Ὀδυσσῆος ἠδ᾽ υἱοῦ κυδαλίμοιο.*

40 *Αὐτὴ δ᾽ αἰθαλόεντος ἀνὰ μεγάροιο μέλαθρον*
*ἕζετ᾽ ἀναΐξασα, χελιδόνι εἰκέλη ἄντην.᾽*
Ταῦτα μὲν εἶπεν Ὀδυσσεὺς φρονήσει τῇ οἰκείᾳ·
οὔπω δὲ νίκην κατ᾽ αὐτῶν εἰργάσατο τελείαν,
ἀλλ᾽ ἔτι ῥώμης τῆς αὐτοῦ καὶ τῆς τοῦ Τηλεμάχου

45 ἀπόπειραν ἐλάμβανε τῇ μάχῃ τῶν μνηστήρων.
Ὁ δ᾽ ἦχος τούτου τῆς φωνῆς ὅμοιος χελιδόνος
ἠχήσας ἐξανέδραμε τῆς στέγης τῆς οἰκίας.

*'Καὶ δή οἱ Μέντωρ μὲν ἔβη κενὰ εὔγματα εἰπών,᾽*
ὡς Ὀδυσσεὺς ἐπλάττετο πρὸς Μέντορά τι λέγειν,

Mentor's likeness? Odysseus, fearing the crowd of suitors,
lest they be defeated by them, as they were only four,
pretends that Mentor was supposedly with them.
That is, along with the others, he speaks to him as well.                    25
   'So he spoke, deeming that it was Athena, the rouser of hosts'
means so Odysseus said, although he knew clearly
that no man, whom he addressed, was there with him;
this, then, is the cunning of his wisdom.
   'So he spoke, and Athena became even angrier in her heart,               30
and rebuked Odysseus with angry words';
this means that he chastised himself, saying this word for
      word;
"I wouldn't be the Odysseus who sacked Troy,
who did this and that in battle with the Trojans then,
if I were to endure this in my house                                        35
and did not send everyone to a fitting death."
   'She spoke, but did not give him strength utterly to turn the
      battle,
but still made trial of the might and valor
of Odysseus and his glorious son.
And she herself flew up to the roof beam of the smoky hall,                 40
and sat there in the form of a swallow.'
In other words, thus did Odysseus speak to his own mind;
he did not yet win a total victory over them,
but still made trial of his own strength
and that of Telemachos in battle with the suitors.                         45
And the sound of his voice, ringing the same
as a swallow's, rose up to the roof of his home.
   'Indeed, Mentor has gone from him, uttering empty boasts'
means that Odysseus pretended to say something to
      Mentor,

50 οἱ δὲ μνηστῆρες ἀπειλὰς ἠπείλουν καὶ ἀπόντι,
νῦν δ᾽ Ὀδυσσεῖ μὴ βλέποντες τὸν Μέντορα συνόντα
οἴονται δειλιάσαντα τούτους ὑποχωρῆσαι,
εἰπόντα τὰ φρυάγματα, Ἀγέλαος ὡς λέγει.
῾Ὁ ῾Ζεὺς δώῃ βεβλῆσθαι᾽ δὲ τανῦν ἡ Εἱμαρμένη.
55 Εἴτ᾽ οὖν ὃν εἶπον λογισμὸν εἴπερ λυσιτελήσει
καὶ Ὀδυσσέα δράσειε παρά τινος βεβλῆσθαι.
῾Ἐτώσια δὲ ἔθηκεν᾽ ἡ φρόνησις ῾Ἀθήνη.᾽
Φρονήσει πρὸς τὰ πρόθυρα καὶ γὰρ ἑστῶτες οὗτοι
πέμποντες μέσον δώματος ἀνήρουν τοὺς μνηστῆρας.
60 Οἱ δὲ μνηστῆρες ἔπεμπον εἰς μάτην ἅπαν βέλος,
ἐκείνων πρὸς τὰ πρόθυρα καὶ τοίχους ἑστηκότων
καὶ κρυπτομένων ταῖς βολαῖς καὶ πάλιν δὲ βαλλόντων.
῾Θεοῖς,᾽ ψυχῆς δυνάμεσιν, ῾ἐπίτρεπε τὸν μῦθον᾽
ἤτοι σὺν νῷ καὶ λογισμῷ λέγε καὶ μὴ φλυάρως.
65 ῾Δὴ τότ᾽ Ἀθηναίη φθισίμβροτον αἰγίδ᾽ ἀνέσχεν
ὑψόθεν ἐξ ὀροφῆς· τῶν δὲ φρένες ἐπτοίηθεν.᾽
Τότε τὴν πανουργίαν δὲ γνόντες τοῦ Ὀδυσσέως,
ὡς οἱ σὺν τούτῳ βάλλοντες κτείνουσι τοὺς μνηστῆρας,
οἱ δὲ μνηστῆρες οὐδαμοῦ δύνανται τούτους βλάπτειν
70 ταῖς παραστάσι, τοίχοις τε καὶ ὅπλοις κρυπτομένους,
οἷα ῾βόες᾽ ἐτράπησαν ῾οἴστρῳ᾽ πεφοβημέναι.
῾Διὸς μεγάλου δὲ βωμὸν᾽ ἀέρος ἢ ἡλίου·
εἶχον στοιχείων γὰρ βωμούς, σοφῶν καὶ βασιλέων,
καὶ ψυχικῶν δυνάμεων καί γε τῆς Εἱμαρμένης.

and the suitors threatened him even though he was absent,    50
and now, not seeing Mentor with Odysseus,
they think that he retreated because he feared them,
having previously spoken boastfully, as Agelaos says.

  'May *Zeus grant* that Odysseus be struck' here means
    Destiny.
Or indeed may the reasoning I spoke about help the suitors    55
and make it so that Odysseus is struck by someone.

  '*Athena* made *vain*' means wisdom.
For due to their wisdom they stood near the doorways and,
shooting into the middle of the room, were killing the
    suitors.
And the suitors were shooting every arrow in vain,    60
as the others were standing near the doorways and the
    walls,
and hiding from the shots and shooting back in turn.

  'To the gods leave the *matter*' means to the powers of the
    soul,
that is, speak with understanding and reason not foolishly.

  '*Then Athena held up her aegis, the bane of mortals,*    65
*on high from the roof, and the suitors' minds were panic-stricken.*'
That is, when they realized Odysseus's cunning then, that
his comrades were killing the suitors by shooting arrows at
    them,
and the suitors were not at all able to harm them,
as they took cover by the entrances, walls, and shields,    70
they fled like '*oxen*' scared 'by a horsefly.'

  '*The altar of great Zeus*' means of the air or the sun;
for they had altars of wise men and kings, and of the
    elements
and of spiritual powers and of Destiny.

247

75    Ὁ ἀοιδὸς ἀείδει δὲ 'θεοῖς τε καὶ ἀνθρώποις.'
       Ἢ βασιλεῦσι καὶ κοινοῖς, σοφοῖς καὶ ἰδιώταις,
       ἢ λέγει τὰ ἀνθρώπων τε ὁμοῦ καὶ τῶν στοιχείων
       καὶ πάντα Εἱμαρμένης δὲ καὶ ἔρωτας καὶ πάθη.
          'Θεὸς δέ μοι ἐδίδαξε' νῦν λογισμὸς οἰκεῖος.
80    Ἀείδω δὲ ὥσπερ θεὸν ὡς Ἥλιον ὑμνῶ σε,
       ὡς ἥλιον, ἀέρα τε ἢ ἕτερα τῶν θείων.
          'Μοῖρα θεῶν ἐδάμασεν' ἀστέρες Εἱμαρμένης.
          'Τῇ Πηνελόπῃ ὕπνον δέ τις τῶν θεῶν ἐπῶρσεν'
       ὑγρότης καταστήματος ἢ φρόνησις οἰκεία.

The singer sings 'to gods and men.'                                    75
That is, either to kings and commoners, to the wise and
    foolish,
or he means the things pertaining to both men and the
    elements
and all the things of Destiny, and love and suffering.
    '*A god* taught *me*' here means my own reason.
I sing and I praise you like the Sun god,                              80
that is, like the sun, the air, or the other divine things.
    'The fate *of the gods* destroyed' means the stars of Destiny.
    'To Penelope some god has sent *sleep*'
means the moisture in the weather or her own wisdom.

Ψ′

Τοῦ Ψῖ τῆς Ὀδυσσείας δὲ ὑπόθεσιν νῦν μάθε.

Ἄνεισιν ἡ Εὐρύκλεια θαλάμῳ Πηνελόπης
καὶ ταύτην ἀνεγείρει δὲ τοῦ ὕπνου Πηνελόπην
καὶ εὐαγγέλιά φησιν, ὡς Ὀδυσσεὺς νῦν ἔνδον
καὶ πάντας ἐξαπέφθειρε κτείνας μνηστῆρας οἴκῳ.
5  Ἐκείνης κατελθούσης δὲ περὶ τὸν Ὀδυσσέα
ἄμφω τινὰ γνωρίσματα εἰπόντες δὲ ἀλλήλων
ἀλλήλοις συνευνάζονται καὶ διηγοῦνται πάντα,
ὁ μέν, ὁπόσα πέπονθε πλανώμενος ἐκ Τροίας,
ἡ δ᾽, ὅσα πάλιν ἐν αὐτοῖς τοῖς οἴκοις καθημένη.
10 Εἶτα αὐτός, Τηλέμαχος, Εὔμαιος καὶ βουκόλος
πρὸς σφὸν ἀγρὸν ἐκτρέχουσι διὰ μνηστήρων φόνους.

    *Μάργην θεοί σε ἔθεσαν᾽ ἤτοι ἡ Εἱμαρμένη.*
    *Ἀλλά τις ἀθανάτων κτεῖνε μνηστῆρας ἀγαυούς.᾽*
    Τὶς ἀθανάτων νῦν σοφός, μάγος, φαρμακεργάτης.
15   *Μαῖα φίλη, χαλεπόν σε θεῶν αἰειγενετάων*
    *δήνεα εἴρυσθαι, μάλα περ πολύϊδριν ἐοῦσαν.᾽*

# Book 23

Here learn the subject matter of the twenty-third book of
the *Odyssey*.

Eurykleia goes up to Penelope's chamber,
rouses Penelope from her sleep,
and tells her the good news, that Odysseus is already inside
and has utterly destroyed all the suitors, killing them in the
    house.
When she came downstairs for Odysseus,                              5
after exchanging with one another certain tokens of
    recognition,
they lie down together and tell one another everything:
he how much he suffered as he was wandering from Troy,
    and
she in turn how much she suffered as she remained in this
    house.
Afterwards, he, Telemachos, Eumaios, and the cowherd             10
run away to his own farm because of the murders of the
    suitors.

  '*The gods* made *you mad*,' that is Destiny.
  '*But one of the immortals has slain the lordly suitors.*'
One of the immortals here is a wise man, a mage, a potion
    maker.
  '*Dear nurse, it is hard for you to comprehend the counsels*      15
*of the eternal gods, no matter how wise you are.*'

Δύσκολον, κἂν πολύϊδρις Εὐρύκλεια τυγχάνῃς,
βουλὰς νοεῖν σε τῶν σοφῶν, μάγων καὶ φαρμακέων.
Τῶν ʻαἰειγενετάωνʼ δὲ τῶν ζώντων ἀεὶ φήμαις.

20  ʻΦρασσόμεθʼ, ὅττι κε κέρδος Ὀλύμπιος ἐγγυαλίξῃ,ʼ
ὁ νοῦς ἐμὸς καὶ βούλευμα εἴτε καὶ Εἱμαρμένη.
ʻΠολὺ δὲ κάλλος ἔχευεν Ἀθήνηʼ πρὶν ἐρρέθη.
Αὐτὸ κατὰ μετάληψιν τὸ δένδρον τῆς ἐλαίας·
μᾶλλον τοῦ δένδρου πλέον νῦν τὸ ἔλαιόν σοι λέγει.

25  ʻἼδρις, ὃν Ἥφαιστος δέδαεν καὶ Παλλὰς Ἀθήνη,ʼ
ὅνπερ τὸ πῦρ ἐδίδαξε καὶ φρόνησις σὺν τούτῳ·
ʻὁμοῖος ἀθανάτοιςʼ δὲ ἀστράσιν ἢ στοιχείοις.
ʻΟἱ τὰ Ὀλύμπου δώματα ἔχοντεςʼ Εἱμαρμένη.
ʻΘεὸς αὐτὸςʼ νῦν ʻἐπελθώνʼ τις ἐκ σοφῶν καὶ μάγων,

30  εἴτε καὶ τῶν στοιχείων δέ, ὥσπερ αὐτὸς νῦν φράσω.
ʻʻʻΤίς μου στρωμνὴν μετέθετο;ʼʼʼ ὁ Ὀδυσσεὺς εἰρήκει,
εἰ μή που μάγος περ ἀνὴρ εἴτε σεισμὸς γῆς μέγας
ἢ θάλασσα λαβράσασα ἢ ἕτερον τοιοῦτον.
ʻΘεοὶ παρεῖχον ὀϊζὺνʼ ἀστέρες Εἱμαρμένης.

35  ʻΔιὸς ἐκγεγαυῖαʼ δὲ παῖς οὖσα βασιλέως,
ʻτὴνʼ ἢν ʻθεὸςʼ παρώρμησε ʻρέξαιʼ κακόν τι ʻἔργον.ʼ
Θεὸς ἡ Εἱμαρμένη νῦν ἢ καὶ ἐπιθυμία.
ʻΕἰ μὴ ἄρʼ ἄλλʼ ἐνόησε θεὰ γλαυκῶπις Ἀθήνη.ʼ
Νύκτα μὲν ἐν περάτῃ δολιχὴν σχέθεν, Ἠῶ δʼ αὖτε,ʼ

40  ʻκαὶ νύ κʼ ὀδυρομένοισιν ἐφάνη <ἡ> ἡμέρα,ʼ

That is, it is difficult, even if you are the very wise
    Eurykleia,
to understand the wishes of the wise men, mages, and
    potion makers.
'*Eternal*' means who are always alive through stories.
    '*We shall devise whatever advantage the Olympian may*     20
    *vouchsafe us,*'
that is, my mind and will or even Destiny.
    '*Athena* shed *abundant beauty*' was explained previously.
This was the olive tree by transference of meaning;
rather he speaks to you here more about the oil than the
    tree.
    '*A cunning workman whom Hephaistos and Pallas Athena*     25
    *taught,*'
that is, whom the fire taught along with wisdom;
'*like* the immortals,' that is, like the stars or the elements.
    'Those who have palaces on Olympos' means Destiny.
    'Some *god himself should come*' means a wise man or mage,
or even one of the elements, as I myself will say here.     30
    '"*Who* moved my bed?"' said Odysseus,
if not a mage or a great earthquake
or the sea rushing violently or some other such thing.
    '*The gods* gave me *sorrow*' means the stars of Destiny.
    '*Daughter of Zeus*' means the daughter of a king,     35
'*whom*' a '*god*' prompted '*to work*' some evil '*deed.*'
God here means Destiny or even desire.
    '*Had not the goddess, flashing-eyed Athena, taken other counsel.*
*The long night she held back at the end of its course, and likewise*
    *Dawn,*'
'*and now would* the day have risen *upon their weeping,*'     40

εἰ μὴ καιρὸς χειμέριος μακραί τε νύκτες ἦσαν.
Οὔπω μὲν οὖν πραγματικῶς νοούμενον λεχθῆναι·
ὁ Ὅμηρος δὲ εἴρηκεν ὁ πάνσοφος ὧδέ που
"εἰ μὴ ἀὴρ καὶ Ἀθηνᾶ χειμέριος ὑπάρχων
45  τὴν νύκτα παρεξέτασε, παρεῖχε τὴν ἡμέραν."
    'Θεοὶ' καὶ Εἱμαρμένη 'σε ἐποίησαν ἱκέσθαι.'
    'Ὁ Ποσειδῶν' ἡ θάλασσα, 'θεοὶ τοῦ οὐρανοῦ' δὲ
ἀήρ, σελήνη, ἥλιος, πῦρ, φύσις τῶν ἀστέρων.
    'Γῆρας τελέουσι θεοὶ' ἀστέρες Εἱμαρμένης.
50  'Θήσειν ἀθάνατον καὶ ἀγήρων ἤματα πάντα'·
ἄρχοντα, βασιλεύοντα, ὑμνούμενον αἰῶσι.
    'Θεὸν δ' ὡς ἐτιμήσαντο' σοφὸν ἢ βασιλέα
ἢ ὡς στοιχείων οὐρανόν, ἀέρα ἢ ἀστέρας.
    'Ἡ δ' αὖτ' ἄλλ' ἐνόησε θεὰ γλαυκῶπις Ἀθήνη·
55  ὁππότε δή ῥ' Ὀδυσσῆα ἐέλπετο ὃν κατὰ θυμὸν
εὐνῆς ἧς ἀλόχου ταρπήμεναι ἠδὲ καὶ ὕπνου,
αὐτίκ' ἀπ' Ὠκεανοῦ χρυσόθρονον ἠριγένειαν.'
Ὁ δὲ ἀὴρ ἐποίησεν ἡμέραν παραυτίκα,
ἅμα τῷ τούτοις συντυχεῖν καὶ ὕπνου κορεσθῆναι.
60  Ὅμηρος δ', ὅπως εἴρηκεν ἐμψύχως καὶ γλυκέως
μύθοις γλυκάζων ἅπαντα τοῖς ἔπεσι, νῦν ὅρα.
    'Φόως' τοῖς ἀθανάτοισιν ὡς 'φέροι,' τοῖς στοιχείοις,
τῇ γῇ, θαλάσσῃ, οὐρανῷ, τοῖς σύμπασι στοιχείοις.
    'Ζεὺς' καὶ 'θεοὶ' 'πεδάασκον,' ἀὴρ καὶ Εἱμαρμένη,
65  εἴτ' οὖν ἀὴρ καὶ θάλασσα καὶ τὰ λοιπὰ στοιχεῖα.
    'Ἤδη μὲν φάος ἦεν ἐπὶ χθόνα, τοὺς δ' ἄρ' Ἀθήνη
νυκτὶ κατακρύψασα θοῶς ἐξῆγε πόληος.'

that is, had not the weather been wintry and the nights
  long.
In no way has a historical thought been expressed;
rather, Homer the most wise said here,
"had not the wintry air, that is, Athena,
stretched the night, producing day." 45
  'Gods,' that is, Destiny, 'have caused *you to come back.*'
  'Poseidon' is the sea, the 'gods in heaven' are
the air, moon, sun, fire, the nature of the stars.
  '*The gods will bring about old age for you*' means the stars of
    Destiny.
  '*That she would make him immortal and ageless all his days,*' 50
that is, a ruler, a king, praised through the centuries.
  'They honored him *like a god*' means like a wise man or
    king
or like the sky of the elements, the air or the stars.
  '*Then the goddess, flashing-eyed Athena, took other counsel.*
*When she judged that the heart of Odysseus had* 55
*had its fill of dalliance with his wife and of sleep,*
*straightway she roused from Okeanos golden-throned Dawn.*'
That is, the air made the day immediately,
as soon as they had their fill of being with each other and of
    sleep.
See now how Homer spoke vividly and sweetly, 60
sweetening with his words everything in the epics.
  '*To bring light*' to the immortals, that is, to the elements,
to the earth, to the sea, to the sky, to all the elements.
  '*Zeus and the other gods bound*' means the air and Destiny,
or else the air and the sea and the other elements. 65
  '*By now there was light over the earth, but Athena*
*hid them in night, and swiftly led them forth from the city.*'

Τούτους δ' ἡ φρόνησις αὐτὴ καὶ ἡ οἰκονομία
ἐξήγαγε τῆς πόλεως παρ' οὐδενὸς γνωσθέντας,
70  εἴτ' οὖν ἡμέρα ἤδη ἦν, ἀὴρ δὲ ὀμιχλώδης
αὐτοὺς ἀγνώστους ἔξωθι τῆς πόλεως ἐξάγει.

That is, wisdom itself and the dispensation of things
led them out from the city without being recognized by
    anyone,
or it was already day, and the foggy air           70
led them out of the city unrecognized.

# Ω′

Τὸ Ω′ τῆς Ὀδυσσείας δὲ τὸ μέγα τάδε γράφει.


Ἑρμῆς κατάγει μὲν ψυχὰς μνηστήρων εἰς νερτέρους.

Τῆς Ἀχιλλέως δὲ ψυχῆς, Πατρόκλου, Ἀντιλόχου

καὶ τῆς ψυχῆς τοῦ Αἴαντος ὁμιλουσῶν ἐκεῖσε

καὶ ἡ τοῦ Ἀγαμέμνονος ἦλθε ψυχὴ πρὸς ταύτας

5 σὺν ταῖς ψυχαῖς τῶν δώμασιν Αἰγίσθου τεθνηκότων.

Καὶ πρὸς τὴν Ἀγαμέμνονος ἡ Ἀχιλλέως λέγει,

ὅπως πᾶσι μακαριστὸς καὶ εὐτυχὴς ἐδόκει,

οἰκτρῷ θανάτῳ δ᾽ εἵμαρτο τοῦτον ἀναιρεθῆναι.

Πάλιν ἡ Ἀγαμέμνονος τῇ Ἀχιλλέως λέγει,

10 ὅσα τῇ τούτου τελευτῇ συμβέβηκε καὶ οἷα,

καὶ πῶς ἐτάφη τε καὶ ποῦ καί γε σὺν τίσι κεῖται.

Τοιαῦτα τούτων αἱ ψυχαὶ ὡμίλουν πρὸς ἀλλήλας

καὶ τὰς ψυχὰς κατεῖδον δὲ τῶν Ὀδυσσεῖ θανόντων.

Τὸν Ἀμφιμέδοντα, υἱὸν ὄντα τοῦ Μελανέως,

15 ὁ Ἀγαμέμνων ἐρωτᾷ καὶ πᾶν λεπτῶς μανθάνει,

καὶ Ὀδυσσέα καὶ αὐτὴν ὀλβίζει Πηνελόπην,

αὐτὸν δὲ καὶ τὴν ἔχιδναν πρεπόντως ταλανίζει.

Ταῦτα πρὸς Ἅιδην αἱ ψυχαί. Οἱ δὲ μετ᾽ Ὀδυσσέως

εἰς τοὺς ἀγροὺς ἐξέρχονται καὶ δρῶσιν εὐωχίαν.

20 Αὐτὸς αὐτοῦ δὲ τοῦ πατρὸς ἀπόπειραν ποιεῖται,

εἶτα γνωρίζεται αὐτῷ καὶ τὰ συμβάντα λέγει.

# Book 24

The great twenty-fourth book of the *Odyssey* writes this.

Hermes leads the shades of the suitors down to the
    underworld.
While the souls of Achilles, Patroklos, Antilochos,
and the soul of Aias were speaking there,
Agamemnon's soul also came toward them,
along with the souls of those who died in the house of      5
    Aigisthos.
And Achilles's soul says to that of Agamemnon
how he seemed to all most blessed and fortunate,
but he was destined to die a pitiable death.
Agamemnon's soul in turn tells Achilles
all that happened at the time of his death and in what way,   10
and how he was buried and where and with whom he lies.
Such things these souls said to one another, and
they looked down upon all who had died by Odysseus's
    hand.
Agamemnon questions Amphimedon, the son of Melaneus,
and learns everything in detail,      15
and he deems Odysseus and Penelope fortunate,
but rightly deems himself and the viper unfortunate.
So much for the souls in Hades. Those with Odysseus
go out into the countryside and feast.
He himself makes trial of his own father,      20
then he is recognized by him and tells him what happened.

Εὐωχουμένων δὲ αὐτῶν ἐν τοῖς ἀγροῖς τῷ τότε
οἱ τῶν μνηστήρων συγγενεῖς γνόντες τὰ πεπραγμένα
μετὰ μυγμῶν καὶ στεναγμῶν καὶ θρήνων καὶ δακρύων
25  ἐκ τῆς αὐλῆς ἐκφέροντες τότε τῆς Ὀδυσσέως
τοὺς τούτων ἔθαπτον νεκρούς. Συνέδριον δὲ θέντες
χωροῦσι πάντες ἔνοπλοι κατὰ τοῦ Ὀδυσσέως
Εὐπείθους τούτων ἄρχοντος, πατρὸς τοῦ Ἀντινόου.
Ὧν τοὺς ἡμίσεις ἔπαυσε Μέδων καὶ Ἁλιθέρσης,
30  οἱ δ' ἄλλοι μετ' Εὐπείθεος χωρήσαντες εἰς μάχην·
ὑπ' Ἀρκεισίου γέροντος πεσόντος τοῦ Εὐπείθους
καὶ μοίρας τούτων οὐ μικρᾶς ἐκ τῶν μετ' Ὀδυσσέως,
βροντῆς αἴφνης καὶ κεραυνῶν βιαίων γινομένων,
—ἅπερ φησὶν ὁ Ὅμηρος νῦν Ἀθηνᾶν ὑπάρχειν—
35  ἀλλήλοις ἐς ὁμόνοιαν καὶ σύμβασιν συνῆλθον.

'Ἑρμῆς δὲ ψυχὰς Κυλλήνιος ἐξεκαλεῖτο.'
Ὁ Ὅμηρος βουλόμενος εἰπεῖν ἐνθάδε δύο·
τοῦ Ἀχιλλέως τὴν ταφήν, ποίῳ ἐπράχθη τρόπῳ,
φοβῆσαι δὲ τοὺς πράττοντας τὰ ἄθεσμα ἐνθάδε.
40  Ἐν τῷ δεικνύειν αἴσθησιν τοῖς κάτω τῶν ἐνθάδε
τὴν εἰδωλοποιΐαν σοι ταύτην τανῦν εἰσφέρει
καὶ πλάττει λόγους τῶν ψυχῶν, οὕσπερ τρανοῖ τὰ ἔπη.
Ἀλλ' ἤδη, τίς ἐστιν Ἑρμῆς ψυχοπομπός, λεκτέον.
Ἑρμῆς Ἀρκάς τις ἄνθρωπος, Ἑρμῆς καὶ ὁ ἀστὴρ δέ.
45  Ἐκ τούτων δὲ ψυχοπομπὸς οὐδείς ἐστι τῶν δύο·
ψυχοπομπὸς δ' Ἑρμῆς ἐστι τῆς προφορᾶς ὁ λόγος.
Ὅπως δ' ἐστὶ ψυχοπομπός, ἀκούων μάνθανέ μου·
πρὸ τῶν θνησκόντων σιωπᾷ καὶ προεκτρέχει λόγος.

While they were feasting in the countryside then,
the suitors' kinsmen, after learning what had been done,
with moans and sighs and laments and tears,
carried their dead out of Odysseus's courtyard                    25
and buried them. After organizing a meeting,
they all advance in arms against Odysseus,
led by Eupeithes, Antinoös's father.
Medon and Halitherses stopped half of them,
but the rest advanced with Eupeithes to battle;                   30
when Eupeithes fell at the hands of old Arkeisios
and many of them fell at the hands of Odysseus's comrades,
there was suddenly thunder and violent lightning,
—which Homer says here was Athena—
and they joined with one another in unity and harmony.            35

   '*Meanwhile Kyllenian Hermes called forth souls.*'
Homer wished here to speak about two things;
the burial of Achilles, in what way it was done,
and to scare those who were doing lawless deeds here.
In giving a sense of the here-on-earth to those below            40
he introduces dead men talking
and he fashions the souls' speeches, which his epics portray
      clearly.
But now I should explain who Hermes is, the conductor of
      souls.
Hermes was an Arkadian man, Hermes is also the star.
Neither of those two is a conductor of souls;                    45
Hermes, the conductor of souls, is the spoken word.
Listen and learn from me how he is the conductor of souls;
speech goes silent and runs out before dying men.

Τὰ ὡς ἐπὶ τὸ πλεῖστόν σοι γινόμενα νῦν λέγω·
50 βραχέα γὰρ συμβέβηκε λαλοῦσιν ἀποθνήσκειν.
Οὕτως Ἑρμῆς ψυχοπομπὸς τῆς προφορᾶς ὁ λόγος.

*Ἀνδρῶν μνηστήρων· ἔχε δὲ ῥάβδον μετὰ χερσὶ*
*καλήν, χρυσείην, τῇ τ᾽ ἀνδρῶν ὄμματα θέλγει,*
*ὧν ἐθέλει, τοὺς δ᾽ αὖτε καὶ ὑπνώοντας ἐγείρει·*
55 *τῇ ῥ᾽ ἄγε κινήσας, ταὶ δὲ τρίζουσαι ἕποντο.᾽*
᾽Ἔχε δὲ ῥάβδον ἐν χερσὶ᾽ τὸ μυθικὸν νοεῖς μοι·
ῥάβδον κατέχων ἐν χερσὶ τοιάνδε καὶ τοιάνδε,
κινῶν ἐσόβει τὰς ψυχάς, ἄγων αὐτὰς ἐς Ἅιδου,
Ὠκεανὸν τὸν ποταμὸν δῆθε διαδραμούσας,
60 πέτραν τινὰ ᾽Λευκάδα᾽ τε καὶ ᾽πύλας᾽ τὰς Ἡλίου
᾽καὶ δῆμον τῶν Ὀνείρων᾽ δὲ συντόμως ἀφιγμένας
᾽λειμῶνα παρ᾽ ἀσφοδελόν,᾽ ὅπου ᾽ψυχαὶ᾽ θανόντων.
Τὰ μὲν τοῦ μύθου τοιαδί, ἅπερ ἀναπτυκτέον.
Ψυχοπομπὸς Ἑρμῆς ἐστι τῆς προφορᾶς ὁ λόγος
65 πρὸ τοῦ θανεῖν τοὺς θνήσκοντας, ὡς ἔφην, προεκτρέχων.
᾽Κατεῖχε᾽ νῦν ἐπέσχηκε, σιγῇ παρεδεδώκει,
ἐν ταῖς χερσὶ καὶ πρακτικῶς τὴν ῥάβδον τὴν τιμίαν,
λόγου σειρὰν προφορικοῦ τὰς λέξεις τὰς συνήθεις,
δι᾽ ὧν τελοῦνται συμβουλαὶ πᾶσιν ἡμῖν ἐν βίῳ,
70 ἀποτροπὴν τῶν φαύλων μὲν πραγμάτων νουθετοῦσαι,
θέλγουσαί τε καὶ ἱλαρὰ τὰ ὄμματα ποιοῦσαι,

Here I am explaining to you how it happens most of the
    time;
for it happened for those who are dying to speak briefly.    50
Thus Hermes, conductor of souls, is the spoken word.
  *'The spirits of the suitors. He held in his hands a beautiful*
*golden wand, with which he lulls to sleep the eyes*
*of whom he will, while others again he rouses even out of slumber;*
*with this he roused and led the spirits, and they followed*    55
    *gibbering.'*
With *'he held* in *his hands a wand'* understand the mythical
    aspect;
holding in his hand a wand so fine and of such kind,
by moving it he pushed about the souls, leading them into
    Hades,
as they supposedly passed through the river Ocean,
a rock, *'Leukas,'* and *'the gates'* of the Sun    60
*'and,'* arriving soon at *'the land of Dreams,'*
'the *meadow* of the *asphodel,'* where are the *'souls'* of the dead.
These are the elements of the myth, which need to be
    unfolded.
Hermes, the conductor of souls, is the spoken word
which anticipates the dying men, before their death, as I    65
    said.
'He held fast' here means he held in his hands the honored
    wand
and relegated it to silence allegorically, that is,
the sequence of uttered speech, the customary words
through which counsels occur for all of us in life,
advising us to avoid evil deeds,    70
delighting us and making the eyes cheerful,

πρὸς δὲ καλὰ προτρέπουσαι πάντας νωθρούς, ῥᾳθύμους.

Τὸ 'τῇ ῥ᾽ ἄγε κινήσας' δὲ τοῦτο σημαίνειν νόει,
τῷ κινηθῆναι ἐκδραμεῖν συνθήκην τὴν τοῦ λόγου·
75 καὶ αἱ ψυχαὶ κατήγοντο εὐθέως τῶν μνηστήρων.

Τὸ 'τρίζουσαι δὲ ἔποντο' καθάπερ 'νυκτερίδες'
δόξα Ἑλλήνων πέφυκε δοξάζουσα τοιάδε,
τῶν βίᾳ σφαττομένων τε καὶ τῶν ἀναιρουμένων
πολλαῖς ἡμέραις τὰς ψυχὰς τρίζουσας παραμένειν.
80 Ὡς καὶ πολέμου πώποτε μεγάλου γεγονότος
καὶ ἑκατέρωθε πολλῶν ἀνδρῶν ἀνηρημένων
εἰς νυχθημέρους [ὅλας] ὥρας τρεῖς μετὰ τρυσμοῦ καὶ ἤχου
μάχην συνάπτειν τὰς ψυχὰς ἀνδρῶν τῶν ἀμφοτέρων.
Ἐν δέλτοις δέ μου τῶν φρενῶν μυρίων σοφῶν ὄντων
85 οὐκ ἔχω λέγειν ἀκριβῶς τὸν ἱστοροῦντα τάδε,
ἢ Καισαρεὺς Προκόπιος εἴτε τίς ἐστιν ἄλλος.

'Ἑρμείας ἦρχε' δὲ αὐτῶν νῦν προλαβὼν εἰρήκειν,
ὡς προεκτρέχει πρῶτον μὲν ἐκ τῶν θνησκόντων λόγος,
εἶτα εὐθὺς καὶ αἱ ψυχαὶ ὥσπερ ἀκολουθοῦσαι.
90 'Ἀκάκητα' τὸν λόγον δὲ ὡς παυστικὸν κακίας,
παύει γὰρ ἔριν καὶ θυμόν, ῥᾳθύμους ἀνεγείρει.

'Πάρισαν' καὶ παρέδραμον ὠκείᾳ δὲ πορεύσει.

'Ῥοὰς' καὶ τὸν εὐμάραντον καὶ εὔροον δὲ βίον
καὶ τὰς Λευκάδας πέτρας δέ, αἷς τὰ λοιπὰ στοιχεῖα,
95 καὶ 'τὰς Ἡλίου πύλας' δὲ καὶ 'δῆμον τῶν Ὀνείρων'
καὶ τὴν ἡμέραν δὲ αὐτὴν παρέδραμον καὶ νύκτα.

and urging all sluggish, lazy men toward good deeds.
    Understand that '*with his hand he roused*' means this,
that rhetorical composition veers off course by being
        moved;
and the souls of the suitors were immediately led down.       75
    '*And they followed gibbering*' like '*bats*'
means there was a belief among the Greeks which held that
the souls of those who are slaughtered and killed violently
stay behind gibbering for many days.
Just as when a great war happens sometimes       80
and many men are killed on both sides,
so during a period of three days and nights, with shrieks and
        screams,
the souls of men on either side engage in battle.
In the books stored in my mind, written by countless wise
        men,
I cannot say accurately who recorded these things;       85
either it is Prokopios of Kaisareia or someone else.
    '*Hermes* led' them here means he spoke to them
        beforehand,
as speech runs out from dying men first,
and then immediately the souls, as if following it.
    He calls speech '*guileless*' as it stops evil,       90
for it stops strife and anger, it rouses the lazy.
    'They went past' means they ran past in swift procession.
    '*The streams,*' that is, life that withers easily and is fast
        forgotten,
and the rocks of Leukas, by which he means the remaining
        elements,
and 'the *gates* of the Sun and *the land of Dreams,*'       95
that is, they ran past day itself and night.

Ὠκύπτεροι 'λειμῶνα δὲ ἀσφοδελὸν' εἰσῆλθον·
ἀσφοδελός τι ἄκαρπον φυτάριον ὑπάρχει.

Ἄκαρποι δὲ καὶ οἱ νεκροί· διὸ συμπλάττει τάδε,
100  ὡς αἱ ψυχαὶ ἀπέδραμον εἰς ἄκαρπον λειμῶνα,
εἰς τὸ μηδὲν ἐχώρησαν, εἰς ἀφανὲς καὶ χάος,
εἴτ' οὖν εἰς τὸν ἀσφοδελὸν ἀσπούδαστον λειμῶνα,
ἢ ὅτι οὐ σπουδάζει τις ἐκεῖσε ἀφικέσθαι,
ἢ ὅτι πόνος καὶ σπουδὴ ἔργων ἐκεῖ οὐκ ἔστι.
105  Τὸ 'σφεδανὸν' καὶ 'σφοδενόν' ἐστι δὲ τὸ σπουδαῖον.

Τὸ Νῦ δ' εἰς Λάμβδα τρέπουσι τῶν Ἀττικῶν τὰ γένη·
τὸν 'πνεύμονα' γὰρ 'πλεύμονα' καὶ 'σφοδελὸν' ὁμοίως
καὶ τἆλλα πάντα λέγουσι Νῦ τρέποντες εἰς Λάμβδα.
Τὸ Λάμβδα τρέπουσιν εἰς Νῦ τὰ Δωριέων γένη,
110  τὸ 'ἦλθον' 'ἤνθον' λέγοντες καὶ τὰ λοιπὰ ὁμοίως.

'Τὸν προτέρη ψυχὴ προσεφώνεε Πηλείωνος·'
τοῦτό ἐστιν, ὡς ἔφημεν, <ἡ> εἰδωλοποιΐα,
ἣν διὰ δύο τρόπους νῦν ὁ Ὅμηρος ἐγράφει·
διὰ τὸ χρήζειν τε εἰπεῖν ταφὴν τὴν Ἀχιλλέως,
115  ἣν τεχνικῶς παρέδραμε τόποις εἰπεῖν προσφόροις,
φοβῶν τε τοὺς τὰ ἄθεσμα πράττοντας ἐν τῷ βίῳ,
ἐν τῷ παρ' Ἅιδην αἴσθησιν τῶν τῇδε παρεισφέρων.

Τὸ 'φίλον ἔμμεναι' 'Διὶ τερπικεραύνῳ' τῇδε
ἢ τῷ ἀέρι, οὐρανῷ καὶ κόσμῳ τῷ ἐνθάδε
120  περιφανῆ, διάσημον, ὀνομαστὸν τυγχάνειν,
εἴτ' αὖ τῇ Εἱμαρμένῃ δὲ τῶν προσφιλῶν τυγχάνειν,
τίμιον καὶ περίβλεπτον τοῖς πᾶσιν ὑπηργμένον.

On swift wings they came into the *'meadow of asphodel'*;
an asphodel is a small plant without fruit.
Dead men are also fruitless; hence he fashions the two
        together,
as the souls ran away into the fruitless meadow,                    100
they advanced into nothingness, into obscurity and chaos,
so into the asphodel meadow means into the one that is not
        zealously sought,
or that someone is not eager to arrive there,
or that there is no toil or eager deeds there.
'Vehemently' and 'with vehemence' means zealously.               105
The Attic people change the letter nu into the letter
        lambda;
for they call 'pneumon' a 'pleumon' and likewise they say
        'sphodelos,'
and they say everything else changing nu into lambda.
The Doric people change lambda into nu,
calling 'elthon' 'enthon' and the rest in likewise manner.       110
    *'And the soul of Peleus's son was first to address him, saying'*
is, as we have said, dead men talking,
which Homer introduced here in two ways:
because he needed to speak of the burial of Achilles,
which he skillfully omitted to relate in suitable passages,      115
and terrifying those doing unlawful deeds in life,
by giving them here a taste of Hades.
    *'You are dear'* 'to Zeus, who delights in thunderbolts'
here means to be conspicuous, eminent, famous,
either to the air, to the sky and to the world here on earth,    120
or again that one is dear to Destiny,
honored and admired by everyone.

Ἦ τ᾽ ἄρα καὶ σοὶ πρῶϊ παραστήσεσθαι ἔμελλε᾽·
πρωῒ καὶ συντομώτερον καὶ ταχυτάτῳ λόγῳ.
125 ‘Θεοῖς δὲ ἐπιείκελε᾽ τοῖς ἄστρασιν ὁμοῖε.
‘Ἀπόλλωνι δαμείς, τὸν ἠΰκομος τέκε Λητώ.᾽
Ἀπόλλων μὲν ὁ ἥλιος, ἡ δὲ Λητὼ τὸ σκότος,
σκότος τὸ ἀρχεγόνιον, τὸ πανταχοῦ κωμάζον,
οὗπερ ῥαγέντος ἥλιος καὶ κόσμος παρυπέστη.
130 Καὶ οἱ ὀξεῖς μὲν θάνατοι λέγονται τοῦ ἡλίου.
Τὸν Ἀχιλλέα δὲ θανεῖν νῦν ὑφ᾽ ἡλίου λέγει,
ἀνθ᾽ ὧν παρὰ τοῦ Πάριδος θνήσκει ναῷ Ἡλίου.
Τὸ σχῆμα δὲ μετάληψιν εἶναι μοι τοῦτο νόει,
μεταφορᾶς μετάβασιν, κλήσεως ὡς πρὸς κλῆσιν,
135 τὸ τοῦ Ἡλίου τὸν ναὸν Ἥλιον ὀνομάζειν,
τὸν οἶνον καὶ τὴν ἄμπελον Διόνυσον δὲ λέγειν
καὶ τὰ λοιπὰ ὁμοίως δὲ κατὰ λεπτόν τοι γράφω.
   Καὶ ‘Ζεὺς᾽ ‘ὁ παύσας πόλεμον᾽ ὁ οὐρανὸς ὑπάρχει,
ἐξ οὐρανοῦ γὰρ λαίλαπες βίαιοι γεγονυῖαι
140 τότε τὴν μάχην ἔπαυσαν Ἑλλήνων καὶ τῶν Τρώων.
   ‘Μήτηρ δ᾽ ἐξ ἁλὸς ἦλθε σὺν ἀθανάτῃς ἁλίῃσιν᾽
θανόντος Ἀχιλλέως γάρ, ὥσπερ Ὅμηρος εἶπεν,
κειμένου ἔτι τοῦ νεκροῦ τοῦ τούτου δὲ ἀτάφου,
ἐξέδραμεν ἡ θάλασσα μυκήματι βιαίῳ,
145 καὶ πάντες φεύγειν ὥρμησαν Ἑλλήνων οἱ παρόντες.

'*But verily on you too was deadly doom to come early in the day.*'

Early in the day means sooner and in the swiftest speech.

'*Similar to the gods*' means similar to the stars.                125

'Tamed *by Apollo, whom fair-haired Leto bore.*'

Apollo is the sun, Leto the darkness,

the primal darkness, reveling everywhere,

and when this was shattered, the sun and the world came
　　forth.

And deaths from acute illness are said to come from the        130
　　sun.

Here he says that Achilles died by the sun,

whence the story that Paris killed him in the temple of the
　　Sun.

Understand that I mean this figure of speech is transference
　　of meaning,

a transition of metaphor, a substitution of name for name,

to call the temple of the Sun 'Sun,'                           135

to call the wine and the grapevine 'Dionysos,'

and the rest similarly I write for you in detail.

And '*Zeus*' who 'stops war' is the sky,

for when violent hurricanes happened in the sky,

they stopped the battle between Greeks and Trojans.            140

'*His mother emerges from the sea with the immortal sea
　　nymphs*'

means that when Achilles died, as Homer said,

while his corpse lay still unburied,

the sea gushed forth with a violent roar,

and all the Greeks who were present rushed to escape.          145

Μόλις αὐτοὺς κατέσχε δὲ 'Νέστωρ' εἰπὼν τοιάδε·
πολλὰ συμβαίνει τελευταῖς ἀνδρῶν τινων ἀρίστων,
καθὼς παρετηρήσαμεν ἐξ ἀκοῆς καὶ χρόνου,
καὶ νῦν ἡ θάλασσα δοκεῖ πενθεῖν τὸν Ἀχιλλέα.
150 Οὕτως εἰπὼν ἐπέσχε μὲν ἐκ τῆς φυγῆς ἐκείνους.
Τὸ δὲ θαλάσσης ἐκβρασθέν, ὃ προειρήκειν, ὕδωρ
ἄχρι τῆς κλίνης ἐπελθὸν τοῦ Ἀχιλλέως τότε
καὶ συγκαλύψαν τὸν νεκρόν, ὃ 'εἵματα' νῦν λέγει
'ἄμβροτα' καὶ ἀμφίασιν τούτου ἐκ Νηρηίδων,
155 καὶ ὥσπερ κλαῦσαν γοερὸν ἐν μυκηθμῷ μεγάλῳ
αὖτις πρὸς κοίτην τὴν αὑτῆς ὑπέστρεψεν ἀθρόως.
    Τίνες 'ἐννέα Μοῦσαι' δὲ θρηνοῦσαι τὸν Πηλέως;
Ἡ συμφωνία σύμπασα τῶν μουσικῶν ὀργάνων,
ᾠδαῖς γὰρ πάσαις μουσικαῖς ὁ Ἀχιλλεὺς ἐτάφη.
160 'Κλαίομεν ἀθάνατοί τε θεοὶ θνητοί τ' ἄνθρωποι'
ὁμοῦ γένος ἀνθρώπων τε καὶ φύσις τῶν στοιχείων
καὶ τῆς θαλάσσης εἴκεσαν τὸν θρῆνον, ὥσπερ εἶπον.
Ἐξ οὐρανοῦ δ' ἦν θύελλα δεινὴ καὶ καταιγίδες,
ἐκλείψεις τοῦ ἡλίου δὲ αὐτοῦ καὶ τῆς σελήνης,
165 ἀστρορυήσεις, χάλαζα, σκηπτοὶ συχνοὶ καὶ ὄμβροι.
    'Θεῶν ἐσθῆτα' λέγει δὲ νῦν βασιλέων κόσμον,
ἤγουν, "λαμπροῖς ἱματισμοῖς σὺ τῷ πυρὶ ἐφλέγου."
    'Χρύσεον ἀμφορέα δὲ δῶρον ἐκ Διονύσου'
ἐξ οἰνεμπόρων, γεωργῶν καὶ ἐργάτων ἀμπέλων,
170 τοὺς οὓς ὁ Θράκης βασιλεὺς ἐξήλαυνε Λυκοῦργος.
Ἡ Ἀχιλλέως δώρημα μήτηρ λαβοῦσα Θέτις

'*Nestor*' barely held them back by saying such things;
this means, many things happen at the death of the best
    men,
as we have observed by hearing and over time,
and here the sea seems to mourn Achilles.
So speaking, he held them from flight.                    150
The water gushing forth from the sea, of which I have
    spoken,
came up to the deathbed where Achilles lay
and completely covered the corpse, which Homer calls here
'*immortal clothing*' and his garment from the Nereids.
And as if the water cried in lamentation and with great    155
    bellowing,
it returned again suddenly to its seabed.
    Who are the '*nine Muses*' grieving for the son of Peleus?
The complete harmony of the musical instruments,
for Achilles was buried accompanied by musical songs.
    '*We lament you, immortal gods and mortal men*' means    160
that the human race together and the nature of the
    elements
and the sea uttered the lamentation, as I have said.
There was a terrible hurricane and squalls from the sky,
eclipses of the sun itself and of the moon,
streams of shooting stars, hail, frequent thunderbolts, and    165
    storms.
    Here he calls the '*gods' garment*' the adornment of kings,
that is, "you were burning with fire in radiant robes."
    With '*golden* urn, *the gift* from Dionysos,'
he means from wine merchants, farmers, and vine workers,
whom the king of Thrace, Lykourgos, drove out.         170
Achilles's mother, Thetis, taking the gift,

τῷ Ἀχιλλεῖ παρέσχηκεν, ᾧ καὶ θανὼν ἐτάφη
σύν γε Πατρόκλῳ καὶ παιδὶ Νέστορος, Ἀντιλόχῳ.
Τὸν ἀμφορέα τὸν χρυσοῦν, ὅνπερ τανῦν εἰρήκειν,
175  δῶρον ἡ Θέτις ἔσχηκεν ἐκ Διονύσου τοῖον.
Ὁ τῆς Σεμέλης γὰρ υἱὸς Διόνυσος ἐκεῖνος
τῆς Θέτιδος ἀνώτερος δύο γοναῖς ὑπῆρχεν.
  'Μήτηρ δ᾽ αἰτήσασα θεοὺς περικαλλέ᾽ ἄεθλα
θῆκε μέσῳ ἐν ἀγῶνι ἀριστήεσσιν Ἀχαιῶν.'
180  Τοῦ Ἀχιλλέως μήτηρ μὲν τοῦ Νηρέως ἡ Θέτις
καὶ Θέτις δέ, ἡ θάλασσα, μήτηρ τοῦ Ἀχιλλέως
δι᾽ οὓς τρόπους εἰρήκειμεν τοῖς ὄπισθε καλεῖται.
Νῦν δ᾽ ὅτι ἐμυκήσατο θρηνῶδες ἐξελθοῦσα
καὶ πάλιν ἀνθυπέστρεψε πρὸς ἑαυτῆς τὴν κοίτην.
185  Ὁ θρῆνος οὗτος οὖν, φησίν, ὁ τότε τῆς θαλάσσης
καὶ τὰ συμβάντα τοῖς λοιποῖς τῇ τελευτῇ στοιχείοις
πέπεικε περὶ θάλασσαν ἀγῶνας ἡμᾶς θεῖναι.
  Ἡ 'Θέτις ἀργυρόπεζα,' ὥσπερ πλειστάκις ἔφην,
ὅτι τὸ ὕδωρ ἔλλευκον, πλέον δὲ πρὸς τοῖς ἄκροις.
190  'Φίλος θεοῖσιν ἦσθα' δὲ στοιχείοις, Εἱμαρμένη,
τοῖς μὲν στοιχείοις θρηνηθεὶς καὶ τούτοις, ὡς εἰρήκειν,
τῇ Εἱμαρμένῃ δ᾽, εὐτυχῆ ἄτε λαχὼν τὸν βίον.
  'Ὁ Ζεὺς ἐμήσατ᾽ ὄλεθρον ἐν ταῖς χερσὶν Αἰγίσθου'
ἡ Εἱμαρμένη τε αὐτὴ καὶ οὐρανὸς ἀήρ τε
195  ὥσταις ἀνέμοις ἐκβαλὼν ἀγροῖς τοῖς τοῦ Αἰγίσθου.
  'Κακὸς δαίμων' καὶ μοῖρα δὲ τῷ γένει τῶν μνηστήρων
'τὸν Ὀδυσσέα ἤγαγεν ἀγροῖς πρὸς τὸν συβώτην.'

gave it to Achilles, and he was buried with it when he died
along with Patroklos and Nestor's son Antilochos.
Thetis received such a gift from Dionysos,
the golden urn, about which I have spoken here.                    175
For that Dionysos, the son of Semele,
was two generations earlier than Thetis.
    '*But your mother asked of the gods beautiful prizes, and
set them in the midst of the contest for the Achaean chiefs.*'
Achilles's mother, Thetis, daughter of Nereus,                     180
and Thetis, the sea, is called the mother of Achilles,
in the ways we have spoken of above.
Here he says that she bellowed a mournful song
as she came out and again she returned to her own bed.
So this lament, which was then from the sea,                       185
and the things done by the other elements at his death
have persuaded us that there were contests near the sea.
    '*Silver-footed Thetis,*' as I said many times,
means that she is the white foam, floating near the shore.
    '*You were dear to the gods*' means to the elements, to        190
        Destiny,
having been lamented by these elements, as I said,
and by Destiny, because he had had a fortunate life.
    '*Zeus* devised *doom* at the *hands of Aigisthos*'
means Destiny itself and the sky and air
pushed him out with windstorms from Aigisthos's lands.             195
    '*Some cruel god*' means the fate of the suitors' ilk
'*brought* Odysseus to the countryside to the swineherd.'

‘Ὅτε δ’ αὐτὸν ἀνήγειρε Διὸς νοῦς αἰγιόχου,’
ἤτοι νοὸς τοῦ ἑαυτοῦ αἱ κρύφιαι βουλήσεις,
200 εἴτ’ οὖν ὁ νοῦς καὶ βούλησις Διὸς καὶ Εἱμαρμένης.
　　‘Θεῶν τις ἐπιτάρροθος’ φρονήσεις, πανουργίαι,
ἢ μαγικῶν δυνάμεων βοήθεια συνῆν τις.
　　‘Χαρίεσσαν ἀθάνατοι τεύξουσιν ἀοιδὴν δέ·’
νῦν οἱ σοφοὶ ἀθάνατοι καὶ ἀοιδὴ οἱ ὕμνοι.
205 　‘Δαίμων’ καὶ μοῖρα ‘ἔπλαγξεν ἀπὸ τῆς Σικανίης.’
　　‘Διὸς δὲ ὥρας’ οὐρανοῦ ἀκούων νῦν μοι νόει.
　　‘Ζεῦ πάτερ, ἦ ῥα ἔτ’ ἐστὲ θεοὶ κατὰ μακρὸν Ὄλυμπον·’
‘Ζεῦ πάτερ’ νῦν οἱ σύμπαντες ἀστέρες Εἱμαρμένης.
　　‘Ἀθήνη’ ‘μέλε’ ἤλδανε’ τὸ χρῖσμα <τοῦ> ἐλαίου·
210 τὸ χρῖσμα νῦν καὶ τὸ λουτρὸν ‘Ἀθήνην’ ὀνομάζει.
　　‘Τοῖς ἀθανάτοις δὲ θεοῖς’ ἀλίγκιον νῦν λέγει
ἄστρασιν ἢ τῷ κάλλει δὲ καὶ τῇ ἐπιθυμίᾳ.
　　‘Θεῶν τις’ νῦν ‘σε ἔθηκε τῶν ἀειγενετάων’
“τὶς Εἱμαρμένη τέθεικεν <σ’> ὡραῖον νῦν, ὦ πάτερ.”
215 　‘Αἲ γάρ, Ζεῦ τε πάτερ καὶ Ἀθηναίη καὶ Ἄπολλον,’
ὦ οὐρανέ τε καὶ ἀὴρ καὶ φῶς λαμπρὸν ἡλίου.
　　‘Θεοὶ δὲ ἤγαγον αὐτοί’ τανῦν ἡ Εἱμαρμένη,
ὁμοίως καὶ τὸ ‘χαῖρε δέ, θεοὶ δ’ ὄλβια δοῖεν.’
　　‘Οὐκ ἀθανάτων ἄνευθεν ὁ Ὀδυσσεὺς τὰ ἔργα.’
220 Νῦν ψυχικῶν δυνάμεων καὶ μαγειῶν δὲ λέγει·
εἴκασμα γὰρ ἐποίησεν ὡς Μέντορα ὁρᾶσθαι.
　　Τοῦτο δ’ ὁ Μέδων οὐκ εἰδὼς ὡς βύρσῃ κεκρυμμένος,
οἴεται καὶ λογίζεται ἀκούειν Ὀδυσσέως
τὸ πλῆθος δειλιάσαντος τότε τὸ τῶν μνηστήρων,
225 καὶ τῇ φρονήσει τῇ αὐτοῦ σύμμαχον παρεστάναι

'When the mind of *Zeus,* the aegis bearer, roused him,'
that is, the secret wishes of his own mind,
or even the mind and the wish of Zeus, that is, Destiny.                    200
   '*Some god* was *their helper*' means their thoughts, their
      trickery,
or that there was some help from magic powers.
   '*The immortals shall make a pleasant song*';
here the immortals are wise men and the song is the hymns.
   '*A god,*' that is, fate, 'drove me *from Sikania.*'                     205
   When you hear '*Zeus's* seasons,' you should understand of
      the sky.
   '*Father Zeus, verily you gods yet hold sway on high Olympos*';
here '*father Zeus*' means all the stars of Destiny.
   '*Athena*' '*made greater the limbs*' is the anointing with oil;
here he calls the anointing and the bath 'Athena.'                         210
   Resembling 'the immortal *gods*' here means
resembling the stars whether in beauty or desire.
   '*Some one of* the *eternal gods* has made *you*' here means
"some Destiny has made <you> handsome now, O father."
   '*I would, O father Zeus, and Athena, and Apollo*'                       215
means, O sky and air and bright light of the sun.
   '*The gods themselves* have brought' here means Destiny,
likewise the '*Welcome, and may the gods grant you happiness.*'
   'Not without the *immortals* did *Odysseus* do these *deeds.*'
Here Homer speaks of powers of the souls and magic;                        220
for Odysseus pretended that Mentor could be seen.
Medon, not knowing this since he was hiding under an ox
      hide,
supposes and reckons that he hears Odysseus
being afraid of the crowd of the suitors then,
and with his own wisdom imagining that Mentor                              225

τὸν Μέντορα συμπλάσαντος καὶ βοηθεῖν καλοῦντος.
'Αὐτὰρ Ἀθηναίη Ζῆνα Κρονίωνα προσηύδα·'
νῦν Ἀθηνᾶ ἐστιν ἀήρ, ὁ οὐρανὸς ὁ Ζεὺς δέ.
Ἀὴρ τὸν Ὀδυσσέα δὲ ἤγαγεν εἰς πατρίδα·
230 εἰς τὴν πατρίδα δ' ἐπελθὼν ἀνεῖλε τοὺς μνηστῆρας,
ὅθε φησὶ τὸν οὐρανὸν πρὸς τὸν ἀέρα λέγειν.
'Εἰ σὺ τοῦτο ἐβούλευσας, ὡς Ὀδυσσεὺς μὲν ἔλθοι
καὶ τοὺς μνηστῆρας τίσεται, ποίησον νῦν ὃ θέλεις.
Λέγω δ', ἐπεὶ νῦν Ὀδυσσεὺς ἀνεῖλε τοὺς μνηστῆρας,
235 εἰρήνην θέντες ἔνορκον ὁ μὲν βασιλευέτω,
ἡμεῖς τῶν φόνων λύσιν δὲ θεῖμεν τοῖς συγγενέσιν.'
'Οὕτως εἰπὼν' ἐκίνησεν εὐθέως τὸν ἀέρα,
ποιῆσαι, ἅπερ εἴρηκε, συμβάσεις καὶ εἰρήνην.
Τοῦτο δ' ἐστὶ προέκθεσις καὶ πρόρρησις τὸ σχῆμα.
240 Μέλλει γενέσθαι τοῦτο δὲ τοῖς ἔμπροσθεν, ὡς μάθῃς·
ὡς γὰρ Εὐπείθης ὑπ' αὐτοῦ πέπτωκε τοῦ Λαέρτου,
καὶ σφάττειν 'πάντας' ἔμελλον οἱ μετὰ Ὀδυσσέως,
ἐκ τοῦ ἀέρος, Ἀθηνᾶς, βροντῆς καταρραγείσης,
βροντῆς ὁμοῦ καὶ κεραυνῶν εὐφρόνως βουλευσάντων,
245 ἀλλήλοις ὅρκους ἔθεντο καὶ σύμβασιν φιλίας.
'Τοῖσι δ' ἐπ' ἀγχίμολον θυγάτηρ Διὸς ἦλθεν Ἀθήνη,
Μέντορι εἰδομένη ἠμὲν δέμας ἠδὲ καὶ αὐδήν'
ἦλθεν αὐτοῖς ἡ φρόνησις τοῦ Μέντορος· ὁ Μέντωρ
τέκνον Διὸς δὲ καὶ νοὸς ἡ φρόνησις ὑπάρχει.
250 'Τὸν δὲ παρισταμένη προσέφη γλαυκῶπις Ἀθήνη·
"ὦ Ἀρκεισιάδη, πάντων πολὺ φίλταθ' ἑταίρων,

was there as his ally and calling him to help.

'*But Athena spoke to Zeus, son of Kronos*';
here Athena is the air, Zeus is the sky.
The air led Odysseus to his homeland;
coming into his homeland, he killed the suitors,                    230
from which he says that the sky talks to the air.

'If you *devised* this, that *Odysseus* was coming
and will take revenge on the suitors, do what you wish.
I say, *since* now *Odysseus* has killed the *suitors,*
after we establish a sworn peace, *let him be king,*              235
and *we* will give absolution for the murder to their
    kinsmen.'

'So *saying,*' he immediately moved the air,
to make what he said, an alliance and peace.
This figure of speech is called a preface and introductory
    statement.

This is about to happen in what follows, so that you             240
    might learn it;
for when Eupeithes fell at the hands of Laertes himself,
and Odysseus's comrades were about to slaughter '*everyone,*'
since from the air, that is, Athena, thunder burst forth
that is, since thunder and lightning counseled them
    reasonably,
they swore oaths and an alliance of friendship with each         245
    other.

'*Then Athena, daughter of Zeus, drew near them*
*in the likeness of Mentor both in form and in voice*'
means the wisdom of Mentor came to them; Mentor
is wisdom, the child of Zeus, that is, of understanding.

'*Then flashing-eyed Athena came near him and said:*            250
"*Son of Arkeisios, by far the dearest of all my friends,*

εὐξάμενος κούρῃ γλαυκώπιδι καὶ Διὶ πατρί,''' 
Λαέρτην Μέντωρ ὤτρυνεν ἢ λογισμὸς οἰκεῖος.
Φρονήσει βέλος δ' ἀφεικὼς ὁμοῦ καὶ εὐτυχίᾳ

255 'βαλὼν' κατὰ 'τῆς κόρυθος' ἀνεῖλε τὸν Εὐπείθην.
'Εἰ μὴ Ἀθηναίη, κούρη Διὸς αἰγιόχοιο,
ἤϋσεν φωνῇ, κατὰ δ' ἔσχεθε λαὸν ἅπαντα.'
Τὴν Ἀθηνᾶν προεῖπον σοι τὴν νῦν τοῖς ἀνωτέρω,
ὡς ἐξ ἀέρος ὑπ' αὐτοὺς βροντῆς καταρραγείσης

260 καὶ κεραυνῶν φλεγόντων δὲ συνῆλθον εἰς συμβάσεις.
'Κὰδ δ' ἔπεσε πρόσθε γλαυκώπιδος ὀβριμοπάτρης.'
Νῦν ὁ ἀὴρ ἡ Ἀθηνᾶ ὑπάρχει, ἡ γλαυκῶπις,
ἡ ἰσχυρὸν τὸν ἥλιον πατέρα κεκτημένη.
'Δὴ τότ' Ὀδυσσῆα προσέφη γλαυκῶπις Ἀθήνη·'

265 ἐκ σημείων ἔγνωκε <δὲ> τινῶν τῶν τοῦ ἀέρος.
Τὸ σχῆμα δὲ μετάβασις ὀνόματος ὑπάρχει.
Νοῆσαι παρεσκεύασε τότε τὸν Ὀδυσσέα,
καλὸν εἶναι τὸ παύσασθαι καὶ μάχης καὶ πολέμου,
μὴ ὀργισθῇ πως κατ' αὐτοῦ ἄδηλος Εἱμαρμένη,

270 καὶ τοῦτον ἀποκτείνωσιν ἄνδρες οἱ τῆς Ἰθάκης.
Οὕτω νοήσας ἔπαυσε τὸν πόλεμον καὶ μάχην.
'Ὅρκια δ' αὖ κατόπισθε μετ' ἀμφοτέροισιν ἔθηκε
Παλλὰς Ἀθηναίη, κούρη Διὸς αἰγιόχοιο,
Μέντορι εἰδομένη ἠμὲν δέμας ἠδὲ καὶ αὐδήν.'

275 Ὅρκοις δ' ὑστέρως ἥρμοσεν ἀλλήλους ἐς φιλίαν
ἡ φρόνησις τοῦ Μέντορος, ἤγουν αὐτὸς ὁ Μέντωρ.

Ἔχεις ἀναπτυχθέντα σοι πάντα σαφεῖ τῇ λέξει
καὶ ταῖς τυχούσαις ἀκοαῖς τελούσῃ τῶν εὐλήπτων,

*after praying to the flashing-eyed maiden and to father Zeus,'"*
means Mentor or his own reason urged on Laertes.
　Releasing his arrow with wisdom and success,
he 'struck the *helmet*' and killed Eupeithes.　　　　　　　255
　*'Had not Athena, the aegis-bearing daughter of Zeus,*
*shouted aloud, and checked all the host.'*
I already explained above what Athena is here,
that as thunder burst forth from the air behind them
and as lightning was blazing, they came to an agreement.　　260
　*'And down it fell before the flashing-eyed daughter of the*
　　*mighty sire.'*
Here Athena, the flashing-eyed, is the air,
who had a powerful father, the sun.
　*'Then flashing-eyed Athena spoke to Odysseus';*
that is, he knew from certain signs in the air.　　　　　　265
This figure of speech is called transition of a name.
Homer made Odysseus understand then
that it was good to cease from battle and war,
lest unknowable Destiny be angry with him somehow
and the men of Ithake kill him.　　　　　　　　　　　270
With this understanding, he ceased war and battle.
　*'Thereafter a solemn oath between the two was made*
*by Pallas Athena, aegis-bearing daughter of Zeus,*
*as she was in the likeness of Mentor both in form and in voice.'*
The wisdom of Mentor, that is, Mentor himself,　　　　　275
joined them in friendship afterward with oaths.

You have had everything revealed to you in clear speech,
which was easy to understand even by a chance audience,

οὐ κομπολακυθούσῃ δὲ καὶ ξένῃ καὶ ἀγνώστῳ.

280 Ὁπόσα χαριζόμενος ταῖς ἀπαλαῖς καρδίαις
ταῖς Ἰλιάσι μάχαις τε καὶ πλάναις Ὀδυσσέως
ὁ Ὅμηρος ὁ πάνσοφος τῷ νέκταρι τοῦ μύθου
φυράματι χρησάμενος καὶ συζυμῶν γλυκαίνει,
τὰ βάθη βλέπειν παρεικὼς ἐν τέχναις βαθυδρόμοις

285 καὶ τοῖς μαργαροθύραις τε τῶν λογικῶν ὀστρέων,
οἵπερ ὑπαναπτύσσοντες ἐκείνων τὰ κελύφη
τοὺς τιμαλφεῖς ἐκφέρουσι καὶ διαυγεῖς μαργάρους.
Ἔχεις τὸ γράμμα τὸ σαφὲς ὡς Ἀριάδνης μίτον
ἐκ Λαβυρίνθου συστροφῶν θηρὸς δὲ Μινωταύρου

290 καὶ ποδηγοῦν σε δεξιῶς καὶ πρὸς τὸ φῶς ἐξάγον.
Ἔχεις καὶ Πασικράτιον τοῦτο δὲ φῶς, εἰ θέλεις,
κάτω θαλάσσης τοῦ βυθοῦ καὶ μέσω τῶν κυμάτων
λάμπον καὶ μὴ σβεννύμενον οἷα χερσαίοις οἴκοις.

with nothing pretentious or foreign or unfamiliar.
By offering so many things to the simple minds           280
with the battles in Troy and the wanderings of Odysseus,
Homer the all-wise, through the nectar of his tale,
uses dough and leavening to make it sweet,
allowing us to see the depths through his arts that penetrate
    deeply,
and through the pearly gates of the rational oysters,           285
which, having cracked open their shells,
bring out their valuable and shiny pearls.
You have this work clear as the thread of Ariadne,
as if it has twisted you out of the beastly Minotaur's
    Labyrinth
and guided you skillfully and led you out to the light.           290
You also have this light of Pasikrates, if you wish,
which shines down into the sea's depths and the midst of
    the waves,
and is not extinguished, just as if it were in houses on dry
    land.

# Abbreviations

*FgrH* = Felix Jacoby, ed. *Die Fragmente der griechischen Historiker* (Berlin, 1923–1958; Leiden, 1954–1964)

*LbG* = Erich Trapp, ed. *Lexikon der byzantinischen Gräzität,* 7 fasc. (Vienna, 1994–2017)

LSJ = Henry G. Liddell, Robert Scott, and Henry S. Jones, eds. *A Greek-English Lexicon, 9th ed. with Supplement* (Oxford, 1968)

*OCD*⁴ = Simon Hornblower and Anthony Spawforth, eds. *Oxford Classical Dictionary,* 4th ed. (Oxford, 2012)

*ODB* = Alexander Kazhdan et al., eds. *Oxford Dictionary of Byzantium,* 3 vols. (New York, N.Y., 1991)

*RE* = *Paulys Real-Encyclopädie der classischen Altertumswissenschaft. Neue Bearbeitung* (Stuttgart, 1894–1980)

*TLG* = *Thesaurus Linguae Graecae, A Digital Library of Greek Literature*

Tz. = Tzetzes

# Note on the Text

We have based our Greek text on the edition prepared and published by Herbert Hunger, "Johannes Tzetzes, *Allegorien zur Odyssee,* Buch 1–12," *Byzantinische Zeitschrift* 49 (1956): 249–310, and "Johannes Tzetzes, *Allegorien zur Odyssee,* Buch 13–24," *Byzantinische Zeitschrift* 48 (1955): 4–48, and thank Walter de Gruyter GMBH & Co. KG for permission to use this publication. Hunger based his edition on four manuscripts. Vaticanus graecus 904 (Va) and Vindobonensis philologicus graecus 118 (P) transmit only the first part of the work (Books 1–12). The entire work, including Books 13 to 24, is transmitted only in Vaticanus Barberinianus graecus 30 (B) and Vaticanus Palatinus graecus 316 (V). That is to say, only B and V contain an (almost) complete version of the *Allegories of the* Odyssey. Since it was Hunger who first discovered B and V, earlier editors could rely only on Va and P (which lacked the second half of the work). The stemma on page 252 of Hunger's 1956 article is a visual rendering of the description that precedes it. There is a further stemma for the BV relationship in Hunger's first article of 1955 (p. 10).

Hunger's text is reproduced in essentially unaltered form, although we have made numerous tacit corrections in punctuation, accentuation, and capitalization, have fixed some typographical errors, and suggested a few emendations to the text. In the few places where Hunger chooses alternate readings of the manuscripts, we have so indicated in a note to the text. Square brackets are used to denote lines that Hunger thought were out of place or should be deleted. In places where Tzetzes quotes the Homeric text verbatim, we have italicized the word, phrase, or lines and placed single quotation marks around them, in both the Greek text and our translation. The references to the Homeric text are given in the Notes to the Translation. Single quotation marks around text that is not italicized signify that Tzetzes is either paraphrasing Homer in twelfth-century Greek, re-ordering his sequence of words, or isolating terms for which he provides an explanation immediately afterward. Double quotation marks indicate direct speech.

SIGLA

< > = added by editor

[ ] = secluded by editor

# Notes to the Text

## BOOK 1

32 *We have emended* ὀθεδήποτε, *which is not attested anywhere, to* ὀθενδήποτε.

304 *We have changed* εἴ τε *to* εἴτε.

## BOOK 2

5 *We have emended* Μενόλαν *to* Μενέλαον.

## BOOK 4

48 *Note that in the Loeb edition of the* Odyssey, *at 4.364,* ἐσάωσε *is the principal reading, with* ἐλέησε *as an alternative reading.*

## BOOK 6

91 *Note that in the Loeb edition* οὔρεος *is an alternative reading for* οὔρεα *in 6.102.*

194a *This line is bracketed in the Hunger edition.*

## BOOK 8

208 *We have corrected* ἠ̈δε *to* ἠδε.

## BOOK 9

13 *We have emended* Ἰλιόθε, *attested only here, to* Ἰλιόθεν.

58 *We have emended* αἰδοῖο *to* αἰδεῖο *as this was clearly a typographical error.*

64 *We have emended* ἄχθος *to* ἔχθος *in accordance with the Homeric original, as this was probably a typographical error.*

115     *We have emended* οὗτω *to* οὗτῳ.

123     *The text of Aristeas has* φάς<αν> *instead of* σφάς.

126     *We have emended* ἕν *to* ἕν'; *we assume this was a typographical error, since the word* ὀφθαλμός *is masculine and therefore would require the masculine form of "one."*

## BOOK 10

103     *We have corrected* ὠκτείρησεν *to* ᾠκτείρησεν *as the first form is grammatically incorrect.*

## BOOK 11

16a–b     *These are alternative lines in the Greek text.*

52     *We have changed the* ἤ *of the Hunger edition to* ἦ, *as in the Homeric text.*

74     *We have corrected* Κάστορα *of the Hunger edition to* Κάστορά *as in the Loeb edition of the* Odyssey *at 11.300.*

77     *We have corrected* αὖτε *to* αὔτε.

79     *We have emended* ζῶντες *to* ζῶντας *as the accusative case makes more sense in this context.*

84     *We have corrected* ἠχμαλώτισαν *of the Hunger edition to* ἠχμαλώτισαν.

131a–b     *These are alternative lines in the Greek text.*

## BOOK 12

27     *This line is bracketed in Hunger's edition.*

101     *This line is bracketed in Hunger's edition.*

## BOOK 17

53     *We have emended* βουλαί *to* βολαί. *The line refers to Od. 17.494, which speaks of Apollo striking men with his arrows.*

## BOOK 18

41     *We have emended* λείψαντες *to* σπείσαντες, *as the latter word is used in the Homeric text at Od. 18.425–26 and makes more sense in this context.*

# Notes to the Translation

## Prolegomena A

1–6     The story is from Herodotus 1.189.

8     *Kalliope*: Kalliope was the Muse of epic poetry.

9     *Catalog of heroes*: That is, the catalog of ships in *Il.* 2.494–759.

12–14     *Not like the river ... vigorous desire*: A strange sentence. It could be that Tzetzes speaks metaphorically of the Ocean of words (perhaps the countless words flooding his mind, his inspiration) attempting to "drown" his vigorous desire to allegorize the Homeric text.

16     *My queen*: Most likely a reference to the empress Eirene, who probably commissioned the work; see Introduction.

19     *Mandrokles*: See Herodotus 4.88. Mandrokles was a Greek architect from the island of Samos in the service of the Persian king Darius. He built a pontoon bridge across the Thracian Bosporos.

21     *Apollodoros*: Another bridge builder who was also responsible for many constructions commissioned by the emperor Trajan (r. 98–117 CE), including Trajan's column, the Odeum, a gymnasium, etc. He was later falsely accused, banished, and put to death by Hadrian. See Cassius Dio 69.4.

24     *Dexiphanes*: Dexiphanes built the causeway connecting the city of Alexandria to the island of Pharos, on which his son Sostratos built the lighthouse of Alexandria. See also Tz. *All. Il.* pro.12.

26–27     *Just as that old ... cross it*: See Herodotus 1.75. Tzetzes here alludes to the common story (as narrated by Herodotus), which pre-

sents Cyrus and his army reaching the river Halys only to find
that there was no bridge to cross. Thales, who was with them,
dug a channel and thus managed to split the river into two
streams, making it easy for the army to get across. The channel
was crescent shaped, allowing the two streams to unite again
further down from the camp. Herodotus, however, states that
he does not believe the story and claims that there was a bridge
there already.

32    *Demo*: Demo (or Damo) was probably Greek and flourished
around the second century CE. There is only one extant short
epigram attributed to her, which was inscribed on the Colossus
of Memnon at Egyptian Thebes. She appears to present her-
self as a protégée of the Muses (Pierides) in her text, employs
Homeric vocabulary and expressions, and uses the Aeolic dia-
lect; see Ian Michael Plant, *Women Writers of Ancient Greece and
Rome: An Anthology* (Norman, Okla., 2004), 157–58, for more
information and an English translation of the epigram.

35    *Herakleitos*: Not to be confused with the pre-Socratic philoso-
pher of the same name. Tzetzes here refers to Herakleitos the
Paradoxographer, author of *On Unbelievable Tales* (possibly first
to second century CE, although very little is known about
him). We possess only one thirteenth-century manuscript of
the work, and Eustathios of Thessalonike refers to him by
name twice. His work contains some allegorical interpreta-
tions of the *Odyssey*. See Jacob Stern, "Heraclitus the Paradox-
ographer: *Peri Apiston, On Unbelievable Tales*," *Transactions of the
American Philological Association* 133 (2003): 51–97.

36    *Cornutus*: Cornutus (Lucius Annaeus Cornutus, in Latin) lived in
the first century CE under the emperor Nero. He composed in
Greek *A Survey of the Theological Traditions of the Greeks,* where
he offers an allegorical explanation of Greek myths, including
the names of the gods. See Jonathan Tate, "Cornutus and
the Poets," *Classical Quarterly* 23 (1929): 41–45; José B. Torres,
"The *Homeric Hymns,* Cornutus, and the Mythological Stream,"
in *The Reception of the Homeric Hymns,* ed. Andrew Faulkner et
al. (Oxford, 2016), 187–202; Cassius Dio 62.29.

*Palaiphatos*: Palaiphatos's identity (including his real name and dates) is uncertain. The *Suda* contains four different entries with that name (Π 69, 70, 71, 72), three of which appear to be referring to the same individual. He is believed to be the author of *On Unbelievable Tales,* a work rationalizing tales from Greek mythology and not to be confused with the work of the same title by Herakleitos the Paradoxographer (see note on line 35, above). For more information and a translation of his text, see Palaephatus, *Peri Apiston: On Unbelievable Tales,* trans. with introduction and commentary by Jacob Stern (Wauconda, Ill., 1996).

*Psellos*: Michael Psellos lived from circa 1018 to circa 1078. As chief philosopher at the court of Constantine IX Monomachos (r. 1042–1055) and personal advisor and tutor to subsequent emperors, he was one of the most influential and prolific Byzantine scholars. In addition to philosophical and theological treatises, several hundred of his letters survive, as do numerous speeches, including funeral orations for his mother and three patriarchs. He is perhaps best known for his *Chronographia,* a history of Byzantine emperors. Psellos was also deeply involved in politics at the highest levels. Tzetzes sardonically refers to him as "that all-wise Psellos" at Tz. *All. II.* 4.48 to mock what Tzetzes views as Psellos's erroneous allegorical interpretations.

54     *The much-traveled man*: That is, Odysseus.

## BOOK I

33    *Od.* 1.10.

34    *Od.* 1.14.

35    *Od.* 1.17.

36    *Od.* 1.19–20.

43    *Od.* 1.22.

48    *Od.* 1.85.

57    *Od.* 1.25.

58    Here Tzetzes is making a pun with the word for "bull" (ταῦρος) and the word meaning "in a bull-like manner" (ταυρωδέστερον), both deriving from the same root. Tzetzes here is referring to an astrological phenomenon. See Hunger 1956 edition, p. 306, note on Book 1, line 58, where he mentions the connection between the swelling of the Nile and the zodiac sign of the Bull; he also adds that the "bull-like manner" of the sound of the river is probably related to the ancient mythological image of the river god appearing in the shape of a bull.

59    See *Od.* 1.23–24.

68    *Od.* 1.27.

69    *Od.* 1.28.

84    *Od.* 1.28.

99–100    *Should now . . . Destiny*: That is, instead of calling it Zeus.

100    *If anyone . . . the past*: Though the meaning is unclear, we interpret this to mean that no one in the past understood the distinction between Destiny and Zeus.

103–4    *With skillful rhetorical technique*: Δεινότης and μέθοδος are technical rhetorical terms, meaning "intensity" and "the rhetorical technique of means or mode of treating," respectively. See LSJ, under "δεινότης" and "μέθοδος," and Tz. *All. Il.* pro.1165.

105    *Od.* 1.28.

108    *Empedokles*: Empedokles was a pre-Socratic philosopher from Akragas, circa 492 to 432 BCE. For his life and thought, see Diogenes Laertios 8. Perhaps Tzetzes here refers to Empedokles's cosmological theory of the four elements, which are mixed and separated by the forces of φιλότης (love) and νεῖκος (strife).

    *Anaxagoras*: A pre-Socratic philosopher from Klazomenai, circa 500–428 BCE. Various fragments survive, where Anaxagoras

explains how life was created from Chaos. On the nature of the
earth in the beginning, see, for instance, fragments 15 and 16.

112 The expression "reason-that-is-beyond-reason" is a periphrasis
signifying Christ.

116 *Historical sense*: See, for instance, Tz. *All. Il.* 18.267.

124 *Od.* 1.31.

126 *Od.* 1.32. Tzetzes here attributes the speech of Zeus to Mentes's
oracular interpretation.

131 In *Od.* 1.38–43 Zeus says that Hermes had been dispatched to
warn Aigisthos not to kill Agamemnon or marry Klytemnestra,
but Aigisthos ignored the warning. Tzetzes speaks of "written
oracles," which is not supported by the text.

132–33 *Having interpreted . . . adultery*: "He" here refers to Hermes (see
previous note). The Hunger 1956 edition, p. 306, note on Book
I, lines 132f., notes that "having interpreted" and "interpreted"
(ἐφερμηνεύσας and ἡρμήνευσε, respectively, in Greek) are an
intentional pun on Hermes (Ἑρμῆς, see *Od.* 1.38).

140 *Od.* 1.45. This is Athena's response to Zeus's speech in the *Odys-
sey*, which Tzetzes allegorizes as the views of other wise men.

145 *Od.* 1.50.

146 *Od.* 1.49.

147 *Od.* 1.51.

148 *Od.* 1.50.

151 *Od.* 1.53.

152 *Od.* 1.52.

164 *Od.* 1.63.

167 *Od.* 1.65.

175 *Od.* 1.68–69.

176–85 These lines are spoken in Mentes's voice as per Tzetzes's inter-
pretation.

181 *Elpe*: There is no reference to a daughter of Polyphemos in the
*Odyssey*. This version of the story can be found in John of
Antioch, fragment 24.35–45, and John Malalas, *Chronography*
5.18.19–33, who speak of an Elpe, daughter of the Cyclops, who
was snatched either by Odysseus or by one of Odysseus's com-
rades. John of Antioch also notes that the blinding of the Cy-

clops was an allegory for the abduction of his only daughter. See Andrew T. Alwine, "The Non-Homeric Cyclops in the Homeric Odyssey," *Greek, Roman, and Byzantine Studies* 49 (2009): 323–33, at 329; Nathaniel E. Griffin, "The Greek Dictys," *American Journal of Philology* 29 (1908): 329–35, at 329–30, who argues that John of Antioch and Malalas might have gotten this story from the Greek version of Diktys's *Ephemeridos belli Trojani*.

182     This is a parenthetical interjection by Tzetzes in authorial voice.

188–89     *Od.* 1.71–73.

189     *Phorkys*: In Hesiod's *Theogony* 233–37, Phorkys is a water god, the son of Pontos (the sea) and Gaia (the earth).

200–201     *Od.* 1.83.

203     *Od.* 1.84. Argeïphontes ("slayer of Argos") is a Homeric epithet for Hermes.

206–7     Tzetzes here speaks again in the voice of Mentes and the wise men.

216     *Od.* 1.96.

217     *Od.* 1.97.

220     *Od.* 1.99–100.

221     *Od.* 1.101.

224     *Od.* 1.102.

236     *Il.* 5.23. A reference to the Trojan Idaios, son of Dares, a priest of Hephaistos, rescued in battle. Homer makes no mention of a tree.

241–43     *Od.* 1.102–4.

250     *Od.* 1.102.

256–59     *Od.* 1.126–29.

260     *Od.* 1.127–28.

268–73     *Od.* 1.194–99.

276     *Od.* 1.194.

279     *Od.* 1.198.

280     *Od.* 1.200.

285     *Od.* 1.201.

292–93     *Od.* 1.222–23.

297     *Od.* 1.263.

299     *Od.* 1.267.

301   *Od.* 1.273.
307   *Od.* 1.282–83.
309   *Od.* 1.320.
312   *Od.* 1.323.
313   *Od.* 1.324.
314–15   *Od.* 1.326–27.
316   *Od.* 1.332.
318   *Od.* 1.329.
319   *Od.* 1.336.
320   *Od.* 1.338.
322   *Od.* 1.348.
323–24   *Od.* 1.363–64.
328   *Od.* 1.364.
329   See 2.84–85 below. Tzetzes uses the adjective ἔγγλαυκος (translated as "blueish" in LSJ), which comes from the same root as γλαυκῶπις ("flashing-eyed," but also "gray-/blue-eyed" in other translations), the standard epithet of Athena.
332   *Od.* 1.371.
333   *Od.* 1.378.
334   *Od.* 1.379.
335   *Od.* 1.384.
337   *Od.* 1.420.
339   *Od.* 1.444.

## BOOK 2

1–2   *Od.* 2.6–79.
3–6   *Od.* 2.349–434.
7   *Od.* 2.1.
11   *Od.* 2.5.
13   *Od.* 2.10.
16   *Od.* 2.12.
17   *That man's counsels*: That is, those of the elderly Aigyptios who first addressed the assembly of suitors in *Od.* 2.15–34.
19   *Zeus*: *Od.* 2.34.
      *Of the gods*: *Od.* 2.66.

*Of Zeus*: *Od.* 2.68.

21     *Od.* 2.66.

24     *Tartaros*: One of the three primordial gods as well as the underworld abyss in which the Titans are imprisoned.

25     *Od.* 2.68.

29     *Od.* 2.116, 125.

31     *Od.* 2.134, 143.

35     *Od.* 2.144.

36     *Od.* 2.146.

37     *Od.* 2.211.

38     *The other elements*: See Book 3.24 below, where the Sun is again called an element.

39     *Od.* 2.216–17.

40     *Od.* 2.261.

41     See, for instance, Book 1.210–18, 266–67 above.

42     *Od.* 2.267–68.

55     *Od.* 2.296.

57     *Od.* 2.297.

58     *Od.* 2.372.

60–62     *Od.* 2.382–84.

69–72     *Od.* 2.393–96.

78     *Od.* 2.420.

79     *Air*: The word ἀήρ is feminine in Homer and Hesiod and masculine from Herodotus onward (see LSJ). Here it is feminine, but in line 84 below the word is masculine.

81–83     *Od.* 2.431–33.


## Book 3

1–2     *Od.* 3.1–50.

3–5     *Od.* 3.79–200, 254–312.

6     *Od.* 3.371–73.

7–9     *Od.* 3.313–28, 475–86.

10–12     *Od.* 3.1–3.

16     See Genesis 1:6, 8, 14, and elsewhere; Psalms 19:1, 150:1, and elsewhere.

17  *Od.* 3.12.

21  *Od.* 3.27.

22  *Od.* 3.28.

23  *Od.* 3.47–48.

28  *Od.* 3.88.

29  *Od.* 3.131. An excerpt from Nestor's speech describing how he and Odysseus were always of one mind during the long siege of Troy, but after the fall of Troy Agamemnon and Menelaos had a harsh disagreement over their return to Greece (*Od.* 3.126–58).

31  *Od.* 3.139.

33  *Od.* 3.132.

41  *Od.* 3.135.

48  *Od.* 3.136.

52  *Od.* 3.141–42.

53–57  *Od.* 3.143–47.

62–63  *Od.* 3.151–52.

67  *Od.* 3.152.

68  *Od.* 3.153–55.

69  *Od.* 3.158.

73  *Od.* 3.160. As is his standard practice, Homer does not use the augment on μήδετο (planned); Tzetzes adds it (ἐμήδετο), but the meaning is the same.

74  *Od.* 3.161.

75  *Od.* 3.173.

76  *Od.* 3.205.

77  *Od.* 3.215.

78  *Od.* 3.218.

79  *Od.* 3.219.

80–81  *Od.* 3.221–22.

84  *Od.* 3.228.

85  *Hyperbole*: For ὑπερβολή (overstrained phrase, hyperbole) as a figure of speech, see LSJ, and Aristotle, *Rhetoric* 1413a29.

86  *Od.* 3.229.

87  *Od.* 3.246, a description of Nestor by Telemachos.

89  *Od.* 3.269.

90  *Od.* 3.273.

91        *Od.* 3.279–80.

94        *Od.* 3.288–89.

96        *Od.* 3.346.

101      Tzetzes seems to change the meaning of 3.346 here. Lines 96 to 100 of *All. Od.* refer to the Homeric passage where Nestor prays that Zeus and the other immortals prevent him from sending away Athena and Telemachos without hospitality and guest gifts. In line 101 Tzetzes seems to suggest that Zeus is being prevented by the other immortal gods, which is not supported by the Homeric text. Could it be that Tzetzes is allegorizing Nestor's mind as "Zeus" being prevented by the other gods (that is, reason or other intellectual powers) from insulting his guests?

105–6   *Od.* 3.371–72.

119–20  *Od.* 3.376.

123      *Od.* 3.378. Tritogeneia is another name for Athena. The meaning of the term is disputed, sometimes translated as "head-born," "the third child," "born thrice in the year," etc. (see LSJ).

126–27  *Od.* 3.380–81. The queen is Athena.

130      *Od.* 3.385.

135      *Od.* 3.489.


## Book 4

1–2       *Od.* 4.1–64.

5         *Proteus*: Proteus, the "Old Man of the Sea," is a god of waters who is also a shape-shifter.

3–7       *Od.* 4.316–560.

8–10     *This happened . . . to kill him*: *Od.* 4.664–73.

10–12   *Learning this . . . her child*: *Od.* 4.675–702, 787–841.

13       *Od.* 4.7.

14       *Od.* 4.14.

15       *Od.* 4.27. The reference is to Peisistratos and Telemachos, both sons of rulers.

17       *Od.* 4.74.

20       *Od.* 4.122.

21    *Od.* 4.160.

22    *Od.* 4.188.

25–26  *Od.* 4.220–21.

35    *Od.* 4.236–37.

36    See *Od.* 4.261.

39    *Od.* 4.289.

41    *Od.* 4.341. This is the beginning of Menelaos's prayer that Odysseus might return to Ithake and kill Penelope's suitors.

45    *Od.* 4.351.

48–50  *Od.* 4.364–66.

51    *Proteus*: For Proteus, see Tz. *All. Il.* 4.5; Eidothea, a sea nymph, is his daughter.

61    This is a pun on the name of Eidothea: εἰδυῖα, meaning knowing, and θέα, meaning goddess.

72    *Od.* 4.409.

73    *Newly skinned*: Νεέκδορος, "newly skinned," is a word found only in Tzetzes, here and in Tz. *Chiliades* 9.64.

76    *Od.* 4.442.

88    *Peisandros*: Peisandros was an Athenian politician in the fifth century BCE, during the Peloponnesian War between Athens and Sparta (431–404 BCE). Initially a democrat belonging to Kleon's party, he then joined the oligarchs after the disastrous defeat of the Sicilian expedition in 413 and organized the oligarchic revolution in 412 (see Thucydides 8.49, 53–54, 63–68). He was thought to be the instigator behind the oligarchic coup of the so-called "Four Hundred." Aristophanes ridiculed him often about his cowardice; Tzetzes here refers to the anecdote seen in Aristophanes, *Birds* 1556. See also Nan Dunbar, ed., *Aristophanes, Birds* (Oxford, 1995), 712–13. The *Suda* quotes Aristophanes's *Birds* as well, in order to explain the expression "more cowardly than Peisandros" (under Πεισάνδρου δειλότερος) as someone who is excessively cowardly (see Hunger 1956 edition, p. 307, note on Book 4, line 88, and *OCD*⁴, under "Pisander").

91    *Became*: The Greek literally means "became seen as," which we assume signifies that he died on the spot.

98      *Od.* 4.376, 378.

99      *Od.* 4.379.

100     *Od.* 4.380.

101     *Od.* 4.462.

102     *Od.* 4.472.

103     *Od.* 4.479.

105     *Zeus's son-in-law*: *Od.* 4.569.

        *King's son-in-law*: As the husband of Helen of Troy, daughter of
        Zeus and Leda.

111     *Swollen by the rain*: The epithet διϊπετής/διειπετής can also
        mean "fallen from Zeus," that is, "from heaven"; see LSJ, under
        "Διϊπετής."

113     *Od.* 4.583.

114     *Od.* 4.520.

115     *Od.* 4.617.

116     *Od.* 4.653–54.

118     *Od.* 4.712.

120     *Od.* 4.755.

123     *Od.* 4.795–809.


# Book 5

1–5     *Od.* 5.3–20.

6–9     See *Od.* 5.22–27.

7       *Just as you advised*: He is probably paraphrasing ὑποτίθημι λό-
        γον, "give advice," here.

10–14   *Od.* 5.29–332, 365–70.

15      *Ino*: At *Od.* 5.333 and following, Homer describes Ino as the mor-
        tal daughter of Kadmos, who became a nymph upon her death.

16      *Od.* 5.333–53, 451–62.

18      See *Od.* 5.3.

21      See Tz. *All. Od.* 2.42–54.

25      *Halitherses*: Halitherses, son of Mastor, is an Ithakan seer who
        warns the suitors to leave off their courtship of Penelope (*Od.*
        2.157–77) and then warns the suitors' fathers against further
        revenge after their deaths (*Od.* 24.451–62). Tzetzes is implying

that Halitherses actually said these things in the *Odyssey*: Hali-
therses's words were spoken by Zeus (which then Tzetzes alle-
gorizes as "a sensible man such as Halitherses," given the rep-
utation of Halitherses as a wise man and a seer). This also
explains lines 28 to 31: it is Zeus who composed the letter to
Hermes.

29      *Od.* 5.28.

41–42   See *Od.* 5.334–35. To escape her husband Athamas, who had gone
mad, Ino jumped into the sea and was transformed into the
goddess Leukothea.

54      *Shearwater*: A shearwater is a bird like a petrel that flies just
above the ocean's surface.

65–66   *Od.* 5.1–2.

72      *Od.* 5.3.

75      *Od.* 5.4.

78      See *Od.* 5.35.

80      *Od.* 5.36.

83      *Basket without knots or braids*: Perhaps a Byzantine idiom; the
word ἀκανίσκος is not found in the *TLG,* and *LbG* does not at-
tempt to provide a definition.

84      *Od.* 5.43; διάκτορος (messenger) is an epithet of Hermes.

85      *Argeïphontes*: *Od.* 5.43. Ἀργειφόντης is a standard epithet for the
god Hermes in Homer, usually translated as "Slayer of Argos."
Here Tzetzes is playing with the compounds of the word, sug-
gesting that it means "clean/purified from murder" (from ἀργός
= "shining," "white," and φόντης, meaning φονεύς = "killer").

90      *Od.* 5.44–46.

93–94   *Od.* 5.47–48.

98      *Od.* 5.49.

99      *Repetition*: Ἐπανάληψις is a rhetorical term, also known as
"anaphora." See Herbert W. Smyth, *Greek Grammar* (Cam-
bridge, Mass., 1956), 673: "anaphora (ἀναφορά, *carrying back*) is
the repetition, with emphasis, of the same word or phrase at
the beginning of several successive clauses. This figure is also
called *epanaphora* or *epanalepsis*)."

103     *Od.* 5.50.

104     *Pierides*: Another name for the Muses: see, for instance, The-
        ocritus, *Idyll* 10.24; Apollonius Rhodius, *Argonautica* 4.1382;
        Euripides, *Medea* 833; etc. They were named after the Macedo-
        nian region of Pieria, where their most ancient seat was situ-
        ated, or after King Pieros of Pella, who was said to be their
        father (although a strand of the tradition says they were the
        daughters of Zeus).

108     *Od.* 5.75.

110     *Od.* 5.79.

112     *Od.* 5.99.

114     *Od.* 5.101–2.

115     *Od.* 5.103–4.

116     *Od.* 5.104.

117     *Od.* 5.118.

118     *Od.* 5.119.

119–20  Although "element" (appearing in line 119) is a neuter noun,
        Tzetzes is probably referring to day, earth, and sea, which are
        all feminine nouns in Greek.

124     *Od.* 5.121. The *Odyssey,* however, speaks of Eos, Dawn, as the
        lover of Orion.

126     Apollodoros (*Library* 1.4.3) claims that this is where Dawn took
        Orion and where he was killed by Artemis. Ortygia is men-
        tioned in Homer, too (*Od.* 5.121–24).

131–32  *Od.* 5.125–28.

134     *Od.* 5.136. "King" refers to Odysseus, as ruler of Ithake.

135     *Men wearing crowns*: A title given to ancient Greek magistrates,
        who had the right to wear a laurel crown; see LSJ, under
        "στεφανηφόρος."

137     *Od.* 5.146.

138     *Od.* 5.148.

139     *Od.* 5.150.

141     *Od.* 5.169.

146     *Od.* 5.199.

152     *Od.* 5.213.

154     *Solymians*: *Od.* 5.283. The Solymoi were inhabitants of Lycia and
        Pisidia in southwestern Asia Minor.

155     *Milyans*: Anatolian Lycians: Herodotus 1.173.

161       *Jebus*: The old name of Jerusalem; see Judges 19:11.
163–64    *Od.* 5.282–83. Poseidon's sojourn among the Ethiopians is first seen at *Od.* 1.22.
167       *Od.* 5.295.
169       *Od.* 5.286–90.
174       *Od.* 5.286.
175       *Od.* 5.291.
177       *Od.* 5.292.
181       *Od.* 5.337.
184       *Od.* 5.356.
188       *Od.* 5.383, 385.
189       *Od.* 5.427.
190       *Od.* 5.447.
193       *Od.* 5.491–92.

## BOOK 6

1–2      *Od.* 6.15–40.
3–5      *Od.* 6.85–118.
6–7      *Od.* 6.149–315.
8–10     *Od.* 6.1–3.
12–13    *Od.* 6.13–14.
26        See *Od.* 6.4, where it is noted that the Phaiakians used to live in Hypereia (Highlands) near the Cyclopes before moving to Scheria. William B. Stanford (*Homer, Odyssey I–XII* [London, 1998], 308) notes that Hypereia should probably be placed in Sicily, since this is generally accepted as the abode of the Cyclopes, but the place-name is probably fictitious. Marina is a village in Sicily.
28        *Godlike*: *Od.* 6.7. See Tz. *All. Il.* 19.103, 24.157, 24.229, and Tz. *All. Od.* 6.112, 8.221, 19.40. Here the epithet is applied to Nausithoös, Odysseus's son by Kalypso.
29        *Od.* 6.10.
29–34    On the five possible interpretations of god in Homer, see Tz. *Exegesis of the Iliad* 45.10, 46.13, 47.15, 48.20, 50.3.
35        *Od.* 6.12.
38        *Of Nausikaa's 'Athena'*: That is, of her prudence.

Nausikaa's . . . her dreams: Od. 6.24–40.

| | |
|---|---|
| 39–40 | Od. 6.41–42. |
| 48 | Od. 6.43. |
| 51 | Od. 6.44. |
| 56–57 | Od. 6.46–47. |
| 62 | The second half of the line is obscure. |
| 73–76 | He is probably referring to the debate between Galen, who argued in favor of the head being the seat of reason, and Aristotle, who argued in favor of the heart; see Aristotle, *Generation of Animals* 738b16f, 743b26f. |
| 83 | *Below*: This is a strange use of μετά + genitive, usually translated "among, together with." |
| 85–90 | Tzetzes here is making a pun on μετάφρενον ("back," literally, "after the midriff"), a compound of μετά + φρήν, by using the prepositional phrase μετὰ φρένας (literally, "after thoughts, thinking"). The Greek word φρήν has multiple meanings, "midriff," "heart," and "mind, thought." |
| 91 | Od. 6.102. |
| 96 | Od. 6.106. Leto was the mortal mother of Apollo and Artemis. |
| 97 | Od. 6.105–6. |
| 106–7 | Od. 6.112–13. |
| 112 | Od. 6.121. |
| 114–15 | Od. 6.139–40. |
| 116 | Od. 6.149. |
| 117 | Od. 6.172. |
| 118 | Od. 6.174. |
| 120 | Od. 6.180. |
| 121 | Od. 6.188. |
| 122 | Od. 6.203. |
| 125 | Od. 6.207–8. |
| 127–29 | Od. 6.229–31. |
| 143 | *Makes it curly*: The verb οὐλίζω is an apparent hapax, not in the *TLG;* it appears to derive from οὖλος, which according to Lampe means "curly" when referring to hair; see also 6.129 with reference to "locks to flow in curls." |
| 148 | Od. 6.233. |

| 150 | *Od.* 6.240. |
| 152 | *Od.* 6.241. |
| 154 | *Od.* 6.243. |
| 155 | *Od.* 6.280–81. |
| 159 | *Od.* 6.291. |
| 174 | *Od.* 6.324. |
| 182 | Interestingly, Homer says she did hear him, but did not rush to help him for fear of her uncle; see below, lines 184–87. |
| 184–87 | *Od.* 6.328–31. |

## BOOK 7

| 1–2 | *Od.* 7.1–6, 142–52. Arete was queen of the Phaiakians. |
| 3–6 | *Od.* 7.228–97. |
| 7 | *Od.* 7.5. |
| 8 | *Od.* 7.11. |
| 11–12 | *Od.* 7.14–15. |
| 15 | *Od.* 7.19–20. |
| 17 | *Od.* 7.39–41. |
| 20 | *Of the weather*: Hunger notes that he could not find the word ἀερόστημος in George of Pisidia ("Pisides," a seventh-century CE poet from Pisidia, Asia Minor) and that perhaps it is related to κατάστημα (weather); see Tz. *All. Od.* 22.84 (Hunger 1956 edition, p. 308, note on Book 7, lines 18–20). The word is not in the *TLG* and seems to be a hapax. |
| 21 | *Od.* 7.47. |
| 23–24 | Tzetzes perhaps considers "Athena" to be a homonym here, since in lines 18–20 it means air and in lines 21–22 it means a girl. |
| 25 | *Name transition*: On the meaning of this term, see note on Tz. *All. Od.* 1.103. |
| 26–27 | *Od.* 7.56–57. |
| 31 | *Od.* 7.64. |
| 32 | *Od.* 7.71. |
| 35 | *Od.* 7.69. |
| 36–37 | Tzetzes here cites two full lines of the *Odyssey*: 7.78 and 7.81. He then explains that he suggests excising the two lines in be- |

tween (79 and 80). The ellipsis indicates that the sentence does not end at 81 but runs on to 82–83, but these lines are not relevant for him to quote.

38 That is, *Od.* 7.79–80.

43 This is a pun with the verb ἐρέχθω (I rend) and the name Ἐρεχθεύς.

45 *City of Erechtheus*: That is, Athens.

47 *Od.* 7.91.

48 *Od.* 7.100.

53 *Od.* 7.94.

54 *Od.* 7.132.

58 *Od.* 7.140.

60 *Od.* 7.164.

61 *Od.* 7.190–91.

62–64 *Od.* 7.199–201.

71 *Od.* 7.245–46.

73 *Od.* 7.250; discussed previously at Tz. *All. Od.* 5.134.

74 *Od.* 7.257.

75 *Od.* 7.263.

76 *Od.* 7.266.

78 *Od.* 7.311. As, for instance, "destiny," "wisdom," and "light," respectively, throughout the poem.

## BOOK 8

1–2 *Od.* 8.4–45.

3–4 *Od.* 8.133–233.

5 *Introduction*: Ἐπιβολή is a rhetorical term, usually translated as "introduction" or "approach to a subject."

5–7 *As an introduction . . . wooden horse*: *Od.* 8.499–520. Demodokos was a minstrel who frequently visited the court of Alkinoös.

8–9 *Od.* 8.521–86.

10–13 *Od.* 8.7–10.

19 *Od.* 8.14.

20 *Od.* 8.20.

25 *Od.* 8.64.

| | |
|---|---|
| 26 | *Od.* 8.76. |
| 28 | *Od.* 8.82. |
| 29 | *Od.* 8.170. |
| 31 | *Od.* 8.193. |
| 34 | *Od.* 8.195. |
| 35 | *Od.* 8.225. |
| 39 | *Od.* 8.224–28. |
| 40 | *Od.* 8.244–245. |
| 41–42 | *Od.* 8.267–68. |
| 43 | See Tz. *Chronicle* 197–527 on allegories of Cosmogony. |
| 48 | See Tz. *All. Il.* pro.291–92 for similar lines. |
| 51 | The ancient mythographer is Paris, as elaborated in Tz. *All. Il.* pro.255–333. |
| 59 | See Tz. *Chronicle* 449–67. |
| 64 | See Anne-Laurence Caudano, "Un univers sphérique ou voûté? Survivance de la cosmologie antiochienne à Byzance (XIe et XIIe siècles)," *Byzantion* 78 (2008): 66–86. |
| 65 | *They*: That is, the elements. |
| 66 | See Tz. *Chronicle* 229, 455. |
| 75 | Erebos was a place of nether darkness, forming a passage from Earth to Hades, while Chaos was the nether abyss, a place of infinite darkness; see LSJ, under "Ἔρεβος" and "χάος." |
| 76 | See Tz. *Chronicle* 352, 277, 506; and also Tz. *All. Od.* 8.121 and 11.62. |
| 88 | *Hemisphere*: Tzetzes here refers to the shape of the sun as it comes up from the sea in the morning. |
| 93 | *Spurious*: The word νόθος usually refers to illegitimate children. Perhaps this is an allusion to Hephaistos's dubious parentage, as according to one tradition he was the son of Hera, but not of Zeus. See also Tz. *Chronicle* 453. |
| 103 | *Od.* 8.273. |
| 104 | *Od.* 8.274. See Tz. *All. Il.* 18.677. |
| 107 | *Od.* 8.274–75. |
| 109 | *Od.* 8.277–80. |
| 111 | *Od.* 8.278–79. |
| 112 | *Od.* 8.280. |
| 115 | *Od.* 8.283. |

| | |
|---|---|
| 118 | Lemnos here means Cosmos: see Tz. *Chronicle* 422, and Hunger 1956 edition, p. 309, Book 8, note on line 118. |
| 125 | *Od.* 8.301. |
| 128 | *Od.* 8.304–5. |
| 131 | *Od.* 8.305. |
| 133 | See Tz. *Chronicle* 397. |
| 140 | *Od.* 8.311. |
| 145 | *Od.* 8.321–24. |
| 150 | See Tz. *Chronicle* 232, 234, 365. |
| 152 | See Hunger 1956 edition, p. 309, note on Book 8, line 152, where he notes a similar construction in Tz. *Chronicle* 460. There we see the compound διᾴττω, "dart through, across" (see LSJ); we assume ᾄττω has a similar meaning here. |
| 156 | *Od.* 8.324, and see Tz. *Chronicle* 457–58. |
| 166 | *Od.* 8.334–42. The term τριστοσαπλοῖς, here rendered as "three times as many," is an apparent hapax invented by Tzetzes; it should perhaps be emended to τριτοσαπλοῖς, but this is also unattested. |
| 176 | *Od.* 8.344. |
| 178 | *Od.* 8.362–63. |
| 200 | *Od.* 8.410. |
| 201 | *Od.* 8.432. |
| 203 | *Od.* 8.457. |
| 204 | *Od.* 8.465. |
| 205 | *Od.* 8.467. |
| 206 | *Od.* 8.488. |
| 207 | *Od.* 8.498. |
| 209 | *Od.* 8.512, 509. |
| 212 | *Od.* 8.520. |
| 213 | *Od.* 8.539. |
| 214 | *Od.* 8.559. |
| 216–17 | *Od.* 8.565–66. |
| 218–19 | *Od.* 8.567–69. |
| 220 | *Od.* 8.570. |
| 221 | *Od.* 8.576. Here Tzetzes uses the form θεοειδής, "godlike," although in the Homeric text it appears as θεουδής, "god- |

fearing." When he alludes to this line below in 9.49, he chooses the θεουδής form; perhaps he considers them interchangeable?

222     *Od.* 8.579.


## BOOK 9

1–2     *Od.* 9.39–61. The Kikonians were a warlike tribe that lived on the south coast of Thrace.

3       *Od.* 9.82–104. The Lotus-Eaters ate a sweet local fruit that so overwhelmed those who tasted it that they became forgetful of anything else.

4–6     *Od.* 9.105–397.

7       *Od.* 9.4.

9       *Od.* 9.15.

10      See *Od.* 9.29, where the word is in the singular.

11      *Od.* 9.38.

13      *Od.* 9.39.

14      *Od.* 9.52.

15      *Od.* 9.67.

16–17   *Od.* 9.94–95.

19      *Gadeira*: The modern city of Cadiz.

35–38   *Od.* 9.106–9.

40      *Od.* 9.111.

41      *Od.* 9.142.

42–43   *Od.* 9.154–55.

47      Tzetzes here is making a pun with the words καταιγίς, "storm," and αἴξ, "goat."

48      *Od.* 9.158.

49      *Od.* 9.176. Here Tzetzes uses the form θεουδής, "god-fearing," as in the Homeric text.

50      *'Apollo' is the sun*: *Od.* 9.198.
        *'Unmixed' wine*: *Od.* 9.205.

52–53   *Od.* 9.240–41.

56      *Od.* 9.262.

58      *Od.* 9.269.

60      *Od.* 9.270.

61–65    *Od.* 9.274–78. This is the Cyclops speaking.

72    *Pity*: Hunger notes that the form οἰκτεριῶ is perhaps a confla-
tion of the forms οἰκτιῶ, the future of the verb οἰκτίζω, and
οἰκτειρήσω, a later future of the form οἰκτίρω (see LSJ, under
"οἰκτίρω"). All forms are variations of the same root "to pity"
(Hunger 1956 edition, p. 309, note on Book 9, line 72).

74    *Od.* 9.291.

77    *He pierced his guts*: The otherwise unattested verb διεντερεύω
seems to be linked to the nouns ἔντερον, "entrails," and διεντέ-
ρευμα, "looking through entrails, being sharp-sighted." Hun-
ger gives the same explanation (Hunger 1956 edition, p. 309,
note on Book 9, line 77).

78    *Od.* 9.294.

79    *Od.* 9.317.

80    *Od.* 9.339.

81    *Od.* 9.358.

82    *Od.* 9.411.

88    *Od.* 9.412.

90    See Tz. *All. Od.* 13.81 for the Cyclops as the child of the sea.

91    *Od.* 9.479.

93–94    *Od.* 9.518–19.

98    *Od.* 9.520. The Cyclops is speaking here of his father, Poseidon.

101    See Tz. *All. Od.* 1.181–83.

103    *Od.* 9.521.

105    A reference to *Od.* 10.80–132, an account of the attack of the gi-
ant Laistrygonians on Odysseus's ships.

114    *Od.* 9.536.

118    *Od.* 9.552.

121–27    The Issedones were an ancient people who lived in Central Asia
near Scythia. Hunger notes that they are mentioned in the *Ari-
maspeia Epics* attributed to Aristeas of Prokonnesos, fragment
4, p. 151. Aristeas was the legendary author of a poem on the
Arimaspeans, a people of the far north. The same quotation
is found in Tz. *Chiliades* 7.678–82. See Hunger 1956 edition,
p. 309, note on Book 9, lines 122ff., although his quotation of
the *Chiliades* is not entirely accurate.

| | |
|---|---|
| 138–39 | These names are not mentioned in the *Odyssey*. |
| 154 | *Smashed . . . into pieces*: The verb συγκαταρράσσω seems to be a compound of καταρράσσω (in the aorist κατήραξα spelled with one -ρ-), which means "to break into pieces, to dash down"; hence the word "cataract." |
| 167 | *Od*. 9.322. |
| 169–70 | Tzetzes speaks of Eros πυρφόρος ("fire-bearing" or "torch-bearing") in his *Chiliades* 5.506. Hunger (1956 edition, p. 309, note on Book 9, line 170) notes that the burning stick with which Odysseus blinded the Cyclops was the torch of the Passions (the little love gods). |

## BOOK 10

| | |
|---|---|
| 1–6 | *Od*. 10.19–75. |
| 7 | *Laistrygonians*: A race of giants who may have lived on Sicily. |
| 7–9 | *Od*. 10.76–132. |
| 10 | *Kirke*: Kirke was a sorceress who turned some of Odysseus's crew into pigs by giving them food laced with a magical drug. |
| 11–13 | *Od*. 10.133–399. |
| 27 | *Interpreter*: A favorite pun of Tzetzes (see, for instance, Tz. *All. Il*. 24.105): Hermes is the interpreter, since it is he who gives Odysseus knowledge of the moly plant. |
| 30 | On moly see *Od*. 10.302–6. |
| 37 | See *Od*. 10.5. |
| 38 | This seems to be a reference to line 45 below, which scornfully presents the theory that Aiolos is the year and his children are the twelve months. |
| 39–42 | Tzetzes seems to list only eleven names, which are not found in Homer. |
| 45 | Tzetzes is probably referring to Heraclitus's *Homeric Problems* 71, where that claim is made. |
| 69 | *Aiolia*: That is, the island of Aiolos. |
| 77 | *Od*. 10.2. |
| 79 | *Od*. 10.3–4. |
| 81 | *Od*. 10.21. |

| | |
|---|---|
| 85 | *Od.* 10.74, a reference to Odysseus. |
| 88 | *Od.* 10.112–13. |
| 90 | *Od.* 10.116. |
| 92 | *Od.* 10.124. |
| 94 | *Od.* 10.136. |
| 99 | This is a confusing expression; Helios is Kirke's father and Okeanos is her maternal grandfather; see *Od.* 10.138–39. |
| 101 | See *Od.* 10.138. |
| 102 | *Od.* 10.141. |
| 103 | *Od.* 10.157. |
| 104 | *Od.* 10.220. |
| 105 | *Od.* 10.222. |
| 106 | *Od.* 10.228. |
| 108 | *Od.* 10.235–36. |
| 110 | See *Od.* 10.237–38. |
| 111 | See *Od.* 10.277. |
| 112 | *Od.* 10.297. |
| 113 | *Od.* 10.305. |
| 115 | *Od.* 10.307. |
| 116 | *Od.* 10.330–32. |
| 118 | *Od.* 10.348–49. |
| 120 | This is a pun with the adverb κιρκαίως and the name Κίρκη, perhaps alluding to her deceitful nature. The adverb is a hapax (see *LbG*, under "κιρκαίως"). |
| 121 | Telegonos was Kirke and Odysseus's son, who, according to the tradition, married Penelope after his father's death; see Proclus, *Chrestomathia* 324–30. |
| 123 | *Od.* 10.389, 392. |
| 125–30 | This passage looks ahead to Book 11 of the *Odyssey,* where Odysseus descends to the Underworld and meets with the seer Teiresias. |
| 131 | *Od.* 10.573–74. |

## Book 11

| | |
|---|---|
| 1–4 | *Od.* 11.90–332. |
| 5 | *Od.* 11.6–8. |

## BOOK II

8–11    *Od.* 11.13–16.

12–13   Kimmerians is the name of an ancient people who lived in Crimea and gave their name to the Kimmerian Bosporos (the present-day Straits of Kerč). The Maeotic Lake is the Sea of Azov, in the northern region of the Black Sea.

16a     *The sun is in Cancer*: That is, the period between June 21 and July 22.

16a–b   These are alternative lines in the text.

18      *Theon*: Theon was a Greek geometer and astronomer who lived in Alexandria in the fourth century CE. He was known for his commentaries on Euclid. His commentary on Ptolemy's *Almagest* survives, although parts of Book 5 and the whole of Book 11 are missing. For more, see Roger Bagnall et al., eds., *The Encyclopedia of Ancient History* (Malden, Mass., 2013), 6685–86.

20      Homer does not say this. This is Tzetzes's own interpretation of the Homeric text.

27      *Siacha*: Siacha is defined as "a Kimmerian name of Lake Avernus near Cumae, preserved by John Tzetzes"; see Robert Owen, *The Kymry: Their Origin, History and International Relations* (Carmarthen, Wales, 1891), 237. For more on Lake Siacha, see Alexander Kazhdan and Ann Wharton Epstein, *Change in Byzantine Culture in the Eleventh and Twelfth Centuries* (Berkeley, Calif., 1985), 135.

35      *Od.* 11.73.

36      *Od.* 11.100–101.

38      *Od.* 11.103.

41–44   *Od.* 11.106–9.

46      *Od.* 1.13.

48      See *Od.* 11.133.

51      *Od.* 11.139.

52      *Od.* 11.172.

60      *Od.* 11.217.

65      *Od.* 11.235. Tyro was the daughter of Salmoneus and the wife of Cretheus.

68      See *Od.* 11.241–42, where Poseidon had intercourse with Tyro at the mouth of the river Enipeus.

69      *Od.* 11.261.

70     *Od.* 11.274.

72     *Od.* 11.292.

73–78  *Od.* 11.299–304.

95–96  *Whom I formerly . . . iambic lines*: He is probably referring to his
       *Theogonia,* line 91 (Pietro Matranga, ed., *Anecdota Graeca e mss
       bibliothecis Vaticana, Angelica, Barberiniana, Vallicelliana, Medicea,
       Vindobonensi deprompta* [Rome, 1850], 577–98, at 580).

97–98  See *Od.* 11.305–20.

99     See *Il.* 5.385–91.

101    *Od.* 11.321–22.

103    See, for example, Diodorus Siculus 4.61, 5.51; Pausanias 1.20,
       9.40, 10.29; Pseudo-Apollodoros, *Biblioteca Epitome* 1.9.

111    *Od.* 11.325.

113    *Od.* 11.341.

114    *Od.* 11.436.

116–17 *Od.* 11.546–47.

122    *Od.* 11.555.

123    *Od.* 11.559–60.

124    *Od.* 11.576.

126–27 *They cut . . . Tityos*: See Apollodoros, *Biblioteca* 1.4.2; scholia on
       the *Argonautica* 1.761; and Strabo, *Geography* 9.3.15. This refers
       to the Caesarean section, explained in *Suda* (under "Καῖσαρ")
       as named after Julius Caesar, who was extracted from his moth-
       er's womb when she died during her ninth month of pregnancy.

128    See *Od.* 11.576.

129    *Od.* 11.580. The miscreant is Tityos.

131a   *Panopeus*: Ancient Greek town in Phokis mentioned in *Od.*
       11.581.

133    Tityos was a son of Gaia, who assaulted Leto and was killed by
       Zeus, Apollo, or Artemis (see *OCD*[4], under "Tityus"); his pun-
       ishment was having his liver eaten by vultures in Hades; see *Od.*
       11.576–81.

138    See Tz. *Chiliades* 5.444–99.

140    *Od.* 11.620.

142    *Eurystheus*: The king of Mycenae.

144    *Hades*: That is, the death.

| 145 | *Land of the Molossians*: A region in Epirus. |
| 146 | The Molossians were famed for their vicious dogs; see Aristophanes, *Thesmophoriazusae* 416; Lucretius, *De Rerum Natura* 5.1063; Horace, *Epodes* 6.5; Grattius, *Cynegetica* p. 169. |
| 152 | *Od.* 11.626. |
| 154 | *Homonymy*: Tzetzes is talking about the similarity between the names of the king of the Molossians, Ἀϊδονεύς, and the Lord of the Underworld, Ἅιδης. |
| 157 | *Od.* 11.634. |

## BOOK 12

| 1–5 | *Od.* 12.33–140. |
| 6–7 | *Od.* 12.3–4. |
| 9 | *Od.* 12.38. |
| 11 | *Od.* 12.39. |
| 18 | *Od.* 12.61. The Planktai are the Wandering Rocks guarding the entrance to the Black Sea, often identified with the Clashing Rocks which Jason and the Argonauts successfully passed on their way to retrieve the Golden Fleece; see also *OCD*[4], under "Symplegades." According to LSJ, the Planktai were originally rocks near Skylla and Charybdis. |
| 19–20 | *Od.* 12.62–63. |
| 21–24 | Antagoras of Rhodes, an epic poet of the third century BCE, was summoned to the Macedonian court. He was a writer of a *Thebais* and some epigrams, very few fragments of which survive. What Tzetzes refers to here is not found in the extant fragments. It is not clear whether he means Ursa Major or Ursa Minor here; if it is the latter, it might be Polaris, the North Star, although we cannot be certain. |
| 25–26 | *Od.* 12.63–64. |
| 28–29 | Hunger (1956 edition, p. 310, note on Book 12, lines 25–29), notes that the infinitives σημαίνειν (to mark) and καταγγέλλειν (to announce) are here probably linked to the expression δοκῶ λέγειν τὸν Ὅμηρον (I think that Homer is saying, 12.21). |
| 30 | *Od.* 12.65. |

| | |
|---|---|
| 31 | *Od.* 12.72. The first "her" refers to Jason's ship, the Argo. |
| 33 | *Od.* 12.85. |
| 49 | *Od.* 12.88. |
| 53 | *Od.* 12.117. |
| 54 | *Od.* 12.118. |
| 57–59 | *Od.* 12.124–26. |
| 60 | *Golden old man:* That is, Homer. |
| 68–72 | *Od.* 12.127–31. |
| 74 | Tz. *All. Od.* 1.13; see also Tz. *All. Od.* 11.45. |
| 84 | *Phaethousa and Lampetie:* These were daughters of the Sun attending the flocks; see *Od.* 12.131–33. |
| 98 | *Od.* 12.395. |
| 101 | This line is bracketed in the Hunger 1956 edition. |
| 102 | *Od.* 12.313. |
| 103 | *Od.* 12.318. |
| 104 | *Od.* 12.337. |
| 105 | *Od.* 12.344. |
| 106 | *Od.* 12.349. |
| 107 | *Od.* 12.371. |
| 109 | *Od.* 12.374–75. |
| 110 | *Od.* 12.399. |
| 112 | *Od.* 12.416. |
| 114 | *Od.* 12.445. |
| 124 | *Od.* 12.448. The island of Ogygia was the home of the nymph Kalypso. |

## Book 13

| | |
|---|---|
| 1–2 | *Od.* 13.70–92, 113–25. |
| 3 | *Od.* 13.159–64. |
| 4–5 | *Od.* 13.363–71, 375–81, 394–96. |
| 6 | *Od.* 13.397–403. |
| 7 | *Od.* 13.25. |
| 8 | *Od.* 13.41. |
| 9 | *Od.* 13.45. |
| 10 | *Od.* 13.51. |

| 12 | *Od.* 13.89. |
|----|----|
| 14 | *Od.* 13.104. |
| 16–17 | *Od.* 13.105–8. |
| 18 | *Entrance*: This refers to the mouths of the cave of the Nymphs. The Greek word is θύραι (plural), which explains the plural articles and verbs in the whole section. |
| 18–20 | *Od.* 13.110–12. |
| 23 | *Od.* 13.121. |
| 25–26 | *Od.* 13.125–26. |
| 32 | *Od.* 13.148. |
| 37 | *Nobles*: Tzetzes's meaning is unclear here. Perhaps he means that Poseidon symbolizes the Phaiakian aristocrats. |
| 38–39 | See *Od.* 13.158. In Homer's *Odyssey* the story is that their city was punished by being surrounded by a great mountain chain. |
| 40 | See *Od.* 13.172–77. |
| 41 | See *Od.* 13.187–89, where she pours mist around him. |
| 45 | See *Od.* 13.200–214. |
| 46 | *Od.* 13.213. |
| 55–56 | *Od.* 13.287–88. |
| 59–61 | Hunger (1955 edition, p. 39, note on Book 13, line 59) rejected the manuscript reading ἐν τῇ χειρί and proposed instead μέν, which can be answered by δέ in line 62. Alternatively, he proposed amending the line to ὁμαλισθεὶς ἐν τῇ φρενί to explain the use of διττολογέω (repeat, say twice) with the deliberate repetition of φρήν. We chose the first solution, because ὁμαλίζω combined with χείρ, meaning "caress with one's hand," appears repeatedly in Tzetzes (see *All. Il.* 1.127, 217). Perhaps διττολογέω refers to the fact that Tzetzes is more or less repeating himself in lines 58 to 60 above, to accentuate the symbolism of Athena as Odysseus's mind. |
| 62–63 | *Od.* 13.288–89. |
| 66 | *These things*: The word σφῶν refers to everything mentioned in line 65. See Hunger 1955 edition, p. 39, note on Book 13, line 66. |
| 70 | *Od.* 13.291. |
| 72–73 | See *Od.* 13.297–98. |
| 74 | *Od.* 13.304. Lines 70 to 74 are spoken by Athena. |

76–78    *Od.* 13.341–43.

79–84    On the Cyclops's daughter, Elpe, see Tz. *All. Od.* 9.99–109, 139, 167–77.

89    See Tz. *All. Il.* 18.137.

97–98    *Od.* 13.344–45. On Phorkys see note on Tz. *All. Od.* 1.189 above.

102    *Neriton*: Mount Neriton was named after Neritos, one of Ithake's legendary founders, the other being Ithakos. See Acusilaus's scholia on the *Odyssey, FgrH* I.A2, fragment 43.2. It is mentioned frequently as the most recognizable landmark on the island. See *Il.* 2.631–32; *Od.* 9.21–22, etc.

103–5    *Od.* 13.366–68.

108    *Od.* 13.377.

110    *Od.* 13.383.

117    See *Od.* 13.398–406.

## BOOK 14

1–2    *Od.* 14.1–4.

3–4    *Od.* 14.199–359.

5–6    *Od.* 14.1–2.

8    *Od.* 14.18. Ἀντίθεος in Homer typically means "godlike," "equal to the gods" (see LSJ). "Hostile to god" is a later translation, especially in Christian context (see LSJ; *LbG,* under "ἀντίθεως"). Tzetzes seems to overlook the Homeric sense and opt for the later meaning.

9    *Od.* 14.39.

10    *Od.* 14.53.

13    *Od.* 14.57.

14    *Od.* 14.61, 65.

17    *Od.* 14.89.

19–22    Hunger (1955 edition, p. 40, note on Book 14, lines 19ff.) notes the three methods of theorizing θεός: (1) pragmatic (wisdom), (2) physical (elements and stars of Destiny), (3) psychological (powers of the soul, justice, etc.).

23    *Od.* 14.119.

24    *Od.* 14.158.

| | |
|---|---|
| 26 | *Od.* 14.175. |
| 27 | *Od.* 14.178. |
| 29 | *Od.* 14.184. |
| 30 | *Od.* 14.198. |
| 32 | *Od.* 14.205. |
| 33 | *Od.* 14.216. |
| 37 | *Od.* 14.235. |
| 39 | *Od.* 14.242. |
| 41 | *Od.* 14.243. |
| 42 | *Od.* 14.251. |
| 43 | *Zeus who hurls thunderbolts*: *Od.* 14.268. |
| | *'Zeus' who 'put it in his thoughts'*: *Od.* 14.273–74. |
| 44 | *Od.* 14.283–84. |
| 45 | *Od.* 14.300. |
| 46 | *Od.* 14.303. |
| 47 | *Od.* 14.305. |
| 48 | *Od.* 14.309, 310–11. |
| 50–51 | *Od.* 14.327–28. |
| 55 | *Od.* 14.348, 357. |
| 56 | *Od.* 14.366, 386. |
| 58 | *Od.* 14.394. |
| 60 | *Od.* 14.406. |
| 64 | *Od.* 14.435. |
| 67 | *Od.* 14.440, 444. "They" in the following line refers to Odysseus and Eumaios. |
| 68 | *Od.* 14.446. |
| 70 | *Od.* 14.457–58. |

## BOOK 15

| | |
|---|---|
| 1–2 | *Od.* 15.1–42. |
| 3–4 | *Od.* 15.111–30, 195–201. |
| 5–6 | *Indeed Peisistratos . . . his father*: *Od.* 15.202–16. |
| 6–8 | *Telemachos . . . supplicated him*: *Od.* 15.256–95. |
| 9–10 | *Od.* 15.351–484. |
| 11–13 | *Od.* 15.1–3. |

18     *Od.* 15.26.

19–20     *Od.* 15.34–35.

19–21     These are Athena's words to Telemachos.

22     *Od.* 15.43.

27–28     *Od.* 15.111–12.

29–30     That is, Homer chose to speak of Zeus and Hera allegorically instead of saying what Tzetzes says in line 30.

31     *Od.* 15.168. A line spoken by Peisistratos, son of Nestor, to Menelaos.

33–34     *Od.* 15.172–73.

37–38     *Od.* 15.180–81.

41     *Od.* 15.187.

44     *Od.* 15.222.

47–48     *Od.* 15.245–46.

53–54     *Od.* 15.250–51.

55–56     See Hunger 1955 edition, p. 40, note on Book 15, lines 55ff.

59     *Od.* 15.252–53. This refers to Kleitos's brother, Polypheides.

63     *Od.* 15.292.

65–66     *Od.* 15.319–20.

68     *Od.* 15.341.

69     *Od.* 15.353.

70     *Od.* 15.372.

72–74     *Od.* 15.409–11.

79     *Od.* 15.414.

81     *Od.* 15.475.

82     *Od.* 15.477.

83     *Restoration:* Ἀποκατάστασις is an astronomical term denoting the return of planets to their former position after completing their orbits. Here, it appears that the restoration of the heavens is day. Hunger 1955 edition, p. 40, note on Book 15, line 83; compare Plutarch, *Concerning the Face Which Appears in the Orb of the Moon* 937f4.

84     *Od.* 15.478.

85     *Od.* 15.488–89.

86     *Od.* 15.520.

87     *Od.* 15.523.

| 88 | *Od.* 15.526. |
|---|---|
| 90 | *Chairemon*: Chairemon of Alexandria (first century CE) was a Stoic philosopher, tutor to Nero, and superintendent of the Library of Alexandria, where he wrote a work on Egyptian astrology. See Pieter Willem van der Horst, *Chaeremon, Egyptian Priest and Stoic Philosopher: The Fragments Collected and Translated* (Leiden, 1984). |
| 91 | *Od.* 15.531. |

## BOOK 16

| 1 | *Od.* 16.4–21. |
|---|---|
| 2–3 | *Od.* 16.130–55. |
| 4 | *Od.* 16.186–212. |
| 5–6 | *Od.* 16.351–57, 363–73. |
| 7 | *Od.* 16.64. |
| 8 | *Od.* 16.96. |
| 9 | *Od.* 16.129. |
| 11 | *Od.* 16.157. |
| 13 | *Od.* 16.161. |
| 14 | That is, people cannot know each other's thoughts. |
| 16 | *Od.* 16.162. "Her" is a reference to Athena. |
| 17–18 | *Od.* 16.456–57. |
| 19–21 | *Od.* 16.162–63. Tzetzes has conflated two passages from the *Od.* here. The dogs were cowed at Athena's appearance and failed to bark at her, not Odysseus. |
| 22 | *Od.* 16.172; compare *Od.* 13.429. However, Tzetzes does not comment on this line in Book 13. |
| 23 | *Od.* 16.179. |
| 25 | *Od.* 16.183. |
| 27 | *Od.* 16.183. |
| 29 | *Od.* 16.184. |
| 32 | *Od.* 16.194. |
| 35–36 | *Od.* 16.199–200. |
| 38 | *Od.* 16.207. |
| 40 | *Od.* 16.211. |

42      *Od.* 16.232.

43      *Od.* 16.260.

45      *Od.* 16.263.

46      *Od.* 16.264.

48      *Od.* 16.298.

50      *Od.* 16.320. Reversed order in Homer.

51      *Od.* 16.364.

52      *Od.* 16.370. The words are identical in the Homeric line, but the order is different.

53      *Od.* 16.402.

56      *Od.* 16.403.

57      *Od.* 16.422–23.

60      *Od.* 16.446–47.

61      *Od.* 16.450–51.

66      *Od.* 16.454–56.

## BOOK 17

1–2      *Od.* 17.107–49.

3–4      *Od.* 17.150–61.

5–6      *Od.* 17.290–327.

7–8      *Od.* 17.574–606.

9      *Od.* 17.37.

12      *Od.* 17.50.

14      *Od.* 17.51.

15      *Od.* 17.63.

16      *Od.* 17.119.

17      *Od.* 17.132.

19      *Od.* 17.143.

23–24      This is a pun on Νύμφη, meaning "Nymph," and νύμφη, meaning "bride." Hunger (1955 edition, p. 41, note on Book 17, lines 19ff.) notes that the etymology of "bride" is given as νεωστὶ φαινομένη, that is, the girl who has been hidden so far and makes her first public appearance at her wedding. Compare Thomas Gaisford, *Etymologicum Magnum* (Oxford, 1848), cols. 1730–31; Friedrich W. Sturz, *Etymologicum Graecae linguae Gudianum et alia grammaticorum scripta e codicibus manuscriptis nunc primum edita* (Leipzig, 1818), 615; Marchinus van der Valk, *Eustathii archiepiscopi Thessalonicensis commentarii ad Homeri Iliadem pertinentes,* vols. 1–4 (Leiden, 1971, 1976, 1979, 1987), 603.34–35.

29      *Od.* 17.148–49.

31      *Od.* 17.155.

33      *Od.* 17.211.

34      *Od.* 17.218.

35      *Od.* 17.240.

36      *Od.* 17.243.

37      *Od.* 17.251.

38      *Od.* 17.270–71.

40      *Od.* 17.322.

42      *Od.* 17.354.

43      *Od.* 17.360–62.

44      *Od.* 17.399.

45      *Od.* 17.424.

46      *Od.* 17.437.

48      *Od.* 17.475.

51      *Od.* 17.484.

53      *Od.* 17.494.

54      *Od.* 17.518–19.

57      *Od.* 17.597.

58      *Od.* 17.601.

## BOOK 18

2       *Public beggar*: *Od.* 18.1.

        *Arnaios, called Iros*: The nickname, which derives from the messenger goddess Iris, was given to him by the suitors because he used to convey messages for them. See *Od.* 18.6–7.

3–4     *Od.* 18.36–99.

5       *Od.* 18.220–25.

6–7     *Od.* 18.281–303. Ὀργάς (here translated "she in her bloom") derives from the verb ὀργάω (literally, "to be ready to bear"), which is mainly used for soil. Hunger (1955 edition, p. 41, note on Book 18, line 7) notes that the noun was a Byzantine euphemism for a girl capable of marriage. Compare Niketas Choniates, *Historia* 508.13.

8–11   *Od.* 18.344–55. Hunger (1955 edition, p. 41, note on Book 18, lines 8ff.) comments that Tzetzes seems to struggle with the idea that Odysseus, the wooer of goddesses, is bald. In the *Odyssey,* the fire glows on Odysseus's bald head, but here Tzetzes states that the red glow comes from Odysseus's hat. In the Homeric text, it is Eurymachos who makes the other suitors laugh.

12–14   *Od.* 18.357.

15   *Od.* 18.19.

16   *Od.* 18.37.

17   *Od.* 18.69–70.

20   *Od.* 18.112.

22   *Od.* 18.133.

23   *Od.* 18.134, 137.

24   *Od.* 18.142.

25   *Od.* 18.155.

26   *Od.* 18.158.

27   *Od.* 18.176.

28   *Od.* 18.180.

29   *Od.* 18.187–96.

32   *Od.* 18.235.

34   *Od.* 18.252, 256.

35   See *Od.* 18.265, 273.

37   *Od.* 18.346. The words are the same as in the Homeric text, but Tzetzes has changed the word order. "Of Odysseus" makes no sense here.

38   *Od.* 18.353.

39   *Od.* 18.376.

40   *Od.* 18.407.

41   *Od.* 18.425–26.


# BOOK 19

1   *Od.* 19.31–34.

2–4   *Od.* 19.16–248.

5–6    *Od.* 19.386–475.

7      *Od.* 19.482–98.

8      *Od.* 19.2.

9      *Od.* 19.10.

10     *Od.* 19.33–34. Compare Tz. *All. Il.* 4.86, 22.83; Tz. *All. Od.* 1.86, 4.42.

12     *Od.* 19.40.

13     *Od.* 19.43.

14     *Od.* 19.54.

16     *Od.* 19.80.

17     *Od.* 19.86.

21     Compare Sophocles, *Oedipus Tyrannus* 1425–26, slightly paraphrased.

22     Hunger (1955 edition, p. 42, note on Book 19, lines 17ff.) argues that this could mean (astrologically) that Telemachos became a man in the year that the Sun was Regent. The word is glossed as ἡλιοδρόμος in LSJ, translated as "sun's messenger," and as ἡλιόδρομος in *LbG,* referring specifically to this passage, and translated as "going through the sun."

23     *Od.* 19.129, 138.

24     *Od.* 19.161.

25–26  *Od.* 19.178–79. Hunger (1955 edition, p. 42, note on Book 19, line 27) notes that Minos should be perceived here as the herald of the Cretan king Zeus; this could be due to the apparent similarity in pronunciation of Minos and "herald" (μηνυτής) in Greek.

27–28  *Od.* 19.201.

29     *Od.* 19.267.

30     *Od.* 19.276.

31     Tzetzes repeatedly calls the Sun an element throughout the *Allegories.*

32     *Od.* 19.279.

33     *Od.* 19.280.

35     *Od.* 19.296–97.

36     We assume he means the will of Destiny. Zeus as Destiny is a recurrent theme throughout the work.

37   *Od.* 19.303.

38   *Giant*: Tzetzes seems to confuse Giants and Titans; Helios is a
     Titan. See Hunger 1955 edition, p. 42, note on Book 19, line 38.

39   See *Od.* 19.363–64, slightly altered.

40   *Od.* 19.364.

41   *Od.* 19.365.

43   *Od.* 19.396–97.

45   *Od.* 19.479.

48   *Od.* 19.485.

50   *Od.* 19.488.

52   *Od.* 19.502.

55–56   *Od.* 19.562–63.

62–65   On the gates of horn and ivory, see Murray's note in the Loeb
        translation: "The play upon the words κέρας, 'horn,' and
        κραίνω, 'fulfil,' and upon ἐλέφας, 'ivory,' and ἐλεφαίρομαι, 'de-
        ceive,' cannot be preserved in English" (Homer, *The Odyssey II*,
        269n1). Hunger (1955 edition, p. 42, note on Book 19, lines 55ff.)
        notes that there have been various attempts at interpretation
        of the imagery and points out that Tzetzes offers only half an
        interpretation (the ivory gate is related not to the spiritual but
        to the somatic aspect of man).

66   *Od.* 19.592–93.

71   *Od.* 19.603–4.

73–76   See *Od.* 14.80–108. On Eumaios loaning Odysseus his cloak to
        keep him warm for the night, see *Od.* 14.518–22. Hunger (1955
        edition, p. 43, note on Book 19, line 74) notes that pig slaugh-
        tering happens in the winter, around November/December.

## BOOK 20

1–2   *Od.* 20.1–3.

3–4   *Seeing the female slaves . . . the women*: *Od.* 20.5–21.

4     *Willed himself to relax and sleep*: *Od.* 20.22–55.

5–6   *Od.* 20.58–90.

7     *Od.* 20.98–101.

8–9   *Od.* 20.102–19.

| | |
|---|---|
| 10–12 | *Od.* 20.165–67, 199–225, 299–300. |
| 13–16 | *Od.* 20.351–72. Peiraios is a friend of Telemachos. |
| 17 | *Od.* 20.376–83. |
| 18–19 | *Od.* 20.30–31. |
| 25 | *Speaks to it*: "It" is the mind of Odysseus. |
| 27–28 | *Od.* 20.42–43. |
| 31–32 | *Od.* 20.54–55. |
| 37 | *Od.* 20.55. |
| 43–44 | For Melitides (not in Homer), see Aristophanes, *Frogs* 991, where Μελιτίδαι is a euphemism for "simpletons." The origin is debated; one etymology links the epithet with the deme of Melite, but it is generally rejected because the first iota in Melitidai is long, whereas the iota in Melite is short. See William B. Stanford, *Aristophanes, Frogs* (London, 1958), 160. The etymology from μέλι (honey), though attractive due to the affinity with modern words using compounds with food to denote soft or spoiled men (such as "sugar baby"), is equally rejected for the same metrical reasons; see Kenneth Dover, *Aristophanes, Frogs* (Oxford, 1997), 186–87. There seems to have been a Byzantine tradition of calling simpletons "Melitides." See Photios, *Lexicon; Suda,* under "γέλοιος"; Hunger 1955 edition, p. 43, note on Book 20, lines 43ff. |
| 44 | *In the world*: βίος (life) is used here instead of κόσμος (world); see Hunger 1955 edition, p. 43, note on Book 20, line 44. |
| 49 | *Od.* 20.61. |
| 51 | *Od.* 20.67, 68. |
| 53 | *Od.* 20.69. The girls are the daughters of Pandareus. After he and his wife died, their daughters were nurtured by Aphrodite, Hera, and Artemis; when it was time for them to get married, they were led in front of Zeus, only to be snatched away and become handmaidens to the Furies. |
| 54 | *Od.* 20.70–71. |
| 60–61 | *Od.* 20.71. |
| 62 | See *Od.* 20.72. |
| 63–66 | *Od.* 20.73–76. |
| 67–68 | The subject in lines 67–68 is καιρός. We believe that it is used in |

the sense of "time" in line 67 and then in the sense of "weather" in line 68 (since it was a whirlwind that snatched the girls away in the Homeric text).

69–70    *Meanwhile . . . deal with*: Od. 20.77–78.

69    *Harpies*: The Greek term for Harpies, Ἅρπυιαι, means "snatchers"; see LSJ.

74    *Od.* 20.87.

76    *Od.* 20.97.

77    *Od.* 20.98.

79    *Od.* 20.101.

81    *Od.* 20.112.

83    *Od.* 20.169.

84    *Od.* 20.195.

85    *Od.* 20.201.

88    *Od.* 20.215.

89    *Od.* 20.230.

90    *Od.* 20.236.

91    *Od.* 20.238.

92    *Od.* 20.273.

93    *Od.* 20.339.

96    *Od.* 20.344.

98    *Od.* 20.345–46.

100    *Od.* 20.393.

## Book 21

1–3    *Od.* 21.67–79.

4–5    *Eumaios . . . began to cry*: Od. 21.82–83.

5–8    *So Odysseus . . . and these men*: Od. 21.188–241. When he says that he turned them into Telemachoi, he refers to Odysseus's declaration that, in his eyes, they are both Telemachos's brothers (*Od.* 21.215–16).

9–11    *Od.* 21.68–423.

12    See *Od.* 21.1.

13    *Od.* 21.14.

17    *Od.* 21.25–26.

| | |
|---|---|
| 19 | *Od.* 21.28. |
| 20 | *Od.* 21.196. |
| 21 | *Od.* 21.200. |
| 22 | *Od.* 21.201. |
| 23 | *Od.* 21.203. |
| 24 | *Od.* 21.213. |
| 25 | *Od.* 21.258. |
| 26 | *Od.* 21.279. |
| 28 | *Od.* 21.280. |
| 29 | *Od.* 21.357–58. This is a reference to Persephone. |
| 32 | *Od.* 21.364–65. |
| 33 | Tzetzes here is making use of the similarity in pronunciation between ἵλεως (propitious) and Ἥλιος (Sun). See Hunger 1955 edition, p. 44, note on Book 21, line 33. |
| 37 | *Od.* 21.413. |

## Book 22

| | |
|---|---|
| 1–4 | *Od.* 22.8–389. |
| 5–9 | *Od.* 22.435–77. |
| 10–11 | *Od.* 22.490–501. |
| 12 | *Od.* 22.7. |
| 17 | *Od.* 22.39. |
| 18 | *Od.* 22.51. |
| 19–20 | *Od.* 22.205–6. |
| 26 | *Od.* 22.210. |
| 28 | *No man*: That is, Mentor. |
| 30–31 | *Od.* 22.224–25. |
| 32 | *Od.* 22.226–35. |
| 37–41 | *Od.* 22.236–40. |
| 48 | *Od.* 22.249. |
| 53 | *Agelaos*: One of Penelope's suitors; see *Od.* 22.241–54. |
| 54 | *Od.* 22.252–53. |
| 55 | *The reasoning*: That is, Zeus. See Tz. *All. Il.* 23.37–38; Tz. *All. Od.* 16.50. |
| 57 | *Od.* 22.256, 273. |

| | |
|---|---|
| 63 | *Od.* 22.288–89. |
| 65–66 | *Od.* 22.297–98. |
| 71 | *Od.* 22.299–300. |
| 72 | *Od.* 22.334. For a parallel passage, see Tz. *All. Od.* 6.29–34. See also the relevant passages from Tz. *Exegesis of the* Iliad, 45–50, and Goldwyn, "Theory and Method," 144–45. |
| 75 | *Od.* 22.346. |
| 79 | *Od.* 22.347. |
| 82 | *Od.* 22.413. |
| 83 | *Od.* 22.429. |

## BOOK 23

| | |
|---|---|
| 1–4 | *Od.* 23.1–57. |
| 5–9 | *Od.* 23.164–206, 300–43. |
| 10–11 | *Od.* 23.359–72. |
| 12 | *Od.* 23.11. |
| 13 | *Od.* 23.63. |
| 15–16 | *Od.* 23.81–82. |
| 19 | *Od.* 23.81. |
| 20 | *Od.* 23.140. |
| 22 | *Od.* 23.156. Compare Tz. *All. Od.* 6.127–29. |
| 23 | *Transference of meaning*: Μετάληψις is a rhetorical term, meaning "transference of meaning," "using one word for another"; see Eustathios, *Commentary on the* Iliad 1.79.44–45. |
| 25 | *Od.* 23.160. |
| 27 | *Like the immortals*: *Od.* 23.163. |
| 28 | *Od.* 23.167. |
| 29 | *Od.* 23.185. |
| 31 | *Od.* 23.184. |
| 34 | *Od.* 23.210. |
| 35 | *Od.* 23.218. |
| 36 | *Od.* 23.222. |
| 38–39 | *Od.* 23.242–43. |
| 40 | *Od.* 23.241. |
| 42 | Tzetzes is here warning against the application of a historical al- |

legory; instead, he says it should be allegorized in natural or climatological terms, which he does in lines 44–45.

46      *Od.* 23.258.

47      *Poseidon: Od.* 23.277.

47–48   *'Gods in heaven' are . . . of the stars: Od.* 23.280.

49      *Od.* 23.286.

50      *Od.* 23.336.

52      *Od.* 23.339.

54–57   *Od.* 23.344–47.

62      *Od.* 23.348. Tzetzes here probably misremembered the Homeric line, as in the *Odyssey* Dawn brings light "to men" (ἀνθρώποισι), not to the immortals.

64      *Od.* 23.352–53.

66–67   *Od.* 23.371–72.

## BOOK 24

1       *Od.* 24.1–14.

2–5     *Od.* 24.15–22.

6–8     *Od.* 24.24–34.

9–11    *Od.* 24.35–97.

12–13   *Od.* 24.98–101.

14–16   *Od.* 24.106–98.

17      *The viper:* That is, Clytemnestra, his wife. She and her lover, Aigisthos (who was Agamemnon's cousin), planned and carried out Agamemnon's death on the day of his return from Troy.

18      *Od.* 24.199–202.

19–20   *Od.* 24.205–15.

20–21   *Od.* 24.216–355.

22–26   *While they . . . and buried them: Od.* 24.413–17.

26–28   *After organizing . . . Antinoös's father: Od.* 24.420–37.

29–30   *Od.* 24.439–69.

31      *Od.* 24.521–25. Homer says that Eupeithes was killed by Laertes, the son of Arkeisios.

32–35   *Od.* 24.526–48.

36      *Od.* 24.1.

39     *Here*: That is, on earth, while still alive.

40     That is, he gave a sense of affairs on earth to the shadows in the
       Underworld.

41     *Dead men talking*: Εἰδωλοποιΐα is a rhetorical term, meaning
       "putting words in the mouth of the dead." See LSJ, under
       "εἰδωλοποιΐα"; Hermogenes, *Progymnasmata* 9.8–12; Aphtho-
       nius, *Progymnasmata* 10.34.1–11.

44     *The star*: That is, Mercury.

46     *The spoken word*: Tzetzes calls Hermes the "spoken word," "ut-
       tered speech" in Tz. *All. Il.* pro.316; 11.63; Tz. *All. Od.* 6.47;
       24.64–65, and the "written word" in Tz. *All. Od.* 5.101.

51     Tzetzes's explanation of the allegory here is convoluted. He
       seems to be arguing that a person's reasoning is silenced in his
       speech and precedes him to the Underworld; hence Hermes,
       the conductor of souls, is speech/spoken word. See Hunger
       1955 edition, p. 46, note on Book 24, lines 43–51.

52–55  *Od.* 24.2–5.

60     *Od.* 24.11, 12.

61     *Od.* 24.12.

62     *Od.* 24.13, 14.

66     *He held fast*: Κατεῖχε here, instead of the Homeric ἔχε (*Od.* 24.2).

73     *Od.* 24.5.

74     *Veer off course*: Ἐκτρέχω (run away, escape) is used here in the
       figurative sense. Tzetzes uses rhetorical terminology, arguing
       that rhetorical composition is violated by excessive move-
       ment. See Hunger 1955 edition, p. 46, note on Book 24, lines
       73–74.

75     That is, to the Underworld.

76     *Od.* 24.5–6.

84     *The books stored in my mind*: Compare Tzetzes's references to his
       memory and his boast that he does not need to consult books,
       as all the information is stored in his mind; see, for example,
       Tz. *All. Il.* 15.87–88.

86     *Prokopios of Kaisareia*: Prokopios of Kaisareia was a sixth-century
       Byzantine historian. Tzetzes here is probably mistaken, as there
       seems to be no reference to the battle he is describing in Pro-
       kopios's work.

87    *Od.* 24.9–10.

90    *Guileless*: *Od.* 24.10; the Greek for "guileless" is ἀκάκητα, an epic
      form of ἄκακος and an epithet of Hermes. The word is a com-
      pound of κακός, "evil."

92    *Od.* 24.11.

93    *Od.* 24.11. For the translation of εὔροος (fair flowing) as "fast for-
      gotten" in this context, see *LbG*.

94    *Rocks of Leukas*: The rock was at the southernmost part of the
      island of Leukas, taking its name from its shining glow in the
      sun. In myth, it was a favorite suicide spot for women over un-
      requited love. For instance, Sappho was said to have commit-
      ted suicide over the love of a man (Menander F 258K), but the
      story was disputed already in antiquity (Strabo 10.2.9); see also
      Hunger 1955 edition, p. 46, note on Book 24, line 94.

95    *Od.* 24.12.

97    *Meadow of asphodel*: *Od.* 24.13. The part of the Underworld where
      the shadows live (see *Od.* 11.539–42).

102–4  Two etymologies of ἀσφόδελος are offered here: (1) not worthy
      of zeal, (2) lack of eagerness. See Hunger 1955 edition, p. 47,
      note on Book 24, lines 102ff.

105   Tzetzes is making a connection here between the words ἀσφό-
      δελος and σφεδανός (vehement).

107   *Pleumon*: This means "lung."

      *Sphodelos*: Σφοδενὸς (vehement) is not attested in the major
      lexica; Tzetzes is trying to make the point that in Attic Greek
      they changed nu into lambda (*sphodelos* into *sphodenos*). He does
      not imply that they change vowels as well. Perhaps *sphodenos*
      was a variation of the now-lost word *sphedanos,* or perhaps it is
      his own mistake or invention.

110   *Elthon*: This means "they came."

111   *Od.* 24.23.

112   *Dead men talking*: See above, Tz. *All. Od.* 24.41.

118   *Od.* 24.24–25.

123   *Od.* 24.28.

125   *Od.* 24.36.

126   This quotation is not taken from the *Odyssey.* The formula ap-
      pears in *Il.* 1.36 without the word δαμείς (tamed). Hunger (1955

edition, p. 47, note on Book 24, line 126) notes that the incident to which Tzetzes refers can be found in *Il.* 21.277, where Achilles fights with the river Xanthos. The use of the particular formula is related to how Achilles is going to die at the hands of Apollo.

127    For Leto as darkness, compare Tz. *All. Il.* 20.236, 21.357, and Tz. *All. Od.* 11.130.

130    Compare Tz. *All. Od.* 7.31, 11.107–8, and 15.77.

131–32    This version of Achilles's death appears in later texts. See Hyginus, *Fabulae* 110; Servius, *Commentary on the Aeneid of Virgil* 3.321, 6.57.

133    *Transference of meaning*: This means the connection of one thing to another by means of the same word, as for example, Hermes as an old man, a star, and spoken word.

138    *Od.* 24.42.

141    *Od.* 24.47.

146    *Od.* 24.52.

154    *Od.* 24.59.

155–56    The gender changes from neuter (κλαῦσαν, "cried") in line 155 to feminine (αὐτῆς, literally, "hers") in line 156. We assume that the neuter refers to water (ὕδωρ, neuter in Greek) and that the feminine refers to the sea (θάλαττα, feminine in Greek).

157    *Od.* 24.60.

160    *Od.* 24.64.

162    See line 160 above.

165    *Streams of shooting stars*: That is, meteor showers. See Tz. *All. Il.* 24.166, where the word appears as ἀστρορρύσεις rather than ἀστρορρυήσεις, as it is here. See also Hunger 1955 edition, p. 48, note on Book 24, line 165.

166    *Od.* 24.67.

168    *Od.* 24.74.

170    *Lykourgos*: Legendary king who drove out Dionysos's attendants, for whom see *Il.* 6.130–40.

171–73    In *Od.* 24.77–79 Homer says the ashes of Achilles and Patroklos were mixed, whereas Antilochos's were placed in a separate urn. See also Hunger 1955 edition, p. 48, note on Book 24, line 173.

| | |
|---|---|
| 178–79 | *Od.* 24.85–86. |
| 182 | See, for example, Tz. *All. Il.* 1.184–203. |
| 187 | *Od.* 24.92. |
| 190 | *Od.* 24.92. |
| 193 | *Od.* 24.96–97. |
| 195 | *With windstorms*: This is Hunger's translation (1955 edition, p. 48, note on Book 24, line 195) of ὥσταις ἀνέμοις, literally, "with thrusting, violent winds." |
| 196 | *Od.* 24.149. |
| 197 | *Od.* 24.149–50. |
| 198 | *Od.* 24.164. |
| 201 | *Od.* 24.182. |
| 203 | *Od.* 24.196–98. |
| 205 | *Od.* 24.306–7. Sikania is an old name of Sicily. See Diodorus Siculus, *Bibliotheca historica* 5.2. |
| 206 | *Od.* 24.344. |
| 207 | *Od.* 24.351. |
| 209 | *Od.* 24.367–68. For Athena as oil, see above, Tz. *All. Od.* 23.22–24. |
| 211 | *Od.* 24.371. |
| 213 | *Od.* 24.373–74. |
| 215 | *Od.* 24.376. |
| 217 | *Od.* 24.401. |
| 218 | *Od.* 24.402. |
| 219 | *Od.* 24.443–44. Hunger (1955 edition, p. 48, note on Book 24, line 219) notes that τὰ is here the demonstrative αὐτὰ (these) rather than the article. |
| 222 | For Medon hiding under the ox hide, see *Od.* 22.361–63. For his speech in defense of Odysseus's killing of the suitors, see *Od.* 24.439–49. |
| 225 | *His own*: That is, Odysseus's. |
| 227 | *Od.* 24.472. |
| 231 | Tzetzes has reversed air and sky here. In line 227 above it was Athena (the air) who spoke to Zeus (the sky), not the other way around, as is implied here. |
| 236 | *Od.* 24.479–85. Zeus is speaking here to Athena. |
| 237 | *Od.* 24.487. The "air" here is Athena. |

239     *Preface and introductory statement*: προέκθεσις (introduction, pref-
        ace) and πρόρρησις (introductory statement, comment given
        beforehand) are rhetorical terms. For the definition of προέκ-
        θεσις, see Hermogenes, Περὶ μεθόδου δεινότητος 12; for πρόρ-
        ρησις, see Pseudo-Aristotle, *Rhetoric to Alexander* 1438b 11
        (Anaximenes, *Ars Rhetorica Quae Vulgo Fertur Aristotelis ad Alex-
        andrum* 31.3).

242     *Od.* 24.521–28.

243     *Od.* 24.529–32, 539–40.

245     *Od.* 24.546.

246–47  *Od.* 24.502–3.

250–52  *Od.* 24.516–18.

255     *Od.* 24.523.

256–57  *Od.* 24.529–30.

261     *Od.* 24.540.

264     *Od.* 24.541.

266     See Tz. *All. Od.* 13.89 above.

272–74  *Od.* 24.546–48.

284     Tzetzes is creating a metaphor of Homer's skills as sailing ves-
        sels with deep draft (βαθυδρόμοις), used to reach the depths of
        the mythical allegory.

291     *Light of Pasikrates*: Hunger (1955 edition, p. 48, note on Book 24,
        lines 277–93) notes that this Pasikrates is probably the king
        of Kourion in Cyprus. In the siege of Tyre in 332 BCE, his ship
        sank during a raid (Arrian, *Anabasis of Alexander* 2.22). The
        legend about the light of Pasikrates is probably related to
        the sunken ship, although there seem to be no sources refer-
        ring to it.

# Bibliography

## Edition of the Greek Text

Hunger, Herbert, ed. "Johannes Tzetzes, *Allegorien zur Odyssee*, Buch 1–12." *Byzantinische Zeitschrift* 49 (1956): 249–310.

———. "Johannes Tzetzes, *Allegorien zur Odyssee*, Buch 13–24." *Byzantinische Zeitschrift* 48 (1955): 4–48.

## Primary Sources

Texts and authors not included in the following list can be found in the Loeb editions.

Acusilaus, Scholia on the *Odyssey* = Jacoby, Felix, ed. *Die Fragmente der griechischen Historiker (FgrH)*, I.A pp. 49–58. Leiden, 1957.

Aphthonius, *Progymnasmata* = Rabe, Hugo, ed. *Aphthonii progymnasmata*. Leipzig, 1926.

Aristeas of Prokonnesos, *Arimaspeia Epics* = Bernabé, Alberto. *Poetarum epicorum Graecorum testimonia et fragmenta*. Editio correctior. Part 1. Stuttgart and Leipzig, 1996.

Aristotle, *Generation of Animals* = Drossaart Lulofs, Hendrik J., ed. *Aristotelis de generatione animalium*. Oxford, 1965.

Eustathios, *Commentary on the* Iliad = van der Valk, Marchinus, ed. *Commentarii ad Homeri Iliadem pertinentes*. 4 vols. Leiden, 1971–1987.

Heraclitus, *Homeric Problems* = Russell, Donald Andrew, and David Konstan, eds. *Heraclitus: Homeric Problems*. Atlanta, 2005.

Hermogenes, Περὶ μεθόδου δεινότητος = Rabe, Hugo, ed. "Περὶ μεθόδου δεινότητος." In *Hermogenis opera*, 414–56. Leipzig, 1913.

Hermogenes, *Progymnasmata* = Rabe, Hugo, ed. "Προγυμνάσματα." In *Hermogenis opera*, 1–27. Leipzig, 1913.

Hyginus, *Fabulae* = Grant, Mary, trans. and ed. *The Myths of Hyginus (Including the Fabulae and the Second Book of the Poetica Astronomica)*. Lawrence, Kan., 1960.

John Malalas, *Chronography* = Thurn, Ioannes, ed. *Ioannis Malalae chronographia* [*Corpus Fontium Historiae Byzantinae. Series Berolinensis* 35]. Berlin and New York, 2000.

John of Antioch = Müller, Karl, ed. "Joannes Antiochenus." In *Fragmenta historicorum Graecorum (FHG)*, vol. 4, pp. 535–622. Paris, 1851.

Niketas Choniates, *Historia* = Bekker, Immanuel, ed. *Nicetae Choniatae historia* [*Corpus Scriptorum Historiae Byzantinae* 35]. Bonn, 1835.

Photios, *Lexicon* = Naber, Samuel Adrian, ed. *Photii Patriarchae Lexicon*. 2 vols. Leiden, 1864–1865.

Proclus, *Chrestomathia* = Severyns, Albert. *Recherches sur la Chrestomathie de Proclus*. 4 vols. Paris, 1938–1963.

Pseudo-Aristotle, *Rhetoric to Alexander* = Fuhrmann, Manfred, ed. *Anaximenis Ars Rhetorica*. Leipzig, 1966.

Servius, *Commentary on the* Aeneid *of Virgil* = Thilo, Georgius, and Hermannus Hagen, eds. *Servii Grammatici qui feruntur in Vergilii carmina commentarii*. 3 vols. Leipzig, 1881–1902.

*Suda* = Adler, Ada, ed. *Suidae Lexicon*. 5 vols. Leipzig, 1928–1938.

Tz. *All. Il.* = Goldwyn, Adam, and Dimitra Kokkini, trans. and eds. *Allegories of the* Iliad. Cambridge, Mass., 2015.

Tz. *All. Od.* = Hunger, Herbert. "Johannes Tzetzes, *Allegorien zur Odyssee*, Buch 1–12." *Byzantinische Zeitschrift* 49 (1956): 249–310.

——. "Johannes Tzetzes, *Allegorien zur Odyssee*, Buch 13–24." *Byzantinische Zeitschrift* 48 (1955): 4–48.

Tz. *Chiliades* = Leone, Pietro L. M., ed. *Ioannis Tzetzae historiae*. Naples, 1968.

Tz. *Chronicle* = Hunger, Herbert. "Johannes Tzetzes, Allegorien aus der Verschronik." *Jahrbuch der Österreichischen Byzantinistik* 4 (1955): 13–49.

Tz. *Exegesis of the* Iliad = Papathomopoulos, Manolis, ed. Εξήγησις Ιωάννου Γραμματικού του Τζέτζου εις την Ομήρου Ιλιάδα. Athens, 2007.

## SECONDARY SOURCES

Agapitos, Panagiotis. "John Tzetzes and the Blemish Examiners: A Byzantine Teacher on Schedography, Everyday Language, and Writerly Disposition." *Medioevo greco* 17 (2017): 1–57.

Browning, Robert. "A Fourteenth-Century Prose Version of the 'Odyssey.'" *Dumbarton Oaks Papers* 46 (1992): 27–36.

———. "Homer in Byzantium." *Viator* 6 (1975): 15–33.

Budelmann, Felix. "Classical Commentary in Byzantium: John Tzetzes on Ancient Greek Literature." In *The Classical Commentary: History, Practices, Theory,* edited by Roy Gibson and Christina Kraus, 141–69. Leiden, 2002.

Cesaretti, Paolo. *Allegoristi di Omero a Bisanzio: Ricerche ermeneutiche (XI–XII secolo).* Milan, 1991.

Cullhed, Eric. "Diving for Pearls and Tzetzes' Death." *Byzantinische Zeitschrift* 108, no. 1 (2015): 53–62.

Ford, Andrew. "Performing Interpretation: Early Allegorical Exegesis of Homer." In *Epic Traditions in the Contemporary World,* edited by Margaret Beissinger, Jane Tylus, and Susanne Wofford, 33–53. Berkeley, Calif., 1999.

Gautier, Paul. "La curieuse ascendance de Jean Tzetzès." *Revue des Études Byzantines* 28 (1970): 207–20.

Goldwyn, Adam J. "Theory and Method in John Tzetzes' *Allegories of the Iliad* and *Allegories of the* Odyssey." *Scandinavian Journal of Byzantine and Modern Greek Studies* 3 (2017): 141–71.

Jeffreys, Michael. "The Nature and Origins of the Political Verse." *Dumbarton Oaks Papers* 28 (1974): 141–95.

Magdalino, Paul. *The Empire of Manuel I Komnenos.* Cambridge, 1993.

Mavroudi, Maria. "Occult Science and Society in Byzantium: Considerations for Future Research." In *The Occult Sciences in Byzantium,* edited by Paul Magdalino and Maria Mavroudi, 39–96. Geneva, 2006.

Rhoby, Andreas. "Ioannes Tzetzes als Auftragsdichter." *Graeco-Latina Brunensia* 15 (2010): 155–70.

# Index

The *Allegories of the* Odyssey contains two sections before Book 1; we have called the first one prolegomena A (pro.A, here in the index) and the second one prolegomena B (pro.B).